OXFORD STUDIES IN
SOCIAL AND CULTURAL ANTHROPOLOGY

Editorial Board

ANTHROPOLOGY AND HISTORY IN FRANCHE-COMTÉ

OXFORD STUDIES IN
SOCIAL AND CULTURAL ANTHROPOLOGY

Oxford Studies in Social and Cultural Anthropology represents the work of authors, new and established, that will set the criteria of excellence in ethnographic description and innovation in analysis. The series serves as an essential source of information about the world and the discipline.

OTHER TITLES IN THIS SERIES

Anthropology and History in Franche-Comté

A Critique of Social Theory

ROBERT LAYTON

OXFORD
UNIVERSITY PRESS

OXFORD

UNIVERSITY PRESS

Great Clarendon Street, Oxford OX2 6DP

Oxford University Press is a department of the University of Oxford.
It furthers the University's objective of excellence in research, scholarship,
and education by publishing worldwide in

Oxford New York

Athens Auckland Bangkok Bogotá Buenos Aires Calcutta
Cape Town Chennai Dar es Salaam Delhi Florence Hong Kong Istanbul
Karachi Kuala Lumpur Madrid Melbourne Mexico City Mumbai
Nairobi Paris São Paulo Shanghai Singapore Taipei Tokyo Toronto Warsaw

and associated companies in Berlin Ibadan

Oxford is a registered trade mark of Oxford University Press
in the UK and in certain other countries

Published in the United States
by Oxford University Press Inc., New York

British Library Cataloguing in Publication Data

Data available

Library of Congress Cataloging in Publication Data

Data applied for
ISBN 0–19–924199–6

1 3 5 7 9 10 8 6 4 2

Typeset in Ehrhardt by
Cambrian Typesetters, Frimley, Surrey
Printed in Great Britain
on acid-free paper by
T.J. International, Padstow, Cornwall

If their bee nothing new, but that which is,
Hath been before, how are our braines beguild,
Which laboring for invention beare amisse
The second burthern of a former child?
Oh that record could with a back-ward looke,
Even of five hundreth courses of the sunne,
Show me your image in some antique booke,
Since minde at first in carrecter was done.
That I might see what the old world could say,
To this composed wonder of your frame,
Whether we are mended, or where better they,
Or whether revolution be the same.

(Shakespeare, from sonnet 59)

ACKNOWLEDGEMENTS

This study could never have been carried out without the friendship, patience and encouragement the community of Pellaport has given me over thirty years. Several people have helped me in fieldwork. Mike Rowlands recorded hay harvesting techniques with me in July 1969. Charles Farr spent three weeks in September 1969 studying a neighbouring village before he began an anthropology degree at Sussex University. Ian Keen and Marga Gervis worked on the comparative study of surrounding villages in July 1972. Freddy Bailey, Phyllis Kaberry, and Peter Ucko gave me the encouragement and inspiration to begin the project. Other members of the Bailey team, especially Riall and Christine Nolan, and Mike and Nanneke Redclift, became good friends as the research developed.

Kathy Fewster took over much of my teaching at Durham during the 1997/8 academic year, while I was writing this book. In the autumn of 1997 I visited the universities of Uppsala and Stockholm to explore the similarities and differences between Scandinavian and French village structure. Hugh Beach, Eva von Hirsch, Mats Widgren, Ulf Sporrong, and Birgitta Roeck Hansen were among those who made me welcome and explained the results of their research. Colleagues in Durham have always made the university a stimulating research environment. In writing this book I have especially benefited from discussions with Malcolm Smith, Catherine Panter-Brick, Tammy Kohn and Charles Gullick, John Bintliff, Bob Johnson, Jonty Rougier, Alan Seheult, Una Strand Vidarsdottir, and Richard Britnell. I also thank Bruce Winterhalder for his consistent encouragement and interest.

The Social Science Research Council funded my Ph.D. research and Durham University awarded the Foundation Fellowship which finally made it possible to write the book.

CONTENTS

LIST OF PLATES

LIST OF FIGURES

LIST OF TABLES

Preamble

In the autumn of 1968 I joined Professor Freddy Bailey's SSRC-funded project to study social change in the Circum-Alpine region of Europe. The Jura was one of the regions not yet studied by a member of Bailey's team and it was enthusiastically recommended to me by Phyllis Kaberry, my M.Phil. supervisor. I spent several weeks in the library of the Royal Geographical Society in London, finding out what French geographers had written about the Jura, and selected a district whose thriving dairy farming and forestry would promise villages that had not suffered serious depopulation. Early in November I went by train to Pontarlier, where I hired a bike and spent a couple of days cycling through some of the villages I had been reading about. I chose one that had a hotel, but was small enough that I could hope to meet members of every household. The following February I returned to Pontarlier, expecting to be able to hire a bike again and cycle to the village. Despite my reading on the region I had not expected to find the town deep in snow. The man at the cycle shop told me to come back in a month's time. Next morning I set off on foot, thumbing a lift as I walked out towards the plain west of Pontarlier. A snow storm soon sprang up but a mother and daughter travelling in a Deux Chevaux stopped to give me and my rucksack a lift. By the time we had reached the turn-off for my chosen village the storm had stopped. I walked through the forest along a road covered in hard-packed snow. The only sounds, apart from my footsteps, were from snow sliding off the branches of the fir trees and occasional French military jets practising flying beneath the radar along the mountains on the Swiss border. Passing through several villages I eventually came to the one of my choice as dusk was falling, only to be told the hotel was closed until Easter. A walk around the village failed to find anyone willing to rent me a room, but the woman in the hotel advised me to walk on to Pellaport, where I would find a Mme Bavarel who could give me accommodation. I walked on through the forest, reaching Pellaport after dark, as more snow began to fall. Mme Bavarel was throwing logs into a cast iron stove when I opened her front door. 'Of course you can stay,' she exclaimed, 'you can't spend a night like this out of doors.' I lived in Pellaport from February to October 1969, and made a return visit in July 1972 to extend my comparative data on other villages in the district. After seven years in Australia, and subsequent time analysing my Australian fieldwork, I was able to revisit the village with my family in 1986. It was a pleasure to be welcomed back by my old friends, and my resolution not to spend the holiday making field-notes was quickly broken. I spent a further three months in Pellaport during the summer of 1995, looking in more detail at the changes that had taken place since my first fieldwork.

Chapter 1 describes everyday life in the village during 1969. Chapter 2 embeds the daily and seasonal routines of villagers in the wider setting of the village as a corporate group, revealing variation in space (between villages) and time (through the history of the village). The conclusion to Ch. 2 outlines the particular moment in the history of anthropological theory in which my Ph.D. research was carried out and looks at the ways in which those issues have been resolved in more recent theoretical work. The remaining chapters analyse social process in the domains of the household, mutual aid, technology, and management of village resources. Analysis is built around a critical evaluation of the work of Marx, Durkheim, Giddens, and Bourdieu. The conclusion to Ch. 7 draws some general conclusions about the features of social life that contribute to continuity or change. Paraphrasing Marx, the object of my research was to find out how, in gaining their subsistence, people are implicated in social relationships (cf. Marx 1971: 20–1). Contrary to Marx, however, it is not my intention to show these relationships are invariably necessary yet beyond the participants' control. Where there *is* choice in relationships the study will also investigate how and why people make certain choices rather than others, how relationships are constructed, and what the consequences of those choices are. In his book *The Rebel*, Camus (1953) argued that authoritarian regimes follow revolution because the old order has been swept away and anarchy must be averted. Yet Pellaport has survived the Revolution of 1789, the agricultural and demographic revolutions of the nineteenth century, and the post-Second World War displacement of the peasantry by commercial farming without losing its fundamental social form. Partible inheritance, the division of the land between commons and private fields, village government by an assembly or elected council, and dairy co-operatives have survived. In this book I aim to show how ordered life has been maintained despite successive transformations.

1

Everyday Life in 1969

Pellaport is situated on the Plateau of Levier, some kilometres west of Pontarlier. The Plateau of Levier falls within the lowest, or *colline* zone, of Alpine environments with an altitude ranging between 500 and 1,000 metres (Viazzo 1989: 17). East of Pontarlier rise the mountains which form the Swiss border. To the west the land descends in a series of limestone plateaux, separated by escarpments. Each plateau is dissected by dry valleys known as *combes*. The Plateau of Levier is close to two ancient roads which lead from Switzerland into France, one running east from Pontarlier through Levier to Dijon, the other heading north-east towards Besançon via Ornans (Fig. 1.1). John Berger's novel *Pig Earth* is set in the same general region. Many of the aspects of village life described here, such as the seasonal cycle of planting and harvesting, mutual aid, nick-names, and partible inheritance have walk-on parts in Berger's trilogy (J. Berger 1992). Playing Stoppard to Berger's Shakespeare, I shall look in detail at their contributions to social process.

Like many villages on the plateaux, Pellaport stands at the foot of a forested escarpment. Privately owned land is located in the dry valleys situated on three sides of the village. Higher, level ground between the valleys is either wooded or occupied by communal pasture. One area of commons is known as la pâture du Seigneur, a reminder of the feudal regime of the Middle Ages. According to village legend, the village's first church was built by the seigneur who owned both this pasture and the wood between it and the village. He liked mass to begin as he entered church with his retinue, but the villagers could not always anticipate the moment of his arrival. Every week a boy was stationed at a window in the church tower to warn the congregation when the seigneur and his party appeared from behind le bois du Seigneur to descend la rue de Croset towards the village. An old footpath leading into le bois de Seigneur has the seemingly paradoxical name of la vie des Morts. *Vie* is the old word for *voie* (way or path). During an epidemic of plague villagers who

FIG. 1.1. Location of the Plateau of Levier

became infected were required to leave the village and remain in the wood awaiting death (see Behar 1986: 268–81; Netting 1981: 9; Rosenberg 1988: p. xiii; and Zonabend 1984: 197–201 for other examples of oral history in European villages).

OCCUPATIONS IN THE VILLAGE

Dairy farming is the core of the village economy. It is indicative of the very different social history of farming in this part of France to that of England, that people do not like to be called *fermiers* (farmers), a term which became current in England during the eighteenth century (Overton 1996: 36). *Un fermier* is a tenant-farmer. There are only two tenant-farmers in the commune, both of whom live on isolated farms outside the village. One brings his milk to the dairy in Pellaport, the other is situated at the extreme edge of the commune and belongs to a different dairy association. The term *paysan* (countryman) is frequently used and has none of the negative connotations of its English equivalent, 'peasant'. As agriculture becomes more mechanized, however, people are beginning to describe themselves as *exploitants* or *cultivateurs*. In 1969 the term *paysan* is never used in government literature. By 1995 *exploitant* or *cultivateur* have become almost universal in conversation, although a few speak of *paysans-exploitants*. I will use *cultivateur* in preference to 'farmer'. *Cultivateurs* are proud of their independence. Several of them remarked to me during 1969 that, although they have to rise early to milk the cows, there is no one to tell them what to do and, unlike a factory worker, they can work at their own pace.

Many of the *cultivateurs* who were in their fifties or sixties in 1969 had been prisoners of war in Germany between 1939 and 1945. Some were spared because they had not been called up before France was defeated. César Maitrugue had the good fortune to be in hospital at that moment. Alexandre Maitrugue, Claude Bavarel, and Felicien Jouffroy were less lucky. All had stories to tell of their experiences (cf. Cole and Wolf 1974: 15; Zonabend 1984: 201). Claude recalls how his unit were force-marched to Germany. Their numbers were counted twenty times a day and anyone who fell by the roadside was immediately shot in the back of the head.

In the remainder of this chapter I present village life during 1969, the year of my first fieldwork, as a moment caught in the 'ethnographic present' of anthropological observation. Close as it seemed in village recollection to the events of the distant past, villagers were equally conscious that their community was rapidly changing. Subsequent chapters will embed this moment in the longer trajectory of Pellaport and villages around it.

Although the proportion of farming households in the village has been declining throughout the century, in 1969 a third of the sixty-six households were *cultivateurs*. An equal number of householders had other occupations. The priest, the husband and wife who taught at the village school, the nun who ran the infants' class, the dairyman and postman, the *cantonnier* who maintained hedges and ditches in the commune, the woman who ran the grocery shop and her brother who maintained the petrol pump, the couple who ran the café, the mason, carpenter, plumber and blacksmith, all worked in the village. Two households were headed by people employed in neighbouring villages and four by people who commuted to work in Pontarlier. A daily bus service provided transport. The remaining twenty-two households consisted of retired people. A few kept a single cow. One couple were part-time *cultivateurs*, the husband also working in a local sawmill.

AGRICULTURE

The House

Apart from the two isolated *fermes*, all the *cultivateurs* live in the village. The oldest house was built in 1613. Felicien Maitrugue and Claude Bavarel, who took a particular interest in the history of the village, told me that when first built it was known as 'the new house'. During the 1630s, however, the village was occupied by Swedish soldiers who made the new house their headquarters and burnt down the rest of the village. The inhabitants fled to a cave in the hills.

Houses built from the seventeenth to the early nineteenth century have wide, square roofs whose two faces reach down to the ground floor windows. To call them *farm*houses is redundant, since all houses in the village were built by *paysans*. Such older buildings typically contain two households, one on each side, an arrangement that ingeniously doubles the volume of hay loft that can be enclosed by a given area of roof (Fig. 1.2).

The family lives in rooms which run the length of the house, facing onto the side walls. The front door opens directly into the kitchen. A large dining-table stands in the centre of the room. A dresser is placed against one wall. Most kitchens have both a wood-fired stove and a gas ring. Two stables run parallel to the living quarters, in the central section of the

PL. 1. Traditional farmhouse

building, one for each household. A side door in the kitchen wall gives people access to the stable, while the animals come and go by an end door. The angle of the roof above forms a vast barn or hayloft, the roof supported by a cathedral-like array of wooden beams. The triangular end walls of the hayloft are formed of loosely-fitting wooden planks, which allow air to circulate. Cattle are housed in the stable from late October to mid–April. The hayloft not only provides insulation against the winter cold, but also allows hay to be passed, by means of a trapdoor, directly to the animals beneath. Grain is stored in wooden bins. A small mill, powered by an electric motor, grinds oats and barley grown on the *exploitation* into a flour that is fed to the cattle during the winter. Farm equipment is stored on the floor of the barn. A ramp, often constructed over a stone arch (*le pont de la grange*), gives access to the barn, unless the building is constructed on sloping ground which provides a natural ramp. Some of the more recent, nineteenth-century farmhouses have two storeys, and house only a single family. The internal layout is similar, with living-rooms on one side of the house and the stable on the other. Two or three bedrooms run parallel to the barn on one side of the first floor (cf. Lebeau 1937; 1949).

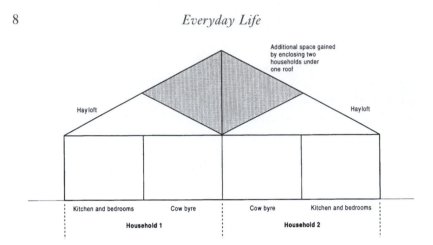

FIG. 1.2. Cross-section through traditional farmhouse

In the stable, each cow's head is separated from the next by a wooden board or *baflanc*. The cows are chained to the stable wall, facing the hayrack that runs the length of the stable. A tiled or concrete floor runs along the far wall of the stable behind the stalls. Most stables are provided with running water, but a few *cultivateurs* still lead their cattle out every morning and evening to drink at one of the cattle troughs located in each corner of the village. Above each stall the cow's name is written. The first letter of a cow's name indicates the year in which she was born. Minette, Montaigne, Nouvelle, Princesse, Plusbelle, Rebelle, and Reveuse are typical names. Some *cultivateurs* also record the date of last calving and insemination and the cow's number assigned by le Contrôle laitier, the organization responsible for improving the local breed of cattle, la race Montbeliarde. Some households have a second stable, parallel to the first, in which the heifers and calves are kept.

Forest, Commons, and Fields

The village and the land around it form a commune, the smallest unit in the system of local government established after the French Revolution. Three broad categories of land-use are recognized: forest, permanent pasture, and plough land. When Claude Bavarel's father's mother, who was born in 1807, married into the village the escarpment behind the village was forested with beech. Now this forest consists almost entirely of fir and Norway spruce. Much of it belongs to the commune. The commune owns almost 400 hectares of forest, including other woodland such as le bois du Seigneur and the wood above les tartes des Fleurs[1], which were still 60 per cent deciduous in 1969. Sale of timber is the commune's main source of income. In principle, poorer than average land belongs to the commune while better than average land is privately owned. The commune owns the 300 hectares of permanent pasture that occupy much of the high ground between the dry valleys. Many of the village cattle graze on the commons during the summer.

Most of the private land, comprising about 50 per cent of the area of the commune, is located in the valleys where the soils are both deeper and richer in clay and sand. In 1969 this land was still divided into long, narrow strips descended from the medieval open-field system. The French government has undertaken a process known as *le remembrement*, in which surveyors visit each village in turn to classify strips according to their quality and redistribute ownership so as to consolidate holdings. Pellaport's strips were grouped into larger fields shortly after my second period of fieldwork in 1972 but each household's land, although less frag-mented, remains scattered across the commune, interspersed with the land cultivated by other households. The village stands at the centre of this patchwork. Each strip, or *parcelle*, is a unit in the system of partible inheritance, through which all children inherit a portion of the family land. Through purchase and exchange, every household has tried to group the *parcelles* it cultivates into larger strips, and this process contin-ued after the *remembrement* of 1972. Even in 1969, Pierre Bavarel was fortunate enough to have one field of 4 hectares, made up of 11 *parcelles*. Another of his strips was more typically composed of three adjacent *parcelles* totalling 60 ares in area.[2] Some *parcelles* belong to members of the household, others to aunts, uncles, brothers, sisters and cousins, while yet others are rented from non-relatives. In 1969 Nicolas Jouffroy's *exploitation* consisted of 30 hectares, comprising 63 *parcelles*. Seven hectares were under permanent pasture. Twenty hectares were under meadow harvested to provide his cattle with hay during the winter. After the harvest half this land became pasture and half was reserved for a second crop of hay. Two hectares and 20 ares had been sown with oats and barley, which will also provide winter cattle-feed. The barley was sown on two fields in different parts of the commune, the oats on a third close to

---

[1] Claude Bavarel explained that *tartes* are fields which, when they start to dry out after rain, develop a dry crust strong enough to support a person's weight but not that of a cow, whose hoofs will break through into the mud below.

[2] An are is one-hundredth of a hectare; one hectare is just less than 2.5 acres.

the village. Felicien Jouffroy had a smaller *exploitation* of 15½ hectares, comprising 38 *parcelles*. He lacked sufficient land to hold any meadow back for a second harvest. One hectare 60 ares, made up of seven *parcelles* grouped into two fields in different parts of the commune, was sown with wheat, oats, and barley. Felicien explained that distributing one's cereal crop around the commune was a traditional way of ensuring against destruction by mice or hail. A quarter of his grassland was permanent pasture, the remainder turned over to pasture after the hay harvest. Alexandre Maitrugue could spare only 30 ares of his *exploitation* for permanent pasture. The rest was needed to provide winter hay. In spring he put all his cows on the commons and moved them progressively to his own land, starting with those that gave the best milk yields, as he completed his harvest. The land that he had most recently cultivated for cereals will provide two crops of hay when it reverts to grass. Alexandre expected to gain a second crop (*un regain*) for the first five years the land is under meadow although Victor Jouffroy expected to harvest *regain* for only two years after the land has reverted to grass. By 1995 the surviving *cultivateurs* had substantially increased their second harvest through the greater use of chemical fertilizers.

Crop Rotation

Almost all the cereals cultivated in 1969 were oats and barley grown to provide cattle-feed. New grain was generally bought each year although one or two, such as the *maire*, retained the best grain from the previous year's harvest to resow. Cereals alternate with pasture, and are cultivated on the same strip for up to five years. Wheat is more demanding of the soil than oats and is sown last. In the fourth or fifth year, grass, trefoil, Lucerne, and sainfoin are sown with the wheat. The wheat shields the more delicate fodder crops while they grow. After the cereal has been harvested the strip will revert to grassland for up to thirty years. Shallow soils close to the margin of the commons cannot be ploughed and these fields are under permanent pasture. Manure and chemical fertilizers are used to improve their quality. They make up between a quarter and a third of the *exploitation*.

Calf Birth

Each cow must give birth once a year to renew the supply of milk. A cow continues to lactate for ten months after calving and, 'like a human', the

TABLE 1.1. *Land-use by four* cultivateurs *in 1969*

	Nicolas Jouffroy	Pierre Bavarel	Felicien Jouffroy	Alexandre Maitrugue
	ha.	*ha.*	*ha.*	*ha.*
Permanent pasture	7.0	5.0	3.5	0.3
Hay > pasture	10.8	17.5	10.3	13.15
Hay > *regain* > pasture	10.0	3.5	—	1.5
Cereals	2.2	2.5	1.6	2.0
Potatoes	—	—	0.1	0.05
TOTAL	30.0	28.5	15.5	17.0
	No.	*No.*	*No.*	*No.*
Milch cattle	20	18	8	11
Placed on commons	6	8	3	10
Heifers	13	10	3	10
Placed on commons	9	10	3	7

cow's pregnancy lasts nine months. The first sign of an approaching birth is the loosening of the cow's pelvis. Many cows give birth during the winter months when they are permanently stabled. Immediately before birth the cow must be made to lie down in her stall. When the calf's front hoofs begin to appear, a rope is tied to them and the calf eased out. It is immediately taken to the calf pen, although it will receive its mother's milk twice a day for two months. The cow is then made to stand, to prevent premature ejection of *la délivrance* (the afterbirth). Felicien Jouffroy gave the cow half a litre of warm, sugared red wine when the birth is complete; I was told this is a traditional practice. Male calves are sold when about 10 days old. Female calves which are kept to maintain the herd will give birth to their first calf after two years. Cows are kept until they are between 10 and 12 years old.

DAIRY PRODUCTION

Milking

Milking is the essential daily task on each *exploitation*, and takes place every morning and evening. The larger *exploitations* had already bought milking machines in 1969, but the smaller households continued to milk by hand. On the smaller *exploitations* hens mingle with the cattle during the evening milking, as they come in to roost. Many households also keep pigs in a pen at one end of the stable, feeding them on the whey which is a by-product of cheese-manufacture in the village dairy. A storeroom contains a boiler for heating water to wash the milking equipment and, where a milking machine is installed, the electric pump. In one corner of Felicien Jouffroy's storeroom hams and *saucissons* hang from the ceiling. The wall beneath is black from the fires he has lit to smoke them. Felicien's wife is content that they have only a small herd. They know their only child, a daughter, does not want to take over the farm and they intend it to give them security until they retire. Felicien puts his tractor in the barn just before 5.30 in the evening and begins to pitchfork hay through the long trapdoor into the rack in front of the cows. His wife has been chopping firewood, but stops to collect the milk churn and take it through into the stable. They each milk three cows in turn, sitting on a wooden stool and holding a pail between their knees (see Pl. 19); the cow's teats are massaged to start the milk flowing and the pail emptied into the churn before they move to the next cow. A 6-day-old calf receives 3 litres of milk from a bucket. Two cows are resting before they give birth. As milking proceeds, the hens come in one by one and take up their positions on poles nailed under the roof beams. The cock arrives last to find there is no room. After a lot of clucking, all the hens shuffle along their perches. A black hen suddenly loses its balance and falls on Mme Jouffroy, taking her headscarf with it. She stands up to identify the culprit and removes it, scolding: 'You're the naughty one; you've all got your places, haven't you?' It takes between 6 and 14 minutes to milk each cow and milking is complete in 45 minutes. Mme Jouffroy washes the pails in the storeroom and gives each cow a ration of flour in a separate bucket. She then rakes out the soiled hay from the stalls, which Felicien removes to the dung heap in a wheelbarrow. The year 1968 was a poor one for hay and much of it became too wet to provide fodder. Every stable in which I watch milking is using *mauvais foin* (bad hay) rather than straw to strew on the floor of the byres. At half-past six, Felicien takes the milk churn to the dairy, pushing it along the street on a small handcart.

Victor Jouffroy and his wife have seventeen cows and have bought a milking machine. They begin to rake out the dirty hay and wheel it to the dung heap before milking begins, then take out the *pots* (stainless steel cans) into which the milk is drawn. Both cans have a tightly fitting lid to which the four cups that fit over the cow's teats are attached. Each cup has two rubber tubes leading from it. One delivers the milk into the *pot*, the other draws a pulsating stream of air from the space between the outer and inner skins of the cup, simulating the sucking of a calf (see Pl. 20). The Jouffroys have two *pots*, allowing the machine to milk two cows at once. They can continue to rake out straw while milking takes place. One cow will not accept the machine and is milked by hand (this is not unusual; Nicolas and Thérèse Jouffroy, who also have a machine, milk two cows by hand). Each cow's teats are washed to stimulate lactation before the cups are fitted. As the flow of milk falls off, the udder is felt and the cups eventually removed. Every 15 minutes the lids of the *pots* are removed to empty the milk into a *bidon* (churn). The *pot* has sufficient capacity to hold the milk of two to three cows. Four calves are given milk and flour as milking continues. Three cows are resting before giving birth. The remainder are milked in just under one hour, although the rather complex equipment remains to be washed. Victor puts two churns on his handcart and wheels it to the dairy, while his wife cleans the delivery tubes of the pots by drawing hot, soapy water through them. The outside of the tubes, together with the lids and their rubber sealing rings are sponged down. This takes a further 10 minutes.

Feeding Cattle

A cow's milk production depends both on its genetic constitution and on its diet. All households supplement the basic ration of hay with flour from cereals grown on the *exploitation*. A local flour-mill supplies cattle-cake and flour enriched with minerals and vitamins which people in Pella-port have been buying since the 1950s. Vache Laitière 124 is a flour made from oats and barley to which lucerne, linseed and rape-seed, vitamins and minerals have been added. In 1969 it cost 57 centimes per kilo. Vache Laitière 500 is a concentrate containing the same elements without the oats and barley, designed to be mixed in equal proportions with flour produced on the *exploitation*. In 1969 it cost 58 centimes per kilo. These are identified as VL 124 and VL 500 in Table 1.2, while 'home' indicates flour from cereals grown on the *exploitation*. The gain in milk from buying these foodstuffs must be balanced against their cost. In 1969 the average value of milk taken to the village dairy was 53 centimes per kilo. Home-produced flour is said to cost half that bought from the mill. A number of farmers supplement home-grown flour with flour from the mill.

TABLE 1.2. *Feed per cow, per day, during the winter months, 1968/9*

Exploitation	Hay (kg.)	Flour (kg.)	Cattle cake (gms.)	Average annual yield per cow (kg.)
a.	12	2 (h-p.)	500 (*VL 500*)	2,404
b.	12	2 (h-p.)	none	2,785
c.	15	2 (h-p.)	350 (*VL 500*)	3,053
		2 (h-p.)	200 (*VL 500*)	
d.	17	2 (*VL 124*)		3,160
		3 (h-p.)		
e.	15–20	3 (*VL 124*)	none	3,442
		2 (h-p.)		
f.	25–30	4 (*VL 124*)	none	3,870
g.	20	5 (h-p.)	800 (*VL 500*)	4,034

Note: h-p. = home-produced.

Cheese Manufacture

As each *cultivateur* arrives in the dairy, the milk is emptied from his churn(s) into a pan where it is weighed, then pumped into one of the three large copper cauldrons which stand in line in the middle of the dairy. The quantity of milk he has delivered is entered in a small note-book. Women and children from other households queue with small *bidons* (cans) to buy milk. The dairy also sells cheese and butter. Although sold in portions of 250 or 500 grammes, people refer to them using the pre-Revolutionary terms, *une livre* (pound) or *demi-livre* (half-pound). The dairy is run by a co-operative association, which rents the building from the commune and employs the dairyman. There are thirty members of the co-operative, including six from the neighbouring hamlet of Montoiseau.

   The evening's milk is left to stand in the cauldron overnight, and the morning's delivery added to it. Two cauldrons are full and will provide enough curds for two cheeses each. The third is half-full of milk and will produce only one cheese. A large wood-fired boiler in the corner of the dairy heats water which circulates between the inner and outer casing of the copper cauldrons, bringing the temperature of the milk to 32 °C. *Caille-lait* (rennet), which contains natural bacteria from calves' stom-achs, is added. The milk is stirred mechanically and, after 30 minutes,

PL. 2. Making cheese in the village dairy

curds begin to form on the surface. These are broken up with a large curd knife consisting of parallel wires mounted in a wooden frame. The temperature of the milk is raised to 54 °C as the milk continues to be stirred for a further hour. Yesterday's cheeses are removed from the cheese-presses and carried down to the cellar. When the mechanical stirrers have finally stopped, whey is drawn out of the vats, leaving the curds behind. The dairyman and his wife take out the curds from each vat using a large muslin cloth. The full cloth is lifted by a small block and tackle. Whey streams out through the fabric. The curds, still in the cloth, are placed in a circular wooden frame beneath a cheese press at the side of the dairy.

In winter sufficient milk is delivered to make five cheeses a day. In summer seven cheeses are made each day. During the next twenty-four hours each cheese will be turned four times. The following morning the mass of curds already cohere sufficiently to be taken out of their frame, forming a cheese weighing between 45 and 50 kilos. The cheese is taken to the cellar, where it spends one day on a wooden rack before being soaked in brine for twenty-four hours. After being left to dry on the rack for a further day, it joins the cheeses which are maturing in the cellar, which are rubbed with salt and turned three times a week. There is insufficient space in the cellar to complete maturation and after three months the cheeses are sold to a wholesaler, who keeps them for a further six months. A small number of cheeses are kept back to be sold in the dairy when they are fully mature.

Cheeses are Collected by the Wholesaler

On 19 March, a lorry arrives from the wholesaler to collect cheeses from the cellar beneath the dairy, so that they can continue to be matured. Several farmers have submitted tenders to help carry the cheeses up and load them into the lorry and they return to the dairy as soon as they have taken their handcarts home from the morning delivery of milk. Even before they have returned, the wholesaler's agent walks into the dairy, dressed smartly in a brown suit. César Maitrugue, Felicien Jouffroy, Maurice Maitrugue, and Étienne Maitrugue return in their working clothes: jeans, pullover, and open-necked shirt, but Jacques Maitrugue arrives last dressed in a new pair of blue overalls. Everyone shakes hands with everyone else as they arrive; Maurice manages to shake my hand and César's simultaneously. When he proffers his hand to the dairyman, however, the latter pretends to spit on it and slaps Maurice on the back instead (this puzzling reaction is interpreted in Ch. 4). The dairyman's wife washes out the scales and pan used to weigh each *cultivateur's* contribution. Maurice helps her dismantle the pipe that takes the milk from the scales to the vat. The others watch the milk being stirred in the cauldron, or talk quietly. Felicien reads the newspaper. Three-quarters of an hour later, the lorry still hasn't arrived. Felicien opens the door to see if it is approaching, letting in a sharp smell of wood smoke mingled with cow dung. 'This is typical,' he remarks. The dairyman removes yesterday's cheese from the presses. Everyone gathers around to watch, looking at the number on the labels. 'The eighteenth; that was yesterday,' says one; 'Today is St Joseph's Day,' adds another.

At ten o'clock the lorry finally arrives. Jacques and Étienne carry the large scales, which will weigh the cheeses, around to the front of the building. The agent insists that the scales are wedged until absolutely level; the others are inclined to feel he is being too fastidious. While the volunteers are putting on coarse aprons and beginning to carry up the cheeses, César and the agent produce notebooks. The cheeses are weighed in batches of eight and carried to the lorry. While the agent wants to query some of the weights announced, César will brook no argument and simply repeats the weight in a louder voice. The agent contents himself with prodding cheeses from time to time, pointing out scratches or black stains. A bottle of wine has appeared and is passed round. The agent declines to drink. '*Nicht trinken?*' demands Felicien, with pretended surprise. It takes an hour to load 140 cheeses. When the job is done, the *cultivateurs* disperse, leaving the agent to take the lorry driver for a drink in the café.

The Accounts

The members of the co-operative are paid once a month. The secretary of the association is schoolteacher in a neighbouring village and brother to two *cultivateurs* in Pellaport. Once a month the management committee meets in the café with the secretary and the dairyman, to make up the accounts over a carafe of red wine. César Maitrugue, the president, has a notebook in which he has recorded the current value of milk at the dairies in neighbouring villages for comparison with that obtained in Pellaport. Payments are in two parts. One is based on the price the wholesaler gives for the cheeses when he buys them, but there is usually a second, smaller sum (the *plus-value*) which the wholesaler provides if he sells the cheeses for a higher price than anticipated when they were bought. Additional income derives from produce sold in the village. Some money is put to one side to cover capital expenditure. The dairyman receives 7 per cent of the co-operative's monthly income as his salary. The remaining income is divided by the quantity of milk delivered during the month to determine the value of a kilogramme of milk that month.

Over the next few days, the secretary calculates the income due to each member. He then arrives at the dairy just before the evening deliveries of milk begin, bringing the pay in his briefcase. Each member's notebook is stamped as he receives his payment.

History of the Dairy

Felicien Maitrugue tells me that during the nineteenth century there was a dairy association, as there is now, that elected a committee to run its affairs. Everyone took their milk to the dairy twice a day, and the quantity was recorded. Instead of receiving money, however, they received dairy produce. When someone had contributed perhaps a thousand kilos of milk, he had the right to receive that day's produce: the cheese, the butter, and the cream. It was then his responsibility to sell them for the best price he could get. These old dairy associations, Felicien recalls, were known as *fruitières*. The difficulty of selling dairy produce in this way led to the disappearance of *fruitières* in about 1910. After that, associations began to sell their milk to entrepreneur dairymen who made the cheeses and under-took to sell them in bulk to recover the cost of buying the milk. At first the price of milk was fixed at the beginning of the year, but this method was abandoned when it was discovered that if the value of cheese rose during the year it was the dairyman and not the *cultivateurs* who kept the profit. Later, the price of milk was determined each month according to the current value of cheese on the Parisian market. The entrepreneurial dairy-men fell into disrepute when, like all shopkeepers, they made illicit profits on the black market during the Second World War. It was César Maitrugue and his brother Eduard who took the lead in re-establishing the co-opera-tive in its present form. Claude Bavarel recalls that in the past each village had two or three *fruitières*. One of those in Pellaport was situated under the school; Felicien says another stood on the site of the present post office.

The Annual General Meeting of the Dairy Co-operative

The Dairy Co-operative's annual general meeting takes place on the evening of 17 April. It is held in the *salle des réunions* (meeting room), over the post office, in a building that belongs to the commune. The president, César Maitrugue, and most of the committee members sit behind a long table at one end of the room, while the ordinary members sit on benches at the opposite end. The middle of the room is occupied only by the cast-iron stove standing on the bare floorboards, and two logs to be put on if the fire dies down. As each person enters, they are handed their *carnet* (account book) for the previous month. Some have put on their sports jackets and flannel trousers, others wear their jeans or overalls. The only member of the committee dressed in working clothes is Felicien Jouffroy.

At half-past eight the meeting begins. The secretary, brother to Alexandre and Étienne Maitrugue and schoolteacher in a neighbouring village, opens the business by announcing the total weight of milk delivered to the dairy during the previous year, followed by the total weight of cheese, butter, and cream produced, the income distributed to members and money remaining in the account. Each is compared with the equivalent figure for 1967. Claude Bavarel borrows my pen to write the figures in his notebook, which are discussed with apparent amusement by those in the back row. Next, the secretary announces the annual production of each *exploitation* for the last two years, identified only by membership number. It is a principle of the association that no one knows how much his neighbours have produced and no one appears to reveal which *exploitation* is theirs by even the smallest reaction. Felicien Jouffroy nods sagely at some, but not his own. After this tense moment, conversation begins again at the back of the room. César bangs on the table to bring people to attention, and the secretary runs through the accounts for each month. At one point, Pierre Bavarel challenges the secretary on how he has calculated TVA (*Taxe Valeur Ajoutée*, i.e. VAT), which has recently been imposed on dairy produce. Several minutes of general discussion ensue. The secretary agrees that it is a lot of money to pay, but justifies his method of calculating the rate payable. 'It should be called TVM, *tout va mal*, not TVA', remarks Felicien. César sits back in his chair impassively, cigarette end in mouth. When the secretary has finished, Felicien distributes the *carnets* of those who arrived late, calling out the account numbers. The owners hold up their hands in turn. César calls for questions on the accounts, but only one question is put and it does not concern the accounts. One of the *cultivateurs* from Montoiseau announces that he has just bought a refrigerated tank and wants to know if he need continue to bring his milk down to Pellaport every day. César is nonplussed by this, protesting that no one has ever asked such a question before. After some discussion, he announces that the matter will have to be put to the committee at its next meeting.

Since three of the nine committee members complete their term of office each year, voting now takes place for three new members. A list of those eligible is passed round. César sets out three piles of slips of paper and three pencils on the committee table and invites everyone to step forward, to place the slip on which they have written their three votes in a wooden box which also stands on the table. A little reluctantly, the first three members step forward. When everyone has sat down again, César points out that Étienne Quintaux hasn't voted. 'Oh, I'll choose the same people as before,' Étienne says. 'Come and write it, then,' responds César. Étienne declines at first, but eventually rises amid some mild clapping. César opens the box and counts the slips. He unfolds each in turn and reads out the three names to the secretary and two committee members. It turns out that Étienne Quintaux has simply written, '*les mêmes*'. One slip is illegible. Only one clear favourite emerges, Victor Jouffroy. Felicien Jouffroy and a *cultivateur* from Montoiseau tie for third place, necessitating another round of voting. Some have not entirely understood whom they should be voting for and a couple have voted again for Victor. César casts his eyes up to the ceiling. 'That's to make really sure,' the *maire* murmurs to Victor. Again, there is one illegible slip. After holding it at various angles to the light and adjusting his glasses, César hands it to the nearest council member, who announces 'Bavarel Jouffroy'. 'Jouffroy, Bavarel', the secretary repeats as he writes it down. Felicien is eventually elected for a second term, and the voting slips are burned in the stove.

Everyone rises to their feet and troops downstairs. The annual dinner will take place in the village café, consisting of soup, cold ham, and hot *saucisse de Morteau*, a local speciality, served with green salad and Algerian wine. Afterwards, people begin to buy more wine for those sitting at their table and, by midnight, everyone is drinking Asti spumante. It isn't always clear whether the corks are intended to fly clear of the fellow guests. Felicien describes how he was once so intent on keeping hold of the cork while he opened a bottle of champagne that the bottle shot out of his other hand and broke on the floor. By half-past one in the morning, people are beginning to think of the morning's milking and the first start to leave.

Annual General Meeting of the Pasture Co-operative

The communal pasture is managed by a second co-operative, which rents the pasture from the commune. Étienne Maitrugue is president. The annual general meeting takes place in the s*alle des réunions* a week after the dairy co-operative has met. The accounts of the co-operative are simpler, but there are some important decisions to be made at the meeting.

Until now, a cowherd has been employed to take milch cows to and from the pasture each day. Étienne begins by announcing that he has been unable to hire a herdsman or woman this year, and asks the meeting how they propose to deal with the situation. The lack of a cowherd is, in fact, well known. People have been discussing the problem for several days, if not weeks. Many are aware that in the neighbouring village of La Combe Sainte-Marie the *cultivateurs* take it in turn to lead the cows to and from the commons. None the less, a heated debate ensues before it is agreed that everyone will have to take it in turns. The meeting decides that each *cultivateur* will work for a number of days in the year proportionate to the number of cattle they are pasturing on the commons this year, but that they will not be expected to discharge their entire obligation on consecutive days. Pierre Bavarel, whose wife comes from La Combe Sainte-Marie, emerges as one of the principle proponents of this scheme. Eventually a vote is taken by show–of–hands. Several fail to vote in its favour but, when Étienne asks who is opposed, only his brother Alexandre holds up his hand. Alexandre is judged to be overruled. There is some joking about whose turn it will be on St John's Day. Saint Jean is the patron saint of cowherds and cheese-making. That day each *cultivateur* places a bouquet of flowers on the stable door and gives a few francs to the cowherd.

Felicien Jouffroy, the co-operative's secretary, deals with the accounts in ten minutes, and the three retiring committee members are each re-elected. A number of jobs which must be done to maintain the quality of the pasture are allocated *par soumission* (by tender). Each of the three areas of commons must be cleared of molehills and brushwood, and chemical fertilizer must be spread. Until piped water was supplied, water tanks had to be driven up to the pasture. Étienne announces the price given to carry out these tasks last year, and invites bids. Some are unchallenged but, where more than one person wants to do the same job, successive bids must be lower than the previous one. Once the jobs have been apportioned, Étienne announces the number of cattle each *cultivateur* wishes to place on the commons, and how the committee proposes to distribute the livestock. Those who would prefer a different allocation then arrange exchanges among themselves which, once agreed, are announced to Étienne. At ten o'clock, Étienne closes the meeting with the announcement '*et voilà, c'est la fin*'. Everyone moves to the café for a drink of wine, but this time no food is served.

THE AGRICULTURAL CALENDAR

The agricultural year begins with the manuring of the strips on which cereals or hay will be cultivated. If lack of snow allows, manuring may be carried out as early as January or February. Ground which is to be sown with cereals is later ploughed but if ploughing takes place too soon after the melting of the snow, the weight of the tractor compacts the soil. After ploughing, lumps of earth are broken up with a *canadienne*, or sprung-tine harrow. Saint Joseph's Day (19 March) is the last day of winter and, in principle, the start of planting season. In 1969, the first oats and barley were sown at the beginning of April and sowing continued throughout the month. Potatoes and beet are planted at the end of April. Several people told me that cereals should be planted during the new moon and root crops during the old moon. If planted during the new moon, potatoes and beet would flower all the time and put nothing into their roots. Leeks and lettuces planted during the new moon would go to seed. Trees are also best felled during the old moon, when the wood is dense but it is easier to trim one's fingernails during the new moon. When I checked actual dates of planting against phases of the moon, however, I found no correlation with phases of the moon and other people with whom I discussed planting remark with a smile, 'you've probably been told those old stories about the moon.' Verdier (1979: 61–7) and Zonabend (1984: 30–1) have recorded a more elaborated form of these traditions in the Burgundy village of Minot.

The cattle are stabled throughout the winter and the first are released in mid-April. Some wait until early May, when the soil has dried and there is less risk that the animals' hooves will churn up the ground, soiling the grass. Those who have run out of hay release their cattle first. At the end of April, heavy wooden or metal frames are used to level molehills on meadow, so that it can be mown for hay more easily.

In principle, meadow grass has grown sufficiently to be harvested for hay in late May, although this depends on the weather. In a dry year, it has passed its best by Bastille Day (14 July). The stalks harden, the leaves turn yellow/red and the seeds fall to the ground. In wet years, harvesting will continue into August. Once the grass has been cut a second, richer growth begins which will be harvested later as the *regain*. The second hay harvest begins in August and continues up to mid-September. As the days shorten there is less time to gather the hay and it takes more than two days to dry in the field, but the second harvest is richer than the first and is particularly valuable for those who have increased their herd size to the maximum their land can support. In 1969 *cultivateurs* often pile the hay into small stacks known locally as *chirons* (*meulons* is said to be the more general term), which gives it better overnight protection from rain. *Chirons* are said to protect the hay from rotting for up to two weeks. Cereals are harvested between mid–August and mid–September.

Winter wheat is planted in October. The cattle are brought down to their stables for winter between 21 October and 15 November, depending on the weather. If there is snow, or so much rain that the cows soil the grass by trampling in mud, they will be stabled earlier.

When I returned to Pellaport in 1995, one *cultivateur* lent me a notebook in which he had recorded the dates of the main events in the agricultural cycle during the years between 1957 and his retirement in 1985. Although the record for each year is incomplete the cumulative record gives a good indication of variation from year to year which complements the account for 1969 in Table 1.3.

TABLE 1.3. *Joseph Bavarel's record of the agricultural calendar, 1957–85*

	Earliest	Latest	Years recorded
Sow cereals	29 March	5 May	17
Release cattle	22 April	7 May	12
Plant potatoes	9 April	7 May	10
Sow beet	5 May	17 May	2*
Saw firewood	10 May	13 June	
	31 August	4 September	8
First hay harvest starts	3 June	27 June	10
First hay harvest ends	12 July	23 August	15
Second hay harvest ends	31 August	19 September	2†
Harvest cereals	20 August	25 September	12
Harvest potatoes	16 September		1
Autumn ploughing	13 September	8 October	3
Sow winter cereals	4 October		1
Return cattle to stable	19 October	21 October	2

* Only mentioned in the first two years' records.
† Two years are also noted in which no second harvest took place.

Manuring Fields

The fourth of March is a bright blue morning, although there is still snow on the more sheltered slopes of the surrounding fields. At the c*antonnier*'s house, the windows have been opened to let in fresh air. The c*antonnier* himself is cutting down some shrubs by the roadside outside the church. Two doors down the road from the c*antonnier*'s Mme Monnier senior is standing in the street outside her front door washing clothes in a metal tub, beating them on a wooden board. Across the street, Jacques Maitrugue has parked his tractor next to his manure heap and is pitch-forking manure onto a wooden trailer hitched to the tractor. The manure is steaming in the mid-morning sun, and hens are picking among the straw. When the trailer is fully loaded, Jacques drives out of the village towards the neighbouring village of Vaux until Pellaport is just out of sight behind the first rise. Here, Jacques's father is waiting on the edge of a strip. The ground is still half-covered with snow but, where it has melted, straw left from earlier manuring can be seen lying on the grass. Jacques's father gets onto the tractor, and his son stands on the trailer, forking the manure onto the ground as his father drives slowly the length of the strip, then returns in the opposite direction. Distant noises can be heard rising from the village on the still air. This strip will be harvested for hay as cattle do not like eating grass which has had manure spread on it. The best fields are manured every year, although the effect of manur-ing can be seen for up to four years.

The *maire*'s son spreads manure on his hayfields a week later. He works on his own, allowing the tractor to run slowly along the strip while he walks beside the trailer, raking off the manure with a *croc*, a long-pronged fork on which the prongs are mounted at right-angles to the shaft. Like the *maire*'s son, Felicien Jouffroy walks beside his trailer while the tractor drives itself along the strip. Others work with their wives. Alexandre Maitrugue is helped by his son, who had returned from sixth-form college in Besançon because he has no lessons that day. Victor Jouf-froy is helped by his second cousin, who lives nearby, and the *cantonnier*, another neighbour. After they have unloaded the manure, some must spread it with a pitchfork, but others use an *éparpilleur*, a machine mounted behind the tractor. The *éparpilleur* is jointly owned by seven farmers, who bought it in 1966. It requires a tractor of 30 horsepower or more to drive its spinning blades, which means those with smaller tractors cannot use it. Pierre Bavarel and his sister's husband Étienne Maitrugue have collaborated to buy an *épandeur*, or muck-spreader; a specially constructed trailer which scatters the manure mechanically and can be driven at a running pace. They can comfortably work alone and complete the job more quickly. The only other *épandeur* in the village belongs to César Maitrugue.

A normal trailer holds $1\frac{1}{2}$ metric tonnes of manure. Hayfields require 15–18 tonnes of manure per hectare; cereal fields about 20 tonnes.

Putting Cattle out to Pasture

Until the end of April, the pastures have not grown sufficiently to feed the cattle, nor has the ground dried out sufficiently from the winter's snow to withstand the trampling of hooves. Nicolas Jouffroy releases his cattle on 25 April, the first fine day after two weeks of snow, followed by rain. As soon as the morning milking is complete, at 7.30, Nicolas begins to unchain the heifers and the cows not currently in milk. He and his wife Thérèse warn me to stand clear of the entrance, because the cattle are a little wild when they first leave the stable. Thérèse stands to one side of the doorway, ready to deflect those who turn the wrong way, while Nicolas's father Alphonse waits at the junction with the road leading to the centre of the village, to direct them towards the pasture. A thunderous mooing begins inside the stable as the cattle realize they are being released. They emerge one by one, gathering in a group outside the door. One kicks up its hind legs, two others immediately begin to butt each other but, suddenly, they all begin to head towards the pasture of their own accord. One of the last to emerge tries to go the wrong way; Thérèse breaks her stick on its back, but Nicolas is carrying a halter which, after a struggle, he gets over the heifer's head, running up the hill with it and rounding up a couple of stragglers who have started to return towards the village. The remainder are waiting at the entrance to the pasture. After herding them in, Nicolas closes the barrier made of lengths of barbed wire nailed to poles.

As we return towards the village, the priest and choirboys pass in a procession. The choirboys are wearing their white surplices. The leader carries a cross. Behind, a group of women and children follow, the widows forming a group dressed in black. They are singing as they pass. Nicolas explains that today is Saint Mark's Day, and they are praying for a good harvest at each of the calvaries placed at the entrances to the village. Nicolas conveys a faint sense of ridicule as he explains what they are doing (he once asked me, while I was watching him milk his cows, 'and do Protestants believe in transmigration of the soul?').

We return to the stable, where Nicolas begins to release the milch cows. They will be put on richer pasture, nearer the village. The cows also seem to know where they are going. Some come out of the stable so quickly that their hooves slip on the concrete ramp and they fall before hurrying to join the others. At the top of the small hill, a few have got into Alexandre Maitrugue's orchard. Nicolas clambers over the barbed wire fence and drives them out through the gate. One turns into the first pasture and, having noticed that the others are continuing, manages to leap over the double strand of barbed wire in the corner of the field. Thérèse is waiting to direct them into the correct strip. Finally the gate is shut, and the Jouffroys contemplate their cattle, some of whom have already begun to eat. The grass is covered thickly in dew, and a cuckoo calls from the forest on the escarpment across the valley. Nicolas's father asks me if I have any money in my pocket: 'if you have a few *sous* left when you hear the cuckoo, you'll never be short of money', he says.

In the next two days, Pierre Bavarel and Victor Jouffroy, who have two of the other largest *exploitations* in the village, also release their cattle. Victor tells me that, fifteen years ago, the cattle spent much more time in the stable and the grass was brought to them, rather than releasing them onto the pasture. Before the introduction of electric fences, cattle could only be released if there was someone in the household free to act as cowherd. It was the job of the *garde-champêtre* (hayward) to make sure no one allowed their livestock to graze on their neighbours' land. When no one had more than five or six cows, it was possible to cut sufficient grass to feed them in the stable.

Repairing Fences on the Communal Pasture

On the day that Nicolas released his cattle onto his own land, seven *cultivateurs* assembled at lunchtime in the village square, in order to repair the fence around the portion of commons known as la pâture du Seigneur. This was not a task for which they had tendered; rather, everyone who was free had been asked to help. Work had begun that morning, and a trailer was already waiting, loaded with tins of nails and staples, sledgehammers, and pliers. Felix Viennet fools around, pretending to hit people on the head with a sledgehammer. We ride on the side of the trailer, up la rue du Croset. Pierre Bavarel joins the party, bringing his cattle-dog, as we pass his house. The track we follow runs past le bois du Seigneur and comes to an end on a large expanse of high, level pasture. César's son Armand Maitrugue has left his tractor and trailer here before lunch, with fresh fencing poles and barbed wire coiled around an old oil drum. The party splits up, and I go with Pierre and Armand to an agreed section of the boundary fence. They work their way along the fence, replacing posts whose bases have rotted and hammering back those which have loosened without rotting. The limestone is not far beneath the surface and it is often impossible to hammer the posts much deeper into the ground. Where undergrowth makes it impossible to reach the fence, Armand cuts it back with a sickle attached to a long pole. He uses a crowbar to make holes for the new posts. Pierre pulls out the staples from posts which are to be replaced and, if the staples are not too bent, puts them in his pocket to use again. Where the wire has slackened, he tightens it by taking a twist around the handles of his pliers. His dog sleeps in the shade of the trailer, or under bushes. Every time a stretch has been completed, Armand drives the tractor forward while Pierre walks with his dog and the sledgehammer, checking the next section. It is already hot. Armand has a bottle of red wine and lemonade wrapped in a wet sack behind his tractor's radiator grill. Every now and then we pause for a drink. After an hour we meet Alexandre Maitrugue, the *maire*'s son and a third *cultivateur* coming the other way. The two drivers steer their tractors on a collision course, braking at the last minute. We share a drink and discuss, good-humouredly, which tractor would have won if each had tried to push the other out of its way. Armand, Pierre, and I then drive to another portion of commons, aux tartes des Fleurs, where they have left some unfinished work from the morning. The others depart in a different direction. Everyone reassembles at five o'clock outside the café, and we go in to order two litres of wine. As we are walking away from the trailer, somebody realizes Felix Viennet is not there. Looking back, we realize he is trapped by his shirt, which has become hooked into the roll of barbed wire. Nicolas Jouffroy goes back to release him, amid general laughter.

Putting Cattle on the Commons

Milch cows are taken up to la pâture du Seigneur for the first time on the seventh of May, and heifers put on another section of the commons the following day. It is a grey, drizzling morning and cloud rises like smoke, in long streamers, out of the forest on the escarpment above the village. Alexandre Maitrugue and his wife Catherine have been asked to lead cows to and from the pasture for the first five days. At about ten minutes past seven, while some farmers are still pushing their handcarts back from the dairy, Alexandre blows a horn in the village square. The horn was formerly used by the hired cowherd. Each *cultivateur* releases the cows that he wants to pasture on the commons, and leads them to the square. From here, the Maitrugues take over, guiding them up la rue de Croset, whacking the stragglers on their rumps and eventually leading them through the gate onto la pâture du Seigneur.

By eight o'clock Alexandre and Catherine are back in the square and ready to take the heifers to their portion of the commons. The rain has stopped and the cloud has lifted above the top of the escarpment. Knowing that the heifers are particularly wild when first released, sixteen *cultivateurs* have assembled to help. Groups of young cows are hurried across the main street. Most are led down the old road out of the village, but *cultivateurs* from the part of Pellaport known as le coin de la Combe take the new road, built in the 1920s, which is closer to their end of the village. The roads meet at the foot of the village. Each animal has its owner's dairy co-operative membership number painted in orange on its flank. As we pass Maurice Maitrugue's house a noise of slapping and shouting comes from inside the stable. Nicolas Jouffroy and the *maire*'s son go in to help. One heifer breaks through the barbed-wire fence of an orchard and is pursued between the trees by Armand Maitrugue and Raphael Mignod, to the amusement of those who see. At the bottom of the dry valley all the heifers are herded across the main road, and up the old track known as la vie des Moutons, from the time this pasture was used to graze sheep (sheep have disappeared as the village economy becomes increasingly specialized in the production of Comté, the local variety of Gruyère). Claude Bavarel explains to me that the commons have been divided into two by a fence so that, while the heifers are grazing one half, the other can regenerate. They will spend fifteen days at a time on each half. He points out the blue *clochettes* (bell flowers) and purple orchis among the grass which, he says, make it particularly good pasture. Animals and men scatter across the hillside, heading in the general direction of the gap in the fence. Pierre Bavarel's cattle-dog snaps at the heels of heifers that stop to graze, making them kick their legs in the air. Once the animals are all herded through the gap, several men struggle to close the barrier made of barbed wire stapled to poles. Unfortunately, the party who had worked on this pasture has cut the wire just too short. Someone spotted some spare wire which had been thrown into a bush out of reach of the cattle and retrieved it, to increase the size of the loop which hooked over the gatepost. Several voices ask who had been responsible for this error. Both Pierre Bavarel and the *maire*'s son claim to have made the barrier but, since they had not been working together, the question remained unanswered.

The entrance to the commons itself is closed by a brand-new orange-painted metal gate made by the village blacksmith. The gateposts have been set in concrete, but the gate has been left to one side while the concrete dried. Just over a week ago General de Gaulle resigned as president and the leading candidates to replace him are Alain Poher, the caretaker president, and Georges Pompidou. As the gate is being hung on its hinges, someone notices that the words 'Poher '69' have been written in the cement on one side. As the laughter dies down, Felicien Jouffroy explains, 'We wanted to write "Pompidou '69" on the right-hand side, but there wasn't enough room on the cement.' When we reach the main road, the *cultivateurs* divide again and those living in le coin de la Combe take the new road. Victor Jouffroy has driven down on his tractor and, as he catches up with the others, he stops to let them all climb onto his trailer. The rest of us are walking up the old road. 'You see,' remarks Pierre Bavarel, '*la commune de la Combe* is quite separate from the rest of the village; we ought to form *une commune de Croset* at our end.'

Sowing Grain

Small quantities of oats and barley are sown every year to feed cattle in winter. A few *cultivateurs* began in early April but, since then, rain has held up sowing. Felicien Jouffroy sows oats on 26 April, sowing the grain on two different strips at opposite ends of the commune. His long, narrow strips of ploughed soil are situated between strips belonging to other *cultivateurs*, which are under grass. Several neighbours are using *rabots étaupinières*, heavy wooden or metal frames towed behind their tractors, to flatten molehills on grass which will be cut for hay. Felicien has picked branches from the hedgerow and inserted them six paces apart, as *jalons* (markers), across the end of his strip. He uses a special long, narrow sack slung over his shoulder. Half the grain is in the bottom of the sack, on his back, half is in a fold on his chest.

Walking just to the left of the first line of markers, Felicien proceeds slowly and deliberately, casting a handful of grain with each step, throwing it across his chest to his left, at waist height. Every now and then he pauses to adjust the sack, bringing more grain forward. When he has reached the far end of the strip he returns along the edge, walking in the opposite direction and thus casting grain onto the same soil. When the first sack is empty he takes a second from his trailer. The same process is

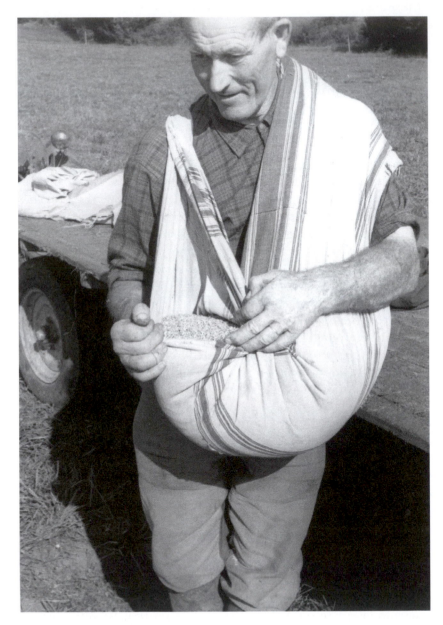

PL. 3. Preparing to broadcast grain

followed between each pair of markers. Having broadcast grain over the whole strip he then takes a bowl containing chemical fertilizer. A cord tied to the bowl allows him to hang it from his neck, and he casts the fertilizer in the same way, although less methodically. Felicien then disconnects his trailer from the tractor and connects *une canadienne* (a sprung-tine harrow) which he tows up and down the strip to bury the grain. The sprung-tine harrow is needed because the soil is still quite damp and must be broken down. An ordinary, spiked harrow (*une herse*) is then driven over the strip to further level the soil. Each harrow is three paces wide, and is driven twice over the same section of the strip, necessitating two runs in each direction between each pair of markers. Finally, Felicien takes a hoe and pulls back lumps of soil which have fallen on his neighbours' strips. I time his work on one of the two strips; it takes Felicien just under 2 hours to sow 15 ares. Raphael Mignot and his father take $2\frac{1}{2}$ hours to sow 40 ares, Raphael driving the tractor and his father broadcasting the grain. In the autumn, Felicien sows 30 ares of winter wheat in 90 minutes.

As we return to the village, after loading the harrows onto Felicien's trailer, he stops to show me a manhole giving access to a pipe taking drinking water to the village. Felicien explains that running water was first piped to the village in the early years of the century. Alexandre Maitrugue later told me that every house used to have an underground cistern fed by rainwater from the roof and pumped back with a hand pump.

Planting Potatoes

Potatoes are planted in mid-May. To plough the furrows, Claude Bavarel uses his old horse-drawn plough, connected to his tractor. Since the plough was designed to be hand-held Claude has asked his sister's husband Eduard Maitrugue to guide the plough. He has also asked his neighbour the retired postman for help. Claude's brother-in-law occasionally directs the plough with one hand but, since the plough seems to guide itself reasonably well, often rides on the back of the tractor watching the plough's progress, signalling to Claude when the ploughshare reaches the end of the strip. To return, the plough must be disconnected. Claude swings the tractor around. The plough is of a reversible Dombasle type. It has two blades and mould boards mounted one above the other. One will throw the soil to the left, one to the right. By rotating them through 180 degrees, the plough can be taken back in the opposite direction and will still throw the ridge of soil to the same side of the furrow. Eduard reverses the plough and reconnects it to the tractor.

Behind them, the retired postman places seed potatoes not *in* the furrow, but on the as yet unturned soil next to it. He measures the distance between each potato with his foot, leaving a sufficient gap that the potatoes will be 30cm. apart. Before returning with the plough, Claude and Eduard help complete the row of potatoes. As the plough is driven back, the soil on which the potatoes lie is turned over and falls into the furrow, burying the potatoes. Claude allows the wheels on one side of the tractor to run in the furrow. This ensures the next furrow will be the correct distance away. After an hour and a half, Mme Bavarel and a friend arrive to help. It takes $2^{1}/_{2}$ hours to plant 9.5 ares.

In July the potatoes must be 'rowed', heaping soil over the potatoes. This is done using a special plough with a V-shaped blade and double mould-board, which throws the soil to both sides at once. The plough is drawn between the rows of potatoes. Unfortunately the tractor is too heavy to be driven over the growing potatoes. After he bought a tractor, Claude used to borrow a neighbour's horse, but the neighbour is now dead. Last year, Claude used *une pioche* (a mattock) but this year he tests an idea he has had. His son has returned from sixth-form college and will drive the tractor across the grass beyond the end of the strip. A length of cable equal to the length of the strip will run between tractor and plough, enabling the tractor to pull the plough. Several unanticipated problems are encountered. It is difficult to knot the steel cable and the cable is not quite long enough. Claude at first suggests his son drive over the last few metres of potatoes then thinks better of it and decides to begin with the tractor just on the grass, and do the first few metres with his mattock. Otherwise the innovation works well. Both father and son are pleased with the results. I began to appreciate that the move from horses to tractors is not necessarily straightforward.

To Dechailles with Prosper Jouffroy

The more I became interested in changing agricultural techniques, the more I wanted to discover a household who still worked with horses. Prosper Jouffroy, Felicien's retired half-brother, offered to help and we made several visits on our bikes to neighbouring villages. One of the first was to the village of Dechailles, where a household consisting of an elderly man called M. Dôle, his wife and his unmarried brother and sister, still worked with a pair of horses.

'They're all *écervelés* (brainless) in Dechailles', Prosper warns me before we set off (cf. Zonabend 1984: 91 and 210 n.). As we cycle through the communal forest he tells me how he had once visited Dechailles before the Second World War with a neighbour who was known for his aggressive temper. When the men of Dechailles saw them approaching they began to throw stones. Prosper and his friend dismounted and threw the stones back. The curé came out of his house and appealed to everyone to stop, but to no avail. Prosper succeeded in knocking the front teeth out of one of his opponents. The following morning a gendarme appeared at Prosper's house, asking him to return to Dechailles: 'He wanted me to pay for the teeth I'd knocked out!' The curé, however, spoke in Prosper's defence, saying they had done well to defend themselves, and he was let off without a fine.

A couple who are first cousins of a woman living in Pellaport helpfully direct us to the right house. We lean our bikes against the house wall. Prosper knocks on the door, and walks straight in without waiting for a reply. At the kitchen table two elderly ladies and a similarly aged man are drinking bowls of coffee and eating slices of bread and cheese. Prosper explains why we have come.

'And where do you come from?' demands the old man.

'Pellaport', replies Prosper, in a tone of voice which implies he wouldn't dream of coming from any other village.

'So you're a Maitrugue, then?'

'No . . .,' Prosper pauses before answering, 'a Jouffroy.'

'Ah,' the man suddenly recognizes Prosper: 'we were mobilized together in '39!'[3]

'Yes, we were indeed.'

'And you're called Propo, no?' says the man, using Prosper's nickname. Everyone laughs. Chairs are produced for us, and glasses. The old man leaves the room to find a bottle of wine while one of the women goes in search of his brother, whom I have already met, but who was reluctant to let me take photographs of him at work. The presence of Prosper is a catalyst. They willingly fetch the horses from the stable, allow me to photograph them harnessed to a wagon, and promise I can return to watch them harvesting the hay.

'You see,' said Prosper as we cycled home, 'everyone knows I'm called Propo; it was thirty years since he and I had seen each other.'

---

[3] This is what my field notes say. They must both have been in their forties when the Second World War began.

The Hay Harvest (la Fenaison)

The first hay harvest extends over a period of four to six weeks, depending on the weather. After the grass has regrown some fields are harvested
a second time. Two days are required to harvest a section of hayfield. The
grass must be cut in the early morning, while the dew still lies on it. Half-
way through the first day it must be turned to allow the underside of the
blades to dry in the sun. Overnight it is put into rows (or in small
haystacks called *chirons*), to protect it from dew and the bleaching effect
of moonlight. It must then be spread out the following morning, turned
a second time at midday, and put in rows to facilitate collection. Since the
cattle spend six months of the year in the stable, harvesting sufficient hay
is crucial to the success of the *exploitation*. The amount of hay that can be
harvested by the household is one of the most significant factors limiting
the expansion of production. It is traditional to hang a bouquet of flowers on the back of the last load of hay to be brought back to the barn.

Harvesting with Horse-Drawn Equipment

The household in Dechailles who still work with horses use harvesting
equipment which was introduced to the region around the time of the
First World War. The *faneuse* was the first mechanical substitute for turning the drying hay with a pitchfork. Their *exploitation* bought its first in
1918. The *faneuse* consists of four mechanically operated forks mounted
side by side between two large, spoked iron wheels. The driver sits on top,
directing the horse, who is harnessed between wooden shafts attached to

TABLE 1.4. *Duration of Joseph Bavarel's first hay harvest, 1966–80*

1966	3 June–1 August
1967	15 June–31 July
1968	18 June–23 August
1969	27 June–4 August
1970	25 June–8 August
1971	27 June–27 July
1975	27 June–1 August
1980	17 June–3 August

Note: During this period Joseph had at first 5 and eventually 7 cows. He bought
a baler in 1974.

P L . 4. *Faneuse*

the axle bearings. As the axle rotates, a crank-shaft lifts the forks up and down, causing them to flick the drying hay into the air.

M. Dôle, wearing a straw hat to protect himself from the sun, drives the horse up and down the strip of meadow. At each end the horse turns by stepping sideways. M. Dôle makes it easier for the horse by running up one edge of the strip, then returning along the opposite edge, creating gradually tighter turns as he approaches the central section. Three strips are worked; it takes 32 minutes to turn 55 ares of hay, but not all the hay is turned because each fork is, of necessity, off the ground part of the time and some hay (I estimate about one-third) is missed. The horse is covered with flies. It flicks its head and sometimes refuses to turn while working on the third strip. M. Dôle lets it rest for a few seconds, explaining that it is tired. He asks if anyone in Pellaport is still using a *faneuse*, and how many have bought the new *pirouettes* that are being introduced from Alsace. Having completed the third strip he returns and repeats the process. On my way back to Pellaport for lunch I meet his sister walking away from the village with a large hand-rake. She is going to rake back the loose hay which has fallen beneath the hedges or onto neighbouring strips. 'Have you seen a baler at work?' She asks, 'It's marvellous how it picks up the hay and turns it into bales, isn't it?'

PL. 5. *Râteleuse*

After lunch I cycle back to watch the hay being loaded. The younger brother uses one horse to draw a large mechanical rake, the *râteleuse*, which gathers the hay into rows across the strip. He sits on a seat over the rake. Each time the teeth have gathered sufficient hay, he pulls on a lever to raise the rake. Having dealt with the first strip, he goes to the next, leaving the others to load it onto a trailer drawn by the other horse. His older brother uses a pitchfork to draw the rows of hay into piles separated by the width of the trailer. His sister stands on the trailer to receive the hay, which is pitchforked up to her by a younger man, whom I fail to identify. The trailer is pulled up and down the strip. A small girl, aged about 10, from the farm next door to the Dôles, drags a large hand-rake back and forth, gathering up loose hay and taking it to the piles. When the first trailer is fully loaded a wooden pole called *une presse* is hooked under the front frame. A rope is looped over the other end of the pole, and wound taut around a winch on the back of the trailer. Loose hay is combed from the sides of the load with a rake, and the horse led to the edge of the field. The loaded trailer is exchanged for an empty one, and the process continues.

PL. 6. Harvesting with horse–drawn trailer

After a while the older brother returns, having finished putting the hay in rows on the other strips, and takes over the job of pitchforking hay up to the trailer. The middle-aged man takes a second hand-rake (which I had been using until then) to help the girl. Later he replaces the sister on top of the waggon. No one is specifically given the job of minding the horse; when it is time to move forward the man with the pitchfork leads it a few paces. If it moves unbidden, everyone shouts together to tell it to stop. At one point it makes a lunge towards some loose hay still caught in the hedge, upsetting the man on top of the loaded trailer. A strip of 22 ares provides two waggon loads, and is harvested in 75 minutes. They tell me this is quick work.

Harvesting with a Tractor but without a Baler

Felicien Jouffroy has owned a tractor since 1956. He replaced his *faneuse* and *râteleuse* the same year, buying a new piece of equipment known as a *râteau faneur* which did the job of both. Although horse-drawn *râteaux faneurs* existed, even two horses were scarcely powerful enough to pull them.

Pʟ. 7. *Râteau faneur*

The great advantage of the *râteau faneur* is that it is no longer necessary to take two pieces of equipment from strip to strip, only one of which
can be transported at a time. The *râteau faneur* functions as a mechanical
pitchfork when the tines rotate in one direction, turning the hay, and as a
rake to put the hay into rows when the tines rotate in the opposite direction. It has the further advantage of creating longitudinal rows, rather
than transverse ones, so that it is no longer necessary to stack the rows
into piles to allow the trailer to pass.

Felicien drives out to his hayfields at eight in the morning, after milking has been completed, to spread the hay which he had left in rows
overnight. He works the *râteau faneur* in the same pattern as M. Dôle,
running up one side of the strip, across the top edge, then down the far
side, gradually converging on the centre. He has spread 33 ares in 20
minutes. Although this is very similar to the rate achieved by M. Dôle, he
does not have to repeat the process to make sure all the hay has been
turned.

Later in the morning Felicien's daughter and her husband come over
from Vaux to help load the hay. His daughter drives the tractor and her
husband stands on the trailer. One trailer is loaded before lunch and two
during the afternoon. The tractor is driven between two lines of hay.

PL. 8. Harvesting with tractor

Felicien pitchforks the hay up from one side while I pitchfork from the other. Felicien's wife follows with the large hand-rake. Felicien calls to his daughter when it is time to drive the tractor forward. When the trailer is fully loaded Felicien and his son-in-law tie the load down with a pole and rope in the same way that the Dôles had done and comb the loose hay from the sides. At the end of the day, the Jouffroys have harvested 60 ares, which produce three trailers of hay. Each trailer takes 20 minutes to load. With eight cows and three heifers in the stable, they normally aim to bring in 40 trailer-loads of hay. During the winter each cow will receive 20 kilos of hay a day. Felicien points out that the yield varies substantially from field to field, according to the quality of the soil. His cousin Victor Jouffroy harvested 11 trailer-loads from 1 hectare, whereas Étienne Maitrugue obtained only 1 trailer-load from a strip of 40 ares. The afternoon's two trailers are hitched in line behind the tractor, and Felicien drives them back to the village.

The hay is lifted into the hayloft using an electrically powered winch. A cradle constructed of poles joined with steel cables was placed on each trailer before it was loaded. Each trailer in turn is driven up the ramp leading to the floor of the barn. The ends of the cables are attached to a hook, and the entire load is raised into the roof. A sliding platform high

PL. 9. *Remy*

PL. 10. *Pirouette*

in the roof beams is brought forward and the hay lowered onto it. Once the hook has been disconnected, the load can be pitchforked into store. It takes between 25 and 30 minutes to put a trailer-load into store.

Harvesting Hay with a Bailer

Nicolas and Victor Jouffroy both harvest their hay with balers, which require a more powerful tractor than Felicien owns. Nicolas is one of several farmers who have increased the carrying capacity of the trailers by nailing temporary extensions to either side which support the end of the bales. Both have replaced their *râteau faneurs* with two newer machines, the *remy* and the *pirouette*. The *pirouette* turns the hay with rapidly spinning metal prongs. Many of the farmers who continue to use a *râteau faneur* are sceptical of the value of the *pirouette*, saying that, while it is good for turning damp grass on the day it has been cut, by the second day the force of the prongs tends to shatter the hay. The *remy* puts the hay in rows. Those who have made the transition say that the benefit of having each job done more quickly outweighs the disadvantage of reverting to two separate machines. Both Nicolas and Victor have bought second, larger tractors but kept their smaller ones.

PL. 11. Harvesting with tractor and bailer

On the afternoon of 15 July, Nicolas bales his hay with the help of a neighbour's teenage son. The baler is connected between the tractor and a trailer. Nicolas drives the tractor, while his helper stands on the trailer. As the bales are delivered, he stacks them behind himself. Once or twice he has to call to Nicolas to stop, because the bales are delivered faster than he can arrange them. Two bales disintegrate as he lifts them; they are thrown back onto the ground. Nicolas drives the baler back over them, jumping out of the tractor to pull the discarded twine away and spread out the hay, as he approaches. When the strip has been harvested, we drive to another, where Nicolas's wife Thérèse is waiting with the old tractor and the *remy*. She takes the driving-seat of the big tractor and Nicolas climbs onto the trailer to receive the bales. Their neighbour's son drives ahead in the small tractor, putting the hay into rows for the baler. At the end of the day they have harvested 7 trailer loads, totalling 489 bales, from 2 hectares and 60 ares. Back at their barn, the bales are unloaded using a conveyor belt (*un monte-bottes*). One trailer takes 7 minutes to unload, the other takes 8 minutes. With twenty cows and thirteen heifers in the stable, they are aiming to harvest a total of about 5,500 bales, or 80 trailer loads.

Victor Jouffroy is helped both by his brother and by his wife's brother's family. They are not *cultivateurs*, but arrange their summer holidays to coincide with the hay harvest. Victor and his wife give them free food and accommodation in return. On the afternoon of 19 July Victor tows four trailers out of the village to the strips of hay he cut on the previous day. When they reach the first strip Victor's son-in-law tows the *remy* behind the old tractor. Victor's wife's brother drives the large tractor, while Victor stands on the trailer to receive the bales. His brother walks between the two tractors, pulling loose hay missed by the *remy* into the waiting rows with a large hand-rake. The first strip of 15 ares is harvested in 15 minutes. The trailer is loaded high with bales, but Victor tells me they will not do so well on the next strip, which has been spoiled by molehills and a plague of mice. When I comment that I am interested in a comparison of mechanized and unmechanized techniques, Victor says that a baler enables the harvest to be carried out almost, but not quite, twice as fast as with a pitchfork. Both he and Nicolas experimented for a few years with elevators, which lifted the hay onto the trailer without baling it, but found this to be a clumsy method and sold their elevators to other farmers. Nicolas's elevator is standing, abandoned, beside the farm track which leads towards les tartes des Fleurs. When we reach the third strip, Victor and his brother change jobs, Victor taking the large hand-rake to retrieve what the *remy* could not reach from the margins of the strip. Later he hands the rake to his son-in-law, and uses a pitchfork to push loose hay that will otherwise be missed into the mouth of the baler. Pierre Bavarel and Jacques Maitrugue, who also have balers, also use a large hand-rake. Étienne Maitrugue dispenses with the rake, but one of his sons walks beside the baler, pushing escaping hay into its path.

Victor completes his harvest on 1 August, having gathered a total of 60 trailer loads for a stable containing seventeen cows and eleven heifers.

The Cereal Harvest (La Moisson)

In the days when almost every family farmered, the commune bought a threshing machine which still stands at the back of the garage beneath the *salle des fêtes* (village hall). Each household cut its own cereal and took the sheaves back to the farmhouse. The thresher was taken from barn to barn. Alexandre Maitrugue described to me how neighbours would work together in each other's barns. He used to help his younger brother Étienne and their neighbour the *maire*. So much dust was generated by the process of separating the grain from the chaff that everyone drank copiously and sometimes people passed out in the stifling heat. Maurice Genre, one of the smaller-scale *cultivateurs* in Pellaport still harvests his cereals with a mechanical scythe and threshes it with a small machine he keeps in his stable. He is a little afraid of being laughed at for his old-fashioned ways, especially as last year he failed to complete his harvest and had to leave some cereal rotting in the field. Everyone else has clubbed together to pay an entrepreneur who brings a combine harvester to the village.

The combine harvester arrives on 31 August. It will work its way around the village fields, harvesting all the grain in each section. All the *cultivateurs* who have sown grain in the section arrive on their tractors to help. The machine discards the stalks of the barley, which will be collected later by each farmer. The grain is stored in a tank in the harvester and transferred to sacks each time the tank is full. To save time, all those present help fill and stack the sacks. By lunchtime seven *cultivateurs* have arrived, including Claude Bavarel, Felicien Jouffroy, Étienne and Maurice Maitrugue. The two Maitrugues have borrowed a seed-drill from a farmer in Vaux and experimented with it. At that moment it was Maurice's strip that was being harvested. He contends that it had taken him half a day to complete sowing 1 hectare 40 ares with the machine, whereas it would have taken him a week had he worked by hand and, moreover, he had only needed half as much seed grain. 'As little as that?'

PL. 12. Waiting for the combine harvester

demands Felicien. 'Well, almost . . .' replies Maurice. (Claude later confides that Maurice was so bad at broadcasting grain that he usually asked Étienne to do it for him). Maurice points out gaps in the barley at the far end of his strip which, he explains, were caused by turning too quickly and not allowing sufficient time for the grain to fall.

After the next load of sacks has been filled from his strip, Maurice produces a bottle of wine, which he hands round. Nicolas Jouffroy arrives with his small daughter; Thérèse is in hospital, having just given birth to their second child and Nicolas chooses to sit on another trailer with his daughter, drinking orange juice, which makes him the butt of jokes shouted across by those who would prefer him to join the party. As the afternoon proceeds, thunderclouds build up and rain starts to fall. One *cultivateur* drives the loaded sacks back to the village. Nicolas goes to find a canvas to cover the remaining sacks but, within ten minutes, the rain is falling so hard that harvesting is abandoned for the day.

Harvesting continues the following afternoon, starting with a strip belonging to the *maire*. He asks me not to time how long it takes to harvest, saying it is a poor year for oats and the figure would be misleading. There is a discussion of the time lost driving the harvester from one strip to the next and the value of farmers exchanging strips to create larger fields (it costs 90 francs an hour to hire the harvester). Felicien Jouffroy sits on a half-full sack and tells the others about the time he was a prisoner-of-war, when the German farmer for whom he was working had overrun his own strip and was harvesting part of his neighbour's. Felicien pointed this out, but the farmer replied that it was irrelevant, since it was all for *La Grande Allemagne*. When the *maire*'s strip has been harvested and the grain discharged into sacks, his son brings out a bottle of beer to pass round, offering it first to the driver of the harvester. It becomes increasingly apparent that it is customary for each *cultivateur* to provide a drink for all present when his strip has been harvested. As the afternoon proceeds some return to the village, but three stay to the end.

The *maire*'s opinion that it had been a bad year for cereals is a general one. As Claude Bavarel puts it, 'Les souris ont rigolé cette année' (the mice had a ball this year). None the less Maurice and Nicolas, who also used a *semoir*, both achieve a harvest of about eighteen times the weight of barley sown whereas those who broadcast their grain achieve an increase of between four and nine times what they had sown.

After the cereals have been harvested the soil is broken up with a *cana-dienne*, to prevent weeds growing, and later ploughed. The commune owns a machine for spreading chemical fertilizer and many fertilize the strips they will be resowing with cereals next year.

The Potato Harvest

Claude Bavarel begins to harvest his potatoes on 17 September, with the help of a neighbour. Once the stems have been pulled up he uses his normal plough to turn over the soil and uncover the potatoes which do not come up with the stems. He drives the tractor while his neighbour guides the plough. The mice have had a ball again, eating the roots (thus preventing some potatoes from growing) and some of the grown potatoes. The surviving potatoes are sorted into piles, the poorer ones to be fed to Claude's pigs, the better ones for human consumption. Rotten ones are thrown to the edge of the strip. Finally, *crocs* are used to rake out any hidden potatoes. As they work, they discuss village affairs. Claude's neighbour asks whether Maurice Genre has joined in hiring the combine harvester this year and clicks her tongue when told 'no'. 'And half his crop was ruined last year,' she adds. Having been shown how to do the work, I am allowed to drive the tractor. After lunch conversation turns to one of the village women who can be seen in the distance tending a large vegetable garden. Although she owns a quantity of land, this woman never says 'Bonjour' when she passes people in the street, nor does she converse with her sister-in-law. She is not *gentille*. Indeed, says Claude, pulling up a potato full of holes, she is a little like this potato. To harvest 2¼ ares, 4 hours and 50 minutes are needed.

Alexandre Maitrugue harvests his potatoes five days later. He has a special plough with a double mould-board on which a series of iron rods are welded, allowing the soil to fall through but throwing the potatoes to the side. It has the advantage of not slicing any potatoes in half, and of leaving fewer to be raked out with *crocs*. Catherine and their son start to pull up the stems. The strip is just below the communal woodland aux tartes des Fleurs. A wild boar has come out of the wood and rooted up some potatoes but fortunately many have survived. It takes them 1¾ hours to harvest 2 ares.

The Second Hay Harvest (Le Regain)

While harvesting the *regain*, Nicolas Jouffroy tries out a rotary *faucheuse*, or mechanical scythe. The manager of his regular garage was on holiday when Nicolas's usual mechanical scythe broke on the last day of the first hay harvest and he borrowed a rotary scythe from the brother of one of the other farmers in the village, who runs a small garage. On the second occasion (22 September), a mechanic brought the rotary scythe from his usual garage. Nicolas is the first in the village to try out the new type of machine, although rumours about its characteristics are well known. As the mechanic is fitting it to Nicolas' bigger tractor, parked next to his stable, Étienne Maitrugue drives past. He is on his way to cut some fresh grass for the cattle he has placed indoors and slows down, taking a long look and pursing his lips. Eventually he stops and walks over to make a closer examination. Nicolas asks Étienne which way he is heading and whether he would like to watch the demonstration. The mechanic makes a trial run on a small patch of grass behind the stable. The blades spin with incredible speed, stirring up dust and causing everyone to step back apprehensively. Nicolas has chosen to try out the machine on a field of poor-quality pasture outside the village. He drives the tractor while the mechanic and I follow in the van. Étienne goes on his way.

Having arrived at the pasture, which is covered with rank grass, this-tles, and molehills, the mechanic demonstrates how to use the machine while Nicolas sits on the wing of the tractor, then dismounts and allows Nicolas to try it for himself. The spinning blades send up a cloud of earth and small stones from the molehills, some of which strike us as we watch.

Claude Bavarel and his neighbour are still harvesting potatoes on higher ground the other side of the road to Vaux. They hear the noise and stop to watch for a few moments. When he has cut a swathe of grass, Nicolas returns, making an exaggerated gesture of wiping his face with his handkerchief. The mechanic reveals a concealed drawer containing spare blades and spanners which is hidden in the frame, but even this is full of grass clippings. Nicolas takes the mechanic back to his house for tea (see Ch. 5). They discuss the relative merits of different types of mechanical scythe but, in the end, Nicolas decided it soils the grass so much that cattle will be unwilling to eat hay cut with the rotary type.

Autumn Manuring: Testing New Equipment

Winter wheat is sown in late September or in October, and manure spread on land which has been ploughed. On 20 September *un comice* (an agricultural show) was held in a neighbouring village. Several farmers who had already shared the cost of buying equipment decided to try out a hydraulic fork, designed to load manure onto trailers, that was on display at the *comice*. Victor Jouffroy contacted the garage and arranged for the demonstration to take place outside the house of his father-in-law, a retired farmer, on the morning of 24 September.

Pierre Bavarel arrives soon after Victor, at about 9.30, and they talk with the older man until Étienne and Maurice Maitrugue, the *maire's* son from Montoiseau, and Nicolas Jouffroy have also arrived. Everyone is then invited in for a drink, while they await the arrival of the lorry from the garage. Eventually Pierre has to leave, to spread *regain* he has left in *chirons*. The lorry arrives an hour later, bringing the hydraulic fork already mounted on a tractor. Several *cultivateurs* have brought empty trailers and Victor Jouffroy tows the first into position next to his father-in-law's manure heap. The mechanic works with a fixed smile on his face, but the villagers are not impressed. It is a little difficult to manœuvre the fork and some manure misses the trailer. The *maire's* son from Montoiseau improvises two sides for the trailer with planks and poles. Victor's father-in-law produces a pitchfork, which Maurice Maitrugue takes from him to clear up what had fallen to the ground.

Nicolas comments that the hydraulic shovel he bought six years ago works better than this. When the first trailer is full, Victor drives it away. Nicolas Jouffroy and Étienne Maitrugue take the opportunity to leave, having decided they have seen enough. When the second trailer is taken away, Maurice is the only villager left. He stands beside the third trailer,

PL. 13. Watching demonstration of hydraulic fork

packing the load down to make sure no more manure falls on the grass. When this too is full the mechanic pauses: 'When did we start?' he asks.

'About eleven o'clock.'

'You see, three trailers loaded in an hour, and it's much easier than working by hand.' Maurice retorts that it has required two people to load the trailer efficiently, and defends his view when the mechanic objects.

The *cultivateurs* decided to test a mechanical shovel like the one Nicolas Jouffroy already owned, and a second demonstration was arranged, with the same garage, for 6 October. The only difference would be that Nicolas's shovel was mounted on the front of the tractor and the new one at the back, where it is easier for the driver to see what he is doing. When I next met Pierre Bavarel, he gives me an accurate account of the objections raised at the time to the first device, even though he had missed the demonstration.

Two days after the first demonstration, an article was published in an agricultural newspaper, *La Terre de chez nous*, which gave a comparative report on the various pieces of machinery available for loading manure. After harvesting, the manual loading and unloading of manure is, according to the author Michel Valladont, the hardest physical task on the farm. For small and medium-sized farms, the cost of equipment is frequently a deterrent, and equipment that can readily be shared should be bought collectively as often as possible. M. Valladont considered that it takes 20 minutes to load a trailer by hand, 5 minutes with a mechanical shovel, and $3\frac{1}{2}$ minutes with a hydraulic fork. Nicolas Jouffroy, who pointed the article out to me, commented that the author was clearly wrong in his assessment of the hydraulic fork. I later asked Pierre if he had seen the article. He had, but could not understand why the author had so seriously underestimated the time required to work with the hydraulic fork. Perhaps there was something wrong with the fork we watched.

The second demonstration takes place outside Étienne Maitrugue's house on 6 October. This time, the garage-owner himself brings the equipment. Unlike the representative from the cheese wholesaler, he seems very much at ease with the villagers, treating them as equals. It takes him some time to attach the shovel to Étienne's tractor without oil leaking from the pipe which operates the hydraulic lift. During this time the *maire* walks up the hill past Étienne's house, carrying a scythe over his shoulder. By the time he has approached within talking distance everyone's heads except mine were bent close to the leaking joint. The *maire* clearly wishes to speak and opens the conversation by commenting that he sees they are buying a piece of equipment manufactured by a local business. A discussion of this firm's equipment ensues, and the *maire* continues up the lane. After he has gone, the garage-owner startles me by quietly ridiculing him. He is clearly crystallizing a general sentiment. One of the others turns to me and says, 'You should go with him and take a photograph; he's going to scythe his peas!' The *maire* was the only person who still planted peas in his fields, even though this was once an essential part of crop rotation.

Étienne begins to load his trailer, with the garage-owner standing on the front bumper, to stop it tipping back under the weight of the manure. The arm of the shovel can be raised or lowered hydraulically, but not rotated, so the tractor must be driven back and forth between the dung heap and the trailer. After 8 minutes the trailer is three-quarters full, but Étienne stops and gets out of the tractor seat, complaining that it is tiring work. 'You must get the hang of it,' says one of the others. Five minutes later the trailer is full and the *cultivateurs* accept the garage-owner's offer to borrow it for a few days while they decide whether or not to buy it.

Two days later, they return to Victor's father-in-law's, to finish loading his old manure heap. They offer advice to the *maire*'s son from Montoiseau, who is driving the tractor: 'The garage-owner said to keep the engine running well, but not to move the tractor too fast.' 'Don't raise the arm too high, or the manure will fall forward over your head.' 'Use the shovel to pack the manure down on the trailer.' Everyone agrees that driving the tractor back and forth is hard work, but that it will become easier with practice. 'Sacrée merde!' exclaims Maurice, sitting on the bank next to me after his turn at the tractor. He also comments that the author of the report in *La Terre de chez nous* was mistaken in his assessment of the hydraulic fork. Somebody asks me how long it has taken to load each trailer and, when we work out the times, it is clear that they are improving. The first took 17 minutes to load, the second and third 14 minutes and the last 9 minutes. 'You see, we were messing around with the first trailer, but after that we got used to it,' says one.

Although Nicolas Jouffroy withdrew from the group, the others bought the shovel. It cost only 2,000 francs, whereas the fork cost 5,000, and they shared the cost equally.

The Cattle return to their Stables for Winter

By 9 October some *cultivateurs*, including Étienne Maitrugue, are leaving their cattle in the stable overnight and only releasing them in daytime. His brother Alexandre prefers to take them back to pasture overnight as long as the weather remains dry because they become less dirty. If they have lain on the straw of the stable overnight, their udders have to be washed before the commencement of the morning milking.

Cows and heifers are brought down from the commons on 13 October. Everyone goes to collect their own animals and the village streets are full of cattle milling in every direction all morning. After Alexandre and his wife Catherine have taken their heifers to one of their own strips of pasture, I go home with them, where we drink bowls of coffee at the kitchen table. Alexandre explains that the young animals, who have been free to wander over the commons all summer without close human contact, are almost wild. They have to be put on a large *parcelle*, or they will start to fight each other, break down the fences, and run away. At that moment he hears hooves coming down the lane from his brother's house and looks up to see one of his heifers heading towards the centre of the village. Catherine has gone out to the vegetable garden behind the house so he calls to her to run around the back of the *maire's* house and head it off. There is no point in chasing it, he explains. Catherine and her younger daughter intercept the heifer from one side, while three of Étienne's sons appear from the other. It is herded back into the Maitrugues' orchard, where we find it has leapt over the gate, breaking two of the uprights supporting the barbed wire.

Later the same morning I walk to Felicien Jouffroy's house to ask if I can return in the evening to identify his *parcelles* on the map of land-holdings and ask what use he makes of each. Felicien is in his workshop in the barn, above the kitchen, repairing a metal harness before going to collect his heifers. He explains that some heifers have no idea what an electric fence is. They burst through leaving broken wires in all directions. Some are wilder than others, his wife adds; Raphael Mignod's are like deer.

Three days later one of Maurice Maitrugue's heifers escapes from the pasture below the commons on which he had constructed a *loge* (cowshed). During the night the heifer unexpectedly gave birth to its first calf and, abandoning the new-born calf, broke through two barbed-wire fences. He first tries to recapture it with the help of Claude Bavarel's younger son and Victor Jouffroy but they are insufficient in number and the beast runs off towards La Combe Sainte-Marie. The next morning Prosper Jouffroy calls in at the café to collect his paper and reports that in the early morning he heard it mooing on the hillside across the Combe, although the mist was too thick to see over the valley. People agree that the heifer has returned to look for her calf. By half-past nine six farmers have assembled at Maurice's house, to be joined by three others during the next half hour. Maurice has taken the calf back to the stable, but he brings it with him when we leave. Victor recommends taking a bale of hay as well, since that helped to pacify an escaped heifer of his three years ago.

Leaving Prosper and me by the junction of the old and new roads at the foot of the *combe*, Nicolas Jouffroy and Raymond Monnier drive towards the point where Prosper heard the heifer, riding on Raymond's tractor and towing a trailer carrying the calf and bale of hay. The others go to collect Maurice's other four heifers, in the hope the escapee will return in a more docile mood if in company. A retired farmer, returning to the village after his morning walk, stops to wait with us. After a while, the four heifers come down the lane that leads to la Haute-Source and are turned up towards the commons. The mason's wife quickly chases their notorious dog into the old stable with a broom and wards the heifers past her vegetable garden. The party has not gone far along la vie des Moutons when Nicolas Jouffroy appears on the skyline shouting that the heifer and her calf are coming towards us along the track. They are herded gently together and allowed to stand for twenty minutes, before we attempt to return to the village.

Unfortunately, just as we reach the mason's house the wild heifer takes fright, breaks through the five men behind and is away up the hillside.

'It's that dog,' says someone; 'it was just the same with Raphael Mignod's heifers yesterday.'

With some despondency, the other four heifers are herded towards Maurice's cowshed while two *cultivateurs* make a wide detour to head off the heifer. Nicolas Jouffroy carries the calf across his shoulders. '*Le Bon Pasteur*,' he explains. Prosper, who has gone ahead to block the road to La Combe Sainte-Marie, fails to see how the heifer escaped and asks why no one was there to stop it. The question is not well received and he continues to explain at length what he thinks should have been done while we wait next to Maurice's cowshed. 'My God, he preaches like Saint Paul,' says someone. Nicolas has put the calf down, and it approaches Prosper from behind. 'Look out!' calls Nicolas, 'she's coming to suckle you.'

When the wild heifer reappears, Nicolas tethers the calf inside the cow shed and everyone retires to a distance. After some anxious moments, all five heifers are inside the strip of pasture and the gate is quietly barred. Victor Jouffroy has converted an old van into a trailer for transporting livestock. He goes to fetch it, accompanied by Raymond Monnier and Maurice. It takes them half an hour, and we can clearly see them across the *combe*, hitching the van to Victor's tractor outside his farmhouse in la rue de la Combe. Finally the heifer and her calf are driven to Maurice's house, and his other heifers returned to their pasture beneath the forest.

Maurice's kitchen is filled with people. He goes in search of some special wine to thank everyone, and returns with three dust-covered bottles. He has difficulty extracting the corks and someone asks how often he actually drinks wine expensive enough to have a cork in the bottle. The wine is soon drunk, and Maurice's packet of cigarettes empty. Everyone returns to their homes for lunch.

WORK IN THE FOREST

Felling Trees for Firewood

Work in the forest takes place between the busiest periods of farm work and has its own annual cycle. Much of the forest belongs to the commune, but some is privately owned. In 1963 Claude Bavarel bought a *parcelle* from someone living in a neighbouring village, near the isolated spring at Haute-Source. On 6 March he takes me up to see it. The track leading to the forest is still deep in snow; in places, the tractor drives itself along the deep ruts he made when he drove into the forest the previous day. As soon as we are out of the sunlight and among the tall trees the temperature drops. The first *parcelles* we pass belong to individuals and the boundary of each is marked with metal plaques nailed to trees at intervals beside the track. After a while we reach a section where the forest to the left of the track belongs to the commune. Claude stops the tractor and leads me down the steep slope where the limestone outcrops at the surface, to see a fir tree which is over 50 metres high.

As we continue uphill, the steep valley to our left becomes shallower. Claude's *parcelle* lies at the head of the valley. Here the shallow slopes are covered with a mixture of deciduous trees, naturally seeded firs of various ages and seedlings planted by Claude two and four years ago. They will take a hundred years to grow to maturity and he has planted them for his grandchildren. Formerly the floor of the valley was pasture. There is a spring at its head which used to feed a cattle-trough and supply drinking-water. Claude shows me a track leading to the site of a farmhouse, but all that can be seen of the ruins is a mound of earth. The wife of the last *cultivateur* was found drowned in the cattle trough many years ago. There used to be two other farmhouses, but they were abandoned even earlier. The spring now contributes to the village's drinking-water supply and is enclosed in a concrete channel with an iron access hatch.

We climb the slope to Claude's *parcelle*. Among the undergrowth is a plant with pale green flowers called *pain au loup* (wolfsbane) which, Claude says, has an unpleasant smell and used to be hung in stables to drive flies away. A buzzard is circling overhead. Someone else is using a chainsaw out of sight on the other side of the valley. Claude uses a *serpe* (a billhook) to clear away the undergrowth, then starts his chainsaw. He fells a small ash tree, two beech, and a fir tree that has begun to rot, clearing the slope for his seedlings. In each case, he first cuts a wedge-shaped section from one side of the trunk to determine which way the tree will fall, then goes to the other side of the tree to make a horizontal cut. The fallen trees are sawn into metre lengths, using a length of hazel sapling as a guide. Claude has a ruler in his pocket, but he puts it back after measuring the sapling, remarking how easy it is to lose things in the forest. A wedge made of *alisier* (service tree) is used to hold the sections apart to prevent the saw becoming trapped. One tree leans to one side, and together we have to push it to make it fall down the slope. Claude explains that, in such cases, you must cut the sides as well as the base before beginning the horizontal cut, otherwise the trunk will split and spring back as it falls. Two or three years ago such a tree had started to fall while he was still cutting it and the trunk sprang back over his head while the saw was still running. Had he been struck, the saw would have fallen across his legs.

Marking Trees for Auction

After more than a week of sunshine, 11 March was cold and wet. The four members of the *Conseil municipal* (village council) who form the forestry subcommittee have agreed to identify fallen or dead trees in the highest part of the communal forest, at the crest of the escarpment overlooking the village, and fixed today as the date on which the expedition to the forest will take place. The trees will be auctioned to villagers and local sawmills. Work started at 8.30 in the morning, but only one car was available for five people and so I had to wait until the afternoon to join them, when a second car was free, after a lunch paid for by the commune had been eaten in the village café. The trees are almost entirely coniferous, a mixture of *sapin* (fir) and *épicea* (Norway spruce), with occasional *hêtre* or *froillard* (beech). The area is a mass of small, dry valleys dissecting the limestone; the tallest trees grow in the valleys. Seedlings and saplings fill the spaces between the mature trees, with an undergrowth of brambles, and ivy. Led by the forest guard, two of the councillors carry axes.

PL. 14. Marking trees in the forest for distribution by lottery

Felicien Jouffroy is in charge of a mace-like hammer which stamps each tree with a number. The forest guard and Alexandre Maitrugue carry notebooks. Each time a tree that is uprooted, withered, or rotten has been identified, two patches of bark are removed and the tree's identifying number stamped on both. The guard and Alexandre note each tree's number, its girth, height, location, and estimated value in their notebooks; the two copies ensure that no mistake will be made. The bigger trees are numbered individually; they will be sold to a sawmill to make planks. The smaller ones are grouped into lots that will be sold for paper manufacture.

Very little leadership is evident. Although the guard is from time to time addressed as *chef*, everyone debates the height and value of each tree in a lively fashion. There is an exuberance which contrasts with the sober tone of those waiting in the dairy for the wholesaler's agent. Unrepeatable jokes are swapped with much laughter; the guard laughing hardest of all. Sometimes Felicien pauses to make sure I have understood. From time to time he also sings in a thunderous voice, and calls out the number of each tree in French, German, and English. At first the party occasionally becomes so dispersed that people are out of sight of each other and must call out to agree which tree to visit first. During lunch at the hotel one man has refilled a bottle of wine he carries in his coat pocket, and we pause to drink from time to time. As everyone grows wetter in the mist and intermittent rain, the party becomes more consolidated, except for Étienne Quintaux, born outside the village, who remains on the edge of the group and continues to wander away on his own. Eventually, he becomes the object of the others' jokes, as they speculate what he is doing when too far away to hear. Finally, the party returns to the café to drink black coffee at 5.30 in the evening, before the farmers disperse to milk their cows.

Deciduous trees can be felled until the sap begins to rise in May. On 20 March, Felicien Jouffroy and his half-brother Prosper work together to fell trees they were allocated in last year's distribution of *affouage* (firewood from the communal forest) in the wood called aux tartes des Fleurs. Felicien drives his tractor, towing a trailer, while Prosper cycles up, with his axe tied to the crossbar and a billhook hanging from the belt of his trousers. Prosper has already located and felled the trees, so Felicien leaves his trailer at the foot of the slope, and tows each trunk down. The trees are again cut into metre lengths, measured with a hazel sapling. Felicien measures the length of the sapling hand over hand, clasping the branch alternately with each hand. Prosper queries the result, giving another by holding the length of sapling up against his body. Felicien accepts Prosper's judgement. While Felicien cuts the trunks with his chainsaw, Prosper and I load the sections of wood onto the trailer, laying them crosswise. Those which are too heavy to lift are split with iron wedges.

The Auction

It was intended to auction the *chablis* on 2 April, but the forest guard discovered that three other communes were holding their sales on the same day, so the *maire* decides to wait. The auction must take place on a Saturday so that those who work in factories can attend. The sale is open to people from other villages, and to sawmill owners. Eventually the sale takes place on 10 May. It is held in the *salle des réunions*. At two o'clock some of the village men have assembled in the street outside the post office and, when it begins to rain lightly, they go upstairs. The forest guard is already waiting, dressed in a dark blue suit. The cast-iron stove has been lit. Men from neighbouring villages begin to arrive within ten minutes, some greeting those from Pellaport whom they know. The forest guard, the *maire*, and César Maitrugue sit behind the long table at one end of the room, and the *maire* declares the meeting open. The forest guard reminds everyone that any lots sold but not felled by the end of the year will revert to the Commune. The less valuable lots are sold first. Each is described by the forest guard, who announces the starting-price that had been agreed during the expedition of 11 March. As soon as someone has indicated their acceptance of the starting-price by calling '*prends*' or '*allez*', bidding began. The less valuable lots are priced in old francs, and bidding advances in increments of 5 or 10 old francs (i.e. 5–10 new centimes). The more valuable lots are priced in new francs and the minimum acceptable increase in bidding is 1 franc. Each sale is concluded when no one has put in a higher bid as the guard repeats the last price offered three times. The *maire* and César Maitrugue each keep a record. After two hours the sale is complete. The *maire* reads out the purchaser of each lot and the price offered. Only once is his record challenged but, since the buyer's record agrees with that noted by César, the *maire*'s record is altered. Although it is still only mid-afternoon, a meal is offered afterwards to all who have attended, hosted by the *maire* and held in the village café.

Claude did not return to collect the wood from la Haute-Source until May. Like many other farmers, however, he spent several of the weeks between sowing grain and harvesting hay in the forest, cutting up trees he had felled earlier and bringing the wood back to the village, where it is sawn into shorter lengths and split for firewood. On 11 August, Victor Jouffroy helps the retired postman bring back two trailer-loads of firewood. Victor collects the trailers from his father-in-law's farmhouse and stops on the way out of the village to use the communal tyre-pump, stored beneath the *salle des fêtes*. The retired postman and I ride on the leading trailer. Victor takes the road towards the neighbouring village of La Combe Sainte-Marie, then turns off along a well-made forest track, whose surface consists of packed rubble. Eventually we have to leave the track and take a narrow, rutted path whose entrance is blocked by a large fir tree, waiting to be collected by a saw mill. Victor ploughs through the undergrowth. The path hardly leaves enough room between the trees for the tractor and trailers to pass, but Victor judges widths and turns to a nicety until the postman finally announces that he thinks we are going the wrong way. He has not seen the logs since he returned to the village on foot in the autumn. They walk away together until the logs have been located, beside another path. Victor returns, and begins to drive the trailers through the forest. A dead fir tree, still standing among the living ones, is caught by the corner of the rear trailer. The trunk snaps, one half bouncing down on the trailer. Victor throws up his hands to protect his head but, fortunately, the lower part of the trunk lodges against another tree.

When we have loaded the first trailer as high as Victor judges to be safe on such uneven ground, he tows it back to the surfaced track. The second trailer is then loaded. The retired postman and I follow the tractor and second trailer on foot, picking wild strawberries as we go, until we pass out of the old clearing in which the logs were stacked, into the gloom of the mature forest.

Affouage

Most of the commune's mature coniferous trees are sold by auction to sawmills, at twice-yearly sales held in Pontarlier. Deciduous trees are offered to the villagers for firewood. Each person who was resident in the village on 1 April is entitled to several *stères* (cubic metres of sawn timber). The entitlement is known as *affouage*. The exact quantity varies from year to year. Until the early 1960s it was generally 4 *stères* per person but the Office national des fôrets decided to clear remaining deciduous wood as quickly as possible, and in Pellaport the allocation was increased to 5 or 6 *stères*. A draw is held in the *Mairie* (Council Chamber) each autumn, at which the head of every household withdraws five or six slips of paper for each member of his household, each marked with a lot number. Lots that are in more inaccessible parts of the forest are rather larger, to compensate for the greater effort of felling and transporting them. Even so, those who draw lots on precipitous slopes pull a long face on opening their slip of paper.

The party that visited the escarpment in the spring reassembles on 6 October to mark the trees which, in this case, have been previously identified by the forest guard as suitable for firewood. They work in woodland on the other side of the commune, aux tartes des Fleurs, where deciduous trees are gradually being replaced by conifers. The two volunteers carrying axes walk ahead, looking for trees the guard has already marked with a single axe-cut while Felicien again carries the hammer. The guard and Alexandre have their notebooks. Trees that are under 20cm. in diameter are classed as *perches* (poles) and grouped together into lots. Larger trees, which will yield more than one *stère*, are measured. Alexandre carries a leather tape-measure and the guard has a table in his notebook that converts height and girth into volume. Étienne Quintaux, who had become the butt of others' jokes in March, now plays the role of forestry expert. He tests the soil to see how dry it is, commenting on its suitability for planting *sapins*, and criticizes his fellow-councillor's placing of the *blanchis* (blazes) for numbering. At first the party accepts this; Alexandre corrects his colleague. Some minutes later, however, the would-be expert protests when Felicien breaks off some twigs around the blaze he has made. 'Can't you mark a tree like that?' he asks. 'Yes,' Felicien responds dryly, 'but I want to mark it with the hammer, not my finger.'

CONCLUSION

A multitude of topics emerged from my daily observations: collective and individual ownership of land, the role of co-operatives, the structure of the household, interpersonal relations, changing agricultural techniques and their effect on other aspects of village life. Each of these themes will be taken up in one of the following chapters and examined in relation to evidence for the way village life had changed before my arrival, and continued to change after my departure at the end of October 1969.

Chapter 1 has given some examples of villagers' sense that their daily routines have grown out of a long history, a way of life that had changed in the past but was now being rapidly transformed as agriculture became mechanized. Chapter 2 looks at continuity and change in the history of management of the village's common land. Comparison of Pellaport with neighbouring villages shows that common principles of social organization exist within a regional culture, yet also reveals variation in the way villages have implemented management of common land and dairy production. The concluding section of Ch. 2 discusses the theoretical implications of this evidence for the reproduction and transformation of cultural practices and outlines the analytical framework to be used in succeeding chapters. Chapter 3 considers the household, the locus of production in a peasant economy. The French industrial revolution transformed household structure, laying the foundations for the mechanization that gathered pace after the Second World War, but the traditional principles of inheritance survived this transformation and continue to contribute to the relatively egalitarian character of village life. Chapter 3 will therefore also show how processes at work within the household contribute to equality or social differentiation in the wider village community. Chapter 4 discusses the network of mutual aid linking households, and the gossip that regulates it, examples of which have already been given in this chapter. Although change in agriculture was the primary object of my research, Ch. 3 documents demographic change associated with the rise in employment outside agriculture, Ch. 4 records the effect on the quality of village life, and Ch. 7 consequent changes in the management of village resources. Chapters 5 and 6 document and analyse mechanization in agriculture. These chapters assess the role of innovators such as Nicolas Jouffroy and present the detailed results of my comparison of alternative techniques in relation to changes in the availability of, and need for, agricultural labour. The transformation of occupational patterns in the village, and the consequences for management of common land, demonstrate the interplay between individual decision-making and the social processes in which it is implicated. Chapter 7 draws some general conclusions about the theory of social process and tests these conclusions through a comparison of the social history of Pellaport and its neighbours on the Plateau of Levier with the history of other villages in Western Europe.

2

Structure and Process in the Corporate Village

The patterns of daily life outlined in Ch. 1 are embedded in the durable social procedures described in this chapter. Despite the many similarities between Pellaport and other villages on the Plateau of Levier, there are significant differences among neighbouring villages. A historical perspective shows that village organization has changed, sometimes slowly, sometimes abruptly. This spatial and temporal variation raises interesting theoretical issues about the construction of social life. The British anthropologist Radcliffe-Brown argued the activities of individuals could be generalized as customs, and that customs were connected by the structure of social relations. Radcliffe-Brown hoped to demonstrate the scientific character of anthropology through the discovery of sociological laws predicting how customs would be related. If descent is through the male line, a man will show respect to his father but have an affectionate relationship with his mother's brother. Radcliffe-Brown's working hypothesis was that customs tended to support each other and produce equilibrium in the social system. Giddens and Bourdieu objected that the structural analysis practised by Radcliffe-Brown and others treated social structure as if it had a life of its own, rather than recognizing it as the product of interaction among socially informed agents. The approach used here benefits from the insights of Bourdieu and Giddens (especially Bourdieu 1990 and Giddens 1984), but will try to make good some of the weaknesses in their method. Both Bourdieu and Giddens perpetuate the tendency of structural analysis to assume social or cultural systems are in equilibrium and do not deal adequately with the conditions that cause instability or change. Both give undue attention to power and social inequality, underemphasizing the role of co-operation and mutual dependence in social relationships. Neither Giddens nor Bourdieu make much use of the idea that social behaviour may be shaped by adaptation to particular circumstances.

The first half of this chapter exemplifies continuity, variation, and change in the social life of the Plateau of Levier through the management of village resources. The second part reviews in more detail the development of relevant theory. Following chapters look at other aspects of social life touched on in Ch. 1 in the light of this body of theory: organization of the household, mutual aid between neighbours, and innovation in agriculture. The final chapter re-examines the changes in management of village resources described below and argues they can be explained in the light of processes identified in Chs. 3 to 6. While not proposing sociological laws of the kind Radcliffe-Brown hoped for, I will argue certain clusters of customs tend to be associated with one another.

Chapter 1 outlined the division of land in Pellaport between the higher, poorer soils which belong to the Commune, and the lower fields that are privately owned. In 1969, the fields still took the form of long, narrow strips descended from the open-field system, although each field was now generally made up of several parallel *parcelles*. Landownership influences many aspects of social life in the village. The forest growing on rocky ground is an important source of income for the village, managed by the National Forestry Office in consultation with the village council. *Cultivateurs* co-operated in the management of the common pasture and frequently helped each other in other aspects of agricultural labour. The dairy co-operative managed the production and sale of cheese on behalf of all *cultivateurs* in Pellaport and Montoiseau. Chapter 2 examines the ownership and management of resources in the villages of the Plateau of Levier, in its geographical and historical context. Chapter 3 will consider the ownership and management of privately owned land.

Like Pellaport and its neighbours on the Plateau of Levier, villages in Switzerland and the neighbouring regions of France and northern Italy are characterized by the corporate ownership of substantial resources and popular participation in village government. A similar system is found in the northern Spanish province of León and in south-west Germany. Such villages present a striking contrast to the weak political organization of the modern English village and also differ greatly from the organization of villages in other parts of France.

Netting (1981: 78) characterized the Swiss village of Törbel as, 'resembling a state in microcosm. The community has . . . its own territory clearly demarcated from that of its neighbours, its own citizenship,

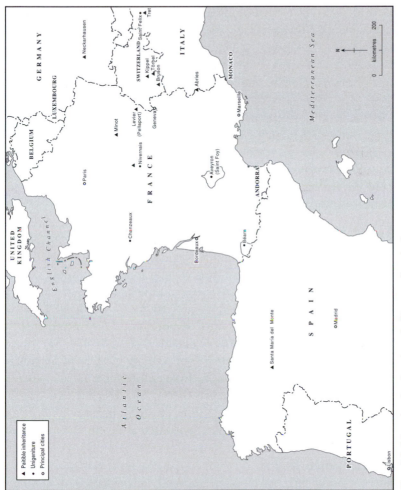

FIG 2.1. Map showing location of village studies cited

and its own political structure with elected representatives and highly democratic town meetings'. In 1483, Torbel already referred to itself as a peasant corporation when it laid down rules for the use of common pasture and forest it owned (ibid. 60). At the time of Netting's study, all the cattle-owning members of the village belonged to an association which managed the alpine pastures and co-ordinated production of cheese from livestock grazed on them (ibid. 65).

La Chable, the Swiss village studied by Weinberg, presents a very similar picture. La Chable is divided into three principal 'neighbour-hoods' (*quartiers*), recalling the three sections of Pellaport known as les coins de l'Église, la Combe, and le Croset, which were described ironically by Pierre Bavarel as *la commune de la Combe* and *la commune de Croset*. Fifty of the seventy-five households in La Chable belong to the *laiterie*, or dairy co-operative. Grazing on alpine pasture is managed by a co-operative *consortage*. In the 1930s the two *consortages* then in existence responded to overgrazing on the high pastures by buying up private land and thus expanding the scale of collective ownership, while simultaneously negotiating an agreement that villagers would reduce the number of cattle they owned. Voter turnout in commune elections is often 100 per cent (Weinberg 1976: 176).

The Swiss Alpine village of Kippel grants each citizen of the village use-rights to those alpine pastures that belong to the community. Other alps are owned and managed by associations of villagers and membership of such associations can be gained by inheritance or purchase. Like the inhabitants of Törbel, the villagers of Kippel long ago decreed that no citizen could sell or lease alp-rights to outsiders (Friedl 1974: 54). In the Burgundy village of Minot, ownership of a house confers use-rights to communal land and communal woods. Collective tenure gives a sense of belonging to the community (Zonabend 1984: 23). To gain access to the commons in Santa María del Monte, León, one must be married and resident in the village (Behar 1986: 271). Tasks such as hearding livestock on the commons are often allocated by rota (Friedl 1974: 55, Behar 1986: 149, 183, 203, 205).

This dense web of social co-operation in the management of common resources contrasts starkly with the political life of English villages and this chapter will explore the basis for co-operation in the joint ownership of resources. 'Belonging' to Elmdon, the Essex village studied by Strathern (1981: 6), is an intangible condition, established by birth in the village, and membership of an 'old' Elmdon family. There is no way in which Elmdon 'unites' as a community of equals, and the powers of the parish council are limited to the provision of recreation grounds, street lighting, and garden allotments, and the award of small grants (ibid. 36, 49). Harris concludes the people of Hennage, a village in north Norfolk, are not a corporate group (Harris 1974: 39). English parish councils suffer from severely restricted powers and financial resources (Havinden 1966: 187). A typical parish council meeting in the two estate villages studied by Havinden is attended only by the chairman (the vicar) and one other member. Only 11 people voted in an election to replace a member of the council and villagers ignore the council's decisions (Harris 1974: 46–7). Williams and Newby reach much the same conclusion in their studies of villages in the Lake District and East Anglia; the functions of the parish council are 'limited, and their potential highly restricted through lack of finance' (Newby *et al.* 1978: 225, cf. Williams 1969: 175, 237–8).

The structure of French local government was laid down at the time of the Revolution of 1789. English parish councils were introduced by the Local Government Act of 1894 (Havinden 1966: 187; Newby *et al.* 1978: 224–5; Wilson and Game 1994: 45). Immediately prior to the Local Government Act Justices of the Peace were responsible for local government (Newby *et al.* 1978: 221–4; Wilson and Game 1994: 42). The JP was often the squire (Plumb 1990: 34–5; Orwin and Orwin 1938: 152). This was not the case in earlier centuries. Under the open-field regime, which dominated a broad region of England from Yorkshire in the north to Dorset and Sussex in the south between the tenth and eighteenth centuries, each village chose a jury at its village court. The court admitted new freeholders and tenants to the community, passed by-laws compelling residents to repair chimneys and clear pathways, and forbidding them to encroach on access tracks by overploughing the edge of strips, or to allow animals to graze on fields before crops had been harvested. The jury also limited the number of animals each household could graze on commons (Ault 1972; Chibnall 1965: 231; Orwin and Orwin 1938: 154–9). According to the Orwins, 'The government of the open-fields is a pure democracy' (ibid. 197). Pellaport and the villages around it, from the Swiss border to the plateaux which descend towards Besançon and Dijon, have retained many of the features of the open–field system that have long disappeared from the typical English village. The following paragraphs review these features. Chapter 7 will look at the long-term political processes that appear to have caused the different trajectories of English and French cultures over the last thousand years.

HISTORY OF THE COLLECTIVE OWNERSHIP OF PROPERTY

Introduction of the Open–Field System to the Study Area

While an impressive degree of historical continuity can be shown in the organization of Pellaport and other villages, they have also experienced repeated change. The nucleated village typical of Western Europe replaced scattered hamlets in the high Middle Ages (Rösener 1994: 62). The co-ordination of village land-management through the three-field system began at about the same time (ibid. 61, 158–9), although the two were not necessarily linked (Behar 1986: 125, 195). Braudel (1990: 357) writes that the open-field system can only be identified with certainty in France from the twelfth and thirteenth centuries. He suggests it was devised to reconcile the conflicting demands of expanding animal husbandry and plough cultivation of cereals. The conflict was resolved by putting all the village's livestock in one herd and grazing them either on the fallow or the currently cultivated fields after harvest, the practice of *vaine pâture* (ibid. 358). Bloch (1966: 50n,) explained the division of cultivated land into long, narrow strips as a response to the difficulty of turning a wheeled plough. The disadvantage of long, narrow strips is that they maximize the length of the boundary enclosing a given area. Social arrangements that made it unnecessary to fence land against livestock alleviated this problem.

Between AD 1000 and 1340 Europe's population almost doubled, rising from 38.5 million to 73.5 million. Population pressure prompted widespread colonization of virgin lands (Rösener 1994: 48). Many of the villages of the Plateau of Levier were first mentioned in eleventh-, twelfth- or early thirteenth-century documents, when grants of feudal tenure were made by kings of Burgundy, or by the lords of Joux whose castle dominates the approach to Switzerland east of Pontarlier (see Chapuis 1958, Courtieu 1982, Gioud 1952). The Black Death, whose course is mapped by Braudel (1990: 157–9), ravaged Franche-Comté in 1349. The population of Les Foncine, studied by Daveau, appears to have been virtually wiped out. A document dated 1373 records the birthplace of thirty heads of households and shows them all to be immigrants from Savoy, Switzerland, and the southern Jura (Daveau 1954: 120). The culture of the region thus draws on traditions from a wide hinterland.

Some villages close to Pontarlier belonged to the *Baroîchage* of Pontarlier. The *Baroîchage* was an quasi-independent political entity, which existed for eight centuries. Members were entitled to chose their own protector, and were absolved from feudal obligations. Members living in the villages had the right to withdraw behind Pontarlier's town walls if the district was invaded. Each village was self-governing. Abriès, the French Alpine village studied by Rosenberg, belonged to a similar confederation of fifty-one villages known as the *Briançonnais*, established in 1343, and Rosenberg (1988: 40) writes that 'such coalitions were not uncommon in French history'. The *Baroîchage* of Pontarlier was dissolved by Louis XIV in 1672, as France conquered the region (cf. Braudel 1988: 198, 321). Beyond the *Baroîchage*, villages such as those of the Val d'Usier fell under the dominion of a single seigneur. Yet others, including Pellaport, were divided by their obligations to different overlords but had an independent existence as corporate communities, reproducing the pattern that Bloch (1961: 242) described as characteristic of Medieval France.

In 1477, the Burgundian region was divided into two. The duchy of Burgundy became part of France. Franche-Comté was inherited by the Habsburgs in 1506. As the property of the Habsburg Philip II of Spain, it became a Spanish province in 1555 (Braudel 1988: 197). One of the principal family names in Pellaport is said to be of Swiss-German origin, while another is traced to immigrants from Spain who arrived while France-Comté was part of the Spanish Netherlands.

The Ten Years War

The Ten Years War was an episode in the Thirty Years War (1618–48). The Swedes of whom Felicien Jouffroy and Claude Bavarel spoke were soldiers in the army of Bernard, duke of Saxe-Weimar. The French government, in the person of Richelieu, employed Bernard to occupy the area as a prelude to French conquest. During 1639 his army of 18,000 Germans and Swedes systematically destroyed every village between Pontarlier and Salins-les-Bains, creating a long-lasting antipathy between the inhabitants and France. In 1995 I was told by a nephew of Felicien's that after the Ten Years War it became customary for people on the Plateau of Levier to ask that they be buried face down, so as to present their backsides to the French invaders. Franche-Comté formally became a French province in 1678 (Braudel 1988: 278).

Population Densities

Rise and fall in the size of village populations is one of the main processes that prompts change in the management of village resources. Records enable population trends to be charted from the late sixteenth century, shortly before the Ten Years' War. The villages of Les Foncine, south of the Plateau of Levier, suffered 200 deaths during the epidemic of plague which accompanied the Ten Years War (Daveau 1954: 120). Lebeau estimated that, after the Ten Years War, the region between Pontarlier and Saint-Claude (within which Les Foncine are situated) supported a similar density of population to that of the mid-twentieth century, that is between twenty and thirty people per square kilometre on the plateaux and under twenty in the mountains of the Swiss border. He attributes this rather low density to the impact of the war, by the end of which, 'the villages had been burned, the inhabitants killed and the countryside so depopulated as to resemble a desert rather than a once-peopled land' (Lebeau 1951: 408). Chapuis calculates that, twenty years after the Ten Years War, the population density on the plateaux bordering the Loue Gorge was only 11 persons per square kilometre, but that it rose to 29 persons per square kilometre by 1790 (Chapuis 1958: 138). More recently, the team compiling the Gazetteer of the *département* have estimated that villages on the Plateau of Levier lost up to 50 per cent of their population during the Ten Years War (Courtieu 1982). Once the war was over, the region experienced steady population growth for 200 years, interrupted only by a brief dip at the time of the Revolution. The population of Les Foncine rose from 554 in 1657 to 2,695 in 1806 (Daveau 1954: 120). Population on the Plateau of Levier peaked in the mid-nineteenth century whereas in the Swiss Alps it continued to rise for another hundred years (Friedl 1974: 72, 91; Netting 1981: 96). Once the Industrial Revolution enabled emigration to cities, a remorseless decline began. In 1851, the biggest village of our survey had over 800 inhabitants, the smallest had 250. Chapuis's figures indicate that the population of the plateaux adjacent to the Upper Loue Valley had increased to a density of 33 persons per square kilometre at its maximum in 1851, but it had been halved again by 1954 (Chapuis 1958: 137, see Fig. 13). By 1962 the largest village in our survey had shrunk to 520 inhabitants, the smallest to 80. Since my first fieldwork in 1969, the growth of private car ownership has allowed people to commute daily to work, and the population of many villages has begun to rise again (see Fig. 2.2). In 1969, only four households in Pellaport had members who worked in Pontarlier. There were few cars in the village. The possibility of insufficient cars being available to take a party to the forest, as was the case in March 1969, is now unthinkable. In 1995 about thirty people commuted to work. Villages within 10 kilometres of Pontarlier experienced their population trough in

FIG. 2.2. Average population in sample villages, 1593–1995

the early 1960s. Those further away continued to suffer declining populations until the late 1970s and early 1980s. In some of the most distant villages the population was still declining in 1994.

The population of Pellaport fell dramatically in 1874, when a fire in le coin de l'Église left thirty-four households, living in fifteen houses, homeless. Only five houses were rebuilt. Claude Bavarel related the event:

There used to be a carpenter there. His house stood where [X's] house now stands. The fire began in the carpenter's kitchen and spread quickly. The surrounding houses soon caught fire because in those days they were all roofed with wooden tiles. Many of the families were too poor to afford the rebuilding of their houses.

Raphael Mignot provided further details:

It began in the kitchen of the carpenter's house. His wife had put more wood on the fire and it flared up. She ran out to find her husband and, while she was out, the house took fire. The blaze stopped at the nuns' house, where there was a statue of the Virgin in the window. Until last year [1994], when the house was rebuilt, you could still see where the beam ends were singed beneath the hayloft roof.

Such fires were common on the Plateau (other examples are given in Malfroy, Olivier, and Guiraud 1981).

In 1886, Gauthier compared the findings of a recent agricultural enquiry with the census of 1688, carried out shortly after the French conquest of Franche-Comté. Since the province had become three approximately equal-sized *départements* at the Revolution, Gauthier divided the figures for 1688 by three, to estimate the scale of livestock holdings in the area that was to become Doubs. He showed how, despite the increase in all types of livestock except goats, the increase in human population had outstripped them. By 1884 310,827 people were living in the area that had been occupied by an estimated population of 110,900 in 1688. Bearing in mind that the population had already been depleted by emigration over the previous thirty years, Gauthier's findings give a good indication on the pressure to improve mid-nineteenth century agricultural productivity, and throw light on the reasons for emigration to the industrializing cities.

Agriculture as an Occupation

Change in the proportion of the community engaged in agriculture is the second principal process provoking change in the way communal resources are managed. Despite rising populations in most villages over

TABLE 2.1. *Livestock in the* département *of Doubs, 1688 and 1884*

	1688 Absolute no. (no. per person)	1884 Absolute no. (no. per person)
Horses, donkeys, mules	16,169 (0.14)	20,926 (0.07)
Oxen	20,097 (0.18)	35,299 (0.11)
Cows, heifers, calves	47,689 (0.42)	106,957 (0.33)
Sheep	37,507 (0.34)	45,141 (0.15)
Pigs	18,050 (0.16)	47,352 (0.15)
Goats	12,381 (0.11)	6,580 (0.02)

Source: Gauthier 1886: 52–4.

the last twenty years, the proportion of people who are *cultivateurs* is continuing to decline.

Data for three villages recorded in the 1872 census show that 66 per cent of the 285 households in these villages were working their own, or rented *exploitations*. A further 11 per cent were headed by agricultural labourers. Most of the remainder (another 19 per cent) were craftsmen and women who almost certainly kept a cow to provide for the household's subsistence and were dependent on agricultural households for their customers. A small proportion of elderly people (the remaining 4 per cent of household heads) described themselves as *rentiers* or landlords, presumably because they were no longer working their own land, but renting it to others (the status of *rentier* will be reconsidered in Ch. 3). In 1972 the proportion of households working their own *exploitations* had declined to 34 per cent. Agricultural labourers had disappeared and rented farms were virtually eliminated.

TABLE 2.2. *Number of* exploitations *in the* département *of Doubs, 1892–1993*

1892	1929	1945	1954	1963	1970	1979	1988	1993
45,000	31,149	16,342	12,866	11,140	9,361	8,070	6,952	5,130

Sources: *Documentation française* (1959); Bidard de la Noe (1970); *Agreste* (1990); *Agreste* (1994).

TABLE 2.3. *Those engaged in agriculture as a percentage of total population in the* département *of Doubs, 1931–93*

1931	1936	1946	1952	1962	1979	1988	1993
17.3	16.0	15.5	14.4	6.8	7.0	5.0	4.0

Sources: *Documentation française* (1959); *Economie rurale* (1967–8); *Agreste* (1994). The criterion on which the figures have been calculated may have changed between 1952 and 1962, since there is not a corresponding drop in the number of *exploitations*.

In eight of the villages surveyed in 1972 and 1995, figures were obtained for the number of household heads engaged in all occupations. Table 2.4 shows the two biggest changes during the intervening twenty-five years have been the continued decline in the number of *cultivateurs* and the rise in those classed as waged or salaried (*ouvriers/employés*). The presence of unemployed household heads (*chomeurs*) is a recent development. Dairy farming is, however, becoming increasingly productive, due to continued improvements in breeding, the quality of pasture, and the supply of cereals in cows' diet. In 1769, one villager wrote to the Subdelegate of his district that his six cows and seven goats produced about twelve 'pints' (15.7 kilos) of milk per day while in 1778 villagers from Chaussenans wrote that each of their cows yielded three 'pints' (4 kilos) of milk per day, in two milkings (Latouche 1938: 778–9). It is difficult to extrapolate an annual yield from these figures, since milk yield will

TABLE 2.4. *Occupations of household heads in eight villages, 1972–95*

	Cultivateurs	Artisan and self-employed	*Ouvriers/* employees	Un-employed	Retired	Total
1972						
no.	145	40	164	0	131	480
%	30	8	35	0	27	
1995						
no.	69	61	312	39	164	645
%	11	10	48	6	25	

TABLE 2.5. *Average milk production per cow*, département *of Doubs, 1929–92*

1929	1952	1965	1992
2,884	2,988	3,178	4,814

Sources: *Documentation française* (1959); *Economie rurale* (1967); Vivot (1994). Figures have been converted from litres to kilos.

decline and eventually cease as the birth of the next calf approaches. Figures recorded for villages on the Plateau of Levier in the mid-nineteenth-century censuses, which range from 1,000 to 1,600 kilos per cow per year, suggest yields had improved since the previous century (see Courtieu 1982). Since the mid-nineteenth century yields have undoubtedly continued to grow, although dramatic increases have occurred only in the last thirty years.

After the State intervened to regulate access to communal forests in 1725 the sheep, goats, and pigs that often relied on the forest for grazing diminished in number, and from that time there was a greater specialization in cattle-husbandry (Chapuis 1958: 80). Latouche considers that the *fruitières* of the eighteenth century received no more than one-tenth of their supply in the form of goat's milk.

Experience had already demonstrated that goat's milk was more watery and provided little or no cream. . . . It was, it seems, from purely humanitarian motives 'to assist the poor' that goat's milk was accepted by *fruitières* (in the eighteenth century). Had it been excluded many individuals who had neither 'the means to purchase cattle nor the wherewithal to feed them, would have been totally excluded from the advantages of the *fruitière*, a resource which greatly assists them in the payment of their taxes'.   (Latouche 1938: 782, quoting from a letter written by the members of a *fruitière* in the village of Chaussenans in 1788)

Artificial pastures were improved with the addition of trefoil, sainfoin, and lucerne from the closing years of the *ancien régime*. As is the practice today, grass mixed with such crops was sown with the wheat that forms the last crop before plough-land reverts to grass. Shaded by the wheat, the more vulnerable fodder crops grow and are left standing when the wheat is harvested (Chapuis 1958: 86–7; cf. Daveau 1959: 233–4, Lebeau 1951: 393). The *départemental* Year Book for 1833 records the widespread seeding of sainfoin and trefoil on the Plateau of Levier.

The impetus to improve the quality of communal terrain, followed by the transformation of agriculture from a universal occupation to the occupation of a specialized, minority group is one of the most important processes driving change in the way resources in the community are managed.

Village Government before the Revolution

Before 1790, French village affairs were regulated by popular assemblies and officers appointed by seigneurs or local government (Gournay, Kesler, and Siwek-Pouydesseau 1967: 115). All household heads, including widows, who held taxable land had the right to attend the pre-Revolutionary assembly in Abriès. Meetings were held in the covered market. The assembly elected consuls to represent its interests before higher courts, used communal funds earned from leasing pasture to employ teachers and lawyers. In 1694, an army engineer wrote 'these people govern themselves like Republicans not recognizing any leader among them nor having to suffer any nobility' (Rosenberg 1988: 39). In Spain, village assemblies were replaced in law by elected councils in 1830, but those of rural León have continued to meet and are usually consulted by the elected council (Behar 1986: 156–9). Communal work parties were regularly recruited, and celebrated afterwards with wine and a meal, to distinguish their work from wage labour (ibid. 173).

In rural León, the most important office was that of *procurador* or village headman, either elected or appointed in rotation between households. It was not an easy job, and was not paid (ibid. 147–51). In the Swiss village of Kippel the *Gewalthabe* convened community assemblies, organized communal work parties to make good avalanche damage etc., and looked after the village's stud bull, but he was never paid more than his expenses, served only for one year, and often ended the year in debt (Friedl 1974: 23). In Pellaport the *échevins* (sheriffs) and *prud'hommes* (arbitrators) played similar roles.

The role of village assemblies on the Plateau of Levier can be illustrated from documents preserved at Pellaport's village hall. One of the main preoccupations of communities during the sixteenth and seventeenth centuries was to fix their boundaries on areas of common land. Mouthier fixed its boundary with Aubonne in 1546, and with Athose in 1677. Ornans and Chantrans divided the forest they had previously shared in 1737 (Chapuis 1958: 9; other examples from the Plateau of Levier are given in Malfroy, Olivier, and Guiraud 1981, and numerous similar boundary

negotiations throughout the district are summarized by Courtieu 1982.).
In 1659 Pellaport's assembly attempted to fix the boundary across
common land up till then shared with the neighbouring village of Vaux.

On the sixth of November 1659 the *prud'hommes* and inhabitants of the village of
Vaux on one part, and those of the village of Pellaport on the other, gave consideration to the delimitation of pasturage and commons which were common
between them, in execution of a judgement delivered in Pontarlier the fourth of
October the same year. There remained certain difficulties on the south side *(le
coste du vent)* but on the other side, being the north (*le coste de la bise*), the parties
suppose that the ancient boundary markers are certain and take them to be recognized as in the former treaty. . . . There were, however, certain difficulties in the
place called Les Tartes des Fleurs.

In 1720, the inhabitants of Pellaport challenged the impartiality of
witnesses who had appeared on Vaux's behalf in the Sovereign Chamber
of Waters and Forests (Les Eaux et Fôrets) on the grounds that they had
married women of Vaux, or had relatives living there. In 1731, the
community appealed to the subdelegate of the *baillage* of Pontarlier,

Saying that the contagion which is upon the beasts of Vaux, some small parts of
whose territory have remained in common with that of the suppliants and therefore each of the said communities has the right to pasture their beasts on the said
common land; but since those of the said community of Vaux might infect those
of the suppliants, which would cause them considerable prejudice, to prevent
which they have recourse to your authority.

If it please you, Sir, order the inhabitants of Vaux to enclose their beasts on
their own territory and forbid them from leading them upon the remaining
common shared by the two communities, as much and as long as the said malady
shall last.

Further attempts to define the boundary between Vaux and Pellaport
were made in 1741 and another court order was made in 1746, preventing
the cattle (*le bétail rouge*) of Vaux from grazing on shared pasture during
an epidemic.

In the seventeenth and eighteenth centuries, such meetings were held
on Sundays, after church. All heads of households had the right to participate and two-thirds of the household heads had to be present for the
assembly's deliberations to be valid. The assembly could legally bind the
community to a seigneur as well as sell common land. It frequently
elected procurators (representatives) where negotiations with other
villages were necessary. On 10 June 1740, for example, the two sheriffs of
Pellaport assembled,

In the public place of Pellaport, with [the names of twenty-six men follow], all inhabitants of the said place, assembled in the accustomed manner of the place, even at the sound of the bell, representing the majority of the inhabitants, even two-thirds of them, who, having deliberated among themselves on the subject of the difficulties they have with the neighbouring communities of Vaux and La Combe Sainte-Marie, and recognizing that it may be difficult for them to reassemble at each difficulty arising hereafter, have therefore named as their general and irrevocable procurators, for and in the name of the said inhabitants, to represent the said community to follow their differences before all judges until a definitive sentence has been secured.

Cultural Repertoires and the Revolution of 1789

The Revolutionary National Assembly enacted legislation abolishing the ancient provinces and introducing municipalities and *départements* in December 1789. Local elections were held in January and February 1790. Officers of the commune were elected by all the active citizens (Hampson 1963: 114). Fitzsimmons quotes a contemporary account of the moment, in the village of Vourez in Dauphiné, when the curé called the villagers together to explain the new legislation and open the elections. 'He reminded his listeners that all citizens now had the same right to the same laws . . . [and] exhorted the inhabitants to make their choices honestly' (Fitzsimmons 1994: 181). The villagers of Pellaport were used to electing temporary representatives for specific purposes, but this was the first time they had elected men who would replace the village assembly. In 1758, the community had successfully challenged a local miller's claim to pay a reduced share of the village's taxes. The sheriff in office who presided over the assembly's drafting of its challenge was Jean Nicolas Jouffroy. He was chosen by the community as one of its two procurators, to represent their case against the miller. He was still sheriff in 1761, when the village opened proceedings against the local seigneur. Pella-port's first *maire*, from 1790 to 1791, was also called Jean Nicolas Jouffroy. Despite the tendency for two or even three men in the village to have the same name, it is quite possible the same man, an existing figure of authority, was elected to the new position (Wylie 1966: 28 gives a similar case).

When the *maire* of Pellaport wrote to seek guidance in locating fire-wood in the forest during October 1790 he was addressing an elected *départemental* council which had been in office for nine months. He explained that 'customarily representatives of the Office of *Les Eaux et Forêts* come even without summons to the community of Pellaport at a time even earlier than the present, in order to mark the allowance of the said community'. Anticipating that some villagers might help themselves to timber, he continued, 'We also desire, Sirs, that for the common good, all offenders found in contravention in our said forests shall be reported to the clerk's office in the municipality [i.e. the village] without thereby presuming upon the rights of the king in giving us authority to judge them.'

The nobility and clergy had renounced their feudal privileges on 4 August the previous year. None the less, the king was still alive and at that time many revolutionary groups saw his support as key to completing the Revolution (Hampson 1963: 100, Fitzsimmons 1994: 70, 94, 181). It was not until the king tried to escape in June 1791 that the Constituent Assembly in Paris began to execute decrees without obtaining the king's signature (Hampson 1963: 104). Pellaport took several years fully to catch up with the discourse of liberty and equality. Fitzsimmons (1994: 203, 209, 231) quotes several declarations from newly elected speakers in *départemental* assemblies extolling the new concept of the citizen during 1790 and 1791. During those years Pellaport's elected representatives still cautiously used the subservient discourse of the old regime: 'Messieurs les administrateurs du *département* de Doubs, suplient humblement les officiers municipaux de la commune de Pellaport et disent . . .' It was not until 1795, when a new *maire* and *adjoint* sought help during a further attempt to divide the land held in common by Pellaport and La Combe Sainte-Marie, that they began, 'Aux citoyens, administrateurs du *département* de Doubs, exposent Claude Joseph V. et Claude François M . . .'

LE CONSEIL MUNICIPAL

The contemporary structure of French local government derives from laws passed during the French Revolution, but the particular procedures in force in 1969 had been established by the law of 5 April 1884 (Gournay, Kesler, and Siwek Pouydesseau 1967: 115). Each commune normally consists of a single village and its surrounding land. It is governed by an elected council. The election of *maires* was introduced in 1789, but suppressed shortly after and reinstated in 1871. The *maire*'s political power is considerable, and council elections are often keenly fought, even though the commune is answerable to higher authorities (Chapman 1953: 83, 125–38). Most communes in our survey elect eleven councillors; those with over 500 inhabitants elect thirteen. In those communes with over 300 inhabitants first cousins and closer relatives are forbidden by law to serve simultaneously as councillors, expressing the principle that the commune is a *local* group which transcends the factional interests in kin. Other studies have none the less suggested nepotism may have an effect. In Chanzeaux, a commune of Anjou dominated by large rented farms, town councillors have significantly more relatives living in the commune than the average inhabitant (Wylie 1966: 192). Even in Törbel, political careers are often built upon a nucleus of support from one's brothers (Netting 1981: 192).

Municipal elections take place every six years. When the results have been calculated, the successful candidates are identified by placing a fir tree decked in tricolour ribbons outside the house of each one. A celebratory banquet is served in the village square.

At the first council meeting following the election, the new councillors elect the *maire* and one or more *adjoints*, the *maire*'s deputies. The council meets a minimum of four times a year. Its meetings are open to the public. The *maire* plays a dual role. In the internal affairs of the commune, he or she is the council's agent and obliged to put the council's decisions into effect. If s/he refuses to do so, the council may appeal to the prefect, head of government in the *département*. In practice, long-serving *maires* may be able to impose their wishes upon less-experienced councillors. The *maire* is also the State's representative in the commune and, in this role, answerable to no one within the commune. It is his or her responsibility to appoint officers who uphold welfare and security in the commune; the *cantonnier*, who maintains hedges and ditches, and the *garde champêtre* (hayward), who polices straying livestock. The *maire*'s position reproduces the tension which Abélès (1991: 111, 115), identifies in the government of the *département*, created by the conflicting policies of the Revolutionary government towards local democracy and a unified state. In 1982 the balance of authority shifted towards the commune, when the State gave communes greater independence in the management of their budgets and reduced the government's right to annul decisions taken at the local level (ibid. 105, 116–8). The occupations of *maires* in the fifteen villages of our survey range from *cultivateur* to sawmill owner, housewife to retired *gendarme*. While some *maires* last only a single term it is common for the same person to be re-elected three or four times and thus to serve for eighteen to twenty-four years. The mayor of La Combe Sainte-Marie was elected to his fifth term of office in 1995 (cf. ibid. 15–19).

Membership of the municipal council is typically representative of the range of occupations pursued in the village: *cultivateurs*, craftsmen, housewives, teachers, bank clerks, shopkeepers, factory workers, and retired people sit together on the same council. Women have begun to be elected to municipal councils since 1972, although they are still in a minority.

Elections, as Abélès found in the *département* of Yonne, are fought on local, not national issues (cf. Rogers 1991: 111). Among communities close to the Swiss border, the development of ski facilities has been a key issue; close to Pontarlier, the sale of communal land for the construction of new houses. In many villages the central issue of the 1995 election was the survival of the village school in the face of declining numbers of pupils (cf. Abélès 1991: 14). When the date of the next election approaches, the mayor in office normally invites candidates who wish to be elected to the council to submit their names at least two weeks before the election. Normally each candidate stands on the basis of his personal reputation, and the eleven (or thirteen) who win the most votes are elected. There is, however, a customary procedure that allows advocates of rival policies to submit alternative lists of candidates. If the electors choose to elect one or other of the parties it is understood the convenor of the successful list will be chosen as mayor. The most common, overtly expressed, opposition is between generations. A new list of *jeunes* (young people) will challenge the old ones who have been re-elected for many years (see Rogers 1991: 169–176 and Wylie 1966: 227–239 for examples). A covert ground for competing lists may be that the established councillors have become identified with a faction, or kin network, in the community. Abélès found that wider issues such as the relationship between church and state sometimes also underlie apparently local contests (Abélès 1991: 14–15, 23–8).

THE BUDGET

The communes in our survey have two principal sources of revenue. One derives from the sale or rent of communal resources, the other from taxation.

The sale of timber from communal forest is the most profitable source of income for most villages. In 1972, every hectare of forest represented an income of between 550 and 650 francs. Many communes gained an income of 100,000 to 250,000 francs a year from the sale of timber (about 500,000 to 1,000,000 fr. expressed in 1994 values). Communal pasture was rented at the value of two or three kilos of milk per are, representing an income of between 100 and 150 francs per hectare. Three communes with about 150 hectares of common, for example, were earning between 15,000 and 17,000 francs a year in 1972 by renting it to the villages' *cultivateurs*. Some communes charged for the supply of water to households, but richer ones covered the cost of water supply out of the income from the communal forest. In 1995 the real revenue from timber sales was about the same, although it had fallen in some communes and risen in others. The rent of pasture, tied as it is to the value of milk, has also remained more or less constant.

Communes received a variable amount of income from taxes upon business activities within their boundaries. Those with sawmills or gravel quarries benefited far more than those with merely artisanal activities such as a mason's yard. In 1972, the State levied VAT and business taxes, and returned a portion of each to the commune. Since 1983, however, the State has made a block grant to each commune (cf. Abélès 1991: 118–19). Communes are also entitled to raise direct taxes, traditionally known as *les centimes additionels* but now called *les produits des contributions directes*. These taxes vary widely between the fifteen communes of our survey. The richest do not impose them at all but for the poorest in communal land they are essential to balance the books. The commune that relied most heavily on direct taxation in 1972 raised 13,000 francs by this means (c.60,000 in 1994 values). Income from taxation and the state grant has risen in proportion to growth in the village's population. In Pellaport and Dechailles the total income for the commune is now, in real terms, one and a half times its value in 1972; in one of the communes close to Pontarlier it is two and a half times its 1972 value.

The commune's principal running expenses arise from management of forest and country roads within its boundaries, the supply of drinking water, the upkeep and heating of communal buildings, the wages of the *cantonnier* and cowherd, the allowances due to *maire* and *adjoint*, and the cost of postage, telephone bills, etc. Some communes make special grants, such as Vuillecin's awards for the construction of new houses in 1972, or the grants to assist students in tertiary education awarded in Pellaport in 1995. Developments such as the construction of ski lifts or holiday accommodation can be financed from the commune's budget.

CORPORATE OWNERSHIP OF LAND

The land surface of the fifteen communes studied ranges from 500 to 1,800 hectares (average 1,100 ha.). An average of 40 per cent of the land within the commune is common land (ranging from 65 per cent to 15 per cent). Between 10 per cent and 30 per cent of land within the commune is covered with communal forest (average 230 ha.). Pellaport is one of the richest in communal forest. All but one commune of the fifteen surveyed has communal pasture, ranging from 5 per cent to 27 per cent of their land surface (average 113 ha.). Most communes also own some fields which they rent to individual *cultivateurs*. These represent between 5 per cent and 9 per cent of the area of the commune (average 88 ha.).The one commune that lacks communal pasture has one of the largest expanses of communally owned fields that are rented by individuals (12 per cent of its land area).

The commune or, before the Revolution of 1789, the general assembly, has the right to sell common land. When Claude Bavarel took me to his parcel of forest at Haute-Source in March 1969, he pointed out the ruins of an old farmhouse (see Ch. 1). The land on which this house (and two others that have disappeared) was built was sold by the commune in 1625. A copy of the document, made in 1712, records that the sale was agreed before a representative of the king by sixty-one men of the village. These men were

all inhabitants of the village who, in the body of the community and as much in their own names as in those of the other inhabitants, and on behalf of their successors, have sold and ceded, purely, perpetually and irrevocably, to Claude Maitrhugue dit Blaize and Claude Syrugue dit Graby of Pellaport and their successors, an area of commons of about thirty *journaux* [i.e. 10 ha.] at the place called Haute Source ... an area of commons which they have held since time immemorial and have always enjoyed and used without payment or contribution ... which they have sold under the following condition, that the said purchasers may not sell, alienate or mortgage the said portion of commons to anyone except those who are born, native and originating in the village of Pellaport.

In 1723, some villagers attempted to sell church land in order to discharge debts incurred by the community. Seventeen men put their names to a document drawn up on 25 April, claiming to represent the other inhabitants of the village. A month later a meeting attended by twenty-one men of the village, who described themselves as 'the inhabitants of Pellaport', assembled 'in the body of the community, in the place where they are accustomed to deliberate upon the affairs of their community'. The meeting noted that five of the six men who had purchased the land had been party to the agreement, and that the land sold was dedicated to the support of the church. They sought permission to have the sale revoked, and were allowed to take their case to Besançon, the provincial capital.

Since the mid-1960s, a number of communes, particularly those close to Pontarlier, have divided areas of common land near the village into lots, and sold them for housing. The earliest of the villages in our survey to take this step was Vuillecin. The previous *maire* had refused to sell communal land for housing but, in 1965, his newly elected successor was alarmed by the continuing decline in population. He not only released land for sale, but offered a grant of 1,500 francs towards the construction of each new house. Between 1965 and 1972 the population increased from 150 to 200. His policy has been continued, and by 1995 the population of the village had risen to 480.

Forest

Communal forests have been managed by the State since 1725, when the National Office of Waters and Forests intervened to restrict the traditional rights to *affouage* and *marrouage* (the rights to firewood and building materials from communal forest; see Gioud 1952: 125; and Chapuis 1958: 95–9). From 1964, management has been conducted according to twenty-year plans of management agreed between the National Forestry Office (Office national des forêts, or ONF) and each commune. The Office's work is paid for jointly by a State subsidy and a tax on timber sales from communal forest. When the first 20-year plans were drawn up many hardwoods had less than half the value of softwoods. In 1972 oak, which takes 140 years to grow to maturity, earned 40 francs per cubic metre, as did ash. Beech, which takes 135 years to reach maturity, sold for 70 francs per cubic metre. Fir and Norway spruce, which need 120 years to mature, sold for between 70–88 francs per cubic metre. The first ONF plan for Pellaport therefore envisaged felling the remaining hardwood, concentrated in le bois du Seigneur and le bois aux Tartes des Fleurs, as quickly as possible. Since then, the value of hardwoods has risen and it has been found that pure stands of fir or Norway spruce do not regenerate as well as mixed stands. The current objective, in 1995, is to create mixed stands containing 25 per cent deciduous and 75 per cent coniferous trees. The value of softwood has fluctuated, falling notably in 1984 and 1992, but ONF policy is to fell a constant volume of timber each year, so as to maintain a sustainable yield.

   In 1968, the commune's income from the sale of timber was about 70 per cent of the total income earned by the dairy co-operative. While the value of timber has remained more or less constant, the increased production of cheese has caused the commune's income from its forest in 1994 to fall to 30 per cent of the income earned by the co-operative.

The principal timber auctions are held in Pontarlier in the spring and autumn. Pellaport keeps back 100 cubic metres to sell at a village auction. The selection of trees and the village auction of 1969 were described in Ch. 1. Most of the timber is bought by local sawmills.

Villagers have a traditional right to obtain firewood (*affouage*) and, in the past, timber for house repairs (also called *affouage,* but sometimes distinguished as *marrouage*) from the communal forest. *Affouage* is measured in *stères*, or cubic metres of cut timber. In the mid–eighteenth century the villagers of Pellaport took their seigneur to court over his claim to have rights of *affouage* in their forest (cf. Abélès 1991: 20). In the letter quoted above, the villagers wrote to the administrators of the new department of Doubs at the midst of the Revolution, saying that normally the officers of Les Eaux et Forêts would already have come to the village.

In order to avoid expenses which could be considerable for a poor village, we make recourse to you, sirs, to discover whether it is possible to mark the trees ourselves, or at least to be told whom we may consult in these times, in order to escape the expenses which can sometimes befall those who act without consultation . . . We hope, sirs, that it will be your pleasure to take action as soon as possible, because the season is already well advanced and no one having made their provisions, if the snows should fall it will be difficult if not impossible to secure subsistence in regard to firewood.

In 1969, each member of the village was entitled to 1 cubic metre of fir wood for house repairs and 5–6 *stères* of hardwood for heating, depending on the accessibility of the trees. Lots which are harder to reach are larger. The firewood allowance had been raised from 4 *stères* in the early 1960s. By 1995, the entitlement had been reduced again, to 3–4 *stères* per person. To qualify for *affouage* the individual must be a French citizen, and have been resident in the village for six months (i.e. from 1 April). *Affouage* is allocated in early October at a lottery in the village hall, when the head of each household draws a slip of paper for each member of his family from an urn. The ONF's forest guard identifies the trees to be allocated, and the municipal council's forest committee numbers the chosen trees, deciding how they are to be divided into lots. This was the purpose of the expedition on 6 October 1969 described in Ch. 1.

In 1995 *affouage* was still distributed in about one-third of the villages surveyed. High villages, whose forest is entirely coniferous, appear to have abandoned *affouage* earliest. In 1969, some villages had adopted the policy of selling the timber designated as *affouage* once a year and distributing the income, which amounted to 60–80 francs per person. By 1995 this policy had ceased.

A number of communes have invested in forest since 1969, buying land which previously belonged to individuals.

Pasture

Until 1790, management of Pellaport's commons was the prerogative of the assembly of household heads. Management was for long hindered by rights of inter-commoning, which allowed adjacent villages to pasture their livestock on the same land. Repeated and eventually successful efforts were made during the eighteenth century to agree the boundaries between the land of adjacent communities and prevent the spread of cattle disease between villages. Before community boundaries had been agreed the commons were probably an open-access resource. Once community assemblies had gained control they were in a position to avoid 'the tragedy of the commons' discussed below in Ch. 7.

Pellaport's commons were managed by the municipal council until a pasture co-operative was established in 1954. I have no information on how the commons were managed by the council in the nineteenth century, but in 1969 older villagers described the system that obtained during their childhood. Part of the commons was given over to pasture, part to hay meadow. La pâture du Seigneur was reserved for grazing. The commune hired a cowherd, who took the cattle to the pasture after the morning and evening milking, and brought them back for the next milking. Other sections were reserved for haymaking. The meadow was divided into lots. Each person born before 1 January that year was entitled to put one cow on the pasture, and harvest one *journal*[1] of meadow. Portions were allocated at a lottery in the village hall attended by the head of each household, who drew one lot for each member of his family. The quality of meadow varied, and the effect of the lottery was to randomize each household's allocation. As Claude Bavarel explained,

Anyone who put cattle to graze on the common pasture was entitled to one portion of meadow, but anyone who did not, who was not a *cultivateur*, had two portions. There were many retired people who had no cows. They scythed their portions, harvested them and sold them at a good price. The army, and urban transport, still needed lots of hay in those days.

---

[1] A *journal*, one-third of a hectare, was the area one could plough in a day, using oxen.

When the hay had been harvested the land reverted to commons and while the *regain* was growing anyone could take their cattle there, although, because the commons were unfenced, they could not be left to graze untended. This difficulty also influenced pasturing on private land. Victor Jouffroy told me that before the introduction of electric fences in 1962 cattle spent more time in their stable and could only be pastured when someone was available to herd them (see Ch. 1). Joseph Bavarel commented on how much more efficiently grass could be exploited after the fences were installed. Cattle could be left to find the best grass on the strip, and one could wait until one section had been fully grazed before moving them to the next.

Vaine pâture is the right to graze one's livestock on others' strips after harvesting has been completed. It is a vestige of the open-field system, and was a response to the difficulty of herding cattle on unfenced strips. *Vaine pâture* persisted in Pellaport and Dechailles until the introduction of electric fences. Before then, the cost and labour of fencing the numerous long, narrow strips would have been prohibitive. The custom first came under threat in the eighteenth century, when maize, millet, and legumes were introduced to the region, and planted on soils that would otherwise have been subject to the fallow phase of the rotation. These crops were protected from grazing livestock by movable fences. They produced substantial yields: lentils and beans produced six times the quantity sown, maize as much as twenty-five times the weight seeded (Chapuis 1958: 65). A document from Pellaport dated 1790 shows that the first village council passed a by-law to fence land below the village on which to cultivate peas, lentils and vetch. The 1912 Year Book for the *département* of Doubs referred to *vaine pâture* in disparaging terms: 'Since time immemorial, *vaine pâture* has been practised in the *département* of Doubs . . . It can only be exercised after all harvests, even *les regains*, have been taken from the fields. Generally regarded disfavourably, because it causes the loss of manure, the destruction of trees and occasions grave abuse, *vaine pâture* is subject to strict municipal and prefectorial regulations' (Pigallet 1912). Claude Bavarel described the custom as follows:

before electric fences, you couldn't allow your cattle to wander anywhere after the hay harvest, you had to have a cowherd. Everyone had to keep their cattle on their own land until October, when the biggest grass from *le regain* had been eaten. In Pellaport the cattle could then go *tout à travers* (right across). That was never the case in Vaux, where cattle were kept on their own land right to the end of October. They had a *garde champêtre* (hayward) who made no mistake.

Clade (1994: 75–6) has described what it was like, as a boy growing up in the 1950s, to be a *berger* in charge of the family's cows and Braudel (1990: 301) himself herded his family's livestock as a child. 'It was hard work,' Joseph Bavarel recalled; 'you had to be out in the open even when it was raining. When the best grass was gone, all the boys would get together, and follow the cattle around in one large herd. But they were never allowed to range over the land belonging to La Combe Sainte-Marie, or fields sown with cereal.' Claude's son told me that on New Year's Day *les conscrits* (the 18-year-old boys) took *brioches* to three people in the village, to wish them a happy new year: the *maire*, his deputy the *adjoint*, and the *garde-champêtre*! In another village, where the right of *vaine pâture* was abolished around 1930, a retired *cultivateur* pointed out what an advantage the custom had been for the poor who had little or no land of their own.

Many adults in Minot recalled minding their parents' cattle when they were children. Each household was forced to begin guarding its own live-stock at the end of the nineteenth century when practice of putting live-stock in a common herd guarded by a communal shepherd, associated with the three-field rotation, came to an end. The children of woodcutters and day-labourers herded for others, earning enough to buy a pair of shoes to wear to school in winter. Children started when 6 or 7, as soon as they were big enough to open the gates. Some started even younger: 'I went off when I was five; I was smaller than the dog,' one villager recalled (Verdier 1979: 162). During April and May the cattle were led to wasteland or meadows that were not going to be harvested. The children set off at seven in the morning and stayed out till midday. Then the cows were led back to the stable to rest and the children went to school in the afternoon. In the evening the cows were led out again until sunset. During the summer each family had to keep strictly to its own pasture. The hayward made regular rounds; if he found anyone's crops damaged, he would make the little cowherds go and apologize to the owner. 'The fields were minuscule and we had the hayward on our heels' (ibid. 171). Fields were declared open to grazing by other proprietors on All Saints' Day. *Vaine pâture* lasted for one month or more; during this period everyone's cattle were mixed together into three or four large herds. As soon as frosts and snow began, at the end of November, they were kept in their stables.

LE BUREAU D'AIDE SOCIALE

Some communes, including Pellaport, own *parcelles* which have been willed by villagers to the commune's Bureau d'aide sociale (formerly called Le Bureau de bienfaisance). These fields are rented to *cultivateurs* at a price expressed in terms of the year's mean value of milk at the dairy; that is, expressed as a number of kilos of milk per hectare, depending on the quality of the land. The income is used to support good works, such as aid to the elderly, or, in 1969, the income of the nun who took the village's infant class. A substantial portion of this land was left to the village by one woman and is situated at la Haute-Source. Perhaps it was part of the land that the community sold in 1625.

COMMUNAL EQUIPMENT AND BUILDINGS

Examples have been given in Ch. 1 of the use of communal equipment such as the threshing machine and tyre pump. Pellaport's municipal council bought a series of threshing machines between 1917 and 1960. The last continued in use until 1965, when everyone except Maurice Genre began to hire a combine harvester. In 1969, the commune also owned a still for making *eau de vie*, a heavy roller used by *cultivateurs*, a bandsaw for cutting firewood, a threshing machine, the tyre pump, and a snow plough. Much of this equipment was agricultural and in 1969 the *maire* decided that no more would be bought, since the declining number of *cultivateurs* rendered it unjust that communal funds should be spent on equipment for a special interest group. Two other villages had taken the same decision. None the less, the commune of Pellaport still owned substantial equipment in 1995, including a computer and other office equipment in the *mairie*, a tractor, strimmer, battery recharger, chainsaw, and snowplough used by the *cantonnier* in his upkeep of roads and hedges, a bandsaw available to all households, a second-hand fire engine, and the firemen's uniforms. It had recently spent 16,000 fr. on constructing tennis courts and 1,000,000 fr. on refurbishing and modernising the *mairie*.

In every village the commune owns its *mairie*, school buildings, a village hall and meeting-room, and the church. Church property was handed to the communes in 1905, after which upkeep of the church became a communal responsibility (the controversy this transfer provoked in the district is described by Malfroy, Olivier, and Guiraud 1981: 214–8). The commune also generally owns the village *fromagerie* or, if not, the land on which it is constructed.

TASKS CARRIED OUT *PAR SOUMISSION*

Much work performed on behalf of the commune is allocated by tender (*par soumission*). In 1972, major works such as relaying drains, piping drinking-water and repairing retaining walls or public buildings were put out to tender from professional contractors. Minor jobs were offered to villagers. The *maire* posted a notice advising the approximate price the municipal council was willing to offer for a named task, and invited people to submit tenders. The lowest tender submitted by someone judged capable of executing the work satisfactorily won the job. Driving the village snowplough, attached to one's own tractor, was paid at a rate of 25 fr. per km. in Pellaport. Breaking stone for resurfacing tracks in the forest or between fields was paid at 25 fr. per cu.m. of stone. Chopping firewood for the church and the nuns' and priest's houses, earned about 18 fr. per *stère* although, in 1969, no one was willing to tender for this work and Alexandre Maitrugue's son did it at a rate offered by the *maire*. Other jobs allocated by tender included cleaning the stone cattle troughs and removing the ice which formed on them every morning in winter, emptying dustbins and removing the rubbish to the village tip, and making coffins. Until 1967, the job of digging graves had been allocated by tender, but since then it had become a regular part of the *cantonnier*'s work. By 1995, the *cantonnier* had taken over many of these jobs, such as driving the snowplough (using the commune's tractor) and clearing the cattle troughs. Public buildings were heated by oil and rubbish collection had been taken over by an intercommunal syndicate based in Pontarlier. All work in the forest was commissioned from professional companies. The same trend away from tendering by villagers had occurred in the other communes although in Dechailles villagers still tender for minor jobs such as cleaning gutters in the village street and pumping sediment from the settling tanks which purify the water supply.

DAIRY CO-OPERATIVES

Agricultural co-operatives are common in France, and widely promoted by government as a means of ensuring viability for family farms. Ulin (1996: 97) wrongly states that the first French agricultural co-operative was established in 1888. The French government introduced *fruitières* to the Hautes-Alpes between 1851 and 1875 (Rosenberg 1988: 116). The majority of the wine-producing co-operatives studied by Ulin in southwest France were founded in the 1930s (Ulin 1996: 76, 86, 174). The legal regulation of co-operatives in 1884 does, however, coincide with their spread to other parts of France. In the district around Chanzeaux in Anjou, for example, agricultural co-operatives have only existed since 1891 (Wylie 1966: 109).

History of les Fruitières

Claude Bavarel and Felicien Jouffroy had told me something about how the traditional dairy associations or *fruitières* were organized in the late nineteenth century. The name *fruitière* comes from the fact that the associations process the 'fruits' of dairy production. Claude recalled that there used to be more than one such association in Pellaport. Although the Year Book for 1856 records the existence of two *fruitières* in Pellaport, by 1891 there was only one. Figures quoted in the departmental Gazetteer (Courtieu 1982) indicate that the number of associations in each village peaked in the mid-nineteenth century, coinciding with the maximum size of village populations.

Dairy associations have considerable antiquity. They spread from Switzerland to the French Jura in the thirteenth century, when *fruitières* were recorded in two villages on the Plateau of Levier in a document of 1264 (Lambert 1953: 175; see also Latouche 1938; Lebeau 1951). By the end of the eighteenth century *fruitières* had spread throughout the region between Morez and Morteau, extending westward to Salins les Bains, Amancy, and Vercel (Daveau 1959: 249). As in the Swiss villages of La Chable and Törbel (Netting 1981: 25), each quarter of French villages used to have their own association, and each member household took it in turn to manufacture cheese from the day's pooled milk, which the household then sold to travelling merchants.

Braudel (1990: 231) dates the quickening of long-distance trade in France to the eleventh and twelfth centuries, while Rösener (1994: 54) states that the four-wheeled wagon, enabling the transport of heavier loads, was introduced at the beginning of the twelfth century. A trade route already existed between Switzerland and Burgundy, following the route of the present RN 72 between Pontarlier and Salins les Bains and crossing the Plateau of Levier (cf. Braudel 1988: 276). A second route, following the line of a roman road, linked Champagne and Italy via Pontarlier and Besançon (ibid. 194, Chapuis 1958: 8). By the thirteenth century timber was being exported from the region and the creation of *fruitières* enabled *paysans* to co-operate in the manufacture of large, durable cheeses which could also be traded for wine and wheat. As late as 1826, 363 of the 546 *fruitières* in the *département* of Doubs were located in the district around Pontarlier delimited by these ancient trade routes. The first *fruitière* in the Loue valley, only 20 km. north of Desérvillers, where one of the first associations was created in 1264, was established in 1823.

FIG. 2.3. Distribution of *fruitières* in the eighteenth century
Source: Lebeau (1951: 393).

At first cheese was made in members' houses and the copper cauldron belonging to the association carried from house to house. A tally was kept of each household's daily contributions. During the eighteenth century professional dairymen arrived from Switzerland, bringing knowledge of the techniques of Gruyère manufacture. *Fruitières* began to construct special dairy buildings, employing dairymen and paying them either a fixed wage or a proportion of the association's income (Latouche 1938: 778). By the end of the nineteenth century almost half the associations had stopped distributing cheeses to members and had begun selling cheese in bulk, distributing the income in proportion to the quantity of milk contributed by each member (Daveau 1959: 282).

Dairy associations are therefore an institution created to facilitate participation in a market economy. They have flourished in this environment for many centuries. A set of rules governing the conduct of *fruitières* compiled in 1787 forbade members from undermining a collective agreement by engaging in private negotiations with cheese merchants (Latouche 1938: 777, 786). During the nineteenth century, if not before, privately owned dairies operated alongside the associations. In 1864 such a dairy was manufacturing 30 kilos of Gruyère a day, from the milk of 51 cows (Laurens 1864). Nine years later Laurens wrote,

The most important centres in France for the production of gruyère are the Departments of Jura, Doubs and Ain, followed by the Vosges. In the Department of Jura these cheeses are manufactured on a grand scale . . . and produced in two ways:

1: in barns or *chalets*
2: in *fruitières*.

The chalets are held by proprietors or their tenants. They are found principally in the high mountains on the Swiss border. The *fruitières*, also known as village chalets since they are located in villages or hamlets, consist of an association established between a certain number of inhabitants who could not, on their own, produce enough milk to make a cheese of 30 to 35 kg. in a single session. (Laurens 1873: 158–9)

Lebeau (1951: 400) has argued that, since *fruitières* were found on the plateaux rather than in the mountains close to the Swiss border, they may have been an independent French invention, and not copied from the earlier cheese-making associations formed by alp management groups in Switzerland. Laurens describes the typical village dairy of the 1870s, containing a reception room where the milk was received and measured, the dairy where cheeses were manufactured, and the cellar where they were salted and stored. The dairyman's bedroom, on the first floor, was reached by a movable ladder. Another observer writing in the 1870s noted that it was the dairyman's responsibility to keep a record of each delivery. Accounts were sometimes entered in a ledger but usually on a tally stick, one stick being held for each member. 'The entry requires no more than a few cuts with the little saw used in the dairy, and is made with surprising rapidity' (Guyétant 1870: 191). The cheese, cream, and whey produced each day were given to the member who, at that moment, had contributed the greatest quantity of milk since last receiving the produce. His cheese was labelled with his name while stored in the dairy building's cellar. Guyétant, a lawyer, noted that it was forbidden to make loans to, or accept milk from, another associate in order to hasten the moment when someone was due their next cheese.

During the eighteenth and nineteenth centuries many *fruitières* suspended production during the winter, when milk production left no surplus above the household's subsistence needs (Daveau 1959: 250). Guyétant took issue with the court in Besançon, which had judged in 1842 that the association itself dissolved, and was renewed each spring with whatever changes to its rules or membership the associates agreed (quoted in Guyétant 1870: 74). Guyétant (ibid. 32–40) conceded that the accounts were closed each autumn but pointed out that the dairy building and its equipment continued to be the shared property of the associates even during times when production had been suspended.

Until 1884, the procedures for managing a *fruitière* had been merely customary, making it difficult for courts to resolve disputes between members. Latouche concluded that *fruitières* were originally managed according to the procedures used in village government. The *échevin* (sheriff) convened the community's general assembly, and it was he who took the initiative in establishing *fruitières*. If there were several associations in one village, the general assembly would try to ensure that each had roughly the same number of members, and might even threaten to punish those who refused to deliver their milk to the association they had been told to join (Latouche 1938: 784). Before the Revolution the *Intendant* (steward) of Franche-Comté decreed that each *fruitière* should annually appoint an *échevin* of its own, to manage its affairs as if he were 'father of the family' (Lebeau 1951: 391). In 1884 the French government passed a law codifying the regulations by which dairy associations were run. Unlike the commune, the *fruitière* has continued to be governed by a general assembly of its members, although since 1884 a permanent committee is elected to manage the association between general meetings.

Management of Dairy Co-operatives Today

The regulations in force in 1969–72 had last been revised in 1964 (*Journaux officials*, 1964). Any co-operative other than one formed to share agricultural equipment must have a minimum of seven members. Anyone living in the commune where a co-operative has been formed is entitled to join unless he is guilty of a criminal offence, has falsified or delivered fraudulent produce to the co-operative, or otherwise previously jeopardized the success of the association. On joining, each *sociétaire* (member) must contribute a minimum sum to the association's capital. He may contribute more, but (unlike a shareholder in a private enterprise), he is not entitled to any additional voting power. Each member is obliged to deliver all he produces of the resource which the co-operative exists to process to the co-operative, apart from what he requires for family or professional purposes. The association is not dissolved by the death or withdrawal of members. The heirs of a deceased member inherit his debts to other members and one who withdraws remains contractually bound in his obligations to other members for five years. If, however, three-quarters or more of the association's declared capital is lost, an extraordinary general meeting must be called to wind up the association. If debts exceed assets, they are divided equally among the members.

A general assembly of members must be convened at least once a year. The association's accounts must be presented to the meeting, and a report made of the year's activities undertaken by the co-operative. One-third of members must be present to render an ordinary general meeting quorate, and two-thirds if an extraordinary meeting is called. Votes at ordinary general meetings must secure a simple majority, those at extraordinary meetings a two-thirds majority. Although a co-operative with less than twenty members may under certain circumstances be managed by a president alone, all the co-operatives in the villages of our survey elected a committee of between two and nine members. Members' periods of office overlap, so that only one half, one-third, or one-quarter of committee members are elected each year. The term of office varies from two to four years. The committee chooses the president from among its members. The law requires that if there are more than fifty members no two people who are affines or ascending, descending, or collateral kin to the second degree, may sit simultaneously on the co-operative's committee, but few of the co-operatives in our 1972 survey had this many members. It was none the less widely recognized to be in members' interests to prevent nepotism. Only one co-operative in the villages surveyed allowed both brothers and father and son to be elected to the committee. Two others were willing to elect brothers, but not father and son, at the same time. At one of the general meetings I attended in 1969 the election of a new committee member was challenged on the grounds that he was first cousin to another member, but this objection was overruled by the president.

The Entrepreneur Dairyman

Many *fruitières* ceased co-operative production of cheese at around the time of the First World War and handed over responsibility for making and selling cheeses to an entrepreneur. In most cases the building remained the property of the association or the commune, but the role of the association was reduced to co-ordinating the delivery of milk and negotiating its price. If the entrepreneur resigned, the association had to find another. Daveau (1959: 286) suggests that an increase in the quantity of Swiss Gruyère imported into France at the turn of the century had depressed the market. American imports and inflation probably also contributed to the uncertainty. The entrepreneur undertook to shoulder the risks of marketing cheese in return for the right to keep any unanticipated profit if the value of cheese rose after he had bought the milk. Rapid inflation occurred during and after the First World War and by 1929 two-thirds of the *fruitières* in Doubs had accepted this arrangement. Pellaport's first entrepreneur, a Swiss-German called Schwartz, was already in control of production at the time of the First World War. After the war he believed he would be liable to pay reparations and returned to Switzerland, but others stayed on in the district and he was replaced. One of those who worked in Pellaport bought a large area of land at the edge of the commune. The disadvantages of entrepreneurial production became apparent during the German occupation of the Second World War, when many entrepreneurs, like shopkeepers, profited from the clandestine sale of dairy produce on the black market, and kept the money for themselves (Lambert 1953: 176). As the secretary of one association told me in 1969, 'Between the wars, many Swiss dairymen arrived with their possessions in a pocket handkerchief yet, within ten years, they were driving large cars. While everyone else were tightening their belts, German officers were arriving at the *fromagerie* for lunch and staying there until after supper.' The danger of relying on middlemen who could keep unanticipated profit became apparent to wine-producers in southwest France during the First World War, but it was the experience of mutual support under extreme danger during the Second World War that prompted the creation of many wine-making co-operatives (Ulin 1996:174–9). After the Liberation there was also a widespread movement in Franche-Comté, in which Pellaport participated, to restore co-operative control over the production and marketing of cheese. Although entrepreneurs retained control in some villages, their actions were limited by competition with neighbouring co-operatives to provide the best price for milk, and the knowledge that they, too, could lose their position. The competition between entrepreneurs and co-operatives explains César Maitrugue's keen interest in the price of milk at neighbouring dairies, two of which were run by entrepreneurs. The prices they gave in 1968 (47 and 50 cts. per kilo) were similar to those offered by neighbouring co-operatives (46 to 49 cts. per kilo).

The Prevalence of Dairy Co-operatives in 1969 and 1995

During 1972, the dairy co-operatives in eleven of the fifteen villages in our survey managed the production and sale of cheese, employing their own *fromager* (cheese-maker/dairyman) in a village *fromagerie* or dairy. At least four of these had restored co-operative control after the Second World War. The remaining four co-operatives still sold their milk to entrepreneur dairymen. One entrepreneur bought his milk from the *cultivateurs* of two neighbouring villages. Two intervillage co-operatives existed in the region, one of which had been established in January 1969. The most recently established co-operative was already collecting milk from eight villages. Each member had installed a refrigerated tank on his *exploitation*, allowing milk to be collected once rather than twice a day. It was this innovation that one of the *cultivateurs* at Montoiseau had emulated, and by 1986 he had withdrawn from Pellaport's co-operative to sell his milk elsewhere. I spoke to the dairyman at the new intervillage co-operative in October 1969. He impressed on me the economies of scale to be gained by a grouping of co-operatives and predicted that independent village dairies would disappear in the next five to ten years. Like other predictions made at the time (see Ch. 6), this overestimated the rate of change. None the less, by 1995 only four of the fifteen villages still had independent village dairies operated by their co-operatives. The entrepreneur who bought milk from the *cultivateurs* of two villages had been succeeded by his son and the two village co-operatives who co-ordinated the sale of milk to him were in the process of merging. Six villages now participated in intervillage co-operatives. In three villages close to the

Swiss border the dairy co-operatives had dissolved. Two had formerly
sold their milk to village-based entrepreneurs, one had controlled
production in its own dairy. The primary cause of dissolution appeared to
be the declining number of *cultivateurs* although, in one, the end of the
co-operative had been hastened by a dispute over the method of recording of milk deliveries after the introduction of milk quotas in 1984. The
cultivateurs of these three villages were now pursuing uncoordinated
strategies. Some sold their milk to entrepreneurs operating at a regional
level, others had joined neighbouring co-operatives.

In 1969 every village dairy, and even the new intervillage co-operative,
sold its cheeses after a period of months to *affineurs*, who kept them until
maturity and then resold the cheeses to retailers. Some belonged to
UCFFC, a regional co-operative (Le Union co-operative des fruitières de
Franche-Comté), which has its own cellars in Besançon and Lons-le-
Saulnier. Others, such as Pellaport, sold their cheese to private businesses.
By 1995 some dairies had begun to make cheeses such as Mont d'Or and
Morbier which required less time to mature and could be kept in cellars
within the village until ready for retail, thus cutting out the *affineur*. The
ability of Gruyère to withstand the long wagon journey on rough roads is
no longer needed, although Comté (the local variety of Gruyère) remains
the region's best-known product.

OTHER CO-OPERATIVES

Since the 1950s, new agricultural co-operatives have been set up to
manage communal pasture, stud bulls, and agricultural machinery.

*Pasture Co-operatives (*Sociétés Pastorales *or* Syndicats de Pâturage*)*

When the pasture co-operative in Pellaport was established in 1954, it
began to rent portions of the commons from the commune, and organize
their management. Money was borrowed from the commune to erect
boundary fences and pipe water to drinking troughs. The co-operative
bought a machine to spread chemical fertilizer and negotiated the bulk
purchase of fertilizer, both for the commons and for members' own fields.
Members were allowed to borrow the machine when it was not in use on
the commons. By 1969 the co-operative was renting all the communal
pasture. That year it had twenty-two members, who between them sent
206 head of cattle to graze on the commons, 73 per cent of the village's

heifers and 30 per cent of its milk cows. The *cultivateurs* of Montoiseau are not members of this co-operative, and one *cultivateur* in Pellaport with a relatively small herd had sufficient land of his own not to need access to the commons.

The affairs of the co-operative were administered, between general meetings, by a nine-man committee, including the president and secretary. In spring, each member declared the number of cattle he wished to place on the commons. The committee decided which animals to place on each pasture. In 1969, milk cows had to be closest to the village, so that they could be brought back for milking. A number of jobs were allocated *par soumission* (by tender), including the clearing of brushwood, levelling molehills, spreading fertilizer, and transporting water to the portions not yet provided with a piped supply. The total expenses of the co-operative in 1968 were 16,203 fr. (equivalent to 91,385 fr. at 1994 prices). The main expenses were the hire of pasture (3,475 fr.), the purchase of fertilizer (3,510 fr.), and paying the cowherd (1,700 fr. wages and 1,746 fr. social insurance). The expenses were recouped by a standard charge of 79 fr. for each animal placed on the pasture. Any money earned working for the co-operative was deducted from the charge levied on the *cultivateur*.

In 1972, management of the commons was still carried out by the mayor and members of the municipal council in five of the fifteen villages surveyed, while pasture co-operatives existed in six. In three others the dairy co-operative rented the pasture from the commune and arranged its management. The price of the annual rent is expressed in terms of the mean value of milk over the year at the dairy, typically between 2 and 3 kilos of milk per are. By 1995, pasture co-operatives existed in all but three communes. Eight villages, however, had divided the commons and arranged for each *cultivateur* to rent one section, either through the co-operative or directly from the council. Two further villages had divided some sections of the commons, but left the remainder as a single high pasture on which the *cultivateurs'* heifers were placed together. This process of enclosure without privatization is a signal example of the difference between the principles ruling the management of resources in English villages and the villages of Franche-Comté. It will be discussed in Ch. 7.

In Pellaport the commons were divided in 1979. The pasture co-operative continues to rent the commons, and to arrange the size of each household's portion. Division of the commons enabled each *cultivateur* to decide whether to graze cattle or harvest hay on their portion and is also considered to reduce the risk of diseases being transmitted between one household's cattle and another's.

Stud Bull Co-operatives (Syndicats d'Insemination)

During the 1950s and 1960s a number of villages created co-operatives whose members shared the ownership of a stud bull. Until the introduction of artificial insemination the only alternative, for many, was to buy the services of a bull belonging to one of the wealthier *cultivateurs*. To have fed and stabled an animal which one needed only four or five times a year was considered too expensive. Once artificial insemination had been introduced by a regional co-operative based in Besançon, the village *syndicats d'insemination* began to disappear. There were none left in the villages of our survey by 1995.

JOINT OWNERSHIP OF EQUIPMENT

CUMA

CUMA (Co-operatives d'utilisations de materiel agricole), co-operatives created to share the cost and ownership of agricultural equipment, have been widely promoted by government agents as a means of reducing the cost of mechanization, and are eligible for reduced rates of interest on bank loans (cf. Gröger 1981: 166). They are legally required to have a minimum of four members (fewer than other types of agricultural co-operative). No CUMA has ever existed in Pellaport, but in 1969–72 there were two among the villages of our comparative survey. One had thirteen members among the *cultivateurs* of a single village (less than half the total in that village), the other linked nine out of twenty *cultivateurs* in one village with five from a neighbouring community. I learned of two other CUMA which had dissolved over arguments about how to share the cost of repairs to damaged equipment. Boichard described a CUMA in the same district which he studied in the late 1950s (Boichard 1960). Sharing hay harvesting equipment is impractical because everyone needs the equipment throughout the harvest period. Tractors are, similarly, required throughout the year. Equipment which is only used occasionally yet wanted by many, whose expense is too great to justify purchase by individual *cultivateurs*, is most suitable for shared purchase. CUMA own items such as ploughs and rotavators, seed-drills and muck-spreaders. I was frequently told that CUMA were difficult to manage successfully and many *cultivateurs* preferred to share equipment without entering into a contractual agreement (see Wright 1964: 166).

Ententes

When I began fieldwork in 1969, three ploughs had recently been bought by sets of kin or neighbours in Pellaport. One was shared between three unrelated neighbours, including Pierre Bavarel and Nicolas Jouffroy, one between two brothers-in-law and a mutual friend in a neighbouring house, and one between four neighbours, two of whom were brothers-in-law. A larger set of seven *cultivateurs*, one living in Montoiseau, had collaborated in the ownership of several items of equipment. In February 1969 they already owned a metal frame for flattening molehills, a sprung-tine harrow, and a muck-spreader. It was these friends who bought a mechanical shovel later in 1969. At the time I left the field that autumn they were planning to buy a seed-drill.

Although one member of this set described them as *un société*, they had no formal constitution. There was no elected committee and no written record of the agreement on which shared ownership was based. The arrangement was explicitly 'unofficial' and, like the arrangement to share the ownership of ploughs, based on *une entente* (an understanding). Similar *ententes* were common in the other villages of our survey. We were told of the existence of between one and four *ententes* in each of eight villages. Only one village was explicitly said to lack such agreements and there may have been other *ententes* of which we were not informed. Gröger (1981) found a similar situation in the southern foothills of the Massif Central during the mid-1970s, where portable machines which are not needed throughout the year proved the most amenable to shared ownership. Her region had experienced substantial rural emigration between the First World War and the 1930s. As in Franche-Comté, the first tractors were bought between the two world wars, but it was not until the 1950s that rapid mechanization began. Since the early 1950s eighty overlapping groups of co-owners had purchased twenty-two different types of machine. Sixty-three of these groups still existed at the time of Gröger's fieldwork, and were preferred to formal co-operatives. CUMA were considered too complicated to administer, and not worth the level of subsidy they attracted (ibid. 166). Rather than speaking of *des ententes*, participants stressed the need *d'être d'accord* (translated by Gröger as 'to be of one mind', ibid. 169). Shared machinery was generally purchased by those who already co-operated, and bought in one person's name.

It is tempting to see the guiding spirit of *ententes* as a continuation of the ethos that sustained the traditional *fruitière*, before they were transformed into agricultural co-operatives by the French government in 1884. Guyétant (1870: 73) quoted a nineteenth-century court ruling which described the basis of the pre-contractual *fruitière* as 'une confiance reciproque et . . . la bonne foi' (reciprocal confidence and good faith). While there is undoubtedly some continuity at the level of organizational procedure, there is also evidence that the ethics of interpersonal life have undergone steady transformation since the nineteenth century (see Ch. 4).

When I returned to Pellaport in 1995 my friends told me that there was less co-operation in the purchase of equipment than had been the case twenty-five years earlier. This claim seemed inaccurate, although it derives from a series of changes in the quality of community life that will be reviewed in Ch. 4. All the surviving *cultivateurs* of the village belonged to *une entente* which shared ownership of a seed-drill, a heavy metal roller, and a crop sprayer, which they had bought between 1971 and 1987. Étienne Maitrugue's son administered the accounts, but the agreement had not been formalized as a *syndicat*. Since the majority of participants were not members of the *entente* that bought the hydraulic shovel in 1969, it does not seem one had descended directly from the other (Pierre Bavarel recalled that the earlier *entente* lasted about five years). Jacques Maitrugue had entered into an additional *entente* with his cousin in La Combe Sainte-Marie. They shared a cement mixer and a tank in which to store *purain* (liquid manure). Armand Maitrugue and his brother had also formed a separate *entente* with Victor Jouffroy, to buy a muck-spreader. *Ententes* were still commonly reported in other villages when I visited them to repeat the 1972 survey.

One of the two successful CUMA of 1969 still existed, its membership now extended to *cultivateurs* from a number of villages, including Nicolas Jouffroy. The president attributed his association's success to the strict check made each time an item of equipment was returned and the insistence that each member cleaned equipment when he had finished using it. Every time an item needed repair, a committee meeting would convene to decide whether the equipment should be repaired or replaced. The village in which this CUMA is based has sustained a significantly slower rate of decline in the number of *exploitations* than in neighbouring villages, having only declined by four (from twenty-seven to twenty-three) between 1972 and 1995. The other CUMA had merged with a larger co-operative in the same canton. One new CUMA had been created in 1985, in Dechailles, and was still working well ten years later.

THEORY AND ETHNOGRAPHY

Theory guides the way in which we separate interesting from trivial events experienced during fieldwork. It helps link the observations that interest us into a coherent ethnographic account and points towards particular interpretations or explanations of what we consider related events. Theories do not, however, blind us completely to the complexity of field experience. Our findings may lead us to modify a useful theory or even reject a theoretical orientation altogether if it appears indifferent to what interested us in the field. The analysis of my field data from Franche-Comté developed into a dialogue between theory and ethnography. A number of theories helped me appreciate the character of the social processes that underlie my observations in Pellaport and surrounding villages.

Anthony Giddens (1979) proposed that action, structure, and contradiction constituted the central problems in social theory. Stephen J. Gould (1999) identified structure, contingency, and history as the primary concepts of social and biological theory. For three-quarters of the twentieth century, structure was taken to be the most important of the three. At the start of the century the great and unexpected variety of societies encountered during European colonial expansion needed to be classified into types, and some general argument was required to indicate how the types were related (Layton 1997*b*: 27–37). Making a virtue of expediency, and perhaps adopting the prevailing political theory of the nation-state that subordinated the citizen to the common good (Foucault 1977), structure was considered to dictate action and (except in the work of Marx) neutralize contradiction or history. Societies were considered inherently stable, enabling what Gould (1999: p.x) calls the schoolchild's version of scientific method: 'remove all distinctiveness of time or place by reducing the overt complexity of a . . . phenomenon to a few repeatable and controllable factors'.

There was also a good methodological reason for emphasizing structure; it highlighted the emergent qualities of social interaction. The French sociologist Durkheim argued that social life displays emergent phenomena that cannot be reduced to the psychological or biological dispositions of individual people. 'Social facts' such as the language we speak, the currency with which we buy and sell, the contract law that regulates our transactions, are 'ways of acting or thinking with the peculiar characteristic of exercising a coercive influence on individual consciousnesses' (Durkheim 1938: p. liii). As an emergent phenomenon, society constrained individual behaviour. Durkheim's dispute with his contemporary, Tarde, concerning the primacy of society over the contingency of individual action, will be discussed in Ch. 5.

Durkheim's first attempt to demonstrate his theory was *The Division of Labour in Society* (1933). Following earlier social theorists, Durkheim argued that there were two common forms of human society. Compound societies were made up of a series of identical units, like a segmented animal organism, in which all the essential 'organs' (institutions) were reproduced in each segment. In complex societies the units became differentiated so that each played a distinct role in the maintenance of the whole social organism, as did the liver, heart, and lungs in a complex animal body. Durkheim implicitly took the French Industrial Revolution as an example of the transition from the first to the second. Formerly self-sufficient villages came into competition as they expanded, as was indeed happening on the Plateau of Levier when disputes broke out over the use of shared common land during a period of population growth. Competition was resolved as each region specialized in the goods to which it was best suited: grain, wine, iron ore, or coal. The emerging railway network ensured each could depend on the others. As people streamed into the cities, the repressive sanctions that had guaranteed uniformity of behaviour in traditional village communities gave way to contract law, regulating the new, complex forms of interdependence that arose.

The British school of anthropology known as the Structural Functionalists and led by Radcliffe-Brown, adopted Durkheim's approach and applied it to the traditional 'compound' or 'segmentary' societies of the Third World. They considered it axiomatic that such societies were inherently stable, that sanctions functioned to restrain deviance, that the function of customs was to preserve society's existing form, and that accounts of variations in the behaviour of individuals had no part in anthropological analysis.

Cognitive structuralism, another strand in Durkheim's thinking, proved more influential on French anthropology. Durkheim (1915) argued that human social life depended on our ability to communicate through symbols. The meaning of any symbol depended on its place in a structured system of thought, the 'collective consciousness'. Communication could only succeed if the collective consciousness successfully imposed itself on the individual minds of society's members. Durkheim's structural approach to meaning was developed during the 1950s and 1960s by Lévi-Strauss (1966), then criticized by Bourdieu

(1977) and, more radically, by Derrida (1976). Both cognitive structuralism and structural–functionalism suppressed history by emphasizing structural constants.

My Ph.D. research in Pellaport was guided by a dissatisfaction with both types of structuralism. The Master's thesis that I wrote under Phyllis Kaberry's supervision was based on a reading of the available literature on myth and ritual in northern Australia (Layton 1968). The ethnography showed, contrary to Lévi-Strauss's assumptions in *The Savage Mind* (1966), that there were both variations in individual interpretations of myth and changeable meanings attributed to objects used in ritual (see Layton 1970). The discovery of variation in individual interpretation of the values and meaning of actions in interpersonal relations in Pellaport gave me a chance to explore the former aspect of culture in the field (see Ch. 4). Fieldwork in Europe gave access to written records, and enabled a deeper study of social change. I chose to study the role of individuals in the adoption of technological innovations (Ch. 5) and the introduction of new co-operatives (Ch. 7) to challenge Radcliffe-Brown's assertion that there was no place for the study of individuals in social anthropology (see Layton 1974). The discovery that no two villages were alike in their structure, but varied according to whether, and for how long, they had relied on co-operatives, entrepreneurs, the village council, and interpersonal *ententes* posed an interesting problem for description: how could I capture the 'structure' of the typical village, where villages varied in space and time?

Far from this being an isolated case of disaffection, there was widespread dissatisfaction with three aspects of the structural-functionalist model of social systems during the 1950s and 1960s: the argument that social systems tended to maintain themselves in equilibrium, the implication that each segment (village or lineage) should have a structure identical to the others, and the claim that the behaviour of individuals was predetermined by the structure of the system which both supplied the positions that people occupied, and dictated the behaviour appropriate to each. Other studies of European villages were prompted by the same theoretical issues.

The assumption that each segment of society should have the same structure was criticized by Leach and Geertz, who showed variability in the structure of Burmese and Balinese villages. Buckley and Easton exploited the development of the theory of cybernetics to gain a more flexible interpretation of how social systems work through time. The third aspect of structural-functionalism, the primacy of the system over individual action was countered by the argument that the behaviour of individuals *generates* the structure of relationships. This argument was advanced by writers as varied as Fortes, Blau, Barth, and Bailey.

Variation in the Structure of Segments

Leach's ethnography of highland Burma and Geertz's account of Balinese village structure influenced my attempts to conceptualize variation in the structure of villages on the Plateau of Levier, but neither provided a complete parallel.

Leach (1954) had found that among the Katchin of northern Burma, some villages were independent, some under the authority of local Katchin chiefs. Leach concluded two ideal forms of political organization were recognized by the Katchin, the egalitarian *gumlao*, and the hierarchical *gumsa*. The two ideologies predicated alternative forms of behaviour which coloured the entire structuring of the village.

The distinction between *gumsa* and *gumlao*, with their attendant ideologies, suggested a parallel of sorts with the difference between villages on the Plateau of Levier which managed dairy production through a co-operative, and those which handed production and marketing of cheese to an entrepreneur. It was not a very convincing parallel because, in other respects, the French villages might be identically organized. They were not riven by a complete set of structural oppositions, as were the villages of highland Burma. As a villager from Pellaport once exclaimed, 'and you know, Robert, there *are* socialists, even here'. In the 1969 Presidential election, the votes from Pellaport were fairly evenly divided between the mainstream candidates of right and left, Pompidou and Poher. The third, far left candidate received a mere handful. None the less, Leach had shown that structure was not necessarily stable and the structure of a village could change through time. Two ideologies could coexist within the cultural repertoire, even though only one was realized in any village.

My supervisor Freddy Bailey drew my attention to Geertz's paper on Balinese village structure. Geertz (1959) describes how he surveyed twenty-five villages on the island of Bali, in the hope of establishing the structure of the typical village, but found none to be exemplary of a type. Communities consisted of variations on a series of organizational themes which regulated worship at a temple, irrigation of rice fields, and so forth. These intersected differently in each village, creating complementary or conflicting obligations. Geertz showed there was no need to construct a 'typical' village for the Plateau of Levier. The Plateau's cultural unity clearly lay in common possession of a number of organizational themes such as mutual aid, co-operatives, entrepreneurial activities, and commune councils. Like the Burmese case, however, the Balinese one did not fit exactly. It would have been as if every village managed its common pasture according to one principle, its dairy according to another, and shared agricultural equipment according to a third. What made the villages of the Plateau particularly interesting was the way in which local politics revolved around choice between one or another way of managing a particular resource.

Society as an Evolving System

During the 1960s, the idea of a social system advocated by Durkheim and Radcliffe-Brown was reassessed. Easton (1965: 26) argued for a model of society as 'an adaptive, self-regulating and self-transforming system of behaviour', whose organization gives it emergent properties. In keeping with contemporary cybernetics, both Buckley and Easton regarded the flow of information as the key to understanding how the organization of social systems is regulated (Buckley 1967: 48–51). The flow of goods and labour, basic to Marx's analysis of social systems, was not mentioned.

Easton argued that social systems are constituted through interaction, and treated political life as a subsystem operating within a natural and social environment, which responds to stress by reinforcing or modifying its members' policies. The ambiguity of this formulation was a weakness in Easton's approach. Is it people (action) or the system (structure) which 'responds'? Stress is generally treated as something the environment inflicts on the system (Easton 1965: 48, 87, but see 114). Although it is difficult to pin down exactly what Easton treats as inputs to, and outputs from a political system (see ibid. 75, 113), he treats feedback as the flow of information to political authorities on the success of their current policies (ibid. 128–9). Bailey's work *Stratagems and Spoils* (1969: 18 n. 10) can be construed as an attempt to flesh out the approach with case studies but, as Silverman later showed, similar weaknesses can be identified in Bailey's analysis.

Easton contended a successful system is one that can preserve an equilibrium in the face of stress, but Buckley gave greater prominence to a system's history. Buckley argued that rather than comparing society to an animal body, a closer parallel with social process could be found in evolving biological populations which typically change in response to modifications of the environment, as villages on the Plateau of Levier were responding to change in the regional economy. The difference lies in the way information is transmitted within the system: in a biological population it is coded in DNA but in a social system it is transmitted through language and other forms of symbolism. Social systems are typically rather fluid; their structures change and there is a thin line between structure and process. The concepts of institutions and social control were not helpful tools for representing such processes. Structure is 'the way in which moving reality is translated, for the observer, into an instantaneous and artificial observation' (Buckley 1967: 21). Societies 'of any complexity' have alternative or counter-norms and areas of uninstitutionalized behaviour. People can choose between them. 'The structure of such a system is thus viewed in terms of sets of alternative actions' (ibid. 128), a description that applied well to village organization on the Plateau of Levier. Whereas natural selection proceeds by blind trial and error, humans can learn from their own previous actions and from each other, and make social decisions. Patterns in society are created not just by rules, but also by '*the interactions* among normatively and purposively oriented individuals and subgroups in an ecological setting' (ibid. 61–2, his emphasis). The concept of a 'step function', in which a variable has no effect on others until its value has changed by a certain amount (ibid. 67) seemed particularly appropriate to the processes of technological change in Pellaport (see Ch. 6).

During the 1990s, the theory of social systems has again been revised. Although some recent writers continue to use the vocabulary of 1960s systems theory, social systems are now considered less predictable than the simple concepts of negative and positive feedback implied. Chaotic movement in complex systems was originally discovered in the turbulent movement of particles that develops in weather patterns or swiftly flowing water (for a general account, see Stewart 1997). The unpredictability of social process has been explained in similar terms (Kiel and Elliott 1996; van der Leeuw and McGlade 1997). Byrne (1997) has shown how the concept of chaotic movement in complex systems can help explain the growing social divisions in British cities as they developed new trajectories during the 1980s. Bintliff (1997) extends Byrne's analysis to explain why some ancient cities survived catastrophic destruction, while others never recovered. Where three or four related variables interact, and where their variability is constrained within certain limits, the state of a system can cycle indefinitely without ever returning exactly to its starting-point. This concept is particularly applicable to the household cycle on the

Plateau of Levier. Households which have a similar composition and economic status at one moment may increasingly diverge in response to demographic variables or the accessibility of alternative employment. Ruelle (1991) points out the difficulty of detecting chaotic movement in human society when historical systems take a very long time to approach, or return to their initial condition. An archaeological timescale may be most appropriate for studying cycles in regional history (see Erwin 1997 and McGlade 1997 for applications of chaos theory to prehistoric economic systems).

Cyclic movement in the social processes discussed in this book can be identified at three levels. The longest are the Braudelian cycles cited in Ch. 7 which have a period of between 500 and 1,000 years. The Kondratiev cycles of production in a capitalist economy, outlined in Ch. 6, take about 50 years to complete. The household cycle analysed in Ch. 3 is driven by a generation span of between 25 and 30 years. Since the three types of cycle interact, the encompassing social system is itself likely to display a chaotic trajectory. The development of increasingly complex agricultural technology is superimposed on all three cycles and, at least at present, seems to have no limit.

The Social System as an Epiphenomenon

All the studies summarized so far could be said to have taken a top–down approach, showing that social structure was more prone to change, and more variable, than classic structural-functionalism allowed. Far more radical was the approach that treated social structure as an 'epiphenomenon', a by-product of people acting in their own self-interest. The writing of Fredrik Barth and Freddy Bailey were breaths of fresh air after the stultifying accounts of social structure that dominated my generation's undergraduate reading. Radcliffe-Brown (1952: 192) had written of social structure as 'the concrete reality . . . which . . . is the set of actually existing relations'. The superficiality of structural-functionalism became clear when I caught myself, as I cycled back to Pellaport after early visits to surrounding villages, wondering 'Where is the structure? Why can't I see it?'

One of the earliest studies to take a bottom–up approach was Fortes's paper on Asante household structure. Rights to land are transmitted by matrilineal descent among the Asante of Ghana. Many marriages take place between men and women of different lineages in the same village. A man's children inherit property from their mother's brother, so a married man must decide whether to live with his wife and children, or with his sister and her children, his own heirs. Children may eat with their fathers and sleep in their mother's house. It would be possible to produce a typology of the alternative structures seen in Asante households (nuclear family, extended family, etc.). These structures are, however, generated by the developing life cycles of household members, and the various ways in which they have tried to resolve the contradictory demands of parenthood and descent. ' "Structure" thus appears as an arrangement of parts brought about by the operation, through a period of time, of principles of social organization' (Fortes 1970: 32). Fortes's paper clarified the significance of the nineteenth-century household census data located during my second period of fieldwork with Ian Keen and Marga Gervis, in 1972, discussed in Ch. 3.

Fredrik Barth also argued that customary patterns of behaviour should be seen as the outcome of the decisions people made about how to allocate their time and resources in particular circumstances. Social structure was an 'epiphenomenon' of people's actions. Focusing on the idea of politics as a game, Barth tried to strip political strategies of their cultural form. Norwegian fishermen and tribesmen from Pakistan were treated alike as rational actors seeking their personal advantage. The relative success of alternative strategies is determined by the technical and ecological conditions in which they are implemented and the constraints imposed or opportunities offered by other actors, pursuing their own strategies (Barth 1959; 1966; 1967). In the United States, Peter Blau (1964) took a rather similar approach in his analysis of the outcomes of exchange in interpersonal relations. Blau's arguments will be taken up in Ch. 4 while the relevance of Barth's approach to household structure in Pellaport will be noted in Ch. 3.

In his seminal work *Stratagems and Spoils* (1969), Bailey took a radical, action-oriented approach to the analysis of politics. He argued that politics is a game: it has a prize worth winning, an uncertain outcome, and is played by relatively evenly matched teams. Occasionally, politics becomes a fight in which the combatants aim to destroy the existing game and establish a different set of rules. In both routine politics and revolutions leaders must attract, reward, and settle disputes among followers. The game always disallows certain strategies, but there are two kinds of rule, *pragmatic* rules tell you how to get things done (for example, 'don't associate yourself with parties the voters don't like') while *normative* rules express publicly acceptable values. Politicians tend to play according to the former, but justify their actions in public according to the latter.

Pragmatic rules are tactics, which fill the gaps between the norms. They tell you what is effective, regardless of what is right and proper. The same pragmatic rules are used in otherwise different societies. Normative rules are used to judge the ethics of a tactic. Bailey acknowledges the influence of Firth's distinction between social structure and social organization on his thinking (cf. Firth 1954; 1955).

Although he borrowed from Easton's use of systems theory, Bailey admitted he found this approach too mechanistic, giving insufficient room for the role of 'man . . . as an entrepreneur' (Bailey 1969: 18 n. 10). It may be possible to write of a political system adjusting to its environment, whether to independent variables in the natural environment such as drought or disease, or to rival political structures in the social environment, but in practice these adjustments are made by politicians who change the rules, not by 'the system'. Social anthropology had moved from the 'vast impersonal forces' in Durkheim's explanation to a 'Bad King John' theory of social process (cf. Carr 1961: 45); from structure to action or contingency.

On the Plateau of Levier, political competition has often taken place over the appropriate strategy to apply in any one case: whether, for example, stud bulls or dairies should be managed by the co-operative or an entrepreneur; whether common pasture should be managed by the village council or by a co-operative. Before the Revolution of 1789, similar competition for the control of resources took place between the corporate village and local feudal lords, although this game was played out in the courts of the Crown, rather than in a village electorate. Bailey's approach brought into focus the difference between variation in village structure on the Plateau of Levier and that in highland Burma or Bali. On the Plateau local politics consisted of competition to implement one or another of the strategies in the cultural repertoire, in the management of particular resources (cf. Cole and Wolf 1974: 282).

Exciting as it was, Bailey's approach left several questions unanswered. It did not show in whose interests it was to uphold the normative rules. Politicians appeared to find them an inconvenience rather than a help. Bailey (1969: 139) argued that the State sometimes provided umpires, such as policemen, while stateless societies relied on the mystical sanctions of umpires such as Muslim 'saints'. Another possibility is that it was in no one's interests to provoke the complete anarchy that would result from annulling all rules. Camus (1953) argued this mistake had caused the French and Russian Revolutions to spawn totalitarian governments in an attempt to reconstitute order, or structure. On the Plateau of Levier, however, political competition arose over *which* rule among several to apply in particular cases. The issue was thus not to distinguish between normative and pragmatic rules, but between procedures and the means to implement them. Both can be described as 'strategies'. In the first sense, both the rules of *gumsa* and *gumlao* in highland Burma, and the planes of village organization on Bali, are administrative strategies for the management of property. 'Norms' are realized in the very implementation of such strategies, which cannot therefore be stripped of their cultural content. Politics, as Bailey pointed out, directs recruitment of support for a policy, outvoting the opposition and implementing the proposal; requiring strategies of a different kind.

Sydel Silverman (1974) subjected the Bailey school to a savage review which, in retrospect, made a number of reasonable points. Bailey and we, his students, reduced politics to contests over reputation. Values are sometimes argued to outweigh economic self-interest. Peasant villages are treated as relatively undifferentiated, face-to-face communities encapsulated within a larger State political structure. History is ignored, and peasant society is treated as timeless. Bailey locates the forces causing change in peasant communities in the social environment, not in the political games they play. Yet it is not clear how or where to draw the boundary between political games and their environment. Worse, analysis of the social environment is excluded and the approach simply considers how political games are played to mitigate its effects. 'The major social science issue—how to explain the structure—is defined as "not our job" ' (ibid. 120). In this regard, the focus on the individual is no better than the structural-functionalism it replaced. In particular, it does not contribute to an understanding of how power is distributed in a society, nor to an identification of the conditions that change the distribution of power. Silverman's critique reflects the shift from interactionist to Marxist anthropology that characterized the 1970s (see Layton 1997*b*: 124–5, 130–2).

Villages on the Plateau of Levier have a degree of closure, both as corporate groups owning property and regulating their affairs through the municipal council, and as communities organized through networks of mutual aid between neighbours, but they are inextricably part of the nation-state, as units in its administration, contributors to its market economy, and observers of its laws. In their daily life, as producers of cheese, as factory or office workers, villagers participate in, and do not just respond to, wider social process (cf. Cole and Wolf 1974: 20; Rosenberg 1988: 15, 49). The distribution of power, based on the control of resources within the village and the opportunities allowed by the State, dictates which strategies are feasible and which cannot be implemented. Chapter 7 will show how changes in the way village resources are managed are generally precipitated either by new state policies or by economic change to which the villages themselves contribute and demonstrate how, in turn, these changes feed back on economic process.

New strategies are derived from older ones (cf. Behar 1986: 162, 218). A historical perspective reveals how and when particular strategies came into existence. The contemporary market economy in agriculture is a product of the rural depopulation which began in the mid-nineteenth century, triggered both by the French industrial revolution in the cities, and by the growth of a rural class system. Co-operatives have only become special interest groups as increasing numbers of people have found employment outside agriculture. The original *fruitières* were created by redeploying the procedures for management of the open fields through the village assembly. It was government legislation in 1884, enacted in response to the spread of *fruitières* after the Industrial Revolution, which clearly distinguished co-operatives from the strategies of mutual aid that continue to enable the sharing of farm machinery (cf. Buckley 1967: 129).

HABITUS AND STRUCTURATION

The interplay between cultural strategy and social or ecological conditions had already been studied in the field, during the 1960s. Wylie and his team worked in France, Cole and Wolf in northern Italy. Both made extensive use of historical evidence. Other anthropologists were beginning their research at about the same time as the team from Sussex University to which I belonged. Zonabend and Verdier regularly visited Minot, in Burgundy, between 1968 and 1975 (Verdier 1979: 11). Three Alpine villages were studied: Friedl conducted his research in Kippel from September 1969 to September 1970 (Friedl 1974: p. vii), Netting carried out fieldwork in Törbel from July 1970 to August 1971 and Rosenberg worked in Abriès between 1972 and 1974.

In the course of the 1970s the theoretical landscape between structure, history, and action that had been explored by Barth, Bailey, Fortes, and Firth was definitively colonized by Bourdieu and Giddens, who gave its principal features names such as 'habitus', 'hexus', practical consciousness, and structuration. The following chapters rely heavily, albeit from a critical perspective, on Bourdieu and Giddens.

What do Bourdieu and Giddens have in common?

Bourdieu (1977: 5) and Giddens (1984: 25) are both critical of the ahistorical quality of the structural analysis promoted by Radcliffe-Brown and Lévi-Strauss. Structural analysis also tends to render variation in individual performances as deviations from an unwritten score (social structure) that is, in fact, an artificial construct built by the analyst. Both argue that order in social relations is not evidence that actors are consciously striving to achieve it, nor does it prove there is a supra-organic entity, 'society', which tries to maintain its own structure. While these arguments are similar to those of the interactionists, Bourdieu and Giddens are equally opposed to treating actors as completely rational, playing the 'pure' strategies of games theory. Instead, they argue, agents' strategies *constitute* local society and culture.

Bourdieu (1977: 2) argued that the ethnographer carries out a structural analysis because s/he lacks a practical mastery or competence in performance of the cultural tradition. Structural analysis is like the study a professional linguist might make of the vocabulary and grammar of a foreign language, in contrast to the mastery of practice in the language that native speakers have. Saussure, the originator of Structural Linguistics, had identified a chicken-and-egg problem: language must exist for speech to be meaningful yet language can only be learned by listening to speech (cf. Giddens 1984: 31). Mere knowledge of the code will not help one appreciate the function of a message used in a practical situation (Bourdieu 1977: 25). Participants in exchange experience it as a sequence of transactions through time, each of which is prompted by the previous offering and seeks to influence subsequent exchanges. To abolish temporal process is to abolish strategy. Giddens (1984: 170) wrote similarly that social systems are created by the situated activities of agents, taking place through time and in space. Social structure is not a constraining force, external to human action. It is the agents' activities which reproduce the conditions that make those activities possible.

Bourdieu devised the concept of 'habitus' to bridge structure and action. Habitus consists of 'structured structures predisposed to function as structuring structures' (Bourdieu 1977: 72): habitus is an egg predisposed to become a chicken. Giddens uses the term 'practical consciousness' to describe this phenomenon. 'Practical consciousness consists of knowing the rules and tactics whereby daily life is constituted and reconstituted across time and space' (Giddens 1984: 90). Habitus is the individual's reconstruction of the rules and tactics deduced from others' actions. Each individual's habitus can be seen as a structural variant of those learned by other members of the community. Variations in the habitus of individuals are best documented in Bourdieu's (1977: 100–9) ethnography of the Kabyle calendar. For Giddens, *agency* is similarly the ability to act in particular ways, where more than one course of action is possible.

The fallacy of inferring actors that strive consciously to achieve social order arises from turning regularities in cognition or behaviour into 'rules', which then presuppose a plan, enforced by a planner (Bourdieu 1977: 120; see Kauffman 1993: 4–8, on similar reasoning in biology). Structure is not a constraining force, external to human action, but something reproduced when the unintended consequences of action feed back to reconstitute the circumstances in which the action occurred, as do the circuits of capitalist production identified by Marx. Giddens argues that most of the time agents acquiesce unreflectively to the constraints imposed by others who exercise their power to act (Giddens 1984: 27, 162, 176).

Giddens and Bourdieu argue that actors do not play the 'pure' strategies of games theory which tend to universalize the particular circumstances of market exchange. Social strategies are bound up with the constitution of meaning and the sanctioning of conduct in particular contexts and agents draw upon the specific rules and resources in their social environment. Bourdieu compares the games theorists' approach to that of Sartre, who advocated 'good faith' as a willingness to confront every fresh situation in itself, without bringing one's accumulated dispositions to bear on it.[2] Giddens objects that 'micro-sociology' (the approach of Barth, Bailey, and others) treats people as 'free agents', assuming it is the job of 'macro-sociology' to analyse the structural constraints on activity, rather than appreciating those constraints are realized even in the smallest and most personal actions of agents. I will assess these arguments when analysing interpersonal relations and the establishment of new co-operatives in Pellaport in Chs. 4 and 7.

Where do Bourdieu and Giddens differ?

Bourdieu's criticism is directed at *cognitive* structuralism, the structuralist approach to the study of meaning. His two main case studies are drawn

---

[2] Bourdieu does Sartre an injustice in not admitting Sartre was preoccupied with the evil perpetrated by Europeans who took refuge from personal responsibility in the name of totalitarian ideologies, whether Stalinist or Fascist.

from his own work on reciprocity and the agricultural cycle among the Kabyle of Algeria. *The Constitution of Society* (Giddens 1984) represents Giddens' critique of structural-functionalism, the structuralist approach to studying social *behaviour*. This difference causes their analyses to diverge.

For communication to succeed, each participant must share *similar*, if not the same, understandings of each other's intended meanings. Social systems, on the other hand, are built on the *differentiation* of roles. For Bourdieu, the primary problem is to explain how the habitus of each individual member of the community converges with that of others. One of the greatest strengths of Bourdieu's analysis is to show that any interaction must take place within the idiom of a culture if agents are to understand each other (cf. Giddens 1984: 331). The capacity of the structures in the Kabyle habitus to generate an indefinite number of new symbolic equations, which none the less follow an existing logic, has a parallel in the ways that villagers of Pellaport construed each other's intentions in mutual aid and efforts to adopt new farm equipment during my initial fieldwork (see Chs. 4 and 5).

Since social systems are built on the differentiation of roles, the problem for Giddens is, on the other hand, to explain how *different* social positions are bound together into a social system, that is to explain how structuration occurs. Agents are 'distributed' through society and Giddens' goal is to explain 'how the limitations of individual "presence" are transcended by the stretching of social relations across time and space' (1979: 35). 'It is the intersection between these forms of positioning and that within the *longue durée* of institutions which creates the overall framework of social positioning' (ibid. 1980: 85). Giddens argues that this framework is built through the exercise of power.

Bourdieu (1977: 76–7) combines a postmodernist (i.e. post-structuralist) desire to show that structures are generated through performance, rather than given in a collective consciousness that precedes and outlasts the individual, with a modernist desire to show the observer's analysis reveals the irrationality of native beliefs. Habitus is situated somewhere between a blind, mechanical reaction and conscious, deliberate intention. It may be accompanied by conscious, strategic calculation, but such calculation is not part of habitus itself (Bourdieu 1977: 76–7).

In contrast to Bourdieu Giddens argues the agent is well-informed, even if much action is unreflective. Although Giddens accepts that much of the 'mutual knowledge' agents draw upon is not consciously accessible to them, and that their actions may have unintended consequences, he contends, in contrast to Bourdieu, that 'all competent members of society . . . are expert "sociologists" ' (Giddens 1984: 26), with a 'theoretical understanding' of the grounds of their activity (ibid. 5). To parody, Bourdieu's agent is cast in the urban intellectual's image of the peasant, unreflectively following age-old traditions, while Giddens' agent is a rational child of entrepreneurial capitalism, who treats power as a means for getting things done, and acts rationally (ibid. 173, 175). It is agents' consciousness that renders them free from the blind forces of social evolution (ibid. 237). I assess this argument in Ch. 6.

Weaknesses in Bourdieu's Approach

Bourdieu's determination to demonstrate the inadequacy of the games theory used by Barth and others leads him to insist that gift-giving is built on a misrecognition of social inequality and power, rather than a rational strategy. There are, however, interesting parallels between the rationales for reciprocity presented by the Kabyle and the people of Pellaport, both of which correspond to Axelrod's predictions about the conditions that are required to enable co-operation. I will return to this question in Ch. 4.

Bourdieu's explanations of why each agent's habitus converges with those of others in the community often approach tautology: 'The homogeneity of the mode of production of habitus . . . produces a homogenisation of dispositions and interests' (1977: 63–4). 'Each member of the same class is more likely than any member of another class to have been confronted with the situations most frequent for members of that class' (ibid. 85; cf. Durkheim's (1938: 55) 'we shall call "normal" those social conditions that are the most generally distributed'). This weakness is related to Bourdieu's tendency to revert to a structural mode of reasoning in his appeals to the 'collectivity'. Habitus is 'constantly reinforced by calls to order from the group, that is . . . the aggregate of individuals endowed with the same dispositions' (Bourdieu 1977: 15). Importantly, Bourdieu also points out that kin groups exist in practice because they derive from a community of interests directed towards undivided ownership of their material and symbolic patrimony (ibid. 35). Since many activities would be impossible without the help of the group, ostracism is a terrible sanction (ibid. 60). The men's assembly could step in and stop someone from becoming richer (ibid. 180). In *The Logic of Practice* Bourdieu argues more forcibly that both the material and symbolic bases of power must be taken into account to explain the transmission of habitus (Bourdieu 1990: 136–140). Subsequent chapters will try to show how consensus over the meaning of behaviour, the management of resources and the regulation of interpersonal relationships is achieved in Pellaport.

Power, Action, and Interaction

Giddens rightly blames Durkheim, and the structural-functionalism he engendered, for underrating the importance of power in social relations but Giddens can himself be faulted for taking only power into account. The absence of co-operation and reciprocity from his analysis allows him to treat social activity as action, rather than interaction. His fascinating case studies of mechanization, the price-fixing cartel, and state provision of services all show how agents are responding to conditions that are generated through interaction (Giddens 1984: 311–7). The case of the declining rates of profit which arise from capitalists competing to mechanize production closely parallels the effect of mechanizing agricultural production on the Plateau of Levier (see Ch. 6), and reveals the emergent qualities of the market economy.

There are four basic forms of social interaction: co-operation, reciprocity, competition, and spite (Trivers 1985: 41–65). Although power may seem to enable action, even power must be exercised against other agents, leading most obviously to competition but least obviously to co-operation and reciprocity. Most people, most of the time, are inhibited from challenging the powerful through fear of compromising their access to resources obtained through exchange, but exchange also creates indispensable links between people of equal status. Giddens (1984: 173) is right to argue that constraint arises from unequal power, and that 'each of the various forms of constraint are thus also, in varying ways, forms of enablement'. This is not, however, the whole story. Few strategies can be carried to conclusion by individual agents. Most depend on chains of relationships stretching across and out of the community and many depend on co-operation or reciprocity rather than unequal power. This has been amply demonstrated through the work of Malinowski, Mauss, and Polanyi (Malinowski 1922; Mauss 1954; Polanyi 1945). Chains of relationships will be most effectively recruited when the strategies are familiar to all involved or if they can, at least, be related to something familiar. They should, in other words, be part of the cultural repertoire. The challenge posed by new strategies is exemplified by the reaction in Pellaport to the French Revolution.

On the Plateau of Levier, relations with the world outside the village have always been predicated on both power and exchange. Power has sometimes been manifest in straightforward aggression, as in the campaign of Bernard of Saxe-Weimar, the subsequent French conquest or, more recently, in the Nazi occupation. More often, power has been expressed through the laws which limit legitimate activities. Since the Middle Ages, the economy has depended on the sale of cheese westward towards Lyon and Dijon; tithes and corvée were extracted before the Revolution of 1789 and taxes have been levied since. Within the village, the flow of mutual aid between households, the pooling of milk through the dairy association, and regulated access to common land have all been the medium for structuring social relationships.

All social behaviour is generated by principles which the actors bring into play, but only some is subject to authoritative interpretation from outside the community. The latter occurs where a superior power intervenes to deem actors' constructions 'legitimate' or 'illegitimate'. The State and, more recently, the European Community, have increasingly intervened in village life. Ulin argues that French nineteenth-century legislation on agricultural co-operatives was *designed* to enable the State to penetrate the working of local organizations (1996: 150, citing Yoon 1973: 174), an approach the European Community has continued with manic determination. Village communities none the less still have some freedom to negotiate social relationships.

Giddens and Theories of Evolution

Giddens' rejection of evolutionary theory is consistent with Durkheim and Radcliffe-Brown's programme for separating social from biological sciences, but Giddens invites challenge when he describes his dismissal of evolutionary theories as strong and controversial (1984: 227). Giddens claims that agents' motives are grounded in a need for 'ontological security' rather than adaptation to their environment (Giddens 1984: 86, 136, 288–293). I argue not only that Giddens' theory of structuration is consistent with aspects of evolutionary theory, but that evolutionary theory can explain why there are limits to the possibilities of structuration. Giddens fails to make a clear distinction between adaptationist and progressive evolutionary theories, and he does not consider whether either type of evolutionary theory might have limited application. Giddens (1984: 232) tilts the playing-field in his favour by setting strict conditions for judging whether a theory of social evolution is successful. It must identify a (single?) mechanism of change, which must be linked to a sequence of changes in which types or aspects of social organization replace each other, and the theory must work across the whole spectrum of human history. Although Giddens acknowledges that some of the anthropologists he criticizes have distinguished adaptation from progress, he does not point out that adaptationist and progressive theories of evolution are radically different. Neo-Darwinian theory deals purely with the adaptation of organisms to their local environment through the chance effect of random variation and does not attempt to explain the emergence of complex forms of order (Kauffman 1993). I will look at developments in Darwinian theory that aim to explain complex interactions between species and their environments in Ch. 6. Progressive theories of evolution, on the other hand, appeal to an internal process within society (or organisms) that tends to induce increasing divergence from an initial condition, often in the form of increasing complexity. One of the best-known dynamics is Marx's analysis of the consequences of the human capacity to produce more than they need to subsist. Surplus labour is harnessed in different ways in different social systems.

Giddens also seems to slip into the structural-functionalist fallacy of supposing it is society that must adapt, not the behaviour of individual agents (1984: 235–6, in contrast to ibid. 294). Even if they adapt through interaction, using social strategies involving power and domination, or reciprocity and co-operation, it is in the end the *individual's* success in acquiring and transmitting these strategies that determines their fate. Giddens (ibid. 237) rightly points out that societies do not have the same degree of closure as biological species, but ignores a large body of literature when he claims there is no equivalent in human 'societies' to the process of natural selection (this literature will be reviewed in Ch. 5). Habitus itself has the qualities needed to behave in an analogous way to the genetic material on which natural selection acts; it can generate an indefinite variety of dispositions and behaviours, and according to Bourdieu habitus tends over time to converge with 'objective' conditions. If Bourdieu is right in his argument that a system must be realized in practice if it is to be learned and transmitted, then, where ecology prevents the realization of a cultural trait, the trait cannot be copied and perpetuated.

Progressive evolutionary theories claim to identify forms of positive feedback that cause increasing deviation from an initial, often supposedly stable condition. For Marx, it was when land ceased to be free for all to use and the powerful appropriated the labour of the weak, that societies moved out of 'primitive communalism' and began to experience progressive change. Rather than lumping adaptation and progression into a single explanation, it would be more interesting to ask what contribution either or both makes to social process in any particular system. Giddens (1984: 238) objects that human history is not a story of continuous growth since 'for the vast bulk of the period during which human beings have existed they have lived in small hunting-and-gathering societies. Over much of this period there is little discernible progression in respect of either social or technological change'. The evidence that hunter-gatherer behaviour has *adapted* to its natural and social environment is, however, quite convincing (see, for example, Torrence 1983 and Layton 1997*b*: 169–183). If, as Giddens points out, early agrarian societies seem to rise and fall in a cyclic pattern, this is because quite different processes of positive feedback come into play, through the accumulation of resources at administrative centres. Human behaviour may continue to adapt to its social and natural environments even when positive feedback is generating progressive change in other aspects of social life. Meat sharing among hunter-gatherers, reciprocal aid between peasant households, the subscription societies of West Africa, and the friendly societies of nineteenth-century England can all be elucidated through the theory of reciprocal altruism (Layton 1997*b*: 176), even though the characters of the wider social systems in which they are embedded are very different. Socioecology suffers, however, from the same weaknesses that Bourdieu and Giddens identify in games theory (on which socioecology draws). It does not explain why strategies (actions) must be clothed in a cultural idiom, nor does it consider the long-term, historical trajectories of social process that strategies may engender. In this regard, the insights of Bourdieu and Giddens are as applicable to socioecology as they are to interactionism and they will be used in the following chapters.

In Ch. 3 I look at the connections between biological reproduction, agricultural work and the inheritance of property. Chapter 4 compares local values concerning mutual aid with the predictions of the theory of reciprocal altruism. Chapter 5 assesses the parallel often drawn between innovations and new genetic traits. Chapter 6 argues innovations must be understood within the context of the economic transformations to which they are a response and to which they contribute. Chapter 7 discusses change in the management of collective resources in relation to the theory of the commons.

CONCLUSION

The first problem in post-structuralist sociological analysis is to explain how cultural dispositions and social strategies are perpetuated. Bourdieu and Giddens are right to address these questions. The durability of the division between private and communal land, the village as a corporation, partible inheritance, and producer co-operatives, all of which have outlasted the successive revolutions of the last two centuries on the Plateau of Levier, is remarkable. There have, none the less, also been radical changes in cultural dispositions and social organization over the same period. The mechanisms that change the content of a socio-cultural tradition therefore also need to be studied, particularly since, given the impossibility of controlled experiments in social behaviour, social change provides the best way of testing hypotheses about the way the socio-cultural order is perpetuated.

All the European village studies mentioned above use historical evidence to understand social process. Netting chose to work in a literate culture because he wished to study the homeostatic tendencies of social systems (1981: pp. x, 27, 58). Netting therefore emphasized continuity rather than change and wrote little about what had happened in Törbel since the Second World War (this gap is filled by Friedl's study of a village on the opposite side of the Rhône Valley); nor does he respond to Cole and Wolf's criticisms of ecological anthropology (1974: 284–5). Törbel is exceptional. Wylie (1966: 9) wrote, 'we see Chanzeaux as a system, but a living system—complex, indistinct, constantly evolving, essentially related to a larger system'. Cole and Wolf (1974) set out to discover how two villages with different cultural histories had adapted to the same alpine environment. They insisted the two villages were neither closed nor homeostatic systems; their unfolding structures were the product of interaction between ideology, local ecology, and relations with the outside world (ibid. 20–2, 119–20). Rosenberg's (1988) study of Abriès, in the French Alps, revealed radical change wrought by interference in village government by the French State. Rosenberg chose to work in a French village because its extensive archives would enable her to integrate history and anthropology through the study of agency. She sets out 'to show how villagers plotted, organized, resisted, seized some opportunities and lost others' (ibid. 6) without committing the Bailey School's error of disregarding the impact of material and political conditions (ibid. 194–5). Rogers (1991: 44) wrote of the Aveyronnais village of Sainte-Foy, 'What I could observe . . . is best explained as the product of ongoing interplay, a kind of mutual acting-upon, among Ste Foyans' notions of appropriate order and meaning, internal tensions and contradictions contained in these, and the shifting range of possibilities contained in practice.' Successive states of disequilibrium in the community's way of life provided scope for human agency while sometimes revealing the misfit between intention and outcome (ibid. 186–7). Behar, who carried out twenty months' fieldwork in the Spanish village of Santa María del Monte between 1978 and 1984, also went with the aim of integrating anthropology and history. Behar (1986: 14) documented how 'the people of Santa María continually recast the forms of the past in the idiom of their historical moment'. 'Villagers are continually looking to the past, to earlier forms of behaviour, for modes of structuring their economy, society and culture in the present' (ibid. 162).

Ulin's field studies of wine-producing co-operatives in the hinterland of Bordeaux were carried out in 1984 and 1989. Like Rosenberg (1988: 49), Ulin aimed to demonstrate that history is not solely created at the centre of world systems; the periphery (in his case, small producers' co-operatives) can have an impact on the core (the large chateaux estates). Rogers (1991: 42–4) and Ulin (1996: 14–38) provide alternative accounts to the one I give above which trace the convergence of anthropology and history upon the question of agency. In Ch. 7 I will draw on the village studies mentioned above to construct a comparative framework through which to explain the success or failure of collective action in European villages.

The most useful aspects of Bourdieu and Giddens' work for the present study are:

1. If there is no 'collective consciousness', then the extent to which the same patterns of thought and behaviour are reproduced, more or less unchanged, within and across generations needs both to be investigated and explained. The values guiding interpersonal relations in Pellaport, their consequences, and the way they are organized and transmitted will be discussed in Ch. 4, and compared with the habitus of interpersonal relations among the Kabyle studied by Bourdieu.

2. Although social strategies can be modelled as 'pure' games, in practice they *must* be clothed in cultural forms to be meaningful. This is not the same as appealing to the norms while covertly pursuing a selfish interest. On the contrary, as Bourdieu and Giddens argue, culture is realized in the very playing of strategies. This insight will be applied to household structure in Ch. 3 and interpersonal relations in Ch. 4, and to the creation of co-operatives in Ch. 7. A comparative study of inheritance rules and household structure in other European village studies reveals the variables crucial to different outcomes in the structuration of social relationships

3. If the structure of society is generated through interaction rather

than preceding it, what are the recursive effects of interaction? The remainder of this study will consider the anticipated and unforeseen consequences of interaction which either reproduce the current structure of relationships or, particularly since 1850, transform it, asking which processes promote negative and positive feedback (stability and progressive change). Chapter 3 will look at transformations in the structure of the household brought about first by local population growth, then by rural emigration, while Chs. 5 to 7 will look at the social and technological consequences of this emigration. Increased participation in national markets, the flow of machines (and information about them) into the village to replace the labour lost through emigration, and the inflationary effect of increasing agricultural production will be shown to set up a complex process of positive feedback which, in turn, precipitates changes in the administration of shared property. Other European village studies will be used in Ch. 7 to reveal the variety of outcomes and the processes responsible.

  4. If any aspect of evolutionary theory is applicable to social interaction, to what extent can the ideas of evolutionary biology be applied to social evolution? Are there objective constraints on the possible outcomes of inheritance rules, mutual aid, and variation in technology? How similar, and how different, are the cultural and genetic transmission of information? In what ways does life in society affect the simple notion of the survival and reproductive success of the individual? These questions will be returned to throughout the remainder of this study.

3

The Household: Inheritance and Structuration

This chapter looks at continuity and change in household structure on the Plateau of Levier in the light of Giddens' concepts of agency and structuration. The processes that contribute to the relatively egalitarian character of village society on the Plateau of Levier during the period of my fieldwork will be identified; these range from the traditional principle of partible inheritance, economic circumstances characterizing a particular historical period, to specific elements of legislation such as the *Statut de fermage*. This chapter also discusses the links between culture and biology which are brought about by production and reproduction within the household. Inheritance rules and work patterns have both social and biological consequences. Darwin regarded the English rule of primogeniture (leaving the entire estate to the eldest son) as both unjust and 'dreadfully opposed to [natural] selection' (Hrdy and Judge 1993: 2). The structure of the household recorded at any moment is the result of patterns of behaviour characteristic of the local cultural repertoire, and those enforced by the state. The outcome of cultural behaviour depends on its suitability to local natural conditions and the way it contributes to wider social relationships beyond and between households.

Children are raised in the household, and the structure of the household typically moves through a cycle that reflects the age and reproductive status of its members. Households can be classified according to their composition, and (like a number of other studies cited below) this chapter will follow the example set by Fortes (1949) in treating household types as stages in a cycle that is partly determined by rules of inheritance and marriage, but through which alternative pathways can be taken that are to some extent the consequence of choices made by its members. The existence of good historical records in many European villages makes it possible to go beyond Fortes's classic analysis, and study the ways in which the changing social environment modifies the opportunities and constraints that shape the household cycle.

THE HOUSEHOLD AS A UNIT OF PRODUCTION

The household (*le ménage*) is a residential unit with its own kitchen. *Feu* (hearth) is an old synonym used in local enumerations compiled during the seventeenth and eighteenth centuries. Despite important exceptions, most households in the pre-industrial economy operated as units of both production and consumption. Even craftsmen and women kept one or two cows to supply their household. During the mid- to late nineteenth century the only households on the Plateau of Levier that were not units of production were those occupied by *journaliers* (day labourers or agricultural workers) and *rentiers* (people receiving income from property). *Cultivateurs, cultivatrices,* craftsmen and women, worked in their own households. One in five households employed resident servants. With the growth of employment in factories and offices many fewer households are units of production. No one now employs servants. These changes have influenced the course of the household cycle and reduced the scale of social differentiation.

While the household is often a unit of production and consumption in peasant communities it rarely functions independently. Where it is not the unit of production and/or consumption its condition may well be an important indicator of social differentiation. Lancaster long ago pointed out the danger of assuming family and household were synonymous (Lancaster 1961: 329–31). Mitterauer and Sieder (1982: 8) write that until the eighteenth century there was no German word equivalent to 'family'. The German root *hus* or *haus* referred both to the building and to the people living in it, but primarily to the people, the household, who were not necessarily a family unit. Sabean (1990: 97–8) illustrates the difficulty of defining the household in the south German village of Neckarhausen. In the nineteenth century, building workers were fed at the local tavern and seamstresses lived in each of their employers' houses for a few days while working there. 'Family' was often used in mid-nineteenth century Neckarhausen discourse to emphasize the contractual aspect of marriage (ibid. 92, 120). The difficulty of identifying the household's limits, where several units are housed in one building, or members are transient, is also discussed by Laslett (1972: 23–8), while Barthelemy (1988: 198) points out that *ménage* was a term developed for bureaucratic purposes. Where it coincides with a family unit, a house and an agricultural holding it may be sociologically significant; but it is less so where temporary employment in other households and networks of mutual aid create wider units of production.

There is a substantial literature on household structure, inheritance, and demography in European village history. A comprehensive discussion of the relevance of this work to the Plateau of Levier would be impossible to achieve within the scope of one chapter; therefore the focus here will be on ways in which household structure, inheritance, and demography throw light on the four topics identified in the conclusion to Ch. 2.

The household's mode of subsistence conditions its composition, determining the viability of particular household types. Household composition and activities have both been radically changed by, and have themselves contributed to, radical changes in the economy since 1850. Massive emigration from the Plateau of Levier occurred during the Industrial Revolution as many, particularly those most disadvantaged by the rural economy, found work outside agriculture. Farming became precarious during the latter half of the nineteenth century. At the turn of the century, however, manual labour began to be replaced by agricultural machines. Between the First and Second World Wars, market production in agriculture increased at the expense of subsistence. Although this trend was set back by the Second World War, it resumed in the 1950s and has continued until the present. Private car ownership has facilitated commuting to work since the 1960s, enabling an increase in the number of people living, but not working, in the village. Since mechanization has reduced the need for manual labour in agriculture, and employment in offices and factories has increased, the birth rate has continuously declined.

I shall look primarily at the impact of social change on farming although I shall also consider the demographic effects of the rise in employment outside agriculture. Land and buildings are the two most expensive types of capital in a farming economy. Most farmhouses are acquired by inheritance, although some have been sold and new houses built from time to time. The household generally owns some of the land it works, but all *exploitations* include rented land, which belongs either to kin of members of the household, to large-scale landowners, or to the commune. Local recollections and government statistics indicate that wholly rented *exploitations* were more common in the past.

Scale of Production

Dairy farming has been the backbone of the agricultural economy since the thirteenth century. The importance of pasture and hay meadow for cattle is apparent in a request drawn up by the people of Pellaport in 1746, asking for the cattle (*le bétail rouge*) of Vaux to be barred from shared pasture during an epidemic.

There are certain cantons which are common to the two communities for pasturage and those of Vaux have not failed to profit from them . . .

Pellaport therefore sought an order to forbid the people of Vaux,

to lead their cattle from their territory, and even from the stables of their houses and, more particularly, to send them to pasture on the cantons common to the two communities, all without prejudice to their rights in the future. It is also just to order that the fruits of grasses and grains shall not be lifted and drawn except with a harness of horses and not one of cattle and also that they may not plough next autumn upon the common land except with a harness of horses.

Although the *fruitières*, or producer co-operatives, allowed specialization in dairy production from the Middle Ages, there was substantial cereal cultivation in the past. The area of land under cereals has declined sharply, particularly since the Second World War. In 1733, villages on the Plateau of Levier were growing about 19 bushels of wheat, 13 bushels of oats and 4 bushels of barley per person (a bushel is 36.4 litres).[1] These data may not be reliable (see Shaffer 1982: 133), and their significance is difficult to assess. Braudel (1990: 367) cites a report compiled in 1785 which stated, 'in the old days' each person required 3 *setiers* of grain per year but, with economic milling, 2.25 *setiers* was enough. Since 1 *setier* varied between 150 and 300 litres the individual's requirements may have been anything between 12.5 and 25 bushels per year. Bians and Goux were producing about 30 bushels per person, Ouhans apparently achieved 50. If these yields are accurate, the villages seem comfortably self-sufficient, but there is no indication how much they had to pay in tithes.

Braudel (ibid. 262) cites a nineteenth-century author who was astonished to see cereals growing above the tree line outside Pontarlier in 1860 (Braudel 1990: 262). From the 1830s to 1910 about one-third of usable farmland was ploughed to cultivate cereals and other crops. Only one-tenth of this land was still cultivated for cereals in 1980 (Courtieu 1982). Subsidiary crops such as potatoes and peas have been abandoned since the 1950s. Cereals are now grown only to provide cattle-feed, whereas until the 1950s they were also cultivated to make bread. According to Claude

---

[1] Production figures for Bians-les-Usiers, Dommartin, Goux-les-Usiers, and Ouhans in Courtieu (1982), with estimate of population from 1688 and 1790 figures.

Bavarel, every household sowed wheat for the family, oats for the horse, and barley for the cattle until after the Second World War.

During the two hundred years between the mid–seventeenth and mid–nineteenth centuries, the population of the region grew rapidly (see Ch. 2), putting increasing pressure on the productivity of the land. There is scattered information on household size before regular censuses were introduced in the nineteenth century, but these only record the number of people in the household, not its structure. Some may be servants, not members of the family. Data collated by Courtieu (1982) and Vignau (1947) for some villages on the Plateau suggest an average household size of 5.7 people in 1593 and 6.0 in 1688.

In 1688 the average household of the district had a single horse. It also had one sheep and one head of cattle (presumably including oxen and calves) per person.[2] Large proprietors were rare among the villages possessing *fruitières*. Few households had more than six cows. In 1778 there were forty-four *cultivateurs* in the village of Songeson. In 1788 there were thirty-five *cultivateurs* in Chaussenans. In each village there was one large proprietor, one with 30 cows, the other with 33. The majority owned between 1 and 3 cows. With a smaller number owning up to 8, the mean number among small proprietors was 3, the mode 2 (Latouche 1938: 781–2). These figures compare well with those declared in Pellaport in 1939 and 1943. In 1939 and 1943 *exploitants* in Pellaport owned between 1 and 7 cows, with an average of 3.6. In 1844–5, most households in the Swiss village of Törbel had 1–3 cows, a few had 7. The average number per household had not changed appreciably in the following 125 years (Netting 1981: 26–7).

Fermiers *(Tenant Farmers)*

The censuses of 1846 and 1872 do not distinguish tenant farmers (*fermiers*) from other *cultivateurs*. Chapuis (1958: 23) found there were few smallholders in the Loue valley, just north of the Plateau of Levier, during the eighteenth century. Many were tenant farmers. In one village 10 per cent of proprietors owned 45 per cent of the land. Daveau analysed the 1790 tax rolls for the two villages of Foncine le Bas and Foncine le Haut, situated in the first of the intermontane valleys which rise towards the Swiss border, about 40 km. south of the Plateau of Levier. She found

---

[2] Based on data for Bians-les-Usiers, Dommartin, Evillers, Fertans, Goux-les-Usiers, Reugney, Saint-Gorgon and Vuillecin published in Courtieu (1982).

that of the 154 villagers whose occupation was in agriculture, 10 were day labourers, 34 were independent farmers (*laboureurs*), but 109 were tenants (*fermiers*) of a landlord; 91 were resident in their landlord's house. Only one person was identified as a domestic servant and Daveau surmises that other servants were listed as members of the household head's 'family'. There may not have been so high a proportion of tenant farmers in Pellaport. In the eighteenth century most large proprietors were located in the mountains along the border, where they operated private dairies. None the less, in a document written in 1790, fifteen men and women of Pellaport describing themselves as *laboureurs* complained to the administrators of the new *département* of Doubs that they had been unfairly penalized under Revolutionary decrees passed in September and November the previous year, and denied they held ancestral wealth derived from owning or renting out land. They demanded their possessions, which had been confiscated, be returned. This suggests a degree of social differentiation in the village that might be disguised in the nineteenth-century household censuses. Some *cultivateurs* might be tenants of landlords who do not live in the village. Seasonal agricultural labourers who came to the region during the hay and cereal harvests would not have been present when the census was taken some time between mid-April and mid-May.

Tenant farmers traditionally took a lease for three, six, or nine years that ended on 20 March, the first day of spring. Even though there was often snow still on the ground, the farmer would lead his livestock on foot to his new tenancy. The agents who checked that tenants were keeping the land in good order were usually very strict. Pierre Bavarel's father-in-law had been a tenant farmer at La Combe Sainte-Marie. Claude Bavarel recalled that in 1945, just after he returned from Germany, he had been standing at his front door as Pierre's father-in-law passed through the village on his way to a new lease. Claude had sold him one of his cows when called up six years previously and, as the herd passed, this cow broke away to head for her old stable. 'You see', Pierre's father-in-law had called, 'she still remembers you.' (This must have been a particularly poignant moment since wartime inflation had destroyed the value of the money Claude banked after selling his livestock.) The economic power of landlords was virtually abolished by the 1945 *Statut de fermage* which introduced state-supervised rent control. If a landlord decides to sell land, his tenant now has first option to buy, and can gain state assistance to do so (Wylie 1966: 81–3). Claude told me the value of agricultural land in relation to the cost of living had fallen dramatically since the Second

World War. Many former *fermiers* had been able to buy the land they once rented. He had bought the land on which he harvested potatoes in 1969 (see Ch. 1) the following year. It had cost him 90 fr. per are but by 1995 was worth only 15 fr. per are. Land prices were at a post-war peak in 1970 (Boinon and Cavailhès 1988). In 1955 20 per cent of *exploitations* in the *département* of Doubs were wholly rented. By 1963 the proportion had declined to 17 per cent (*Économie Rurale* 1969; cf. Chapuis 1970: 117; Lambert 1953: 171). Two of the nine *cultivateurs* of Pellaport included in the 1969 survey of landownership discussed below rented most, but not all of their land from single proprietors. Both landowners were descended from farming families in the village, although neither lived in Pellaport. One was the son of a man who was forced to abandon farming after being badly wounded in a shooting accident.

Demographic Trends: Infant Mortality, Family Size, Adult Celibacy

Household censuses and records of births, marriages, and deaths provide complementary evidence of demographic trends, which will be charted through the registers from Dechailles and La Combe Sainte-Marie from 1898 to 1969. The French demographer Bonneuil (1997: 5, 7, 35, 47) considers the registers of death to be generally accurate, although he believes births to have been under-registered and notes that throughout the nineteenth century the term 'stillborn' included live-born children who died before their birth had been registered.

In 1872 there were 222 women of childbearing age (16–40 years) in Pellaport, Dechailles, and La Combe Sainte-Marie. There were 226 living children born to these women (1018 per 1000). Only 34 per cent of women had actually borne surviving children, an average of 3.4 surviving births per person. Our own survey of four villages in 1972 found 107 women of childbearing age and 140 living children (1308 per 1000). Although the aggregate birth rate had risen, this was due to a higher proportion of women bearing children. 54 per cent of women had surviving children, an average of 2.4 per person. Over this period, women's average age at their first childbirth has fallen from 26.6 years to 23.7 (see Fig. 3.1). The main effect of fertility limitation in the West since 1900 has been to compress childbearing into the early years of married life, whereas previously births were spread fairly evenly over the whole fertile period (Anderson 1980: 20). By 1972, many women on the Plateau of Levier started and completed their families while young, whereas a hundred years earlier many began later and all continued to give birth

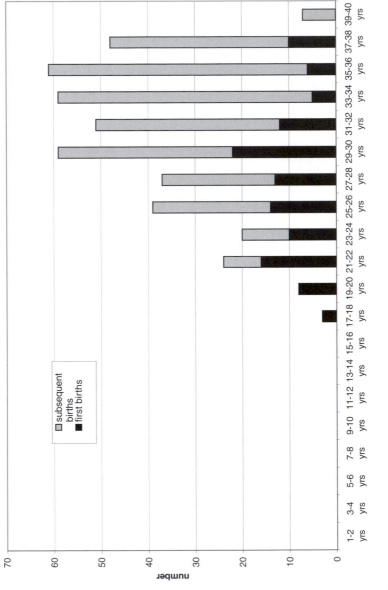

FIG. 3.1. Women's age at birth of first child

Source: 1872 census and 1972 survey.

(a) 1872 census data

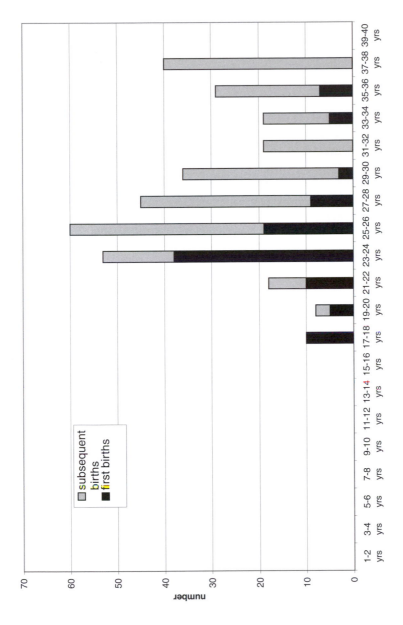

(b) 1972 survey data

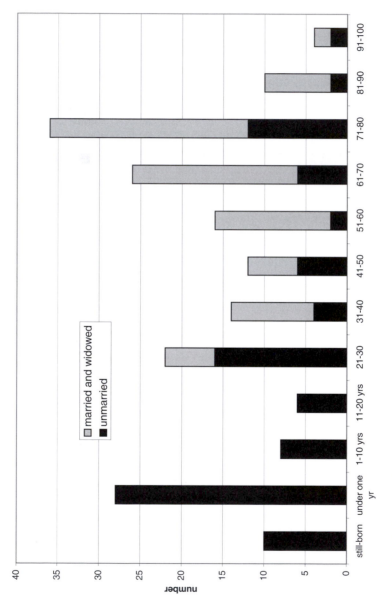

FIG. 3.2. Age and marital status at death

Source: Church records 1910–69.

(a) 1910–1921

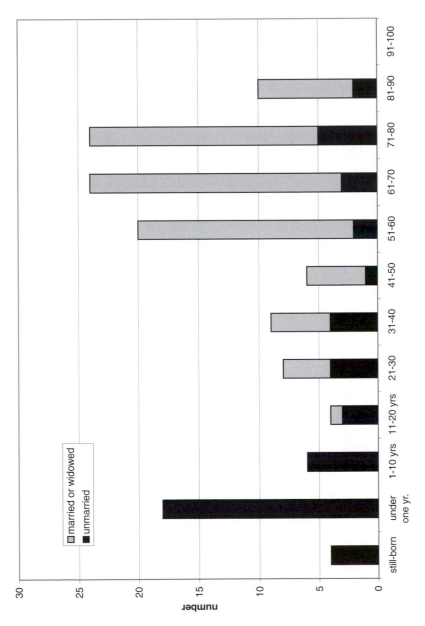

(b) 1930–1949

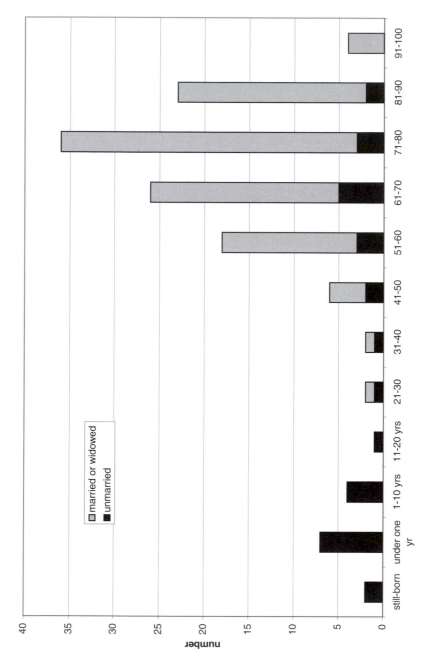

(c) 1950–1969

throughout their childbearing years. Life expectancy has risen, due primarily to the dramatic fall in infant mortality and stillbirths, but also to a decline in the death rate among young adults (see Fig. 3.2).

Documentary and demographic evidence for voluntary birth control in France exists from the mid–eighteenth century, a hundred years before it appeared in neighbouring countries. Beginning in the cities, the practice of limiting the birth rate by practising *coitus interruptus* reached the countryside in 1780s. Contraception may have been a response to over-population, since it developed in parallel with late marriage and celibacy (Braudel 1990: 189–201).

Although the 'demographic revolution' seemed to have been completed by 1972, Fig. 3.1(*b*) shows a minority of women were still continuing to have children into their late thirties. Since 1972 household and family size have continued to decline. In 1986, the diminishing number of children in the village was already a talking-point. The school, like those in some surrounding villages, had reduced the age of entry from 5 to 4, to keep numbers up to the level at which it would be allowed to stay open. The average household size in the fifteen villages of our comparative survey fell from 3.6 in 1972 to 3.0 in 1995. During that period the number of households in Dechailles, Pellaport, and La Combe Sainte-Marie has risen from 167 to 262, but the total population has only risen from 690 to 805, a decline in average household size from 4.1 to 3.0 persons.

The decline of the subsistence economy and rise of employment in factories and offices at first had the effect of reducing the number of women participating as partners in family enterprises, as many women became housewives while their husbands went out to work. More recently there has been an increase in women office and factory workers. Eleven of the thirty-six adults in Pellaport who commuted daily to work in Pontarlier during 1995 were women with school-age children. Two years later a young woman councillor was establishing childminding facilities (Yoshimoto 1997). Yoshimoto points out the particular problem faced by parents of children aged from 3 to 6 years who attend school in a neigh-bouring village but are brought back for lunch. She suggests retired grandparents have taken on a new importance where they are the only relatives available to meet these children, feed them, and return them to the bus for their afternoon schooling (cf. Segalen 1991: 278). Yoshimoto suggests the lack of childcare facilities may contribute to the continuing decline in the number of children born, a decline that was itself respon-sible for the grouping of Pellaport's primary school with those of several surrounding villages, each village keeping responsibility for one or two classes.

Pellaport and surrounding villages have become desirable places to live. Rents are half those in Pontarlier and the *maire* reported that in 1995 he was receiving about one enquiry a month (after the meeting a young counsellor remarked wryly that those who were not young, married couples with children might as well not enquire about housing at the Mairie). Some of those renting houses or flats in Pellaport had heard about them through friends. Building land is scarce. The commune had sold all the land it owned near the village for building plots some years earlier. Village families were willing for their own children to build on privately owned land, but reluctant to sell to 'strangers' who might dilute the dense web of kinship and friendship in the village (I will return to this issue in Ch. 4). The wealth of villages, outlined in Ch. 2, which allowed them to charge little or nothing in local taxes, and provide free firewood and refuse collection, was also suspected to attract would-be residents. About thirty building permits had been issued in Pellaport between 1989 and 1995.

Household Censuses

The French government has carried out regular, 5-yearly household censuses since 1801. The first exhaustive census was that of 1851, although the conditions under which the 1846 census was conducted were an improvement on previous ones (Bonneuil 1997: 6). These censuses record the composition of every household, giving each person's name, relationship to the household head, place of birth, and age. The occupations of family members other than the household head are not normally given and seem to be supplied only if they differ from the head's. Ages are not always consistent over successive enumerations. Bonneuil (1997: 39) argues that the 20–4 age group usually tends to be inflated by adolescents who want to make themselves older, and adults who want to make themselves younger, but men are likely to be under-recorded during times of war such as the 1848 Revolution and the 1870–1 Franco-Prussian War (ibid. 3). The censuses none the less give an extremely useful record of social process over a period of 150 years, from the dawn of the Industrial Revolution to the present. This chapter will draw heavily on the 1846 census in the village of Dechailles, and the 1872 censuses in Dechailles, Pellaport, and La Combe Sainte-Marie. Subsequent censuses up to 1921 will be used to reconstruct the trajectories of particular households in La Combe Sainte-Marie. The 1872 census should have been taken the previous year, but was delayed by the Franco-Prussian War and eventually conducted between 15 April and 15 May 1872 (ibid. 37). The war swept across the Plateau of Levier in January 1871.

Household Typology

Studies of European household structure usually follow Laslett's typology, which is presented below in slightly simplified form (for a complete list of variants, see Laslett 1972: 41–2). In an extended family there is only one married couple, while in a joint family there are two or more. Both extended and joint families can develop vertically or laterally. Vertical development includes a widowed parent (extended family) or married grandparents (joint family); lateral development adds an unmarried sibling of either spouse (extended) or a married sibling and his/her partner (joint). The particular type in which two or more married brothers live in the same household independently of their father is known as *un frérèche*. In the Nivernais, *frérèches* were established by legal contract, but elsewhere they may be nothing more than a stage in the household cycle which follows the death of co-resident parents.

Household Structure in the Nineteenth and Twentieth Centuries

Household censuses are slices out of a process of continuous change. This can be seen by comparing data from 1846, 1872, 1969, and 1995 (Tables 3.1 and 3.13).

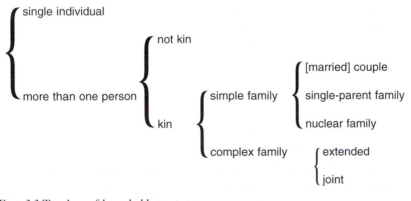

FIG. 3.3 Typology of household structures
Source: Laslett (1972).

TABLE 3.1. *Household structure in Dechailles, Pellaport, and La Combe Sainte-Marie, 1872 and 1972*

	1872 (%)	1972 (%)
Single person	11	17
Married couple without children	16.5	20
Single parent, all children under 20	13.5	5
Nuclear family, all children under 20	25.5	40
Nuclear family, at least one child over 20	15	5
Unmarried, adult siblings (some with widowed parent)	8	2
Adult siblings, one married	5	2
Parent(s) with married child and grandchild(ren)	5.5	5
Other	—	4
N =	*307*	*173*

During the hundred years between these two samples, the occupational structure of the community has changed considerably. The first impression created by the nineteenth-century censuses is of a rural class structure at whose head stand *les rentiers*, leisured landowners who do not work for a living. Beneath them are *cultivateurs* and craftsmen and women. Servants (*domestiques*) living in farming households, and the day labourers (*journaliers*) who although they may have their own households work for *cultivateurs*, are at the bottom of the social hierarchy. According to Maurice Petithuguenin of Eternoz, half the farm workforce in the early twentieth century was provided by *journaliers*. During the winter the men felled wood in the forest while their wives earned money as washerwomen. Felicien Jouffroy recalled that *journaliers* were common before the Second World War. Many were former factory workers hiding from the law by working on isolated farms. They would eat with the family that hired them, but sleep in the stable. They often only stayed for about three months before moving on. Both Maurice and Felicien commented that it was the development of farm machinery that had put an end to day labouring; Claude Bavarel considered *journaliers* were already becoming rare by the time of the Second World War. In 1950 Lebeau found that 10 per cent of those working in agriculture on the Plateau of Levier were *journaliers*, a proportion comparable with that for the *département* as a whole, whereas by 1970 the proportion of wage labourers on the plateau had fallen to 4 per cent of the agricultural work force (Lebeau 1952: 364

TABLE 3.2. *Occupations of household heads in three villages, 1872 and 1972*

	1872		1972
Landlords *(rentiers)*	10 (3.5%)	Landlords	0
Chef d'entreprise	1	*Chefs d'entreprises**	6 (3.5%)
Cultivateurs	187 (64%)	*Cultivateurs*	55 (33%)
Farm labourers	34 (12%)	Factory and office workers:	
		(locally employed)	26 (15.5%)
		(commuting)	9 (5.5%)
Services and crafts	42 (15%)	Services and crafts	29 (17.5%)
Beggar	1	Unemployed	0
Without profession	1		
Unspecified	7 (2.5%)		
Retired	8 (2.5%)	Retired	42 (25%)
TOTAL	*291*		*167*
Employed in farming households			
Servants	48		0
Labourers	17		0

* Three sawmill owners, entrepreneur dairyman, garage-owner, public works contractor.

and Fig 3; Chapuis 1970: 116). I don't know where this 4 per cent were working; it was certainly not in Pellaport.

The self-sufficient character of the nineteenth-century village is underlined by the wide variety of crafts and services provided in the three villages: *blanchisseuse* (laundress), *charron* (wheelwright), *cordonnier* (cobbler), *couturière* (seamstress), *marechal ferrant* (shoeing smith), *sage femme* (midwife), *serrurier* (locksmith), and *tisserand* (weaver). Some households combined craft production with agriculture, either as *cultivateurs* or *journaliers*. One man ran a business, a flour mill. Claude Bavarel recalled that when he was a boy there had been a cobbler in Pellaport. Although his shoes were expensive they lasted for two to three years, even with all the walking people did in those days. There had also been a midwife who wove sheets of hemp when not delivering children, but the sheets were uncomfortable and scratched your skin.

Since 1972, the number of *cultivateurs* has continued to decline, as has been true throughout the *département* (see Tables 2.3 and 2.4). Starting in the mid-1960s, however, the population of some villages began to increase as private car ownership enabled people who worked in Pontarlier and other local towns to remain in their natal villages, or even move out of town to settle in the countryside. By 1995 there were 249 households in the three villages. Only 27 were still farming (11 per cent), but 88 household heads were factory or office workers (35 per cent). A further 35 per cent of households were occupied by retired persons, while 4 per cent of household heads were now unemployed.

In 1969, the nuclear family household was very common in Pellaport but earlier census data show its frequency had increased as extended-family and single-parent households diminished over the previous hundred years. Single-parent households have since reappeared. Two types of complex family household existed in 1969 and both are more commonly recorded in nineteenth-century censuses. The three-generation household almost always included one or both of the husband's parents, as well as the younger couple's children. Only one included the wife's parents. This pattern arises from the patrilineal inheritance of houses. One joint family household consisted of a father and son, with their wives, who ran a forge, the remainder were farmers. In most cases, the older couple had their own kitchen and such arrangements would have been recorded as two households under one roof in the nineteenth-century censuses. Villagers held that it was easier for a father and son to work together in the fields than it was for a woman and her daughter-in-law to work together in the kitchen. One young farmer told me he had left the family home on marriage to rent a flat nearby rather than make his wife share a kitchen with his mother. The second type of extended-family household contained adult brothers and sisters. The only instance recorded in Pellaport in 1969 consisted of three brothers and their sister, only one of whom had married. Until their retirement, shortly before my arrival, they had continued to work with oxen and were remarked upon as the last in the village to be fluent in the local dialect, reinforcing the sense that their household represented the last example of an earlier pattern. One farming household in Montoiseau consisted of three adult brothers, two unmarried, one married with three children. The Dôle family of Dechailles also exemplified this form of extended family; a married household head living with his wife and his unmarried brother and sister. A second farming household in Montoiseau was headed by two elderly brothers who had married two sisters because, as one explained, there were often quarrels when two brothers married 'in different directions' but continued to live under one roof. Both men were now retired, but one son of each had remained at home and the *exploitation* was run by the two first cousins. The decline in the frequency of co-resident adult brothers and sisters is one of the most significant changes in household structure. By 1969 it was expected that one child would inherit the house and responsibility for the *exploitation*; his (or her) siblings would leave and find other work. In two cases a family holding had been divided between two sons (César and Eduard Maitrugue, Étienne and Alexandre Maitrugue), but in both cases, one son had been favoured, the other had returned to the village on the father's retirement. By 1995, Armand Maitrugue's brother had returned to help work the land they and their sisters inherited from César.

In 1969 10 of the 62 households in Pellaport consisted of single elderly people, but there were another 4 in which pairs of elderly women had chosen to live together for mutual support. The curé lived with his house-keeper and one widow lived with her unmarried son.

INHERITANCE OF THE HOUSE AND LAND

The Napoleonic Code

While custom and law do not necessarily coincide in France, the Napoleonic Civil Code, enacted in 1804, is the basis for subsequent French law (Weill 1968). The code distinguished between fixed and movable property and determined that a married couple's property is jointly owned. Both principles already existed in pre-Revolutionary law. The distinction between fixed and movable property was based on the premiss that fixed property was the source of a person's wealth; only fixed property could be mortgaged, and mere possession was insufficient to establish ownership. Agricultural equipment was deemed to be a form of fixed property, as it was essential for the running of the *exploitation*. The wife's position was little changed by the Napoleonic Code. Her husband was still 'lord and master of their patrimony'. He could manage and dispose of property his wife brought to the marriage as he wished, unless a contract had been drawn up before the marriage ceremony, spec-ifying that all or part of her dowry remained her personal property. The wife could also go to court at a later date to demand the patrimony be divided between them on the grounds of her husband's mismanagement. Under current French law, the property brought by each spouse to the marriage remains his or hers and only that acquired after the marriage is conjugal property.

During the *ancien régime* nobles and commoners were subject to different laws of inheritance. Aristocratic estates generally passed intact to the eldest son, whereas in many parts of France commoners were required to divide their property equally between their children (partible inheritance is discussed in more detail in the following section). Napoleon's Code abolished this distinction and sought to make partible inheritance universal, with the intention of fragmenting the large land-holdings of the nobility. The Civil Code required that property normally be divided between heirs in parts that were equal in kind, not merely value. If the deceased had children, they were his heirs. If not, his property was divided equally between his siblings and their descendants. When first enacted, the Civil Code gave collateral relatives up to the twelfth degree priority over a dead man's wife, but the law was changed in 1891 and 1925 to provide widows with rights of usufruct and since 1930 they have been entitled to inherit full rights in their husband's property.

France can broadly be divided into a northern zone where partible inheritance was already customary before introduction of the Napoleonic Code, and a southern zone where peasant farmers have often succeeded in retaining the rule that one child inherits the entire holding (Augustins 1989: 59–65; Flandrin 1979: 74–6; Le Roy Ladurie 1976: 41–5, 52–6). In Pellaport land is divided equally among all children but, since the decline of co-inheritance by siblings who continue to live on the holding, the house has been inherited by a single heir, who succeeds to management of the *exploitation*.

INHERITANCE OF FARMHOUSES

Ideally, and in practice most frequently, farmhouses in Pellaport are inherited by a son of the previous owners. Livestock and equipment are inherited with the house. In the years leading to 1969 it had rarely been the oldest son who succeeded to the *exploitation*. Villagers insisted that it was customary for the holding to pass to a younger son. A *cultivateur* could not afford to support all his children as they grew up. When the older children reached adulthood their parents would be too young to retire, and they would have to leave the village to find work elsewhere. Jacques Maitrugue's two older brothers both left home. One found work in a chocolate factory in Pontarlier and was able to continue living in the village, the other moved away. Jacques began to help his father while the fourth, youngest brother was doing his military service. When the young man returned he had, as Jacques put it, 'missed his chance'. Alexandre Maitrugue worked as a carpenter in Pontarlier for a number of years.

TABLE 3.3. *Transmission of ownership of farmhouses in Pellaport up to 1969*

Father to son	31	Made up of	8 inherited by only son
Father to daughter	6		8 inherited by oldest son
Bought	5		15 inherited by younger son
TOTAL	42		

When his father retired he handed the *exploitation* to his younger son Étienne but was wealthy enough to leave Alexandre a second farmhouse, close to the family home, allowing Alexandre to return to the village and cultivate his share of the land. Although three-quarters of the farmhouses in Pellaport in 1969 had passed from father to son, five had been bought and six had been inherited from the wife's father (Table 3.3). This form of inheritance occurred where a couple had no son and left the house to their daughter. In one case, the house had been bought by the wife's uncles and presented to the couple as a dowry.

Although the possibility of partible inheritance of buildings existed, farmhouses were rarely divided in 1969. The farmhouse attached to the *exploitation* worked by two cousins at Montoiseau had been divided between the two heirs on their fathers' retirement. Claude Bavarel and his next-door neighbour César Maitrugue owned a patchwork of rooms in each other's buildings. The routes through which ownership had passed were equally complex. Sometime in the nineteenth century both buildings had belonged to one man. He divided his inheritance between his two daughters. One woman became Claude's mother's mother, the other was the father's mother of César's wife. By 1995 ownership of the two buildings had been rationalized so that Claude owned one and César's son Armand owned the other.

Family Nicknames

The three surnames Maitrugue, Bavarel, and Jouffroy predominate in the village. All are commonly recorded in eighteenth-century documents. None are confined to Pellaport but other surnames often predominate in neighbouring villages. Possession of a common surname is not necessarily taken as evidence of common descent. Villagers argued that there were Maitrugues, Bavarels, and Jouffroys in many villages and it was merely by chance that certain families with the same name found themselves living in the same village. Three Maitrugue families were recognized, two

Jouffroys and three Bavarels. Each tended to be restricted to a particular corner of the village. When people wanted to signify that two people belonged to the same family they often used the family sobriquet or nick-name. My early encounters with this custom are described in Ch. 4. Such sobriquets are applied at two levels. At an inclusive level inheritance of the same nickname is presumed to indicate descent through male lines from an unknown common ancestor. Such nicknames are prefixed *dit* (called). They appear in the record of the sale of common land at la Haute-Source (quoted in Ch. 2). Smaller sets of kin are differentiated by their descent from known ancestors through a sobriquet with the prefix *chez* (of the home of). Villagers said that when there was a limited pool of Christian names and many households bore the same surname, sobriquets were needed to distinguish between people who would otherwise have the same name. Family nicknames were said to be falling out of use in 1969 because houses were now numbered, making it easier to identify house-holds, and because people were taking more care not to give their children names already held by people with the same surname. While useful, these explanations are insufficient to explain all usages, as some of the follow-ing examples demonstrate. Family nicknames were still sometimes used during conversation in 1995.

Between the 1930s and 1950s there were two *exploitants* called Jules Sirugue living opposite each other in le coin de Croset, although they believed themselves to be unrelated. One was the son of Cherubim Sirugue and was known, by virtue of his father's personal nickname, as Jules *chez* Bubin. The other was known as Jules *chez* Budon, a nickname whose origin I was unable to discover. It may simply have been an alliter-ative play upon his neighbour's name, but he is said often to have referred to himself as Jules Budon and he is listed as Sirugue, Budon in the wartime requisition lists quoted in Ch. 6.

Family nicknames do not only serve the purpose of distinguishing people with the same name. Jacques Maitrugue, his brother and their father's brother's son in la rue de la Combe, were known as les Maitrugues *chez* Jean-Louis, after their father's father. The brothers César and Eduard Maitrugue, and their cousin Maurice Maitrugue acknowledge a common grandfather, Louis. Louis had two sons, Marcel and Denis. When others spoke about them, César and Eduard were iden-tified as César (or Eduard) *chez* Marcel, while Maurice, his brother and sister were distinguished as *chez* Denis. Since Marcel's personal nickname was 'the seigneur', Eduard and César were also sometimes known as *chez le Seigneur*. Personal nicknames are discussed in the following chapter.

The term *chez* does not necessarily signify that someone is living in the household after which he or she is named. Of the five Maitrugues *chez* Marcel and *chez* Denis, only Maurice was actually living in his father's house. His brother and sister had moved to other houses in the same quarter of the village. Marcel's house, ironically known as The Château, had been inherited by César, but it was occupied by César's sister and her husband. By 1995, the sister's husband had died, and César's sister had moved to a small, new house nearby. The family home had been inherited by César's son Armand, but was occupied by his sister's daughter Odile and her husband. At a municipal council meeting, Armand referred to the area between The Château and Étienne Maitrugue's house as *entre chez* Odile *et chez* Étienne. His niece, also a councillor, retorted smartly that, since he refused to sell her house, he would do better to call it *chez* Armand.

When a house has been inherited from the wife's, rather than the husband's father, the children will frequently be known as *chez* their mother. Claude Bavarel's father and his wife lived in a house that had passed to them from the wife's mother. Claude told me his father had usually been known as Joseph *chez* La Sophie, after his wife's mother. Claude himself was used to being referred to as Claude *chez* La Sophie as a boy, but the appellation had fallen out of use when he grew up. Jules Sirugue Budon left his house to his widow Luce, who managed the *exploitation* for a number of years before assigning responsibility to her daughter and daughter's husband. The son-in-law bore a surname otherwise unrepresented in the village, yet there were several occasions when I heard this man referred to, in his absence, as *chez* La Luce.

Claude Bavarel and his second cousin the mayor belong to the Bavarel *dit* Luron family. Joseph Bavarel and his father's brother's sons in Montoiseau belong to the Bavarels *dit* Toto. Joseph's uncle married a girl from Montoiseau and moved to the hamlet. The Bavarel *dit* Toto *maison paternelle*, next door to Joseph's house, was inherited by another of Joseph's father's brothers, and passed first to his daughter, thence to his daughter's son Maurice Genre. Pierre Bavarel and his brother the mason belong to the Bavarels *dit* Croset, named after the land on which the family home is built. Pierre and his brother were also sometimes known as *chez* le Coucou because, when they were children, their parents had a cuckoo clock hanging in the kitchen.

Étienne and Alexandre Maitrugue belong to the Maitrugue *dit* Didier family. The only other living member of this family in 1969 was their father's brother's son, the schoolteacher at Dechailles and secretary to the dairy association. When he retired, the schoolteacher came back to Pella-port, to live in the home he had inherited from his father, in the same building as Alexandre Maitrugue. In 1995, his widow still lived there, while his daughter and her husband had built a new house nearby on family land. Another, once numerous Maitrugue family was in 1969 represented only by a widow, Christine, who was still known by her family nickname as Christine les Dolorises. Other nicknames, held by lines that were remembered but now extinct were the Maitrugues *dit* Niavi, the Maitrugues *dit* Lesbesses, and the Bavarels *dit* Iodont.

It is possible some sobriquets that originate as references to known forebears become transformed into appellations applied indefinitely to future generations. When we were discussing sobriquets in 1969 Claude Bavarel drew my attention to one family known as *chez* Bebet. He recalled that the term had first been applied to the current bearer's father's father, whose mother (or father's mother, he was uncertain) had been called Eliz-abeth. Her diminutive, Babette, had over time been shortened to Bebet, but was still current. There is, in fact, someone of this surname and sobriquet listed in the 1834 cadastral survey. Claude speculated that family nicknames such as *dit* Toto and *dit* l'Etaine (a contraction of Étienne) had also originated as diminutives.

It is difficult to say how old these sobriquets are. Family sobriquets are used inconsistently in seventeenth- and eighteenth-century documents. Men listed as present at public meetings are sometimes attributed sobri-quets, but not invariably. A sobriquet seems to be given only when another man with the same Christian name and surname has already been listed as present at the meeting. A Bavarel *dit* Croset is named in an early seventeenth-century document.

Claude Bavarel's oldest son traced his family line in the church regis-ters, identifying Claude and the *maire*'s common father's father's father Felix, born in 1797, and through a further four generations to Jacque Bavarel, born in 1650. None of the other Bavarel lines in the village were descended from Jacque. In 1969 I was told that the Jouffroys had no family nicknames because there were fewer of them and confusion was less likely. In 1995, Felicien's nephew showed me the very detailed genealogical research he had undertaken, which demonstrated that all the Jouffroys in the village were descended from a common ancestor, Jean-François Jouffroy, born in 1682. He told me that, while it was true there were no sobriquets of the *dit* kind applied among the Jouffroys, the two principal branches were known respectively as les grosses Jouffroys and les Philiberts, after Philibert Jouffroy, the founding ancestor of one branch. Prosper Jouffroy had told me in 1969 that his father had been known as le gros Jouffroy, but Prosper had interpreted this as a personal nickname.

Anthropologists have debated whether family and personal nicknames should be treated as aspects of a single practice (Gilmore 1982; Pina-Cabral 1984). Pina-Cabral rightly argues their structural implications are different and cites Maranda's argument that the only thing which distinguishes surnames from family nicknames is that the former are recognized by the State. Since it is common for surnames to derive from father's name, place of residence, or occupation, surnames arguably constitute nothing more than a 'snapshot', taken and printed by the State, of a process whose continuing vitality is demonstrated by the appearance of new family nicknames. Breen contrasts the durability of family nicknames in two Irish communities, arguing they are less common and less durable where inheritance is by unigeniture[3] since they would have the confusing effect of giving inheriting and disinherited households the same nickname (Breen 1982). In systems of unigeniture families are frequently known by their association with particular houses (Cole and Wolf 1974: 240; Behar 1986: 34, 54; Rogers 1991: 75–9; Sabean 1990: 249), but partible inheritance often breaks down any association between family lines and houses, particularly where the house itself is divided between heritors. A single building may contain several unrelated households (Behar 1986: 283; Cole and Wolf 1974: 143; Friedl 1974: 11; Netting 1981: 192–3; Sabean 1990: 253–4, 369). Such residential flux does not prevent the recognition of durable family lines. Family nicknames are associated with partible inheritance in Tret, in northern Italy (Cole and Wolf 1974: 9, 241). and continuity in family lines is recognized elsewhere. Residents of Kippel belong to thirteen separate family groups (*Stämme*), each tracing descent from a common ancestor or *Stämmvater* (Friedl 1974: 23). Weinberg (1975: 88) found a stable core of fourteen family names in Bruson from 1910 to 1969.

---

[3] Unigeniture (where the entire holding passes to a single heir) is sometimes called impartible inheritance. I have not used the latter term because cases where children all inherit a share, but remain co-owners of an undivided patrimony, could also be called 'impartible' inheritance. In Bohuslän, which was part of Norway until 1658, each sibling's inheritance was intended not to be realized as an actual portion of the holding but rather as a share in the whole. Shareholders were often farmers or farmers' wives working on other farms in the district (Widgren 1997 and pers. comm.).

Are there Patrilineages in Pellaport?

In 1969 I mapped the distribution of households belonging to families sharing the same nickname, and was struck by how they tended to form local clusters. One family had apparently undergone fission, a segment moving to the other end of the village (Fig. 3.4). Use of the term '*maison paternelle*' suggests an awareness that families are rooted in certain houses despite the effects of partible inheritance, but villages expressed surprise that so neat a pattern emerged when I showed them the map. None the less, inheritance through women, and purchase, upset such continuity. What is now considered the Maitrugue *dit* Didier *maison paternelle* belonged to a Claude François Bavarel *dit* Luron when the 1834 cadastral survey was compiled. At that time two Maitrugues *dit* Didier owned houses that were among those burnt down in the disastrous fire of 1874. The widow of an Étienne Maitrugue *dit* Didier owned one of the houses which now belongs to the Maitrugues *chez* Marcel in the coin de la Combe. Opinion was divided over whether the Maitrugues *chez* Marcel were descended from a branch of the Didier family.

Members of same named 'patrilineage' did not co-operate preferentially in *entr'aide* (see Ch. 4). The spate of building that has occurred over the last twenty years suggests one cause of the clustering of houses belonging to members of the same family may be the saving gained by building on family land. Forty houses have sprung up around the edge of the village and in twenty-one cases they have been placed next to the house of the owner's parents. In eleven instances this has led to extension of patrilineal clusters noted in 1969, but in another ten the house has been built on the wife's parents' land, which would not be recorded in the distribution of surnames.

INHERITANCE OF LAND

Inheritance rules have important recursive effects upon long-term trajectories of social process. Chapter 1 noted that the *cultivateur* works land belonging to his aunts, uncles, and cousins. Unlike the house, farmland is always divided among a couple's children. Each son and daughter inherits a portion equal in value. Salitot reports that in the village she studied near Besançon sons receive preferential treatment (Salitot 1988). This is not the case on the Plateau of Levier although land inherited by married women is held jointly, in the husband's name. Only widows and unmarried women hold land in their own names. In my sample of 346 pieces of

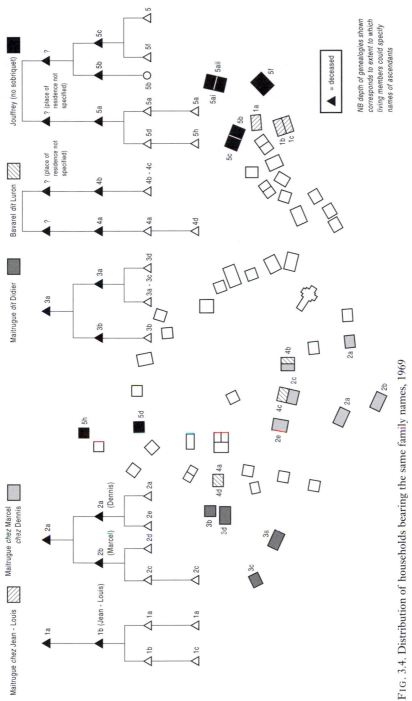

F𝙸ɢ. 3.4. Distribution of households bearing the same family names, 1969

rented land, 70 per cent are reported to be rented from men but this includes cases where the speaker knew the land had been inherited by the wife. The unit of inheritance is the *parcelle*, a small portion of land registered in the cadastral survey. In 1969 each *parcelle* was a narrow strip, typically between 20 and 40 ares in size. The son who inherits the farmhouse receives less land than his brothers and sisters but his siblings are legally obliged to rent him their shares. If none of the heirs remains a *cultivateur* they are free to rent their land to anyone. The *cultivateurs* I interviewed in 1969 had all bought back some of the land inherited by their brothers and sisters, or more distant relatives, but intended to divide the property again upon their own retirement. The practice of dividing land among children has indeed continued up to 1995. The effect can be measured by comparing ownership of land worked on three *exploitations* shortly before *partage*, with ownership on six *exploitations* after *partage*. In the first three cases the father had not yet retired but was helped by his son, the other six were worked by younger or middle-aged men without the help of a son (Table 3.4).

Ownership of the *exploitation* thus pulses slowly through the span of each generation, spreading to its widest at the moment a *cultivateur* retires and gradually contracting as his heir reassembles the inheritance. The

TABLE 3.4. *Ownership of the* exploitation, *Pellaport, 1969*

	% of *exploitation* owned	
	Partage not carried out	*Partage* carried out
Kin of the *cultivateur*		
Parents	49	1
Parents' siblings and their spouses	26	2
Ego (the *cultivateur*)	2	33
Ego's siblings and their spouses	1	18
First cousins	0	11
More distant cousins	0	0
Ego's wife's parents	0	4
Other owners		
Individuals	10	25
The commune	12	6
$N =$	*152 parcelles*	*307 parcelles*

TABLE 3.5. *Sources of land owned by the* cultivateur, *Pellaport, 1969*

	% of total
Inherited from	
Parents	55
Parents' siblings	6
Purchased from	
Parents' siblings	3
Own siblings and their spouses	6
First and second cousins	10
Other individuals	20
The *commune*	0
N =	166 parcelles

children of *cultivateurs* who leave the village expect the son who remains on the farm to provide them with food and accommodation when they visit. During 1969, the brothers of two *cultivateurs* arranged their summer holidays so that they could help with the harvest. The heir to the house is also expected to look after the parents when they retire.

Table 3.5 shows that people are more likely to buy land from cousins than from siblings. This may be because cousins are not obliged to rent the land they have inherited to the heir to the *exploitation*. The emergence of a widening kindred consisting of those with a share in a particular *exploitation* is thus inhibited. When land is offered for sale, the current user has first option on its purchase and is protected from eviction if it is bought by someone else. When Felicien Jouffroy's half-brother Prosper sold strips he had inherited from their father, Felicien bought as many as he could afford, but could not buy them all.

In t he long term, partible inheritance has not caused progressive division of *parcelles*. A comparison of the cadastral maps compiled in 1834 and 1965 shows that an area divided into 304 *parcelles* in 1834 consisted of 254 *parcelles* in 1965 (a small section of this area is shown in Fig. 3.5). In some cases, individual *parcelles* have been divided, but in others they have been amalgamated. By 1969 division of individual *parcelles* was illegal. During the period between the two cadastral surveys, however, the strategies used to prevent division have changed radically. Repurchase is the strategy of *cultivateurs* operating in an industrial market economy associated with rural depopulation. In Neckarhausen, which has long been integrated into a

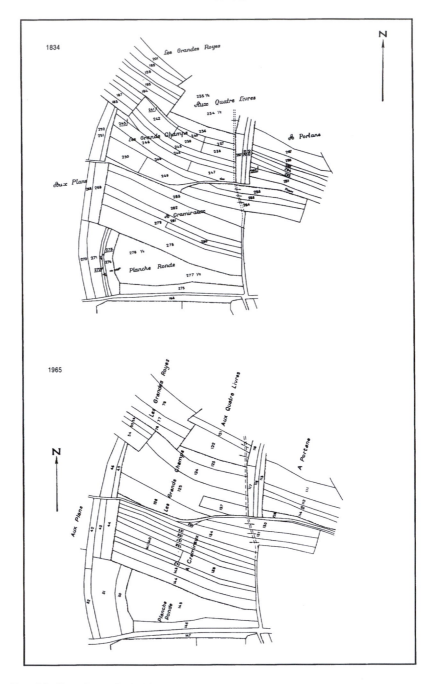

FIG 3.5. Size of *parcelles* in 1834 and 1965

market economy, land has been exchanged, bought, and sold to regroup holdings after partition from the first decade of the eighteenth century (Sabean 1990: 379, 400). On the Plateau of Levier, the surviving extended family households characterized by frequent adult celibacy are relics of an older strategy in which most children remained at home and over-division was precluded by limiting the number of heirs.

The higher proportion of extended family households recorded in the 1846 and 1872 censuses correlates with the high rates of celibacy and late marriage recorded in church registers. They correspond to Hajnal's 'European marriage pattern':

The marriage pattern of most of Europe as it existed for at least two centuries up to 1940 was, so far as we can tell, unique in the world. . . . The distinctive marks of the 'European' pattern are (1) a high age at marriage and (2) a high proportion of people who never marry at all. The 'European' pattern pervaded the whole of Europe except for the eastern and south–eastern portion. (Hajnal 1965: 101).

Hajnal's claims will be reassessed below.

Marriage Strategies and Dispersal of the Exploitation

Although *partage* does not cause the division of *parcelles* it can lead to the dispersal of the land which makes up an *exploitation* as some strips are brought to it through marriage and others lost through the marriage of heirs. Pierre Bavarel's father had worked a strip which now belonged to Étienne Maitrugue's *exploitation*, having been inherited by Pierre's sister, Étienne's wife. Claude Bavarel's father had left several *parcelles* to his daughter and some of the strips Claude worked as a young man were now cultivated by his sister's daughter's husband. Dispersed holdings were not necessarily a disadvantage. They reduced the risk of losing crops through fire, drought, or flood, but they increased the time needed to work the land since *cultivateurs* had to move their equipment through the lanes from one end of the *commune* to the other, and bring hay back to the farmhouse from many scattered strips (McCloskey 1976; Winterhalder 1990). Felicien Jouffroy told me his father had always taken care to sow some grain on clay soil in the valley floor and some on limestone soil on the valley side. In a wet year the latter would do better, in a dry year the former (see Ch. 1).

Marriage between first cousins was considered forbidden (Catholics must obtain a dispensation from the Vatican if they wish to marry a first cousin), but marriages between two brothers and two sisters, or two brother–sister pairs, was a recognized custom (*une coutume courante au pays*). I found one case in Montoiseau, four in Pellaport, and two cases where two siblings had married a pair of first cousins. None of the cases in Pellaport involved people who lived in the same household after marriage. People tended to explain the custom as the result of couples meeting at their siblings' weddings. Such marriages allow the distribution of land at *partages* to be arranged in a way that reduces the dispersal of *exploitations*. According to Bede, St Augustine discovered this practice in Anglo-Saxon England and wrote to the Pope to find out whether it was forbidden in church law (Goody 1983: 30). Anthropologists studying Minot used the term 'relinking' to describe double brother–sister marriages (Segalen 1991: 95). Relinking marriages were prevalent in Bigouden where there was a patrimony or prestige to be preserved (ibid. 119, 286). Marriage between pairs of siblings has also been very common in the Dalarna region of Sweden, where partible inheritance is practised (Sporrong and Wennersten 1995). Augustins (1989: 138–9) discusses the phenomenon generally in relation to unigeniture and partibility.

The need for inherited land also influences the frequency with which *cultivateurs* marry within the village (Table 3.6). *Cultivateurs* born elsewhere tend to marry into the village rather than bring their wives with them. Five of the seven who had married into Pellaport before 1969 had bought their farmhouse, but had inherited most cultivated land from their wife's father. In one case, 35 per cent of the *exploitation* had been inherited from the wife's father. On another small *exploitation* the 16 *parcelles* cultivated consisted of 9 inherited by the wife and 7 that had been bought. Chapter 4 will show that *cultivateurs*' dependence on the network of mutual aid also favoured residence in the community native to one or both partners. A wider survey carried out three years later gave similar results, although the preference for village endogamy among *cultivateurs* was not so marked (Table 3.7). The importance of village endogamy for *cultivateurs* is also evident in the 1872 census data, although the higher proportion of resident *cultivateurs* where neither husband nor wife was born in the village may be a symptom of tenant farmers who have moved into the village to lease an *exploitation*. It was, however, already the case that people whose occupations lay outside agriculture (schoolteachers, dairymen, craftsmen) were most likely to live in a village where neither partner had been born (Table 3.8). The general effect of village endogamy among *cultivateurs* is to create a slow current in which ownership of *parcelles* circulates among the village's *exploitations*. A high rate of endogamy is common in communities practising partible inheritance (cf. Friedl 1974: 25–7).

TABLE 3.6. *Marriage and residence in Pellaport, 1969*

	Cultivateurs	Others
Men born in the village		
Wife born in village	23	5
Wife born elsewhere	16	7
Men born elsewhere		
Wife born in village	7	0
Wife born elsewhere	1	10
TOTAL:	47	22

In the years before 1969, *cultivateurs* in Pellaport had been consolidating their holdings through the exchange of *parcelles* of equivalent value. I was told these exchanges had been carried out since the First World War, in other words, since about the time of the first wave of mechanization (see Ch. 5). Adjacent strips owned by the same person were amalgamated into single *parcelles* by the surveyors who carried out the 1965 cadastral survey, a rather high-handed action which prevented their subsequent division at *partage*. When land is sold, a *cultivateur* who already owns adjacent strips will be willing to pay more than someone who has no land in the vicinity. Land sales therefore also tend to promote the consolidation of *exploitations*.

TABLE 3.7. *Marriage and residence in six villages (including Pellaport), 1972*

	Cultivateurs %	Others %
Men born in the village		
Wife born in village	41	23
Wife born elsewhere	45	24
Men born elsewhere		
Wife born in village	9	15
Wife born elsewhere	5	38
N =	148	128

TABLE 3.8. *Marriage and residence in Pellaport, Dechailles, and La Combe Sainte-Marie, 1872*

	Cultivateurs %	Others %
Men born in the village		
Wife born in village	49	22
Wife born elsewhere	28	32
Men born elsewhere		
Wife born in village	8	12
Wife born elsewhere	15	34
N =	141	50

Since the 1950s, the French Ministry of Agriculture has been engaged in a lengthy process of reorganizing the distribution of land known as *le remembrement*. The *remembrement* aimed to place *parcelles* which were worked by the same *cultivateur* in groups, even if they belonged to several proprietors. Throughout the vast area in which partible inheritance applies, surveyors visit each village in turn and group strips together so that once widely scattered *exploitations* are reconstituted into a small number of larger fields. The variable nature of the terrain makes it difficult to satisfy everyone that they have received land as good as that which they previously owned or rented. The *remembrement* in Pellaport took place between two of my visits to the field. The government agent redrew the *parcelle* boundaries on the cadastral survey, disregarding the talus or slope created between adjacent strips on sloping land through centuries of ploughing. Some people had hedgerows running diagonally across their new fields. Felicien Jouffroy's nephew insisted on taking the agent to see his strips for himself and in later years this became a general practice in other villages (cf. Behar 1986: 286–300 on the *remembrement* in Santa María del Monte). The new fields should not be subdivided at partage. Although some people have done so the division is unofficial, since no formal survey to establish the boundaries of the divisions is allowed. In 1969 Nicolas Jouffroy's *exploitation* comprised 63 *parcelles* with a total area of 30 hectares. In 1995 his *exploitation* consisted of 25 *parcelles* whose total area was 37 hectares (excluding in both cases the communal pasture he rented). Jacques Maitrugue's *exploitation* was reduced from more than 20 blocks of land to 6.

PL. 15. Before the *remembrement*

PL. 16. After the *remembrement*

In order to 'stabilize' the transmission of *exploitations* the French government had recently introduced GAEC (*Groupements agricoles d'exploitation en commun*), in which members of the family become shareholders in a limited company. While the shares may be reallocated at inheritance, the land and equipment remain a single unit. Three of the *exploitations* in Pellaport had been reconstituted as GAEC. There are about 250 in the *département* (Agreste 1994). Jacques Maitrugue and his son, for example, both hold 50 per cent of the capital in their *exploitation*. When Jacques retires he will divide his holding between his three children, but his son's share will remain unchanged, introducing a form of *préciput* (defined below). Nicolas Jouffroy, who had not yet established which of his children would take over the *exploitation*, envisaged each of his four children becoming equal shareholders.

LABOUR, INHERITANCE, AND HOUSEHOLD STRUCTURE

The Debate since Le Play

Previous sections of this chapter have documented the declining frequency of complex family households on the Plateau of Levier. The nineteenth-century French political philosopher Le Play initiated a lengthy and continuing debate on the causes and effects of complex family households. The key questions concern their possible correlation with inheritance rules, whether they develop in response to particular historical circumstances, and their implications for social process on a larger (village) scale.

Le Play concluded that partible inheritance repeatedly fragmented the household, as each child established an independent unit based on their own portion of the inheritance. He wrongly thought partible inheritance had been imposed on northern France by the laws of the Revolutionary Constituent Assembly, whereas it had in fact long been customary in that region (see Flandrin 1979: 74). Unigeniture, in Le Play's assessment, tended to create extended family households in which non-inheriting siblings remained dependent upon the sole heir. Le Play regarded the 'stem family' (*la famille souche*) as a compromise between the two extremes, in which some non-inheriting children were sent out into the world, while those whom the parents judged most able to work with them stayed behind on the farm (Sabean 1990: 89 n.).[4] Le Play considered the stem families associated with unigeniture in southern France to be a traditional institution. Studies of communities practising unigeniture confirm Le Play's argument that (where there are no opportunities for employment outside agriculture) unigeniture does indeed lead to celibate adult brothers and sisters living with the heir on the family farm (Cole

---

[4] For other reviews of Le Play's work see Laslett 1972: 16–21 and Flandrin 1979: 50–3, 68.

and Wolf 1974: 196–7, Rogers 1991: 68, 80), but the link between inheritance and household structure is more complex and less benign than Le Play appreciated.

In 1965, Hajnal proposed an alternative explanation for extended family households, arguing they were the product of a particular historical period. He did not claim a correlation with rules of inheritance and maintained that they were found across most of Europe (Hajnal 1965). Hajnal's first point, that high age at marriage was characteristic of a distinct historic period, is generally accepted. Hajnal found evidence that in fourteenth-century England, children were betrothed and adults married young. These customs had almost entirely disappeared by the eighteenth century (Hajnal 1965: 120). Burguière (1976: 243) considers late marriage may have begun in the sixteenth century, and increased to reach a peak in the eighteenth, reducing a woman's period of reproductive activity by ten years. High rates of adult celibacy during the nineteenth century are documented in many village studies. Hajnal argued that what he called the 'European marriage pattern' contributed to the Industrial Revolution, by greatly increasing the productivity of peasant agriculture. It did so by creating households in which there was a high ratio of adults to children (in order to explore Hajnal's hypothesis I have distinguished, in this chapter's tables, between nuclear families in which all children are juveniles and those in which at least one is adult). Extended family households were generated by celibate adults living with their married brother. Burguière took the argument further by suggesting that the sexual abstinence encouraged by late marriage created a Protestant asceticism among peasants, who presumably diverted their sexual energies into tilling the fields (ibid. 250). The combination of late marriage and widespread adult celibacy has since also been documented in Tibet and Nepal, leading demographers to look for common causes in Europe and the Himalayas (see Viazzo 1989).

While not mentioning Hajnal's work, Laslett made a general attack on the idea that households had been larger and more complex in the past, and that the dominance of the nuclear family was a recent development. Laslett (1972: 60) recognized large family households had existed in the past in southern France, but argued extended families were otherwise rarer during sixteenth- to nineteenth-century Europe than they are today. Mitterauer and Sieder ((1982: 31) similarly argued the nuclear family household was general throughout northern Europe before the Industrial Revolution. Laslett (1972: 31, 49–51) took the frequency of nuclear family households recorded in English censuses as a norm and was sceptical of any 'arrangement which reads very strangely to an Englishman'. He proposed the null hypothesis that all 'departures from the simple household form of the co-resident group in England must be regarded as the fortuitous outcomes of demographic eventualities and economic conveniences, and of particularly strong personal attachments as well' (ibid. 1972: 73). Not surprisingly, this ethnocentric approach provoked an adverse response from French historical demographers. Under criticism from Berkner and Flandrin, Laslett conceded that a high frequency of nuclear family households in pre-industrial Europe was compatible with the coexistence of various kinds of extended family (see Rogers 1991: 38–9). As Laslett acknowledged, a high frequency of complex families does not necessarily increase the average size of households proportionately (Laslett 1972: 54, Viazzo 1989: 97). While Laslett tested for correlations between family size, household composition, and the prevalence of servants, he did not look for any correlation between household structure and inheritance rules (as proposed by Le Play), nor for a correlation with labour recruitment (implied by Hajnal).

The Household Cycle

The household cycle illustrates how cultural strategies are translated into action, and exemplifies ways in which such strategies may alter their social environment, or be themselves changed in response to environmental conditions. This section looks at how households respond to external conditions. Fortes interpreted the variety of household structures he found in two Asante villages as the outcome of the life cycles of individual members, the labour needs of peasant households and men's decisions whether to live with their lineage segment or their nuclear family. In Western Europe, the variety of household structures can be interpreted as the outcome of several variables: members' life cycles, the allocation and transmission of authority, local inheritance customs, the labour force required to form an independent unit of production under particular technological and ecological conditions, rules imposed by those in power, and the availability of alternatives to work and residence in the natal household (cf. Anderson 1980: 69–70). In some cases the structure of the household may be deliberately sought. In other cases it may be an 'epiphenomenon' (Barth 1967). Census data that record household composition may not be enough to identify the strategies or constraints responsible for documented forms. A three-generation household may, for example, be an unintended by-product of the lack of alternative housing for children or grandparents, as in late nineteenth-century Törbel (Netting 1981: 216), or it may result from the father's wilful refusal to hand over control of the family holding to his married son. 'Simple statistics on household composition (or anything else) can never tell us the meaning and expectations associated with behavioural acts' (Anderson 1980: 35).

1. *Demography.* Demography alone can drastically limit the frequency and duration of joint families, and hence their appearance in surveys. In the Provençal Alps heirs could marry long before their succession to headship, thus generating long-lasting stem-family households, whereas the opposite was the case in Austria (Viazzo 1989: 234, 254). Laslett (1972: 6, 20) recognized that, even if older people expect to live with their married child(ren) and grandchildren, a three-generation family will only be present during part of the household cycle, since the members of the older generation will almost certainly die during their grandchildren's childhood. Increasing life expectancy could increase the frequency with which three-generation family households appear in census data, unless the age at which women bear their first child also rises (cf. Rogers 1991: 136–7). Berkner (1972: 406) concluded that under pre-industrial demographic conditions, three-generation households could never exceed 30 per cent of the total and that economic limitations would prevent smaller holdings from ever supporting three generations.

2. *The allocation and transmission of authority.* In the Italian Tyrol the father has power over work schedules, purchase of clothing, even permission to attend a dance (Cole and Wolf 1974: 183–6). If the father will not relinquish authority to his heir(s) before death, a three-generation family household may develop, whereas elsewhere parents may retire to a separate household if a child is allowed to take over control of production during their lifetime. In the early 1960s, the French government introduced a retirement pension for farmers, the *rente viagère*, intended to make small farmers sell or rent out their land, or hand over management to their sons. In order to qualify for the pension, a number of elderly couples in Pellaport had retired to flats within the farm building, handing responsibility for managing the *exploitation* to their sons. Gröger found that in Aveyron, many had allowed heirs to take over the family holding rather than sell or rent the land. An uneasy compromise over the transfer of *de facto* authority had usually been achieved (Gröger 1982: 122–4, cf. Rogers 1991: 69, 79). In Heidenreichstein, Lower Austria, fathers stipulated their son's obligations to provide free housing, a vegetable garden, and firewood in a written contract signed when the property was handed over (Berkner 1972: 401–3). In Törbel each couple quickly sets up its own

home (Netting 1981: 171), but the family estate is rarely divided at the time of children's marriage. In Minot parents retire to a separate household nearby when their first grandchild is born (Zonabend 1984: 115–17)

3. *Local inheritance customs*. Inheritance strategies are determined by two conflicting goals: conserving a holding adequate to perpetuate the family line, and giving all children the best possible start in life (Cole and Wolf 1974: 176). Unigeniture gives priority to the first, partible inheritance gives priority to the second. Augustins argued that partible inheritance and unigeniture have fundamentally different goals. Unigeniture aims to perpetuate the *house (maison, casa,* or *ostal)* associated with a family line at the expense of disinherited kin, partible inheritance aims to perpetuate a wider kindred (*parentèle)* even if it entails sacrificing the continuing association between a family line and its ancestral home (Augustins 1989: 59, cf. Barthelemy 1988: 199). Inheritance rules therefore have a profound effect on inter-household relations. Partible inheritance on the Plateau of Levier is connected with the network of mutual aid discussed in the following chapter. Barthelemy argues that the *ostal* system constitutes (in Lévi-Strauss's typology) an elementary kinship structure, with women and dowries circulating between independent units, whereas partible inheritance is associated with preferential marriage within a kindred, intended to limit the dispersion of ownership of *parcelles*. The stem kindreds of Tory Island (Ireland), which have overlapping membership but separate land holdings, are a third solution to these conflicting goals (Fox 1978).

Unigeniture and partible inheritance are polar positions. Practice may fall somewhere between the extremes. In southern France the principle of *le préciput* allows one heir to receive the bulk of the inheritance, while the remainder is divided equally between all children (Bourdieu 1990: 147–150). Even a rule of partibility may allow one or more heirs to be preferentially treated (Cole and Wolf 1974: 180; Sabean 1990: 186). Communities where, as in Pellaport and neighbouring villages, sons and daughters receive equal shares of the land include Neckarhausen in southern Germany (Sabean 1990: 13), Kippel and Bruson in the Swiss Alps (Friedl 1974: 60; Weinberg 1975: 102), German-speaking Valais, including Viazzo's village of Alagna (Viazzo 1989), and Santa María del Monte in the Spanish province of Léon (Behar 1986: 34). In all these villages, heirs expected to receive a portion of each type of terrain, often necessitating dividing already tiny plots even further (e.g. ibid. 83; Weinberg 1975: 102–4). The same is true in the Romance-speaking communities of the Italian Alps, where the strong zonation of land according to altitude determines what can be done with it (Cole and Wolf 1974). In Norway and Sweden, however, daughters inherited shares half the size of those inherited by sons (Sporrong and Wennersten 1995; Widgren 1997) and Salitot (1988) reports a similar custom in a village near Besançon, less than 50 km. from the Plateau of Levier. Regions practising unigeniture include Galicia (Behar 1986: 34), Lower Austria (Berkner 1972), Béarn in the French Pyrenees (Bourdieu 1990: 152–8), Germanic communities in the Italian Tyrol (Cole and Wolf 1974), Aveyron (Rogers 1991), the large farms in Anjou (Wylie 1966) and parts of the Nivernais (Shaffer 1982).

4. *The need or ability to recruit sufficient labour to work the holding.* Panter-Brick (1993) following Erasmus (1965), identifies several ways in which a peasant household can recruit labour, and assesses the relative cost of each source. These are summarized in Table 3.9. Only the first and last sources of labour will be discussed in this chapter; the others will be discussed in Ch. 4.

Differential access to labour and land are the two determinants of social inequality in a peasant society. The more active adults there are in the household, and the fewer non-productive elderly, or very young people, the greater the household's output, as long as they have enough land to work. The smaller the workforce in the household, the lower the output. Single-parent families with young children will be particularly vulnerable. A freeholding household will keep more of its output than a tenant household which has to pay rent or a share of produce or provide

TABLE 3.9. *Recruitment of labour and the peasant household*

Labour type	Advantages	Disadvantages
Household	Low cost, reliable, flexible	Long time required to complete tasks
Free assistance from other households	Useful in emergencies	Limited availability
Festive labour	Low direct cost (not rewarded with cash)	Often poorly carried out Host must supply food and drink
Reciprocal exchange	Efficient	Incurs reciprocal obligation
Hired labour	Convenient	Costly; only the rich can afford it

corvée labour. Working in the Italian Alps prior to the introduction of tractors, Cole and Wolf (1974: 171–2) found that larger holdings in both the villages they studied sometimes hired agricultural labourers, while medium ones managed through reciprocal labour. The smallest landholders were most likely to hire themselves out to others. A similar trend can be seen in nineteenth-century censuses from the Plateau of Levier.

Labour requirements vary according to the agricultural regime. Mitterauer argued cereal cultivation is associated with day labourers hired for peak labour periods, whereas stock-raising requires a permanent labour force provided by family members and/or resident servants (quoted in Viazzo 1989: 255). Flandrin and Shaffer agree that different types of agriculture have different labour requirements, but claim larger, joint-family households tend to be found in zones where cereal cultivation predominates (Flandrin 1979: 85).

A collective herd is more efficient than separate pasturage of each household's livestock. The demand for children's labour in Pellaport and Minot, created by the abolition of the open-field system and its replacement by a regime in which each household independently manages its fields, has been noted in Ch. 2. In most Alpine communities, as on the Plateau of Levier, the high pastures are still grazed by a common herd. Viazzo (1989: 22, 115) argues the optimal ratio of cattle to herders may be as high as 30–40:1, considerably more than any single household on the Plateau of Levier owned until very recently. There was no common herd in Alagna, and each household managed its own portion of the alps. The resulting demand for labour may explain the unusually high frequency of complex households in Alagna during the period between 1700 and 1850 (ibid. 241, 247).

5. *Rules imposed by those in power.* In parts of southern France during the seventeenth and eighteenth centuries, more than 20 per cent of households were of multiple types. They were common in the Auvergne and Franche-Comté as well as the Nivernais. Flandrin argued they formed in response to the feudal law of mortmain, which permitted a tenancy to be inherited only if the heir was resident at the time of his father's death. In response, marriage contracts stipulated that couples should live with the husband's parents, holding property in common with them (Flandrin 1979: 78–81). Flandrin's explanation does not account for the persistence of complex households after the abolition of mortmain. In southern France before the Revolution of 1789 unigeniture was customary and the currency of Roman law allowed fathers to make a will favouring one heir (ibid. 75). Flandrin points out the key issue is not whether the father is free to choose how to transmit his property, but how he uses that freedom

to enact local custom (ibid. 78). Implementation of the law requiring universal partible inheritance at the time of the French Revolution was resisted in many parts of southern France. In Béarn application of *le préciput* allowed one son to inherit the holding, while creating an illusion of partibility. In Sainte-Foy, disinherited siblings continue to be promised small sums of cash, which they often do not receive (Rogers 1991: 95–6).

In England and Germany, unigeniture was imposed on populations which previously practised partibility (see Faith 1966 for a map of the distribution of inheritance rules in England, and Le Roy Ladurie 1976 for their distribution in France). Partible inheritance was the rule in England during Anglo-Saxon and early Norman times, as it was in Celtic customary law. From the thirteenth century, however, feudal lords required fiefs to be transmitted undivided, imposing unigeniture on their tenants (Faith 1966: 79, Flandrin 1979: 76, Goody 1983: 121). Both Faith and Goody argue that partible inheritance was abolished in medieval England because feudal landlords saw it as a threat to the productivity of their fiefs. If villeins divided up the land among their heirs, progressively smaller holdings would increasingly cater only for their tenants' subsistence and yield lower profits. 'Primogeniture, the system most favourable to seigneurial interests, developed, probably under seigneurial pressure, where lordship was strong and where demesne farming became important' (Faith 1966: 85). There are many instances of manorial systems evolving towards primogeniture, but extremely few of customs changing from primogeniture to something else (ibid. 81).

Unigeniture in the German-speaking Italian Tyrol was established early during colonization, beginning in the eleventh century. The population was rising and feudal lords agreed to hereditary tenure of tenancies in exchange for tenants' undertaking not to divide their holdings between heirs (Cole and Wolf 1974: 31–2, 69–70). Viazzo (1989: 264) similarly argues that the impartible inheritance rule characteristic of the Austrian Alps is a legacy of the mode of colonization (Viazzo 1989: 264).

Sabean considers current inheritance rules in southern Germany to have been established during a period of renewed population growth and market expansion around the sixteenth century. In Upper Swabia, whose ecology is suited to pasture, grain production and forestry, lords throughout the region took steps to enforce unigeniture. In most of nearby Württemburg, however, wine production required intensive production, and considerable risk, favouring densely populated villages and small units of production. Partible inheritance remained the law (Sabean 1990: 15, cf. Cole and Wolf 1974: 72, 80).

6. *The availability of alternative accommodation or employment.* If no employment outside agriculture is available, or if there is no additional housing, large or complex families may occupy single households. Lack of opportunities outside the household may compel siblings to remain, unmarried, in their natal household, as seems to have been the case on the Plateau of Levier during the first half of the nineteenth century.

I argue that the persistence of complex family households on the Plateau of Levier until the late nineteenth century was due to the conjunction of partible inheritance with a growing population. Hajnal pointed out that the more active adults there are in a household, the greater the household's output. Partible inheritance, on the other hand, makes large families a threat to the future of the *exploitation*. A successful household will maximize the available labour but minimize the number of heirs. 'Agricultural wealth could disappear within a generation through the system of partible inheritance' (Friedl 1974: 73).

A strategy directed towards restricting heirs is likely to generate extended family households, while one directed at increasing the labour force can allow more than one child to marry, creating joint family households. The prevalence of extended rather than joint households on the Plateau of Levier in the nineteenth century suggests limiting division of the holding was the primary goal and increasing available labour a secondary one. There were nineteen three-generation family households in the three villages whose 1872 surveys have been analysed (Table 3.1), but only two of these were joint households, including married parents and grandparents. Fourteen included a widowed grandparent while in three there were no extant marriages. None of the cases where adult siblings were living together contained more than one married couple and in many all were celibate. Contrary to Le Play's theory, partible inheritance is here associated with complex family households. Sharecroppers in the cereal-cultivating Nivernais, on the other hand, needed a large labour force to work tenant farms and, since they could not afford hired labour, they were forced to recruit more than one nuclear family to work the large *domaines*. As tenants, inheritance of land was not an issue. This, rather than the rule of inheritance alone, explains the prevalence of large joint families or *communautés* during the eighteenth century (Shaffer 1982: 72). Tenant farmers in coastal Brittany also married young (Segalen 1991: 43–8; 66). Declining labour needs may conversely have been responsible for the rise of nuclear family households in northern France which Le Play decried, where the proportion of extended family households fell from 10 per cent to 4 per cent as agriculture and weaving were displaced by professional, commercial, and building or quarrying work (Blayo 1972).

Although Hajnal considered the high level of adult labour available during the nineteenth century had contributed to the Industrial Revolution he was unaware of the existence of a similar pattern in Nepal, where partible inheritance has also been practised without stimulating an industrial revolution. In order to reduce the number of heirs, peasant farmers in Nepal practice polyandry, one wife marrying a set of brothers. Many women remain celibate. Since the woman's child-bearing capacity is the critical element limiting the number of heirs, the effect on the household's reproductive capacity is the same as if one brother had married and the others remained celibate (Crook 1995, Durham 1991). Durham (ibid. 85) used a computer programme to model the effect of allowing more than one wife to marry into the Nepalese household would have, and concluded so many heirs would be produced that starvation would extinguish the family line after two generations.

Household Structure and Social Differentiation on the Plateau of Levier

In this section I move from considering how the household responds to the constraints it experiences to the consequences of the strategies its members adopt. The occupations of household heads listed in Table 3.2 seem to show a stratified society on the Plateau of Levier in 1872, with landlords at the top, *cultivateurs* and craftsmen in the middle, and farm labourers at the base. A minority of households among *cultivateurs* and craftsmen employ domestic servants. This may be evidence for a process of social differentiation, similar to those documented by Sabean (see Ch. 7) and Flandrin (below), and driven by the tendency for unchecked partible inheritance to produce holdings too small to be viable. It is also possible, however, that the apparent stratification is illusory, and merely the result of capturing data on households at different points in the household cycle.

Until the early twentieth century, agriculture on the Plateau of Levier was labour intensive. The households of *cultivateurs* were bigger than those of craftsmen and women. The appropriate strategy for *cultivateurs* might have been to have many children, to create a large labour force. But the Plateau was overpopulated in the nineteenth century, and the rule of partible inheritance meant that large numbers of children threatened the future viability of the *exploitation*. Nineteenth-century censuses suggest two strategies were used to overcome this danger. One was to enforce life-long celibacy on some members of the family and the other was to exploit the labour of other people who worked as *domestiques* and *journaliers*. If servants and older children have equal value as sources of labour, but different consequences for inheritance, households that can reduce the number of children and make up the shortfall by employing servants will maintain or increase their wealth. Households with many children, who fail to impose celibacy, will see their holding fragmented.

To avoid dividing the *exploitation* one had to limit the number of legit-imate heirs, not the total number of offspring. All but one of the eight households containing illegitimate children in 1872 were those of agri-cultural labourers. Some occupations were more vulnerable to sexual exploitation than others. In Minot there were many more illegitimate births, and single mothers who never married, among dressmakers and day labourers than there were among farming and woodcutting families. Verdier argues dressmakers and day labourers were at risk because they worked day by day on short-term contracts in others' houses, as if they were available 'to the world' (Verdier 1979: 224–7).

Sixty-four per cent of the eighty-one farming households in Dechailles in 1846 consist of nuclear families or widowed parents with their juvenile children, but another 25 per cent contain celibate adults aged 30 or over and 11 per cent contain three-generation families. Flan-drin (1979: 90) calculates the general frequency of extended family households in northern France ranged from 7 to 14 per cent. The larger sample available from the 1872 censuses for Pellaport, Dechailles, and La Combe Sainte-Marie demonstrates that *cultivateurs* have both the largest households, and also the highest rate of celibacy. Twenty four per cent of *cultivateurs* aged over 30 are celibate; but only 16 per cent of craftspeople. *Journaliers* have even smaller households than crafts people. Thirty-seven per cent of farming households employ servants, but only 15 per cent of craftsmen's households. Those farming households that employ servants have fewer family members than those who do not (Table 3.10).

While these data suggest servants and day labourers are being exploited by some households as an alternative source of labour to family members, it is also possible that the employment of servants is merely a stage in the household cycle. Berkner demonstrated that servants in eight-eenth-century Heidenreichstein were not a social class but an age-group. Less than 10 per cent were over 30 years old and only two were married. He also showed servants were more likely to be found in households where the children were too young to work. Servants were often therefore

TABLE 3.10. *Household size in Pellaport, Dechailles, and La Combe Sainte-Marie, 1872 and 1972*

	Av. size of household		Number	
	1872	1972	1872	1972
Cultivateurs				
Without resident employees	4.5	4.6	136	85
With resident employees				
Family size	3.8			
Total household size	5.1	none	51	0
Craftsmen (and factory workers, 1972)				
Without resident employees	3.8	3.5	47	105
With resident employees				
Family size	2.7			
Total household size	3.7	none	7	0
Day labourers	2.6	none	31	0
Rentiers	3.0	none	18	0

a temporary substitute for the labour of family members. As the household's children grew up their labour capacity increased and some might, in turn, be sent out to work for others as servants (Berkner 1972: 410–13). During the 1520s, up to 60 per cent of the rural population in England aged between 15 and 24 were servants (Overton 1996: 41).

A closer look at the 1872 census data shows that several occupations on the Plateau of Levier are more characteristic of phases in the life cycle than of social class (Table 3.11). Most domestic servants are aged between 11 and 25 and only seven are over 30. Ian Keen's analysis of the censuses taken in La Combe Sainte-Marie shows that domestic servants rarely stayed in a household for many years. Day labourers and landlords, on the other hand, tend to be older than average. *Journaliers* are most prevalent among those aged between 60 and 70, while the average age of *rentiers* is 58. Both live in relatively small households. Many day labourers are single parents, widowed or unmarried, who have children living with them. *Rentiers* are frequently single, elderly people although one lived with a family of *cultivateurs* who were presumably her tenants. These two occupations appear to be the strategies of the wealthiest and most vulnerable

TABLE 3.11. *Domestic servants, agricultural labourers, and landlords as percentage of people in age bands, Dechailles, Pellaport, and La Combe Sainte-Marie, 1872*

Age	11–20	21–30	31–40	41–50	51–60	61–70	71–80
Domestiques	13	12	3	1			
Journaliers	2	3	5	3	7	16	9
Rentiers				2	5	3	9

among the elderly, who lack the support of a large family. An alternative route into old age is illustrated by the fate of Aimiable L., a *cultivateur* who had married into La Combe Sainte-Marie and was in his late forties in 1872. Two sons were born. In 1881 one was described as a soldier on leave but in 1886 both sons were single and working with their parents. By 1891, one son had left, the other had married and brought his wife to the household. Aimiable was a widower, but still head. By 1901, however, Aimiable's son and daughter-in-law had a son of 9 and employed an 18-year-old *domestique*. Aimiable was no longer head of the household; aged 78 he was listed last except for the servant.

Notwithstanding the evidence that apparent social difference is partly an artefact of the household cycle, there is also evidence for real differentiation. The average age of the children in the thirty-five households with both children and servants is 11.7 years, whereas in the 151 households with children but without servants, the average age of children is little higher, at 13.0 years. It seems likely that, as Berkner acknowledges, only some households have sufficient wealth or land to capture more labour by employing servants and that this factor is at least as important as the age of their children. At the other extreme, day labourers have the smallest households and may be prevented by an inadequate labour force from working an independent holding. It thus appears that both a regular cycle in household structure and social differentiation are at work on the Plateau of Levier. Their combined effect creates a risk that the trajectories of households on the margins move away from the typical cycle seen at the core, a point made by Flandrin in criticism of Laslett. Comparative studies suggest however that partible inheritance counteracted this tendency. Attempts by some families to develop a village élite by delaying marriage, enforcing celibacy, and marrying among themselves are usually undermined by partible inheritance (Viazzo 1989: 268–70).

Ian Keen traced the history of some households in La Combe Sainte-Marie through successive censuses during the second half of the nineteenth and early twentieth century. These show the variety of trajectories poorer households might follow. In 1872, Maximin A. was living on a farm on the hillside beyond the village with his domestic servant Marie B., who had been born in a village sixteen km. away. Although Maximin's occupation was recorded as *cultivateur*, the farm has been a rented one throughout living memory (in 1969) and he was probably *un fermier*. By 1881 they had married, and moved to the village, where they continued to work as *cultivateurs*. They had two young children and employed a *domestique*. In 1886 they had a different *domestique*, and another in 1891. By 1901 the two children were aged 21 and 19, and there was no domestic servant. By 1921 Marie was widowed, *une cultivatrice* living with her unmarried son. This case is consistent with Berkner's argument that servants are a substitute for the labour of family members.

In 1872 François G. was a 34-year-old *journalier* living with his wife Adeline C., the daughter of a retired customs official. They had three children, aged 8, 7, and 2. Arsène B., a 33-year-old *cultivateur* born in the village of Largilliat, lived under the same roof with his 26-year-old *domestique* Josephine. Ferdinand L., his wife and five children, were *cultivateurs* who also lived in the same building. They employed Émile B. from Largilliat, who may well have been Arsène's younger brother, as a *domestique*. Another house in the village was occupied by Hillaire G. and his wife, *cultivateurs* in their sixties. By 1881 Hillaire was a widower of 73. Although still described as a *cultivateur* he had moved to a separate household under the same roof as François. No longer a *journalier*, François himself was now both *cultivateur* and village hayward. By 1886 Hillaire had become a dependent member of François's household, implying he was François's father. There were now four daughters and a son. In 1886 the oldest daughter worked as a dressmaker but by 1891 she was a domestic servant. In 1901, three daughters had left the village and there is no trace of the family in the 1921 census. The varied occupations of the household, the fact that François had to work as a labourer until his father was in his seventies, and then supplement his income with the job of hayward, all suggest this was a household whose independence as *cultivateurs* was precarious. Another household living under difficult conditions was that of Hélène B., a widow in her fifties when the 1872 census was compiled. Her 20-year-old daughter worked as a washerwoman while Hélène and her two younger, teenage daughters were agricultural labourers. Onezine, the oldest daughter, was employed as *domestique* elsewhere in the village. During the 1880s, Hélène and her daughters were *cultiva-teurs* but by 1901 Hélène had died and only two daughters were left in the village. Living together, one worked as a milliner the other, a single supporting mother, as a day labourer. 'The fact that many small dramas repeat stereotypical performances attests to the power of the syntax established by property dynamics. But, like any language, its structure provides endless opportunity for innovation and creativity' (Sabean 1990: 33). Unlike forms of speech however, the variants enacted engage directly with their social environment; in Giddens' terms, they have different recursive effects.

THE RECURSIVE EFFECTS OF INTERACTION

Inheritance and Social Status

Viazzo, following Braudel, argues that history is the outcome of interaction between ecological forces on one hand, and political and economic forces on the other (Viazzo 1989: 221–3). This was famously demonstrated by Cole and Wolf, who discovered that, once division had reduced holdings to the minimum viable, the practice of partible inheritance and unigeniture converged. Viazzo reached the same conclusion (Cole and Wolf 1974: 179–82; Viazzo 1989: 93, 225). But, as Cole and Wolf (ibid. 243) again first documented, the two systems continue to have different consequences in other areas of village life, including mutual aid (I return to this in Ch. 7). The recursive effects of interaction cause a pattern gradually to emerge from repeated enactments of social strategies, a process of structuration that either stabilizes the social order (as argued by Giddens) or moves it progressively further from an earlier state (as argued by Marx).

Celibacy is found in communities practising both unigeniture and partible inheritance, but celibacy cannot simply be treated as a *response* to population pressure without also considering its recursive effects. Division of the land may be averted by forming a joint holding in which all children have equal shares, although only one son is allowed to marry. This practice is recorded in the Italian Tyrol (Cole and Wolf 1974: 158), in León (Behar 1986: 109), and in the Swiss Alps, where siblings form associations called *erbgemeinschaft* (Friedl 1974: 60–1, 67–8; Netting 1981: 174). Where unigeniture is practised, however, the status of disinherited siblings is no better than that of servants (Bourdieu 1990: 158; Rogers 1991: 80, cf. Cole and Wolf 1974: 242). Disinherited siblings in Sainte-Foy who marry and set up their own households suffer lower status, but where partibility is the rule children who leave home continue to own their share of the holding (Cole and Wolf 1974: 159, 195; Netting 1981: 172; Behar 1986: 55).

Partibility, unlike unigeniture, acts as a levelling mechanism within and between households and creates greater gender equality. In the Spanish village of Santa María del Monte, widows become household heads and can attend the village assembly (Behar 1986: 121). In the French Alpine valley of Queyras village endogamy, encouraged by women's inheritance of land, strengthened women's position because they did not have to sever ties with their natal family (Rosenberg 1988: 27). In the long run, the consequences of partible and impartible inheritance on the structuration of social relationships are, therefore, very different. Sabean (1990: 24) concludes: 'The closer one looks, the more kinship and the family appear to be the operative structures in which values are formed and meaningful action takes place.' 'But', he continues, 'we do not yet have the tools to generate theories about this kind of thing. Practice remains at the level of family and theory at the level of class'. I shall take a similar line, not in the sense used in 'culture of poverty' theory, that claims the poor forget how to inculcate the virtues of hard work in their children, but by arguing that, where the household normally constitutes the unit of production and consumption, any deviation from this norm will be implicated in processes leading to social differentiation. If some households lack sufficient labour to constitute a unit of production, and if others succeed in capturing their labour, social differentiation is occurring at the margins of the modal forms. Structuration is the process that links household strategies with the formation of social classes. The developmental cycle of households does not take place in isolation, but interacts with those of other households, with ecology, the market and the state (Cole and Wolf 1974: 176). Contrary to Giddens's claim, structuration arises through interaction, not action. Flandrin argued that, by focusing on the average size of the household, Laslett failed to appreciate the significance of variations from the mean. One of Laslett's English village censuses from 1676 reveals that although the average size of households was 4.47 persons, over half the population of the village was living in the households of the twelve men who owned almost all the land, provided employment for other families, and were the political leaders of the village (Flandrin 1979: 57). The households of the poor were, on the other hand, very small. The poor had fewer children and only two of the twelve poorest households contained adult couples.

Flandrin concludes, 'the households of the poor were generally former households of [agricultural] labourers which had sunk into poverty on the death of the father of the family'. This unequal social structure was the consequence of enclosing the commons (ibid. 58–9).

Interaction between the Household and Longer Cycles

Households are not implicated merely in processes within the village. They also contribute to the global cycles identified by Braudel and Kondratiev. In all but the most urbanized *départements*, where it had already begun, migration within France got under way from 1856 as the French Industrial Revolution gathered pace (Bonneuil 1997: 76–9). Doubs emerges as part of the large region of population decline surrounding the city of Lyon (ibid. Fig. 9.2, 139). In 1855 Rousset noted that 'young people of both sexes, especially girls . . . [are emigrating] to become servants in Lyon or Paris, or primary school teachers in the *département*' (Rousset 1855, quoted in Daveau 1954: 129). Rousset observed a more alarming trend in 1863, reporting 'Cultivators are not attached to their status (*état*) and leave as soon as they expect to make a little more working in another profession. The price of an agricultural labourer's day's work has almost doubled' (Rousset 1863 [1992]: 23). By 1873 the region's agriculture was in crisis:

Complaints about the lack of capital are to be heard almost everywhere but for large and medium-scale agriculture the scarcity of rural labourers and the conse-quent rise in wages are considerable sources of difficulty and embarrassment. The scarcity of labour is undoubtedly the open wound (*la plaie vive*) in our agricul-tural system and the Agricultural Enquiry of 1866 has revealed no effective remedy. . . .

   The powerful attraction of the towns is incontrovertibly the principle cause, especially since railways have rendered them so easy of access. . . . The same phenomenon is manifest throughout most of Europe. It can only be corrected . . . in the course of time, when conditions enable great and novel advances allowing a greater reward for labour in agriculture.   (Laurens 1873: 161–2)

The strength of this author's language implies that rural life was under-going a transformation as keenly felt as that which has taken place since the 1950s.

   The alternative pathways through the household cycle recorded in late nineteenth-century households were not being followed in a stable social environment. In 1872 the Plateau of Levier was already experiencing rapid change. The population, which had risen more or less steadily since

TABLE 3.12. *Marital status and occupation in Dechailles, Pellaport, and La Combe Sainte-Marie, 1872 and 1972*

	Single (%)	Married (%)	Widowed (%)	Total no.
Cultivateurs, 1872	34	59	7	485
Cultivateurs, 1972	17	81.5	1.5	130
Labourers and servants, 1872	61	13	26	87
Factory workers, 1972	25	73.5	1.5	61

the Thirty Years War had begun to drop equally rapidly after 1850, when railways reached the region, and factories began to appear in towns such as Lyon and Besançon (cf. Netting 1981: 96). Whatever processes of social differentiation were at work in the second half of the nineteenth century have been overtaken by the intervention of the Industrial Revolution. The factory workers, who are (literally or by analogy) the descendants of the nineteenth-century agricultural labourers, have particularly benefited from the new economic conditions, achieving a higher rate of nuclear family households. The decline in adult celibacy has transformed the age structure of households over the last hundred years (see Table 3.12, and also Fig. 3.2).

Although the population of the Plateau of Levier began to decline sharply after 1850, the 1872 censuses seem at first to show little apparent change in household structure or occupation. The same crafts are represented (in fact, there are more craftsmen and women than in 1846). The increasing cost of hiring agricultural labourers may, however, have destroyed the viability of the smallest *exploitations*. In 1846 there were five *cultivateurs* living alone in Dechailles and seven *cultivateurs* who were single supporting parents with children under 18 years old (one man and six women). In 1872, only three people living alone were *cultivateurs* but another five were *journaliers*. All five single supporting mothers with children under 18 have become *journaliers*. The number of domestic servants has doubled and whereas only two households employed 2 servants in 1846, by 1872 eight households were employing 2 servants, perhaps because more households were compelled to send some children out to work.

The proportion of extended family households, and adult children

TABLE 3.13. *Household structure in Dechailles, 1846 and 1872*

	1846 (%)	1872 (%)
Single person	10	11
Married couple without children	11	16.5
Single parent, all children under 20	7	13.5
Nuclear family, all children under 20	27	25.5
Nuclear family, at least one child over 20	13	15
Unmarried, adult siblings (some with widowed parent)	12	8
Adult siblings, one married	4	5
Parent(s) with married child and grandchild(ren)	12	5.5
Other	4	
N =	114	112

resident in nuclear family households did not change dramatically between 1846 and 1872 (Table 3.13). Since mechanization in agriculture had not yet begun, and the cost of hiring *journaliers* had increased, there was all the more reason for *cultivateurs* to rely on their own family for labour. I will return to the history of household structure and agricultural labour in Ch. 6, which looks at how machines replaced manual work.

CONCLUSION: PRACTICAL CONSCIOUSNESS AND STRUCTURATION

Chapter 3 has explored continuity and change in household structure in the light of Giddens's concepts of agency and structuration. It has shown how the development of the household cycle exemplifies ways in which cultural strategies are translated into action. Contrary to Bourdieu's characterization of 'habitus', there is good evidence that cultural strategies are consciously pursued, even if their full effects may not be immediately apparent.

In Ch. 2 I argued that evolutionary theory can explain why there are limits to the possibilities of structuration. Historical variation in Europe supports the hypothesis that cultural strategies for household organiza-tion tend to converge on those which provide an effective adaptation to limited natural resources.

Hrdy and Judge (1993) found that, in North America, colonial farmers practised partible inheritance while land was plentiful, but switched to primogeniture when there was insufficient land to guarantee the success of each child on a separate holding. Franche-Comté, like many regions of the Alps, has continued to practice partible inheritance during periods of population increase yet even these regions took steps to prevent the uneconomic division of holdings. During the period when the 'European Marriage Pattern' emerged population density in the region of Pellaport trebled (see Ch. 2). The solution was not to abolish partible inheritance, but to impose celibacy on adult co-heirs, only allowing one son and one daughter to marry (Netting 1981: 169–85; Flandrin 1982: 79–81). Netting considered reduction in the birth rate to be one of the principal homeostatic mechanisms ensuring continuity in Törbel's social system. Three centuries of demographic data encompassing ten mortality crises showed that fertility rose to counter-balance high mortality and declined during periods of population growth (Netting 1981: 131–3, cf. Friedl 1974: 73).

In his 1803 *Essay on the Principle of Population,* Malthus proposed a homeostatic regulatory mechanism for mountain populations very similar to that later proposed by Netting, which forestalled the usual 'Malthusian cycle' of overpopulation cut back by famine and disease (Viazzo 1989: 7). Malthus argued that the peak demand for labour in the Alpine dairy economy occurred at harvest time, to obtain sufficient hay to feed stabled livestock through the winter. Since the productivity of meadows was determined by supply of manure, the available hay and livestock each limited the other. The number of livestock in turn limited the number of people who could survive and hence the available labour force. A peasant to whom Malthus spoke near the lac de Joux (only 20 km. from Levier) explained that, even though he himself had married young, late marriage was needed to prevent overpopulation and bring birth and death rates into equilibrium. Malthus noted that where cottage industry had provided alternative income, age at marriage fell and the population increased (Malthus 1973: 210–12; Viazzo 1989: 43–7).

It is consistent with Darwinian theory that disinherited younger brothers in Béarn could stay at home, and were considered ideal domestic servants, but were expected to invest time and emotion in helping to look after their older brother's children (Bourdieu 1990: 158). Celibates depend on their siblings' children to transmit their own genes (Hamilton 1964). Unigeniture is the rule in much of Austria, and the increased demand for labour during the first half of the nineteenth century was met by celibate siblings and servants. A massive surge in illegitimate births also occurred. Mitterauer argued that illegitimate children were a welcome addition to the rural lower stratum, from which the farmers could draw servants (Viazzo 1989: 188–92, cf. Mitterauer and Sieder 1982: 125–6). However, human social behaviour here passes beyond the limits of conventional Darwinian theory, since the notion of legitimate inheritance is a cultural construct. Servants and illegitimate children could not claim a share of the patrimony. The intervention of culture, in the definition of rights over property, causes social and genetic inheritance patterns to diverge. The social entitlement conferred by legitimacy, not genetic paternity, was critical in inheritance. Reproductive success cannot therefore be measured in simple biological terms, but must be related to the web of social relations that conditioned life-chances. For the purpose of working an *exploitation* the labour power of genetically unrelated labourers is as productive as that of heirs. *Cultivateurs* could enhance their own children's chances of survival and successful reproduction by harnessing the labour of labourers and servants (cf. Borgerhoff Mulder 1987).

The persistence of partible inheritance in northern France, and unigeniture in the south, shows how durable cultural strategies may be. Given the range of terrains across which the two modes of inheritance are practised, it would be difficult to argue they represent specific adaptations (Viazzo 1989: 221–3). It is more likely that they constitute alternative resolutions of the conflicting goals of catering for all heirs while preserving a viable holding. Where they are practised under similar ecological and demographic conditions the two strategies are modified to produce similar practices, but they continue to have different effects on the structuration of social relationships. Social interaction, not action, is the key to understanding how people's life-chances vary through time as local culture is enacted in a social and natural environment.

The conclusion to Ch. 2 noted the implication of Giddens's and Bourdieu's work for the study of the formation of shared meanings and interconnected roles. If there is no collective consciousness, how are patterns of thought and behaviour reproduced, and how do they converge to form a 'culture' or social system? Laslett (1972: 65) considered the habitual structures formed by households to be the outcome of socialization. People will tend to value and reproduce the family forms they experienced as children. How often, or for how long, must an element of habitus or practical consciousness be manifest for it to be transmitted? Laslett posed the question, how long, during the household cycle, must a three-generation family be realized for it to remain a known strategy? Shaffer argues that the rapid disappearance of large *communautés* on owner-occupied holdings after 1790 shows, contrary to Le Play's claim, that the institution had not been sustained by values inculcated in children but by parents' right to enforce unigeniture (Shaffer 1982: 83–90).

Partible inheritance is, none the less, preferred by those who practice it to the impartible inheritance known from neighbouring regions. The inhabitants of German-speaking Valais considered the impartible system of Tyrol 'unjust and inhuman' (Viazzo 1989: 95). Villagers in the Spanish province of León look upon the impartible inheritance practised in neighbouring Galicia 'with distaste' (Behar 1986: 34). Shaffer (1982: 7, 144, 197), arguing against Le Play and Laslett, disputes whether household types are norms valued in themselves; arguing they are instead the outcome of strategies. Household structure will change if a different strategy becomes more appropriate. Joint family households are readily abandoned when they no longer serve a purpose (ibid. 18). This does not deny the strategies' origin in culture. Sabean (1990: 184) criticizes the 'raw strategy' approach which replaced functionalism in anthropology, producing 'models of strategy or power and resistance at every point'. Property, he contended, can only be understood as the basis of arguments, of 'claims and obligations ranging from publicly backed principles embodied in codes to demands or requests on the most informal basis'. Strategies are not 'raw' but part of a cultural repertoire. The Nivernais, where Shaffer worked, straddles the boundary between open fields and bocage. The open field zone is associated with nucleated villages while the large multiple family households (*communautés*) were only found in the bocage zone (Shaffer 1982: 51–2). As Barthelemy (1988: 204) puts it, culture intervenes to provide (alternative) solutions to the problems posed by shelter, labour recruitment, the transmission of rights, and the extraction of surplus.

There is no doubt the enforcement of adult celibacy was a conscious policy, rather than merely the unintended outcome of a shortage of land, on the Plateau of Levier. In 1972 the *maire* of one village managed an *exploitation* jointly with his brother and their wives. The brothers had inherited the property when their parents retired to Pontarlier. Living in separate households under one roof, the two families had separate household budgets but a single budget for the *exploitation*. The *maire* contrasted this arrangement with the older pattern in which one brother married and the others were obliged to remain single for the good of the family. The latter had been common among richer families where there was a patrimony to preserve (*où il y avait un patrimoine à conserver*). Such households generally treated their inheritance as a joint holding, even though each nominally owned a certain part. In the old days the father had been a more authoritarian figure and it was usually he who arranged the single marriage. It is therefore vital to discover how cultural traits are transmitted. This topic is addressed in Chs. 4 and 5.

4

Habitus and the Quality of Community Life

Chapter 4 assesses the usefulness of Bourdieu's concept of habitus for the analysis of interpersonal relations and the rituals of daily life in Pellaport. Bourdieu introduced the concept of habitus to explain the connection between cognition and action. Habitus is similar to Giddens's concept of practical consciousness, that is, knowledge of the rules and tactics which constantly regenerate daily social routines. Bourdieu illustrates the way in which cognitive structures in the Kabyle habitus generate an indefinite number of new symbolic equations, which none the less follow an existing 'logic'. Each individual's habitus seems to be a structural variant of those learned by other members of the community. Bourdieu begins to explain why the habitus of each member of the Kabyle community converges with that of others and I try to take Bourdieu's argument further through the concept of evolutionarily stable strategies (Maynard Smith 1982). According to Bourdieu habitus is learned and used unreflectively, not through conscious, strategic calculation. Indeed, Bourdieu argues the habitus of gift-exchange among the Kabyle is built on a misrecognition of social inequality and power, rather than on a rational strategy. This chapter argues to the contrary that gift-giving has a rational basis which is usefully distinguished from market transactions and which contributes to the convergence of villagers' practical consciousness.

VALUES AND INTERACTION

Learning by Experience

Two days after I arrived in Pellaport in mid-February 1969, I visited Maurice Genre and his wife, a couple of *cultivateurs* in their thirties. The husband's aunt, who lived in a first-floor flat, was talking with them in their kitchen. She told me forthrightly that the English should stay in England and the French in France. The young today are far too inquisitive, she said. Why did I want to see their stable? During the Second World War there had been people like me in the village asking questions and making them all work like beasts. Although the latter remark had some historical justification, her behaviour struck me as out of keeping with the way in which I had been received in other households. Six days later I visited a household where the husband, M. Jouffroy, worked as a mason in a neighbouring village. When asked how I had been received in Pellaport I replied that, with one exception, everyone had been friendly. Next time I visited M. Jouffroy's his mother confided she knew exactly who it was who had been hostile to me. 'Don't worry,' she said, 'that woman is not quite right in the head; she is not *gentille* (gracious).' It occurred to me that *gentil* was a word I had taken to using myself during the intervening fortnight although, on reflection, it was not one that figured in my O Level French course. Prosper Jouffroy and his wife also soon told me the old lady was not solid in the head, and not *gentille*. They imitated how she had waved her arms in the air as she told them about all the questions I had asked her nephew, and told me not to worry about her. They asked if I had been able to return to the stable where I had felt ill during milking (see Ch. 6). I said no, they had refused to let me in again. Prosper responded that he was not surprised, they were *fier* (proud) in that household.

One week after my arrival I described to Alexandre and Catherine Maitrugue how my original plan to work in Vaux had been thwarted by the unavailability of lodgings, and how Mme Bavarel had taken me in. Catherine consoled me with the remark that people in Vaux were *fier* because they had larger *exploitations* than the people of Pellaport. On the other hand, she continued, one would have to go many miles to find a woman as thoughtful and gracious as Mme Bavarel. It quickly became clear that the three terms *gentil, fier,* and *fou* (crazy) were key to understanding the way that interpersonal relationships in the village were constructed and evaluated. Many told me that people in Vaux were *fier*. The fact that I had failed to find accommodation in Vaux cemented my relationships with people in Pellaport. The only person who told me I would have done better to work in Vaux was a mechanic I met servicing someone's milking machine, who said agriculture in Vaux was far more advanced than in Pellaport.

During my first visit to M. Jouffroy the mason, I asked how the Jouffroys of the village were related. They told me that, unlike the Bavarels and Maitrugues, there were no family nicknames among the

Jouffroys, although they could not say exactly how they were all related. I followed this up the same evening, while watching milking in Victor Jouffroy's stable. Victor's wife told me it was true that there were no family nicknames among the Jouffroys but, strictly within the family and never to Felicien's face, his household was known as *chez* le Turk, because Felicien could be pretty fierce when he lost his temper. Soon after, I learnt that César Maitrugue's father had been known as Le Seigneur, which had given rise to the custom of calling the family house Le Château. Derogatory nicknames are commonly used in Mediterranean communities (Gilmore 1982: 686), although it has been argued that family nicknames predominate in northern or 'Atlantic' Europe (Pina-Cabral 1984: 149). Both Gilmore and Pina-Cabral associate the prevalence of offensive nicknames with 'honour cultures'.

Prosper Jouffroy explained to me that many people in the village had nicknames. Some were diminutives (although Prosper did not use this term himself) that originated within the family. Nicolas Jouffroy was known as Nounou, because that was what his mother called him when he was a child. Mme Bavarel was known as Bebette, Victor Jouffroy as Vicci, Prosper himself was called Propo. These were names which were used between friends. Other nicknames were descriptive. One man had been known as Le Pipe, because he always smoked a pipe. Pierre Bavarel and his brother, the village mason, were sometimes referred to as *chez* le Coucou because there had been a cuckoo clock in the family home when they were growing up. Other nicknames were more insulting and not to be used to people's faces. César Maitrugue's father had been known as Le Seigneur partly because his house overlooked the village, but partly because he was a proud man. César's wife's father had been known as Le Douanier (the customs officer) because of his officiousness. Yet, Prosper, emphasized, neither Le Seigneur nor Le Douanier had been *méchant* (malicious). Other such nicknames included Le Cerf (the stag), applied to Jacques Maitrugue's father, who walked with his head held high, Le Deputé (The MP, or Member of Parliament), and Le Pasha.

Despite Prosper's disclaimer, such ironic titles should not be used to a person's face. Claude Bavarel told me how a group of men had been drinking in the café one Sunday morning. Someone stood up to buy the next round and asked what everyone wanted. '*Et toi, Deputé?*' he enquired. Le Deputé promptly punched him in the face for using the offensive nickname. Everybody rushed to calm the two men and someone else began to take the next order instead. Slightly inebriated, he too forgot himself in the excitement: '*Et toi, Deputé?*' he asked. . . .

It was these values that generated people's reactions to even the smallest of gestures that might be construed as setting oneself apart from the body of the community, such as Étienne Quintaux's wandering away from the group in the forest, Felix Viennet's becoming caught on the roll of barbed wire after working on the commons, and Nicolas Jouffroy's sitting apart with his young daughter during the cereal harvest (see Ch. 1). Many other examples came to light during the year. Two cousins living in the coin de la Combe had argued over the cost of building a retaining wall between their manure piles and eventually built two walls, side by side. Their neighbours remarked on the pride of one, Le Deputé, which had prevented him reaching an agreement (unfortunately it was in this man's stable that I felt ill while watching milking). César Maitrugue's brother Eduard, who had worked most of his adult life as baker in another village, returned to Pellaport on retirement and immediately fell out not only with his brother César, but also with his brother-in-law Claude Bavarel and his neighbour the *maire*. Various malicious acts such as the breaking of a water conduit and the slashing of tyres on a trailer, which subsequently came to light, were attributed to this irascible man. Eduard bought a cow and, although he did not join the dairy co-operative, he managed a small *exploitation* with the help of César and Claude. I was surprised they were still willing to help him. Claude's son told me his father was keeping the memory of Eduard's past activities in his head. People did draw the line at some behaviour. One man told me whom he had worked for recently, including Maurice Genre. 'But never again,' he added, 'after what Maurice's aunt said to me.' He went on to suggest other people I might talk to on the subject of *entr'aide* (mutual help), including Maurice. 'Not him,' his wife interjected, '*ils sont fous là*'. Long after 1969 Eduard Maitrugue committed suicide having, I was told, eventually alienated himself from all his relatives and neighbours. Interestingly, women are not given ironic titles. Gilmore (1982: 687) reports this also to be the case in Mediterranean communities. Even the 'crazy' old woman was referred to simply by prefixing her Christian name with 'la' (La Thérèse).

Key Terms in the Discourse on Community Life

When I felt that I knew people sufficiently well, I began to interview them in more detail about the meanings of the words *gentil*, *fier*, and *fou*. Some were nonplussed by my question, 'Qu'est-ce que c'est d'être gentil?', replying, 'Mais c'est la gentillesse, quoi!' Others were more reflective.

Prosper Jouffroy said that it was easy to explain what it meant to be *gentil*: it meant to respect people, and even animals; to like everyone, to be aimiable towards your neighbours, to say good-day to those whom you meet. Being *gentil* also entailed helping those in need, such as someone who was ill by the roadside, or whose car had broken down. In agriculture, although the practice had almost disappeared, if you have already completed a task you help others who are still working at it.

What it meant to be *fier* was, he thought, harder to fathom (*approfondir*). There were different ways of demonstrating pride. The crucial question was whether one was *méchant* (malicious). The first thing was to consider whether a person had pride in themselves. Did they dress well, and keep their house in good order? Did they take a pride in their work? If one did not take pride in oneself, one's work would never be good. Those who are *fou* work like pigs. On the other hand, some are proud without justification. Those who were *orgueilleux* (haughty or arrogant) were worthless. I asked what kind of pride had led to men being given nicknames such as Le Deputé or Le Pasha. They were the people who wanted to dominate others, Prosper replied. Le Pasha, for example, always spoke slowly and ponderously, as if he wished to give his words greater weight than they deserved. There were many ways of being proud. One policeman could be proud that he had never sent anyone to prison, another could take pride in meticulously noting the faults of each offender. Jealousy was worse than pride. It was jealousy that led people to call their neighbour a pig just because he owned a bigger tractor. Jealousy always leads to malice and rancour (*la rancune*). Rancour causes you to find fault with everything your neighbour does and results in actions such as slashing your neighbour's trailer tyres, as had happened in Pellaport not many years before.

When I asked about the meaning of the word *fou* Prosper at first questioned its relevance, saying there were many ways of being mad: through love, through drink, through being driven by overweening pride to work with *colère* (fury, passion). Poor work is caused by negligence, not madness, he said. But, he added, he could tell me who were mad in Pellaport. Maurice Genre, who refused to hire the combine harvester, was a good case. It ran in the family: I already knew his aunt and I could ask Claude Bavarel about his father, if I wished. Felix Viennet planted potatoes but did nothing to tend them afterwards, not even ploughing furrows between the rows. Both Maurice and Felix were *fou*, because they worked in a fashion entirely contrary to everybody else.

The curé gave similar characterizations. To be *gentil* meant to be at others' service, to have relations with everyone, not just one's friends; willing to accept others as they were, regardless of their faults and idio-syncrasies. Everyone has their worries, but that should not deter them from smiling and being cheerful. To be *gentil* is to be *mignon* (sweet or neat). *La fierté* is not wholly bad, 'il faut une certaine fierté, mais non pas d'être glorieux' (one must have a certain pride, but not be vainglorious). The opposite of graciousness is to be morose, 'On n'est pas bien avec lui' (one is not at ease with such a person). Thinking one had no need of others underlay *l'orgueil* (arrogance); the day there is no arrogance it will be heaven on earth.

Nicolas and Colette Jouffroy told me that if you are *gentil* you do not refuse when someone asks for help, even if you have your own work to do. The important thing was to be *serviable* (willing, obliging). The opposite of *la gentillesse* is *la méchanceté* (malice, spitefulness). 'Who is to say who is *gentil* and who isn't?' Nicolas asked, rhetorically, 'one person may find you *gentil* and another not.' 'We are proud enough,' he continued, on the subject of *la fierté*, 'everyone is proud of their own courage, of their labour. Perhaps there is something arrogant *(orgueilleux)* about it, who knows? He who is the most intrepid is the proudest.' Nicolas considered jealousy to be worse than envy, although according to the dictionary the latter was a greater sin (he looked it up as we were talking). Jealousy is more malicious. When you want for yourself what others have, you become *fou*. If one is *fou*, 'On ne répond plus à ses actes' (one is no longer answerable for one's actions), a very unfortunate condition. It was not just jealousy that could drive you crazy; happiness could have the same effect.

Alexandre Maitrugue considered that to be *gentil* meant to be calm, to be gracious towards your wife and children, to be content and not pick quarrels with your neighbours. Arrogance, surliness, and malice were the opposites of graciousness; these were the qualities that led someone to pick quarrels. I asked Alexandre about jealousy. He was of the opinion that you could be jealous of your neighbour having twenty cows when you only had ten, yet still invite him in for a drink. Some people keep their jealousy to themselves and others let it show. Catherine, his wife, ques-tioned whether this was possible. Many recognized that the number of machines or cattle someone owned might cause jealousy but, as Claude Bavarel put it, I may be proud of my cattle; the important thing is not to draw attention to the fact.

Prosper was not alone in thinking that social traits ran in families. The secretary of the dairy co-operative and his wife referred to one family who were not disagreeable, but who stood on their dignity. It was their *allure* (demeanour). They were ready enough to help when asked. Pride made one distant, cold towards others, unsociable, interested in oneself but not others. Pride was similar to egoism. Graciousness, on the other hand, was demonstrated in amiability, cheerfulness, politeness, willingness to help. Bebette Bavarel and her brothers were outstanding examples. The secretary went on to discuss a man who was *gentil*, but whose daughter was quite the opposite, saying it was bizarre to find such differences in one family (many also remarked in 1995 that Bebette Bavarel's *gentillesse* had been inherited by her son). Abélès (1991) recorded a similar belief in Burgundy concerning families' eligibility for public office (and see Wylie 1966: 194). When I began to read the documents preserved in the village hall I discovered that the antipathy towards Vaux went back at least to the eighteenth century, when the two villages were engaged in a series of disputes over access to shared high pasture and forest (some examples were quoted in Ch. 2).

Felicien Jouffroy and his wife told me that *la gentillesse* was above all a matter of goodwill, although it could be applied to anything that gave pleasure, even a small creature such as a kitten (the word *mignon*, cited by the curé, can also be used of kittens). Claude Bavarel described how, when he sold his livestock on being called up at the start of the Second World War, his mother had said to him, 'There's one little cow there who is 3 years old, *elle est bien gentille* (really gracious), easy to milk.' She asked him to let them keep that one, even though they were too old to look after the others.

Like his half-brother Prosper, Felicien distinguished between the pride in one's work that gave one pleasure, and the conceitedness that made people think they were better than others. Pierre Bavarel drew the same distinction when I spoke to him later the same day, saying 'C'est la fierté de l'un contre l'autre qui fait du mal.' Those who think themselves better than others pride themselves above their neighbours and won't say good-day to you in the street. Felicien and his wife said the term *fou* could be applied to anyone who behaved bizarrely. If you saw someone doing something unreasonable, you would dismiss his actions by saying, 'Oh, he's crazy!' But, Felicien added, this kind of foolishness should not be confused with the folly of a madman. Someone else referred to the occasion when a man from another village had wandered into the forest and become lost, initiating a large-scale search. No one in Pellaport, he said, is that mad: 'Les fous ne sont pas tellement malins' (*malin* means sharp).

Hints of a similar system appear in the ethnography of Minot. Newly wedded couples who successfully hide from the wedding guests are said to be '*fier*' because they have refused to join in the game (Verdier 1979: 292). An untidy forecourt in Minot attracts criticism. Celibate adults become the butt of jokes and take up the role of village clown (Zonabend 1984: 20, 100). Fickle girls may have a tub of manure deposited on their doorstep (Verdier 1979: 68).

Intersubjective Understanding

Before postmodern anthropology had drawn attention to the fictitious character of Durkheim's 'collective consciousness', George Kelly investigated personal variation in subjective experience through his theory of Personal Constructs (Kelly 1963).[1] Kelly argued that individuals represent their environment by means of a hierarchy of constructs which are strengthened, revised, or abandoned in the light of subsequent experience. Personal constructs are said to be based on similarity and contrast; the individual opposes good to bad, black to white. They differ from the constructs of conventional logic to the extent that conventional logic would oppose *white* to *not-white*, including within the latter category both the contrasting and the irrelevant. Personal constructs, according to Kelly, have a specified range of applicability and exclude the irrelevant. It is meaningful to say one's shoes are *white*, but not to say this of the time of day. Kelly described two ways in which one constructed opposition may subsume another. It may do so by making one opposition analogous to another, so that *intelligent* is to *good* as *stupid* is to *bad*:

$$\frac{\text{good} : \text{bad}}{\text{intelligent} : \text{stupid}}$$

or it may subsume one opposition under one term in an overarching opposition:

```
   evaluation : description
    /     \      /      \
good  :  bad   black  :  white
```

Individuals articulate their hierarchy of personal constructs in different ways; for some the *white : not white* opposition is purely descriptive, as in the above example, but for racists it becomes an evaluative opposition.

---

[1] Barbara Lloyd, of the Psychology Department at the University of Sussex, drew my attention to the usefulness of Kelly's theory as a means of analysing variations in the way that people in Pellaport constructed the oppositions between *gentil, fier*, and *fou* (see Layton 1971: 108–11).

Kelly also argued that an apparently agreed term, such as *kind* may in fact be construed differently, according to the terms which are opposed to it in individuals' personal constructs.

kind : { cruel
         tough
         critical

Kelly's theory usefully identifies two sources of variation in the personal construction of meaning in Pellaport, within the general framework provided by the terms *gentil, fier,* and *fou*. One results from the ambiguous position of the term *fier*, which tends to stray across the *sociable : non-sociable* opposition. In one construction, the terms are opposed as follows:

sociable : non–sociable
   | /   \
gentil fier : fou

In another, the oppositions appear as follows:

sociable : non–sociable
gentil : pas gentil
fierté de soi-même : fierté de l'un contre l'autre

The second lies in the way that different terms are opposed to the key construct *gentil*, or the varying synonyms for *fou*, implying different degrees of tolerance towards the behaviour of others:

gentil is not: { aloof
                   arrogant   *fou* is { different to others
                   malicious   irresponsible
                                             bizarre

Kelly (1963: 94) argued that the potential diversity of personal constructs is limited by a common cultural background.

The psychology of personal constructs (is) an anticipatory theory of behaviour . . . not only in terms of personal outlook . . . but also in terms of what the individual anticipates others will do and, in turn, what he thinks they are expecting him to do. . . . People belong to the same cultural group not merely because they behave alike, nor because they expect the same things of others, but especially because they construe their experience the same way

From an interactionist, or postmodern viewpoint, this is at best only half the story, since the cultural background must itself be seen as the product of past negotiation and constantly liable to decompose if the negotiation of intersubjective understanding breaks down. Other members of the Sussex University research project reported different usages in other regions of France (Hutson 1971; Blaxter 1971). The Austrian sociologist Schutz (1972 [1932]: 139) coined the term 'intersubjectivity' to describe the condition in which we experience the world as something whose significance we share with others. To intuit the subjective meanings another person attributes to the world, Schutz argued, we try to imagine the 'project' in which the other is engaged but, to the extent that our previous experiences differ, we can never fully achieve intersubjective understanding. The concluding sections of the chapter will return to the kinds of clues villagers have to each others' 'projects', and how these might be identified by the anthropologist.

INTERPERSONAL BEHAVIOUR

There are two aspects to interpersonal relations in Pellaport, providing reciprocal help (*entr'aide*) and signalling sociability through greetings or other forms of signifying behaviour.

Mutual Aid

From time to time every household needs help from neighbours or relatives. Although labour should first come from within the household, sooner or later illness, the size of a task, or the kind of equipment needed stretch a household's resources beyond its limits. In 1969, people often helped each other in agricultural tasks, house repairs, or felling and transporting firewood from the forest for the winter months. Some examples have been given in Ch. 1. Augustins and Barthelemey argued that one of the aims of partible inheritance was to create a network of interpersonal links in a community (see Ch. 7) and the patrilineal links highlighted through the use of family sobriquets were not given particular weight in Pellaport's network of mutual aid. The dense network of bilateral kinship relationships in Pellaport is shown in Fig. 4.1. When Victor Jouffroy put two heifers in his wife's father's orchard he asked his wife's mother's brother to help. I asked the older man why he had been called upon. 'Because I'm his uncle,' he replied. Brothers-in-law often worked together. Maurice Maitrugue helped his wife's brother plant potatoes. In return, his brother-in-law helped Maurice repair his roof. Pierre Bavarel and his sister's husband Étienne Maitrugue shared a muck-spreader. Another villager once commented, 'those two run their *exploitations* almost as one'. Although this was an exaggeration, it was noticeable that

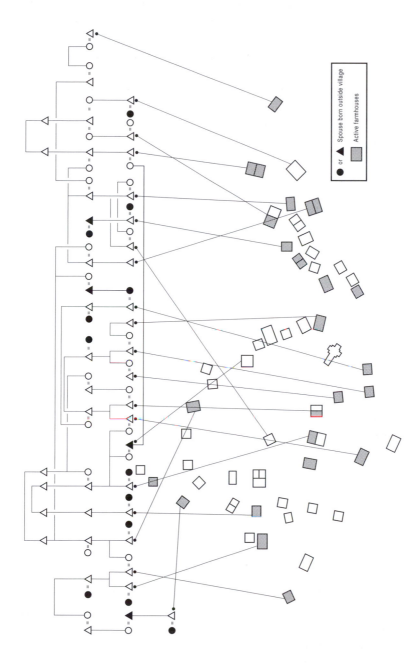

FIG. 4.1. The ties of kinship and affinity linking farming families

Étienne preferred to work with Pierre, who had a similar-sized *exploita-tion*, than with his brother Alexandre whose *exploitation* was smaller and less mechanized. Victor Jouffroy preferred to work with his mother's brother's son Jacques Maitrugue than with his older second cousin Feli-cien. Victor justified this on the grounds that Jacques was a *cousin germain* and his own age (they also had two of the largest *exploitations* in the village).

In principle, kin are expected to provide help before unrelated neigh-bours. One *cultivateur* told me that people most often helped those who were *de la même parenté* (kin). Although one might help unrelated neigh-bours from time to time he himself would only assist his cousins. Although *reciprocité* was normal, once one began to work for unrelated neighbours they might demand too much and he did not have enough free time for that. Claude Bavarel told me that, while you would first ask a kinsman for help, you might then go to an unrelated neighbour. I asked if this imposed a greater obligation to reciprocate but Claude replied, 'Non, rendre service, c'est quand même rendre service' (no, to give help is, after all, to give help). He recalled having mown 30 ares of hay for Felix Vien-net's unmarried uncle when the old man was ill, and he had expected nothing in return. 'In any case,' Claude added, 'he's dead now.' When I suggested that Felix might have inherited his uncle's debts, Claude retorted that Felix himself was indebted to him. A third *cultivateur* with whom I discussed this issue said that one might work as well with kin or neighbours. The important factor was that there should be *une bonne entente* (a good understanding) between the participants. Life in Pellaport is not all friendly co-operation. Disputes sometimes break out and it is usually kin and neighbours who quarrel.

Occasionally there were more serious demands for non-reciprocal help. During 1967 Felix Viennet had to go into hospital for an operation and 'the whole village' helped with his harvest. In the summer of 1968 Maurice Maitrugue fell from a ladder while repairing his roof and broke his leg in several places. He and his wife had no children and his father died in 1948. 'The whole village' turned out to harvest his hay. Then, at the beginning of winter, snow fell earlier than expected while Pierre Bavarel was enlarging his stable. He had demolished a large part of one wall and, as snow drifted against the part which was still standing, it collapsed leaving half of his house in ruins. Again, I was told, 'the whole village' came to help. Some *cultivateurs* came down from Montoiseau. Pierre's wife's brother travelled over from La Combe Sainte-Marie (4 km. away). Mme Bavarel provided meals for everyone while they worked. The phrase 'the whole village' distinguishes this kind of assistance from the reciprocal exchanges which create continuing relationships between kin and neighbours. Barth (1976*b*) describes a similar distinction between reciprocal beer parties in Darfur, at which routine agricultural tasks are performed, and non-reciprocal beer parties organized for special activities such as house building. Networks of reciprocal, non-contractual assistance are integral to peasant life throughout the world (Panter-Brick 1993; Erasmus 1955). They constitute what Scott (1976) called 'the moral economy of the peasant'.

Blau (1964) argued that there are only three possible outcomes from social exchange. An individual for whom a service has been performed is expected to return the service on another occasion. If he does, then the other is encouraged to offer further services and a bond is established between the two. A person who persists in seeking help even though he is unable to reciprocate subordinates himself to the other who provides what he seeks. One who has the means to reciprocate but refuses to do so asserts his superiority. Blau's three possible outcomes correspond to the three terms current in Pellaport, *gentil, fou*, and *fier*: the person who reciprocates is *gentil*, the person who is incapable of doing so is *fou*, the person who wilfully refuses to do so is *fier*.

Unlike the relationships undertaken at marriage or when joining an agricultural co-operative, those established through mutual aid are not contractual. The distinction was deliberately upheld by villagers, who emphasized that both contractual and non-contractual relationships have their proper place in village life. When I first analysed mutual aid in the village (Layton 1971), I referred to the relationships built up as 'informal' relationships. This now seems a misleading term. Non-contractual relationships do not lack formalities. Rather, because they are non-contractual, villagers are free to create, and contest, them without interference from beyond the village. It is a field where it is within the power of villagers to construct 'authorized interpretations' of the validity of each others' actions.

Entr'aide (mutual aid) is expressly not conducted for financial reward, nor should a precise check be kept upon one's debt or credit in terms of hours of labour contributed. The important thing is that there should *une bonne entente* (a good understanding) between those involved. Although the obligation to return services rendered is not made explicit, it is undeniably recognized. Those who seek help without later returning it are either mocked for their foolishness, if they seem incapable of recognizing their obligations, or, if they seem to withhold reciprocal aid they could well have provided, they are criticized for their pride.

If one is *fou, on ne repond plus à ses actes* (one is no longer answerable for one's actions). Someone who is willing to pay the cost of being ridiculed can take advantage of this waiver. It excuses people who constantly need help but are not in a position to return it. For example Felix Viennet, the village fool, had a small *exploitation* but many young children, and frequently needed help with his agricultural tasks.

It would be virtually impossible to quantify the amount of interpersonal assistance given and received on the basis of one person's field observation. Fortunately, and notwithstanding the rule that no account should be kept of hours worked in the course of giving or receiving mutual aid, Joseph Bavarel's *Livre de Mémoire* for the years between 1957 and 1981 notes assistance received from friends and neighbours, and help he gave to others. The totals per year range from zero to eight man/days' help received and from zero to three man/days' help rendered. Joseph did not have a reputation for taking more than he gave. If the completeness of his records of mutual aid is of the same order as his records of the essential elements of the agricultural year, I estimate that it is likely he gave and received up to twelve man/days' help a year. The kind of work involved included clearing brushwood from fields after the *remembrement*, sawing firewood, setting up electric fences, conversions to his cellar and cow byre, sowing, and harvesting.

RITUALS IN VILLAGE LIFE

A comparison of the rituals of daily life with the more elaborate local rites of passage throws light on their capacity to communicate information about people's dispositions and intentions. I compare the two types of ritual and then analyse them in light of communication theory.

Signalling Intentions

The three terms *gentil, fier,* and *fou* refer to states of mind which are themselves unknowable to others and only revealed in outward behaviour. Two kinds of behaviour are symptomatic of the actor's state of mind; the substantial transactions that form the content of interpersonal relations, and the more frequent but less energy-consuming signals that constitute interpersonal ritual.

The essential signals of the person who is *gentil* are those of a friendly greeting. Acquaintances nod and call out 'Bonjour'. If they make bodily contact it is by shaking hands. There is a limit to how often one can do this. As Nicolas Jouffroy put it, 'How many people are there in this village? You can't shake hands with the same person ten times in a morning!' It is better, he explained, to make a joke (*une boutade*) to ease the situation.

> *Vous l'avez vu?* (Did you see it?) one calls out as he passes.
> *Quoi ?* (What?) demands the other.
> *Mon cul!* (My bum!), slapping his backside as he hurries away.

Some jokes had been so overused that it was no longer witty (*une affaire de l'esprit*) to produce them. The three retired brothers over the road, who had been the last to use oxen, were for ever calling out, if you were loading a trailer with manure, *Ça charge?* Or, if you were cutting firewood, *Ça coupe?* He found that irritating. Another overused expression, if you saw someone picking apples in a tree, was to call out, 'It'll be fine weather tomorrow'. When the other asked why, you reply, 'Because the monkeys are climbing!' (The joke is a play on the saying that when *escargots* climb trees, dry weather is on the way.) *Copains* (close friends) slap each other on the back rather than shake hands. This is why the dairyman refused to shake Maurice Maitrugue's hand on the morning the wholesaler's lorry arrived to collect the cheese (see Ch. 1). The distinction between acquaintance and friend corresponds to that between individuals who have built up a relationship based on regular mutual aid, and membership of a community who can all be called upon to help in a crisis.

It was recognized by those with whom I discussed interpersonal relations that one's signals might be misleading. People can be friendly to your face, but malicious behind your back. People can appear proud through their demeanour, yet prove willing to help when the need arises. I met two cases where relationships had broken down, one between an uncle and nephew, the other between two women who were neighbours, in which both parties to the relationship claimed it had come to an end when the other stopped calling out a greeting in the street. Children are as well aware as anyone of the fact that producing the right signals is a social skill and can rapidly switch to the appropriate behaviour on the arrival of adults. This is no doubt because they are taught to adopt the correct 'front' (cf. Goffman 1969). In 1969 one commonly heard verbal exchanges such as the following:

> Mother, on meeting neighbour, to child: *Dis 'Bonjour' au monsieur.*
> The child (coyly): *Bonjour.*
> The neighbour: *Mais, comme elle est gentille, la petite.*

The proud person deliberately avoids interaction by staying indoors or, if he goes out, walks down the street with chin up and eyes ahead, avoiding the acknowledgement of others. Beyond these agreed core signals, a host of deeds or statements can be interpreted as symptoms of overweening pride: campaigning too loudly for election to office, telling others how to do their work, demanding respect by virtue of holding an elected position. Being one of the largest-scale *cultivateurs*, Nicolas was well aware of the ambiguity of actions which might be construed as justifiable pride in oneself, or unjustifiable pride over others, as he showed in his explanation of what it meant to be *fier*.

As far as I could discover, there was no standard way of signalling that one was *fou*, perhaps because the condition was held to be involuntary. The nearest equivalent was talking or singing to oneself. Felix Viennet was nicknamed Aline, after his fondness for singing a song which began 'Aline dans son jardin fleuri', as he went about his work. Although it was a universal practice in the early years of the century (Bouveresse 1989: 80–1, Clade 1994: 80), people who left their piles of manure in the street in 1969 risked being characterized as *fou*. 'They live like pigs.' Many idiosyncratic actions can become symptomatic of irresponsibility. One of Felix's neighbours told me he had once watched Felix wheel the tank he used to take water to his cattle up to the stone trough behind the church, fill it, and wheel it back, without apparently thinking of connecting it to his tractor.

The Celebration of Marriage

Marriage is a contractual relationship whose obligations are defined in law. In the total ceremony there are three strands: the civil marriage, the celebration of mass, and local rituals. Civil marriage (entering the legal contract) is conducted in the Mairie, the offices of the municipal council. The *maire* officiates. Civil marriage almost invariably then receives Catholic blessing at a special mass. The local rituals performed in 1969 were expected to begin outside the Mairie and continue through the day into the early hours of the following morning.

The only wedding at which I observed the initial elements of the rituals described to me was at the marriage of the daughter of the *maire* of Montoiseau to a man from a village 7 km. away. These are performed by *les conscrits*, the youths who were 18 at the New Year. Because there were so few *conscrits* in the community the youths of Pellaport and Montoiseau called on their younger brothers and the 17-year-olds to help them. When the couple make their marriage vows at the Mairie, the *conscrits*, who are stationed outside the building, fire blank cartridges (which they have prepared the previous evening by emptying out the shot) from their shot-guns. In 1969 the *conscrits* waited in Pellaport for the procession of cars to come down the hill from Montoiseau and hid behind the buttresses of the church to fire their guns. When the couple emerge from the church after mass the *conscrits* hold a white ribbon across the churchyard gate and demand money from the groom.

When the couple have been released everyone retires to the bride's father's house and festivities begin. In the evening the *conscrits* milk his cattle and clean out the stable before joining the guests. On the first night of their marriage the newly wedded couple are expected to sleep in the bride's village. They secretly arrange a bed for the night with a sympathetic household and somehow manage to leave the festivities unobserved at around midnight. Two hours later the guests set out with *le garçon et la fille d'honneur*, the boy and girl who accompanied the bride to church, and exercise their right to enter any house in the village in search of the couple. Should they be found, the mattress is overturned and the bride and groom are rolled out of bed then obliged to drink champagne from a chamber-pot in which float bananas or chocolate fondue. If the couple are successful in hiding, the guests turn instead upon *le garçon et fille d'honneur*, transporting them through the streets in one of the wheelbarrows normally used to carry dung out of the stables, and overturning any wagons which they find standing out of doors. Clade writes that in the neighbouring *département* of Haute-Saône the couple are themselves wheeled through the village by *le garçon d'honneur* (Clade 1994: 162–3). Recalling an episode at the New Year when the *conscrits* had behaved too exuberantly at Montoiseau, the bride's father insisted the couple sleep at the groom's village, to which the guests drove at two in the morning. In 1972, another wedding took place while I was in Pellaport. There were no *conscrits* (they were away at school or work), but the search through the village took place with great vigour. It was foiled by the couple's having arranged with the bride's uncle Maurice Maitrugue to sleep in his barn, climbing in through a ladder he had casually left standing, some days previously, at a window to the hayloft.

Firing guns and binding the couple at the churchyard gate were said to have originated in the distant past as a means of expressing disapproval at men from other villages who took the community's girls in marriage. Now, however, they were done at all marriages. A man whose daughter's wedding was not marked in this way would consider it a gesture of ostracism by his fellow villagers. Was the firing of the guns simply a way of celebrating, or are all couples treated in effect as if they were 'outsiders' passing through what van Gennep called a liminal or marginal phase? The hunt through the village and the overturning of the bed were explained as good-humoured entertainment: 'C'est simplement une plaisanterie, une farce que l'on fait aux jeunes mariés, car dans le noces on aime bien rire et faire des farces.' It is true that marriage is an occasion for verbal jokes. At the 1969 wedding the bride's father repeatedly pointed out to the guests that he was both *maire* and *père* to his daughter.

Pellaport is not the only place where the young, unmarried men of the village occupied a privileged role in ridiculing the unpopular (Behar 1986: 47; Verdier 1979: 210). Perhaps this was a consequence of their marginal status, between child and adult. The firing of guns, the search, and drinking from the chamber-pot are all known in Minot (see Verdier 1979: 290–2; Zonabend 1984: 104, 110). Both Verdier (ibid. 294) and van Gennep note the custom of searching out the newly wedded couple and giving them something special to eat or drink is widespread in France and recorded from the Middle Ages onwards. In Minot, the couple used to be given sugared wine called *la gruotte*. The name has now been transferred to the contents of the chamber-pot that replaced sugared wine three-quarters of a century ago. The search has itself been brought to an end in Minot by the custom of holding the wedding feast in a restaurant some miles from the village (ibid. 332). Before the Second World War van Gennep (1946: 442) reported it had been customary in Franche-Comté to barricade the Mairie door or entrance to the church with rocks or sticks, to hinder the couple's entry. These obstructions had been replaced more recently with a ribbon. He considered the firing of guns to be one of the most characteristic elements of French weddings over the last three centuries, but only since 1870 had it been organized by *les conscrits*. Van Gennep's survey suggested the custom was disappearing rapidly by the end of the nineteenth century since, in his view, military service had taught the young to be more careful with their guns and the price of powder and shooting permits had increased (431–3). On the other hand, all efforts to ban the search for the couple, on the grounds of its immorality, had failed. He interpreted drinking from the chamber-pot filled with white wine and chocolate as truly 'primitive', part of a magical system in which excrement was eaten as protection against the evil eye or malevolent spirits. Curiously, although the custom was very widespread in France, the only part of Franche-Comté in which it was reported to van Gennep was the district of Montbéliard (ibid. 561–70).

When I returned in 1986 Renée Bavarel told me the old wedding customs, even holding the ribbon across the churchyard gate, had been 'suppressed'. The house-to-house search was, however, alive and well. Perhaps surprisingly, it was still flourishing in 1995. Specially decorated souvenir chamber-pots can be bought in Pontarlier and young couples proudly display them on their dressers. A new custom, symptomatic of the rise in private car ownership, had appeared: the couple and their guests drove noisily round and round the village in ribbon-bedecked cars. The first time I saw this, in 1986, a decorated bed was towed behind the leading car. By 1995, the firing of guns had been forgotten, although car horns made plenty of noise. When I asked why no guns were fired at the wedding of the son and daughter of two village families during my field-work, the sons of Pierre Bavarel and Jacques Maitrugue denied that the custom had ever existed. Claude Bavarel's youngest son attributed the custom's disappearance to the declining number of *conscrits*. In his year there were thirteen but nowadays only one or two children are born in the village each year. Forgetting that guns were ever fired in Pellaport shows how quickly traits can disappear from the cultural repertoire once they are no longer performed, contrasting markedly with the durability of customs such as partible inheritance.

Reading Signals

The concepts represented by *la gentillesse, la fierté*, and *la folie* enable people to generate their own realm of meaning out of their neighbours' actions. This entails the interpretation of both deliberate signals and the unintentional display of symptoms indicative of mental states (Goffman 1969: 22). The rituals of interpersonal life and those accompanying marriage differ in the extent to which they convey information. The status of those getting married and the legal obligations they incur are clear, but the standing of one's kin and neighbours in interpersonal relations and the rights and duties they acknowledge is less certain. Signals are therefore expected to convey much-needed information in an area of social life where there is considerable doubt about others' intentions. None the less, the rituals that signal personal disposition are less formalized; more choice is possible in the way one seeks to convey one's disposition and the significatory value of signals is more ambiguous.

The following paragraphs consider how it is that signals acquire meaning, and they are organized into a structure of alternative messages. The rituals of marriage and interpersonal life appear to differ from language inasmuch as the meanings of many of the acts are determined by general cultural associations that lie outside the specific structure of the ritual. Drinking from a chamber-pot has significance because this is a manifest reversal of the pot's normal function, a point made all the more overt by the inclusion of imitation faeces. Pigs are representative of asocial behaviour because their habits mark them as unsocialized. Pigs feed largely on the whey that is a waste product of cheese manufacture in the village dairy. Unlike cattle, dogs, and horses, they are not given individual names. This reflects the lack of close contact the *cultivateur* has with them during the short time they are reared. They are not milked, nor are they trained to respond to the farmer's orders; they are simply machines converting refuse to meat. It is offensive to ask a *cultivateur* how many *cochons* he has; they are spoken of in terms of their produce, as *porcs*.

Although the simplest gestures of greeting used in Pellaport (the smile and handshake, meeting or avoiding the other's gaze) are widespread if not universal, much of the ritual of both marriage and interpersonal relations draws on a repertoire of meanings specific to French culture. The marriage rituals current in 1969 consisted of a determined string of actions resembling Saussure's (1959: 124) 'pat phrases [in speech] in which any change is prohibited by usage, even if we can single out their meaningful elements'. The rituals of interpersonal relations, however, form an open system which can construe and hence absorb new actions as vehicles of communication. The meaning of actions is sometimes transformed in different directions once they are incorporated into the two ritual systems. The significance of associating the married couple with human or animal excrement in the ritual chamber-pot, or the ride through the village, is categorically different to the association of households who seem unable to recognize their obligations to neighbours and relatives, with pigs. The only time when the systems dangerously converge is during the *charivari* or ridiculing of unpopular marriages described by van Gennep (1946: 614–35).

Rituals make statements about actors' standing in the community by assimilating their position to one or another of the cultural categories represented in the ritual system. The amount of information conveyed in a message is measured by the extent to which prior doubt in the mind of the receiver is removed, and signals 'have an information content by virtue of their potential for making selections' (Cherry 1966:171). The structure of the ritual system determines the number of possible selections which can be made. If ritual acts are communicating information, they do so by removing uncertainty in a situation where there is initial doubt as to the location of a particular actor or event within a structure of possible positions (Shannon and Weaver 1949: 95 n., 103).

The two types of ritual differ considerably in their semantic structure. Whereas there are at least six positions in the structure of interpersonal ritual, wedding rituals consist almost entirely of a paradigmatic series of images each of which gains its force by representing a common opposition to the normal state of cultural affairs. A single binary opposition between the usual and the abnormal is set up, and the newly wedded couple assimilated to the latter. In a series of incongruous juxtapositions lightly described as 'jokes', they are symbolically threatened with guns, their bedroom (and, indeed, anybody else's during the night of licence) is invaded, the bed is overturned, and they are made to drink from a receptacle for excrement. If the couple manage to hide, then the *garçon* and *fille d'honneur* become their surrogates. Guests turn upon them and wheel them through the village on the wheelbarrow normally used to muck-out the stable. Any other wheeled vehicles they find are overturned. The cumulative result is, as van Gennep pointed out, a forceful statement that the newly wedded couple pass through a marginal state when they undergo their *rite de passage*. In the 1960s similar rituals took place at New Year, when the *conscrits* travelled through the streets after midnight, overturning any wagons that they found out of doors. They had the licence to mock anyone who had made themselves unpopular during the year. A few years earlier one *cultivateur* in Montoiseau had complained when he found his wagon upside down on New Year's morning. On 2 January, he got up to find his front door blocked with snow. During one legendary occasion at the end of the nineteenth century, the *conscrits* managed to haul a wagon onto the roof beams of a half-built house and load it with cattle dung. Only the binding of the couple at the churchyard gate and the demanding of money for drinks (the one time when a member of the couple reciprocates) seem to convey a different message to the rest of the marriage rituals.

The capacity of the marriage ritual to 'make selections', in Cherry's sense, is further limited by the fact that there exists no set of specifically ritual acts to convey the other position in the normal : abnormal opposition. The only alternative to performing the ritual is not performing the ritual; by implication denying that the wedding is a remarkable or notable event. Were that the case everyone would continue to fire their guns at *gibier* (game), roll their wagons through the streets, sleep peacefully in their beds, and from time to time make use of their chamber-pots, but (among the multitude of other daily customs) these actions would have particular significance only if they indicated ostracism of the bride's family. The wedding ritual is essentially an elaborate celebration of a single ritual 'statement': that those entering marriage step momentarily outside the course of everyday community life.

The ritual of interpersonal relations is quite different. All three of the basic constructs are signified through distinct rituals and all three categories can be subdivided into finer semantic distinctions. One can distinguish, in greeting, between relationships of acquaintances and closer friends. Among the proud one can distinguish between withdrawal from community life and aggression towards neighbours. Villagers also seemed to distinguish between different kinds of irrationality among those they considered *fou* according to whether they were simply eccentric or incapable of recognizing social obligations. While no position in this structure was signified by an unchangeable set of ritual actions, the ability of interpersonal ritual to convey a greater amount of information was limited by the apparent lack of a syntax. If each message contains only a single signal, the number of possible messages will be equal to the number of terms in the semantic structure. Since it is assumed that all semantic structures have a finite number of terms, 'a semantic system in which the set of all possible messages is [alleged to be] infinite ... can only be achieved through sequential ordering' in which the meaning of each term is qualified by those preceding and following it (Reynolds 1968: 303–4). Although greetings often consist of whole phrases and sentences, their semantic value as greetings is a global one: 'I am your friend/acquaintance' or 'I can manage without you'. The number of signifiers in interpersonal ritual can be increased by incorporating innovative acts such as mechanizing an *exploitation* into one of the existing categories, but there is no way of stringing together terms indicative of different positions in the semantic structure. To do so would simply be to give contradictory signals. The number of bits of information the system can convey is thus effectively limited to the number of opposed terms in the semantic structure.

In this respect the ritual of interpersonal relations in Pellaport parallels what Hockett, writing on primate communication, called a 'closed-signal call system'. According to Hockett, such 'call systems' are characterized by a repertoire of about half a dozen distinct signals, each the appropriate vocal response to a recurring, biologically important type of situation. In any such situation the animal can only respond with one or another of the calls or with silence (Hockett and Ascher 1964:139, cf. Marler 1998). To the extent that success in maintaining an *exploitation* depends on access to reciprocal aid, the 'situations' (i.e. personal dispositions) communicated in interpersonal ritual can be characterized as 'biologically important', even though the nature of the status positions signalled varies from culture to culture and is sustained by more complex patterns of interaction than are found in primate societies (see Silverman 1966 for an account of a different status structure but similar interpersonal rituals in an Italian village). Two types of communication system with analogous functions, one human and one non-human, appear to have similar structures. Bateson has pointed out that human gesture systems resemble primate communication, at the same time arguing that human language is not derived in any simple way from such systems since, were this so, they would have been displaced as language developed. Clearly they have not. 'Rather', he comments, 'the kinesics of man have become richer and more complex, and paralanguage has blossomed side by side with the evolution of verbal language' (Bateson 1968: 614, cf. Marler 1998). Since I first considered the parallels between interpersonal ritual in Pellaport and primate call-systems, Dunbar has argued that language itself evolved in response to the selective advantage of sustaining larger social groups than could be held together by primate communication (Layton 1981; Dunbar 1993).

Without placing as much demand on the actor's energy or resources as rendering mutual aid itself would demand, everyday ritual alerts people to whether or not those around them recognize acquaintanceship or a closer relationship and, if they do not, provides (through the concepts of pride and foolishness) two or more possible explanations, each of which will affect ego's response in a certain way. Axelrod (1990: 10–13) pointed out that people will be willing to give through reciprocal exchanges only if they expect to receive in future. The tit-for-tat strategy, outlined later in the chapter, requires an assessment of the likelihood the participants will interact again. The higher they estimate this probability to be, the more likely they are to co-operate. Axelrod's observation that reciprocal altruism depends upon the expectation that relationships will extend indefinitely into the future, combined with the uncertainty induced by a changing economy, helps explain why the rituals of interpersonal relations in Pellaport in 1969 were called upon to provide a relatively large quantity of information. To the extent that personal dispositions are believed to be passed from one generation of a family to the next, they constitute a valuable form of *symbolic capital* (Bourdieu 1977: 179). Despite its apparently greater elaboration, the more formalized ritual accompanying the marriage contract seems rather to celebrate what is known and accepted, and is therefore organized in a way that, while rich in allusions, communicates less information.

CHANGE IN THE CHARACTER OF COMMUNITY LIFE BETWEEN
1969 AND 1995

Discourse on Sociality in 1995

When I returned in 1995, one of my priorities was to discover how use of the three key terms had changed during the 25 year interval. I found the term *gentil* was still used quite frequently (and it is a current word throughout rural France) but, to my surprise, the opposing terms *fier* and *fou* were hardly used at all. The same themes featured in criticism of anti-social behaviour: eccentricities such as the inability to recognize limits of normal behaviour when meeting in the street, the bad design of new farm buildings, or putting one's selfish interests above those of the community were all related to me, but such behaviour was not characterized as *fier* or *fou*. Although I heard the terms *méchant* and *hargneux* (surly) used to describe those who were not *gentil* the only mention of *fier* was, curiously, reported by one of the newest arrivals in the village. She told me that one of her new neighbours had said, 'You will like it in Pellaport, there aren't many here who are *fier*'; a remark which, she said, puzzled her at the time. Pellaport was still spoken of among my old friends as *gentil* and Vaux as *fier*. 'You can talk to anyone here,' said César's son Armand, 'not like in Vaux.' The continuing perfidy of Vaux was demonstrated by an event during the *remembrement*. When field boundaries were replotted, a strip on either side of the major roads was put aside to allow for future road widening. Compensation was paid. Vaux used the compensation it received for lost common land to buy Pellaport's half of the long-disputed common land above les tartes des Fleurs. The *maire* appeared to have agreed to the sale without realizing its historical resonance. A young man who had married into Pellaport from Dechailles told me he thought I would have found it harder to work in Dechailles, which has a different mentality, although not like that of Vaux.

In 1995 I asked several of the young adults who had been children in 1969 what it meant to be *gentil*. Jacques Maitrugue's son was nonplussed, joking, 'It's to be like me, isn't it?' Others told me it meant to be *serviable* (willing, obliging), ready to help when asked, to be tolerant, not to force your opinions on others. 'What I don't like in the village today,' said one 'is people who stay at home and watch what their neighbours are doing from their windows.' But he continued, 'It isn't malicious and it even has a good aspect because, if you know your neighbour usually goes to work at eight o'clock and one day he doesn't appear, you will realize he is ill and go to help.' Pierre Bavarel's daughter-in-law remarked to me how *gentil* it was of Pierre to work all day with his son, driving the tractor during the hay harvest, until she had learned how to operate the equipment.

Rather than using the terms I had learnt in 1969, several people asked me, soon after I returned, whether I thought the spirit of the community had become 'colder' over the last 25 years. The survival of community life had become people's principal concern, not whether a minority conformed to its values. On the one hand there was a sense that the community had become more 'open' and no longer so ready to pass judgement on its members, although younger people felt that newcomers must still feel the weight of community opinion. On the other hand, several indices of declining community spirit were often cited. Jacques Maitrugue told me that people now work more for themselves. Since the commons had been divided and rented out to *cultivateurs* there was no longer any need to go out to the communal pasture together to repair fences, or lead cattle to and from the village each day. He also considered that people now work faster, keeping their heads down and no longer pausing for a break. Pierre's nephew the mason's son recalled the days when it had been common for people to work for the community. One hard winter, the pipe supplying water from la Haute-Source to their end of the village had frozen. He remembered how lots of men had gone up to the forest to dig through the snow and light fires to thaw the pipe (this was one of the jobs that used to be allocated *par soumission*). He had visited them with his sledge to take his father soup. Naturally everyone also stopped once in a while to share a warming drink of mulled wine.

These themes were repeated by others. People have less need of each other than they used to, and are in more of a hurry; they drive their car to the post office to post a letter, rather than walk. 'The only thing I know about Mme X' (who had lived in the village for about six years), said one women, 'is that she wears glasses. I see her wearing them when she drives past.' Jacques's brother cited two indications of the changing *ambience* of the community: people no longer shake hands when they meet in the street, and when they work for each other they now count the cost. Pierre Bavarel's son cited the same two symptoms. The dairyman's son added that greetings have been reduced to a wave of the hand; no one now crosses the road to exchange a joke. Like others, he considered television was partly responsible. When he was a boy his parents often invited friends round on winter evenings to play tarot, then eat a supper of *saucisse de Morteau* and green salad. Now people stay in their own homes and watch television. The mason's son blamed milk quotas for setting

cultivateurs against each other. Older residents regarded the arrival of
new families as a threat to traditional values, although younger ones
tended to welcome new households as a means of combating the effect of
fewer births within the village. The passing of *la veillée*, the evening gathering at which kin and neighbours played cards or told stories, has been
widely regretted in French villages (Rogers 1991: 12; Rosenberg 1988: 30;
Zonabend 1984: 4).

Continuity and Change in the Content of Community Life

In 1969, César Maitrugue and I were the only two adults who did not
attend church every Sunday; I because I was a Protestant, César because
he considered the church had colluded with the Nazis during the war (he
used to circle the church noisily in his tractor before driving off to the
fields). After church, all the men of the village would meet to drink in the
village café.[2] It had struck me that noting who sat at each table would be
an excellent way of plotting friendships and, one Sunday morning in
1969, I began mapping the bar in my notebook. Nicolas Jouffroy spotted
what I was doing and firmly took the notebook. 'What's this?' he asked,
'NJ, that's me, isn't it? PB is Pierre Bavarel and VJ Victor Jouffroy.' He
tossed my notebook aside, reminding me it was Sunday. In 1995, the
weekly gathering in the bar was sadly diminished to between five and
fifteen people. When Jacques Maitrugue's son stood for election to the
municipal council his grandmother told him he did not stand a chance
because he did not go to church. When he *was* elected, she contented
herself by saying, 'Well, you'll never become *maire*, anyway.'

Jacques Maitrugue's observation that *cultivateurs* had less reason to
work together was echoed by others. One man, who moved to Pellaport
from another village about ten years ago, reflected that agriculture had
changed so much that a husband and wife team could now manage the
entire *exploitation* without help. The grandson of the last man to keep
oxen in Pellaport lived in Pontarlier before moving back to the village. He
remarked that, as people had less need of each other, so they had become
more *égoïste*. Despite the pervasive sense that people now preferred to
work for themselves, however, they *do* still help each other. The commu-

---

[2] The village wash-house sometimes used to provide women with a place where they
could gather, counterbalancing the exclusive male gatherings in the village café (Friedl 1974:
37; Zonabend 1984: 126). Tales of adultery and abortion were related in the wash-house at
Minot. Men who approached the wash-house were repelled with obscene banter (Verdier
1979: 132–4).

nal bandsaw is passed from house to house and neighbours help each other to collect and cut firewood. The practice of informally sharing the cost of agricultural equipment continues. *Cultivateurs* help each other lead cattle through the village when they are moved to a different pasture. Raymond Monnier's sister's sons helped him put 300 *boules* of hay into his hayloft in the course of a single day. Nicolas Jouffroy told me that, when his baler broke down the previous year, a friend from Vaux had lent him his baler.

People were as welcoming as ever in their homes. Jacques Maitrugue pointed out that, although he and his wife had renovated an old *ferme* which stood on their land and stabled their livestock there, they (like Nicolas Jouffroy and Raphael Mignod) had chosen to continue living in the village. Two of the newer residents, who had lived ten and eighteen years respectively in Pellaport, remarked that the continuing web of kinship between established families helped to bind the community together. The commune owns little land adjacent to the village and it has been unable to provide much land for new houses. A woman who had moved back to Pellaport when she inherited her uncle's house pointed out that many of the new houses had been built on private land and belonged to the children of village families. Twenty-five years ago they would have migrated from the village but now private car ownership has become so common they all drive to work each morning. One man refused to exchange a field for common land further from the village, to allow more houses to be built, because he feared the arrival of too many newcomers would kill the spirit of the community. I interviewed people in fifteen of the new households. Those who had moved into the village during the 1980s considered the community had become more welcoming since their arrival, particularly (as one remarked) if you had children of primary school age. Those who had arrived during the last two to three years all commented favourably on the sympathetic character of the village.

People agreed about the threats to community life. Raphael Mignod told me the three things a village needed were a *fromagerie* (dairy), a school, and a café. Pierre Bavarel's son said how much he valued the twice-daily meeting with other *cultivateurs* at the village dairy, when news and views were exchanged. Raphael Mignod and Armand Maitrugue told me that everyone in Montoiseau had quarrelled and, for one *cultivateur*, the twice-daily visit to the dairy in Pellaport was his only opportunity to talk to anyone! One of the village's newer residents, who had lived in Pellaport for ten years, considered there were three things crucial to the life of a community: a shop, a school, and a café.

During the most recent municipal elections, which took place shortly before my return, the main issue was the survival of the school. It was felt that the previous council had not done enough to protect the school. Declining numbers of children posed a problem throughout the region and a common solution was to regroup schools to ensure that at least some classes were taught in each village. When the nun who had taken Pellaport's infant class for many years retired, the council had agreed to let the infants be bussed to a neighbouring village. With the imminent retirement of one of the two teachers, there was a risk the school would close completely. Election campaign notices posted beside each of the roads leading into the village stated succinctly, *une école ferme, un désert s'ouvre.*

The same themes were identified by people I spoke to in other villages. In Dechailles the *adjoint* told me, 'when a village loses its dairy, its school and café it ceases to be a village'. The retired *maire* of another village, whom I had known well, said how much he regretted the recent grouping of their co-operative with those of two other villages. *Cultivateurs* would no longer meet twice a day at the dairy now their milk was to be collected by a tanker. This was particularly serious because his village lacked a café. A school, he added, is another important focus for community life. The *adjoint* of a third village spoke of the 'desertification' that afflicts villages where the school and shop have closed and no houses are available to attract new residents.

Apparently disparate aspects of contemporary life have thus converged to erode community interaction. Although I did not count the number of cars in the village in 1969, I doubt if there were more than ten. The few people who worked in Pontarlier caught the daily bus known as *Le Service ouvrier* (The Workers' Service). Now that almost every household owns at least one car more people commute to work (see Ch. 3) and people drive through the village rather than walk. Milk is no longer taken to the dairy on handcarts, but towed in large stainless steel containers behind the *cultivateur*'s car. Households have declined in size as the birthrate falls, and the remaining *exploitations* are generally managed by a two-person team, husband and wife or father and son. There was a striking scarcity of family groups working in the fields during the harvest, which has indeed become harder work, requiring longer hours to complete, even though current machines are designed to be operated single-handedly (see Ch. 6). People in their thirties pointed to the decline in the number of *conscrits,* which had caused the institution to lose much of its significance. In 1981 there were thirteen *conscrits,* in 1985 there were ten; now only one or two children are born each year. Although *conscrits* still go from house to house collecting money on New Year's Day, they no longer have any role to play at weddings. Contract work in the village is given to professional businesses rather than village men, and the forest is maintained by professional foresters. In 1969 50 per cent of active households were *cultivateurs*; now only 10 per cent are. In 1969 only four people worked outside the village; now the majority do.

The remarkable consensus revealed by people's statements about the threats to community life implies that a common discourse about recent social change has been negotiated at a regional, if not national level. This discourse gives primacy to the declining opportunities to *express* sociality. One of the younger municipal councillors described how he had organized a skating trip across the Swiss border. Not expecting many to be interested, he had only booked a minibus. When eighty villagers arrived in the village square he had quickly to telephone for a larger coach. Whether the *need* for interpersonal relationships has also declined generally received less attention, although a number of the statements quoted above shrewdly identify this as a second issue. The contexts in which it is felt community interaction can gain expression are now those that allow gossip and the expression of friendship, but not substantive exchanges of labour. The discourse that crystallized in the three words *gentil*, *fier*, and *fou*, on the other hand, focused on people's willingness to work for each other when asked. Although this discourse has partly survived, it has been pushed into the background. It is questionable whether I would have identified such a 'muted' discourse at all, if my fieldwork had begun in 1995.

Before 1969

The discovery that community values had changed considerably since 1969 led me to reflect upon the evidence I had been given in 1969 that values had already changed considerably, within older people's memory. In 1995 I remarked to Claude Bavarel that I was trying not to think of 1969 as a Golden Age. 'Indeed not,' he retorted, 'life had already changed considerably by then.' Prosper's story of how he and a friend had cycled to Dechailles to be met with stones implied the community had been much more closed before the Second World War. Prosper told me how fights often used to break out between the men of different communities during the annual village fairs. Villages used to have nicknames derived from alliterative play on the name of the village: The Sheeps' Bums, The Sweets' Bums, The Brainless, The Rods (to beat oxen), The Wolves.

During the 1930s, a wealthy *cultivateur* from Pellaport decided to marry a girl from another village. People concluded he was too proud to marry a village girl. According to the account I was given in 1969, he stopped at a roadside inn on the way to the wedding, where he met an old friend he hadn't seen for some time. 'Where are you going today, dressed so smartly?' enquired the friend. 'Oh', Augustin replied, 'I'm going to village C to get married.' The friend had shaken his head, 'Turn back before it's too late,' he warned. But Augustin thought he had no need of anyone's advice, and went on to the wedding (compare the use of cautionary tales in Santa María del Monte and Minot (Behar 1986: 92; Zonabend 1984: 96)). The daughter of the secretary to Pellaport's dairy co-operative said that her grandmother, who came from Paris, had never been accepted into the village. The retired postman had given me a graphic illustration of the difficulties facing incomers. When he arrived, the man who was then *maire* warned him that villagers were buried on one side of the cemetery, strangers on the other. Claude Bavarel's son had heard that if one wanted to marry a girl from another village before the Second World War, one had to go to her house on the pretext of buying a calf, hoping to see her. Inevitably, there was one occasion when the young man asked, 'and how much is your dau—, er, calf?'

Until the1920s, I was told, adults used to go round the village on Mardi Gras (Shrove Tuesday) calling on each others' houses in disguise to demand gifts. The man who was then curé forbade this on the grounds it was a pagan custom and since then only young children have continued the practice. At about the same time, and for the same reason, the custom of lighting a bonfire on the hill opposite the village on *la fête des Rois* (Twelfth Night) is said to have come an end. People used to sing around the bonfire and one man renowned for his horsemanship gave displays of horse-riding. There used to be a wooden cross on the hill. It is said the cross was chopped down one night by young people (one of whom was Felicien Jouffroy's grandfather) and that the curé laid the mutilated cross in the church porch so that everyone who came to mass had to make a penance.

Mocking the proud with ironic titles was already on the wane in 1969. All such personal nicknames I learned of were applied to elderly men, or people who had already died. Many stories told how outsiders, unfamiliar with village nicknames, had in the past been tricked. A stranger arrives in the village and asks the way to someone's house. He is told the way, and also told: 'but don't call him Monsieur A., he prefers to be known as Le B—.' When one makes a successful bid for timber at a village auction, one must give someone's name as surety against one's ability to pay the tax on timber sales. Pierre Bavarel, whose family sobriquet is Bavarel *dit* Croset, recalled that one year the tax-collector asked him who was his guarantor and, before Pierre could think of an answer, the *maire* interjected, 'Le Croset'. None the wiser, the tax-collector duly noted the name down. For many years the baker who brought bread to the village every day caused amusement by addressing one man as 'Monsieur Bubin', not knowing this was his family nickname.

In retrospect, it is only possible to construe such anecdotes as reflections on a time when the values held in 1969 were upheld with greater strength. Had I carried out fieldwork in 1930, I might have reached a different conclusion. It is therefore difficult to say whether my observations on community values during 1969 recorded a tradition as old as the three-field agricultural system that, over the centuries, gave rise to *fruitières, entr'aide*, the sharing of equipment, and so forth, or a transient phenomenon that was the product of a unique moment of rapid change. It is probable that a hundred years ago every household would have had at least one cow, extending the value of mutual aid, but the employment of servants and labourers would have transformed inter-household relationships. In the days within living memory, when sections of the communal meadow were allotted to each person in the village, everyone except the two or three richest households (who had sufficient land of their own) worked side by side on the commons as they harvested their hay. Even those who had no livestock could sell their share to the army, or to businesses in town that relied on horse transport. By 1969, only a third of households still kept cattle and they were renting the entire commons from the commune through the Pasture Co-operative. The 1950s and 1960s were a critical period of change in agriculture, when *cultivateurs* had to decide first whether to buy tractors and, later, balers and milking machines. Much of the discourse on interpersonal relations which I recorded during 1969 concerned those who were either deemed *fier* because they spent too much money on machinery or *fou* because they persisted too long with traditional techniques (see Ch. 5). Those who did not mechanize were in fact condemned, sooner or later, to withdraw from farming. The last to work without milking machines or balers retired during the mid-1980s, leaving a small number of much larger and more highly mechanized *exploitations* in production. In 1969 many of the older and respected *cultivateurs* such as César Maitrugue, Claude Bavarel, Alexandre Maitrugue, and Felicien Jouffroy were either each others' *conscrits*, or born within a year or so of each other, and most had experienced deportation to Germany during the war.

SYMBOLS AND THE CONSTRUCTION OF CULTURE

Floating Signifiers?

Both the symbols expressed during wedding rituals and the symbolism of interpersonal relationships in Pellaport have changed during the past hundred years. Sabean traced a similar process in documents recording terms of abuse used during domestic disputes in Neckarhausen. The meaning attached to the crucial term *hausen* (to live together) changed over time, and usage in a village only 30 km. away anticipated discourse in Neckarhausen by fifty years. 'Talking about the house was an activity: an argument, an expression of value, a claim, an acceptance of obligation' (Sabean 1990: 113). Separation and divorce increased between 1805 and 1840. Requests came overwhelmingly from women, mainly those in their late twenties. Records of marital disputes give a tantalizing glimpse of domestic politics. 'Reading historical documents . . . is a little like catching snatches of conversation while moving along a crowded street. We know pretty much what the words signify, but their specific effect eludes us just because words only have meaning in the context of particular relations' (ibid. 147). In the eighteenth century, husbands in Neckarhausen had only two recorded terms of abuse for wives (witch, dog) while wives had ten for husbands (sorcerer, pack of witches, trash, trashy householder, trashy lot, thief, scoundrel, dog, pig's belly, bird/fool). By the nineteenth century men's reported vocabulary had increased to seven. Women still had ten, but their repertoire included some new epithets, including gypsy, randy stud, rogue, and dissolute fellow.

Derrida argued that language changes randomly through time. Those who use language transform it as current meanings subvert or exploit those of the immediate past. Meanings change uncontrollably, constantly undermining existing practice. Like Durkheim's theory of the collective consciousness, Derrida's theory of meaning is an unstated presence in Bourdieu's thinking, and it is relevant to the construction of symbolism in the habitus. Derrida (1976: 49–50) claimed that, since we could know the world only in terms of its meaning for us, knowledge is an artefact of language and as arbitrary as language itself. Does the flow of particular symbols in and out of discourse in Pellaport or Neckarhausen support Derrida's claim? The following paragraphs will argue, to the contrary, that discourse is to a significant extent anchored by the references it makes to practical behaviour (cf. Layton 1995; 1997*a*). The proliferation of domestic disputes in Neckarhausen coincided with the early nineteenth-century

transformation of agriculture, and was not a case of random drift in signification. In the eighteenth century women were not much involved in
field crop production and had little say in agricultural production and
sale. When production techniques changed, their influence increased.
Once stall feeding began, women had to carry fodder from fields more
than 2 km. away. The new root crops were cultivated with the hoe, and
hoeing seems to have been mainly women's work. Extension of hoe crops
began in the 1760s, coinciding with an increase of female labour in the
fields, and grew substantially around 1815 (Sabean 1990: 149–51). As
women became producers of goods exchanged for cash they began to
demand a greater say in household finances. Men's complaints generally
concerned their wives' failure to do housework, but men were not
compensating women for the additional labour in the fields by taking over
any part of women's traditional work, so it is not surprising that women
also complained.

One way in which the 'free play' of signifiers is minimized in Pellaport
is through the anchoring of signification in those people who epitomize
particular terms. People can fall in with current usage, as I did when I
found myself using the term *gentil*, thanks to the existence of certain individuals who are agreed to exemplify (provide reference points for) the
three polar positions. Bebette Bavarel was the paragon of *la gentillesse*,
Felix Viennet the village fool, Maurice Genre's aunt and Eduard
Maitrugue were the archetypal grouches. The quality of *la fierté* can be
debated by holding it up against alternative patterns of behaviour. The
position of other people is open to negotiation. Popular ones find their
diminutives, which began as terms of affection within the household, are
becoming used by a widening circle of friends. Unpopular people
discover, to their dismay, that they have been given an ironic title.
Consensus is apparently being negotiated as others consent to a pattern of
behaviour deserving such nicknames. Wilkins (1964: 63–8) suggested that
village communities have much greater experience of their members as
total personalities and are therefore more tolerant of deviance than urban
communities, but at the cost of allowing individuals less latitude in the
way each plays out the allotted role. He argued that rejection of a deviant
subgroup has a self-fulfilling effect: as the deviants perceive themselves to
be rejected, so they will tend to conform more closely to a deviant subcul-
ture (ibid. 90). In 1995, one of my new acquaintances told me how much
he and his friends, when they were children, had enjoyed dropping
lighted *pétards* (bangers) into the postbox belonging to Maurice Genre's
aunt. Not only did the *pétard* make a satisfyingly loud bang in the

confined space of the post-box, there was a second and equally predictable explosion moments later as the old lady burst out of her front door, with her wild hair flying in all directions. It would be naïve to think that Felix Viennet did not sometimes contrive situations such as the moment when he became entangled with the barbed wire during the work party's return from the high pastures, in order to reinforce the status more or less charitably extended to him by his fellow villagers. In a similar way, Nicolas Jouffroy seemed to revel in his reputation as a wayward innovator when he sat in the back row at meetings of the village co-operatives, hands in pockets and feet on the bench in front of him.

Chapter 5 will show that, where the terms are used to assess people's approach to technological change, experience may cause evaluations to be revised. What was once widely judged to be arrogance becomes interpreted as good sense. The considerable change which had taken place in the use of these terms by 1995 has already been outlined. Archer (1985: 346) blames anthropology for what she considers one of the most deep-seated fallacies of sociology, that culture displays a high degree of consistency in the interpretations produced by members of society. 'Far from a coherent cultural system being passively received,' she argues, 'its active mediation is required if it is to be translated into a semblance of social coherence'. Deviant practices could provide a fund of alternatives that are 'sorted into those modifications that most closely match the environment' (ibid. 347).

While reference to exemplary individuals can clarify current usage, it does not overcome the difficulty that symbols and theories are always underdetermined by experience (Puttnam 1995: 17, 61; cf. Layton 1997*b*: 207–8). We use culture to propose logical propositions concerning cause and effect and to construct figures of speech but, as Sahlins (1985: p. ix) put it, 'culture is a gamble played with nature'. Where mutual aid is concerned, the gamble is that current cultural constructs predict who is a reliable partner and detect those who cannot be trusted. *Une bonne entente* depends on the mutual intelligibility of people's signals and the predictability of their behaviour.

Bourdieu's (1990) analysis of gift exchange among the Kabyle aims to demonstrate that such exchange is based on a form of false consciousness. The analysis is central to his claim that habitus is unreflective. The motor driving challenge and riposte, gift and counter-gift is not a rule but a disposition, the sense of honour, learned as a child, reinforced by the group, and inscribed in gestures and poses of the body (ibid. 103–4). Habitus seems to become self-perpetuating without ever making any contact with the world of objects. Submission to collective rhythms is demanded both because that is how the group represents the world and because the group orders itself according to that representation (Bourdieu 1977: 163). Kabyle gift exchange rests on symbolic labour, but takes place as if 'it cannot explicitly acknowledge the economic ends' towards which the researcher can see it is directed. Monetary exchange reveals the rationale that gift exchange works so hard to conceal. The development of the market ensures 'the unstable, artificially maintained structures of the good-faith economy break up and make way for the clear, economic . . . concepts of the undisguised self-interest economy' (ibid. 172).

Contrary to this apparent denial that acting according to the habitus can have beneficial practical consequences, Bourdieu also claimed that the strategies predicated by habitus can cope with unforeseen situations because the same strategies have worked before, and they work because they have been shaped by material conditions in the past, even if agents are unaware of this (ibid. 72). Elsewhere (1990: 62) he even described a habitus that has outlived the conditions in which it originated as 'misadaptive'. Bourdieu (1977: 186) also acknowledges that gift exchange has a different goal from market transactions, describing how Kabyle try to minimize the risk of market exchange 'by transforming the impersonal relationships of commercial transactions, which have neither past nor future, into lasting relationships of reciprocity', and in his later work he distances himself from attempts to give the rationality of the market universal applicability (1990: 50–1). By treating gift exchange as nothing more than an exchange of symbolic capital, Bourdieu has none the less given a misleading impression that it is not a distinctive economic activity (1977: 179) and seems to be committing the mistake he accused Saussure of perpetrating, namely assuming the participants are asking the same questions as the observer (1990: 31).

The Comparative Ethnography of Mutual Aid

The parallels between the principles of reciprocity among the Kabyle and on the Plateau of Levier are sufficiently close to suggest they are not arbitrary cultural constructs. The changing symbols expressed in interpersonal relations and weddings flow in and out of a relatively stable structure (cf. Bourdieu 1977: 100–9), and the structure's durability needs explanation.

As in Pellaport, Kabyle parents reward children for producing the desired forms of symbolic behaviour (Bourdieu 1990: 221). Boys watch men in the assembly deploying eloquence and ritual strategies, children encounter a meaningfully structured space in the Kabyle house. Hence they grow up developing a *hexis*, or disposition to stand, walk, and speak in certain ways (Bourdieu 1977: 89–93). As in Pellaport, the eccentric who does everything differently is given a special term, *amkhalef*. A man who gets up late, or who gets up early but achieves nothing, is mocked (ibid. 161–2). Bourdieu writes that the nearest equivalent in French to Kabyle ritual oppositions is the system of adjectives heavy:light, cold:hot, dull:brilliant, in which each term can be opposed to different terms according to the field of use, as when cold may be equated with calm or indifferent. Each usage is only meaningful in relation to a universe of practice (ibid. 121–2), just as is true of the terms *gentil*, *fier*, and *fou*.

Bourdieu (1990: 100) offers a simple generative model that explains the logic of practice. A challenge, gift, or insult calls one's honour into question, allowing three possible responses:

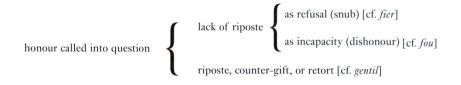

Not only does this model have the same structure as Blau's 'culture-free model', supporting Blau's argument that there are in principle only three possible outcomes of exchange, it also demonstrates how action *must* be clothed in a cultural idiom to become meaningful, that is, to establish the value attached to each of the three logically possible outcomes. Although the three outcomes correspond, as I have indicated, to the core terms in Pellaport, their Kabyle interpretation is in the idiom of honour rather than graciousness.

Parallels to the pattern of *entr'aide* in Pellaport can be found in other communities. In general, mutual aid takes two forms: reciprocal exchanges between individual households, often linked by kinship, and occasions when the entire community comes together to help one person in need. In Kippel any individual could call on the community for help to build an alp hut, or during a crisis caused by death or illness. Communal work-parties tend to take on a festive air (Friedl 1974: 63–7). These two forms of aid correspond to two of the types identified by Panter-Brick (1993) and Erasmus (1956) and were the two discussed in detail by Erasmus; see Table 3.9. Erasmus (ibid. 447–8) argued that while reciprocal labour exchanges took place between equals, the wealthy could use festive labour to recruit the labour of the poor. A substantial proportion of gift exchange among the Kabyle takes place between patrons and clients, not between equals. The idiom of honour conveys a stronger sense that among the Kabyle parity is precariously maintained, a greater fear of slipping into dependence, and respect for those who can maintain their standing. This appears to be an important difference between the Kabyle and communities on the Plateau of Levier. The difference recalls Goody's (1977: 180) argument that there is a deep-rooted distinction between a pan-Mediterranean culture of patronage and a northern European culture of free peasantry. 'Great families' among the Kabyle recruited the labour of clients during peak times in the agricultural calendar. The rich were expected to make the greatest contribution to ceremonial exchange, do most to help the poor, lodge strangers, and organize festivals, but the great families never missed a chance to display their symbolic capital, for this renewed their claim legitimately to dominate others and appropriate their labour. While it is beyond the scope of this study to enter the debate on honour and patronage in the Mediterranean, Ch. 7 will examine its counterpart, the recursive social practices that help to sustain a relatively egalitarian ethos in many northern European villages.

Where unigeniture and patronage prevail, anthropologists working in Europe describe an unequal pattern of exchange. Rogers (1991: 106) found labour flowed disproportionately from small to large holdings in Aveyron, while farm equipment was loaned in the opposite direction. Groger (1981: 173) interpreted the principle of 'not counting hours' in Aveyron as a mystification of such unequal exchange (Groger 1981: 173). In Saint Felix, it was the large landowners who organized 'hay-mowing bees' attended by all the young men of the village, who were rewarded with food, drink, and a small wage (Cole and Wolf 1974: 173–4). Wylie (1966: 119) found mutual aid in Chanzeaux was tainted by the suspicion of patronage favouring one, larger farmer. Bourdieu's analysis of festive labour as a mystification of patronage is supported by these examples, but the importance the Kabyle attach to maintaining parity in encounters where their honour is called into question implies many other exchanges take place between equals, or near-equals.

While Bourdieu does not detail the content of exchange between equals, the principle that mutual aid must be disassociated from commercial transactions is widespread among communities with an egalitarian ethos, recorded by Behar in Léon, Friedl in Kippel, and Zonabend in Minot. A close account can still be kept of the current state of debt and credit between kin or neighbours (Behar 1986: 31; Friedl 1974: 63; Zonabend 1984: 53). Ulin (1996: 136) found that among the wine growers of south-west France, 'the general rule of thumb was that no immediate reciprocity was expected. However it was widely recognised that favours would be returned when a particular need should arise'. Zonabend (1984: 46) writes similarly of Minot that the obligation to return gifts is not pressing. A continuing relationship is intrinsic to the success of reciprocal exchange, whereas commercial transactions can be concluded between parties who do not know each other and will never meet again. The insistence that the value of reciprocal exchange must not be calculated in money asserts they are governed by different principles.

RECIPROCITY AND EVOLUTIONARILY STABLE STRATEGIES

The traditional view in anthropology is that continuing relationships built through reciprocal exchange are necessary to build up society. Mauss (1954: 77–8) put forward this argument, and it is echoed by Zonabend (1984: 168); debts between households linked by mutual aid 'are never liquidated and the series of exchanges never ends'. Unless one accepts the structural-functionalist argument that society is sustained for its own sake, however, the benefit of these exchanges to the participants must be identified.

Interpersonal aid in Pellaport is a good example of reciprocal altruism. According to socioecological theory, reciprocal altruism is adaptive when there is a risk of death from (for example) starvation, no individual can predict who will next be successful in the food quest, but those who are successful obtain more than they require for their own immediate subsistence. If the successful share their food, and can rely on recipients sharing when those who received are, in turn, unexpectedly successful, then the reproductive success of each individual will be increased (Trivers 1985: 363–6). While the risks are not so stark in Pellaport, people are confronted with the unpredictability of illness and the unreliability of equipment which may, at any time, stretch the resources of a household beyond its limits. When they are in good health and their farm machinery is operating normally, they have time to spare which can be invested in helping others, providing they can count on the recipient acknowledging the obligation to reciprocate. Axelrod showed that such relationships of mutual obligation must be conceived of as extending indefinitely into the future, to ensure that current obligations are discharged. If participants anticipate the relationships are about to come to an end they will no longer feel obliged to honour their debts (Axelrod 1990: 10–13). Any means by which people can reassure each other of their willingness to help and their intention to honour obligations in future will increase the probability that the network of relationships built on mutual aid persists. Erasmus (1955: 454) gives examples of how the timing of work-schedules between neighbours can be deliberately staggered to exploit the value of reciprocity.

The problem for the giver, of knowing whether their gifts will be returned, is represented in the Prisoner's Dilemma. The Prisoner's Dilemma uses the model of two suspects who have been arrested and are being interrogated in different rooms. Like the giver who wonders whether his gift will be returned, the prisoner wonders whether he can trust the other to remain silent. Each is told that, if they alone implicate the other in the crime, they will be given a token sentence. If both confess, both will receive a moderate sentence, since their confession helped the police solve the crime. If one refuses to confess ('defect'), even though the other has done so, his sentence will be heavier. Each prisoner knows that, if the other has remained silent, the best strategy is to remain silent too, because both will then be released without charge. If, on the other hand, the other prisoner is suspected of having confessed, it will be better to take the same course oneself (Trivers 1985: 389–90). At first sight, defection (non-reciprocation) appears to be the most rational strategy, because it draws against itself, and wins against remaining silent. Defection is, however, a more costly strategy than reciprocity, because it still earns a small sentence. Each prisoner faces the dilemma that, although defection is less risky than reciprocity, if both defect they will both do worse than if they had co-operated with each other. Axelrod (1990) realized that reciprocity can only develop if the prisoners can anticipate each other's intentions. Since they are secluded from one another in the cells, anticipation must be based on prior knowledge. If the game is played once the stable strategy will be to defect, but if it is played repeatedly by the same players the stable strategy may be to reciprocate.

Axelrod (ibid. 54) found the most stable long-term strategy is one called 'tit-for-tat'. He identified four qualities that made the strategy successful: it is nice, retaliatory, forgiving, and clear. It is nice because it begins by anticipating reciprocity, but it is retaliatory in that it punishes defection. It is forgiving in reverting to reciprocity if the punished player mends his ways. It is clear in the sense that it is intelligible to the other player. In tit-for-tat the player begins by anticipating the other will reciprocate (not confess) and then, in subsequent moves, does what the other player did in their previous move. In this way other players who reciprocate are rewarded, but those who defect are punished. The cumulative benefits of reciprocity are greater than those of defecting, so those playing tit-for-tat win against those playing 'always defect'. This discovery can be extended to real-life situations of reciprocal exchange where the return is delayed, and the dilemma is whether one can trust the other to make a return gift when one is in need. Ridley (1996: 75–8) reviews recent research which shows that in a more realistic situation, where people make mistakes, a strategy a little more forgiving than tit-for-tat may score even more highly. In fact, since the success of each strategy varies according to those played against it, increasingly generous strategies do better than others until eventually they themselves succumb to the short-term strategy 'always defect', allowing tit-for-tat to succeed once more. The time required for such a cycle of strategies to be completed has yet to be discovered.

Tit-for-tat does not explain what Erasmus called 'festive labour', since it predicts that partners who regularly exchange goods or services will form small clusters who can monitor each others' behaviour (Winterhalder 1990: 79). The willingness of the whole community in Pellaport to help someone in distress can be interpreted as a 'friendly society' in which contributions are made in labour rather than money and anyone can 'withdraw' accumulated credit when in need. Signals of *la gentillesse* range from general expressions of sociability to confirmation of specific friendships. The tit-for-tat model of reciprocity only explains the latter. The former probably signals the wish to be considered a member of the community's 'friendly society', although a recent paper by Nowak and Sigmund (1998) offers an alternative explanation based on 'indirect reciprocity'.

There are several possible explanations for the sharing of resources in human communities (see review in Winterhalder 1996). 'Tolerated theft' or 'scrounging', which has been observed in non-human species, can take place if an individual has caught so much food that the surplus is not worth defending and scroungers are allowed to take some. The success of this strategy will depend on the proportion of scroungers to producers (Vickery *et al.* 1991). The lower the frequency of scroungers the more profitable scrounging is. Faced with too much scrounging, producers will produce less. Like Ridley, Winterhalder emphasizes that there may always be more than one strategy in play at any time; the reciprocal altruists can probably never eliminate scrounging or opportunism entirely, but it is in their interests to minimize competing strategies if they are to get the fullest benefits from reciprocity. Nowak and Sigmund (1998: 575) report a similar finding. In Pellaport and among the Kabyle the three culturally identified strategies are, willingness to reciprocate (*gentil*/honour preserved), acceptance without the ability to reciprocate (*fou*/loss of honour) and refusal to give despite holding the resources (*fier*/snub). In Pellaport the first is rewarded, the second tolerated, and the third ridiculed. Among the Kabyle honour is tolerated, but loss of honour is ridiculed and a snub commands respect. The recursive effect on networks of mutual aid will clearly be different, yet they are consistent with the relatively even distribution of resources between households in Pellaport, and social inequality among the Kabyle.

If the cultural constructs of the Kabyle and people of Pellaport have independently converged on the predictions of Axelrod and other socio-ecologists, this is quite good evidence that, contrary to the views of Bourdieu and Giddens their behaviour has been subject to some form of selection. It does not determine the extent to which the convergence was unwitting or reflexive. Axelrod none the less provides a more satisfying representation of Kabyle reciprocity than does Bourdieu because Axelrod's explanation renders Kabyle practice as rational, whereas Bourdieu's renders it as mystification. The variety of interpretations of what is means to be *gentil*, *fier*, and *fou* offered in Pellaport can also be treated as hypotheses about the kind of behaviour that indicates a reliable member of the community. The terms are not a source of ontological security (*contra* Giddens 1984: 136) but a reflection on patterns of co-operation essential to economic survival. Socioecological constructs such as the Prisoner's Dilemma are academic models of the same reality.

This chapter has examined patterns of mutual aid in Pellaport. It has shown that, although individuals differ both in the standards they apply to each others' behaviour and in their interpretation of symbolic actions, there is substantial agreement. Bourdieu's concept of habitus provides a useful basis for understanding this convergence of individual dispositions, but analysis must also take account of the practical costs and benefits of behaviour in order to explain why people's values and dispositions tend to converge. The declining need for mutual aid, and diminishing opportunities to express neighbourliness, explain the changes that have taken place in the quality of Pellaport's community life between 1969 and 1995.

5

Memes and Machines

STRUCTURE AND AGENCY

Bourdieu argued that each individual carried his or her own habitus. In Ch. 4 I argued that variations in individuals' dispositions towards community life (i.e. their habitus) had practical consequences for their inclusion in, or rejection from, the network of mutual aid. Darwin demonstrated that adaptation occurred as a result of chance variation between individual organisms. Natural selection was driven by the effect of such variations in an environment where some variants increased their bearers' chances of survival more than others. Giddens questioned, however, whether theories of evolution had any relevance to sociology. Social and biological anthropology have long been divided over the relative importance of the individual and the social system (see Layton 1989), indeed, the relationship between the structure of institutions and individual action has been debated since the Enlightenment. Rousseau countered Hobbes's theory of natural emotions with the argument that selfishness and greed were the consequence of socially constituted rights to property. He argued society is a 'sum of forces [which] can only arise when several persons come together' (Rousseau 1963: 12–13). Adam Smith, on the other hand, regarded the social order as a by-product of exchange between individuals acting in their private self-interest (A. Smith 1976: 22). Durkheim argued persuasively that the form of society was created through interaction and that it had its own momentum which could not be reduced to the universal psychological dispositions of human beings (Durkheim 1938; 1915). Giddens reformulated the issue in terms of structure and agency, recognizing the self-interest of individual agents is expressed through social action. Structure emerges from the stretching of social relations across time and space, as the 'unintended consequences of actions feed back to reconstitute the initiating circumstances' (Giddens 1984: 27). How, then, can social change be explained? As soon as one examines the place of individual farmers within a regional pattern of technological change on the Plateau of Levier it becomes clear that different actors are behaving in different ways. Some readily accept the latest machines, crop varieties, and cattle-feeding techniques. Others change more slowly. Some, again, have decided to continue with long-established methods. The case for explaining social change as the result of variation in the behaviour of individuals has been most extensively and persuasively argued in relation to innovation. Parallels have repeatedly been drawn between cultural innovations and new genetic variants. In this chapter I look at the theory of innovation and its relevance to technological change in farming on the Plateau of Levier. In the following chapter I will consider the case for the claim that technological change is the outcome of collective social processes. Individuals not only depend on each other to achieve their goals, and must adjust their behaviour accordingly (as in mutual aid), but the actions of individuals can also change the economic circumstances against which they judged the rationality of their original action. The decisions taken by one *cultivateur* can therefore also influence the options available to others.

Durkheim and Tarde

The primacy of individual action or social process was vigorously debated during the late nineteenth century by Durkheim and Tarde. The Industrial Revolution had caused a phenomenal acceleration in the rate of technological innovation. The Spinning Jenny, mechanical loom, steam engine, and other inventions had been devised in quick succession. Invention came to be considered the primary cause of social change and people began to wonder which prehistoric genius had discovered fire or invented the wheel. Oldenziel suggests the idea technology could be used to measure societies' relative development took hold in the West during the nineteenth century (Basalla 1988: 60; Oldenziel 1996: 55–6). The inventor as hero has also been identified as a nineteenth-century icon (Basalla 1988: 57; Latour 1988: 13–15; Overton 1996: 3–4). Tarde (1969: 150–7, 177–89) strongly opposed the view that the inventor was merely a product of his social milieu who materialized a social current. He regarded the inventor as an individual with a special psychology, who combined existing ideas or practices in a novel yet logical fashion. He accepted that one must study the inventor's social environment to understand why certain inventions are forgotten while others become widely copied, but for Tarde the environment consisted of a series of chain reactions passing from one individual to the next. Innovations spread because individuals imitate each other and they stop spreading when individuals contest or reject new ideas. Tarde argued that people imitate those whom they admire, or those with whom they have regular social contact.

A particularly interesting test case, the spread of the practices to restrict disease advocated by Pasteur, had taken place during the previous decade. Latour (1988) uses this case to refute the type of explanation advocated by Tarde (Latour 1988). Tarde's ideas were strenuously opposed in his own time by Durkheim, who sought to separate sociology and psychology. Following Rousseau, Durkheim (1938: p. liii) defined social facts as 'ways of acting or thinking with the peculiar characteristics of exercising a coercive influence on individual consciousnesses'. He explained the Industrial Revolution as the consequence of a social process. Just as animal populations adapted to competition by finding specialized ecological niches, so human communities responded by adapting specialized economies (Durkheim 1933 [1893]). Rather than taking the individual as the unit of analysis in both cases, however, he compared society to the body of an animal. If individual roles also became more differentiated this was not the consequence of psychological variation, but was favoured because such differentiation helped the social organism to adapt.

Durkheim's approach entered the anthropological mainstream through the work of Radcliffe-Brown, and Tarde had little impact on British anthropology, but his ideas concerning the diffusion of innovations stimulated a school of thought in the United States, founded by Boas, taken up by Park during the 1920s and continued through the work of Linton, Rogers, and others (Park 1928; Linton 1936 esp. 308–10; Rogers 1962; Rogers and Shoemaker 1971). Tarde's theory that innovations were achieved by combining existing ideas in a novel fashion was also developed, or reinvented, by several writers. During the 1930s, Harrison (1930: 114) compared innovations to genetic changes, distinguishing between *substitution*, in which a new technique is used in the construction of a known artefact (as when metal is substituted for stone) and *cross-mutation*, when a known technique is transferred from one context to another. Barnett regarded innovation as a conceptual rather than a practical activity. In his model of innovation (1953: 188–92) two culturally established configurations can be represented as Ar^1B and Xr^2Y, where A, B, X, and Y represent 'ideas of things', and r^1 and r^2 the relationships between them. An innovation takes place when the idea occurs of substituting one thing or relationship for another. If A and X are conceived of as in some way equivalent, a new configuration can be derived by substituting X for A, thus creating the pattern Xr^1B. Alternatively, a relationship may be transferred from one configuration to another. If r^1 and r^2 are perceived as equivalent in certain ways, then the new pattern Ar^2B can be envisaged. Barnett influenced my attempts to analyse innovation, while the systems theory of Buckley (1967) guided my early analyses of its social ramifications (Layton 1973; 1974). The theory of co-evolution or dual inheritance has been developed since my first fieldwork, beginning with Cavalli-Sforza (1971), and taken up by Boyd and Richerson (1985), Durham (1991), Alexander (1979), and Rindos (1985).

Innovation and Evolution

The argument that variations in the forms of artefacts are a cultural analogue of the variations in bodily form subjected to natural selection is almost as old as Darwin's theory of evolution. 'We may call it social evolution when an invention quietly spreads through imitation' (Tarde 1969: 184; see Basalla 1988: 15–18; Cavalli-Sforza and Feldman 1981: 29, 357, and Elster 1983: 136–7 for other early uses of the analogy). The mental processes responsible for innovation are, it is argued, analogous to the genetic processes of recombination and mutation that generate physical variety among members of a species. Selection exerted on variant forms of artefacts may be the result of constraints applied by the natural environment or by a social one such as the market economy (Basalla 1988: 6, 14).

One of the curious features of writing on innovation and diffusion is that, although it is generally agreed that the flow of ideas between people is crucial, people frequently fail to point out in support of their argument that others have written on the same topic. In this field, revolution often proves to be the same. Recent exponents of the approach pioneered by Tarde include Cavalli-Sforza, Dawkins, and Durham.

CAVALLI-SFORZA: In biological evolution, the source of hereditary variation is mutation . . . the equivalent of a mutant, in sociocultural evolution, is a new idea. (1971: 535–6).

DAWKINS: Cultural transmission is analogous to genetic evolution in that, although basically conservative, it can give rise to a form of evolution. (1976: 189).

DURHAM: Genes and culture are distinct but interacting 'tracks' of evolutionary change. Cultural values may enhance inclusive fitness of bearers, be neutral, or reduce inclusive fitness. (1991: 206–7, 40).

The analogy with genetic evolution has given rise to two models of cultural evolution, the 'co-evolution' (Durham 1991: 40) or 'dual inheritance' (Boyd and Richerson 1985: 2) model, and the 'epidemic' model. Co-evolution or 'dual inheritance' proposes that culture aids human adaptation by paralleling the processes of natural selection. The alternative 'epidemic' model proposes that cultural traits 'infect' individuals, compelling them to behave as the trait dictates, regardless of its effects on the bearer's own reproductive fitness. The epidemic model has been used by Tarde (1969: 186), Cavalli-Sforza (1971: 537), Cloak (1975: 172), and Dawkins. Dawkins (1976: 191) argued that the idea that culture might have 'biological advantages' is unsatisfactory. Blind faith can justify anything, including an unpleasant death for its bearer. When we talk about the survival value of culture traits, Dawkins argues, we must be clear whose survival we are talking about: a successful meme is *advantageous to itself*.

The epidemic model is an attractive way of representing the mechanisms which allow maladaptive traits such as eating relatives' brains, wearing stiletto heels, or accepting religious beliefs that promote suicide, to spread. If the epidemic model were accurate, however, it would suggest the hypothesis that natural selection favours those who are resistant to 'infection' by local forms of culture. Human evolution would move away from, rather than towards, the capacity for culture. The co-evolution/dual inheritance model predicts that an enhanced capacity to acquire culture will be adaptive. Given the importance of culture in human behaviour, the latter theory seems most plausible. Cavalli-Sforza and Feldman (1981: 216) make the fascinating observation that human genetic variation occurs mainly within populations, while cultural variation occurs mainly between populations (cf. Lewontin 1982: 120–3). Chapter 5 will consider reasons for this dichotomy. No universal mechanism comparable to differential reproductive success has been identified in culture. The feedback mechanism that causes cultural change must therefore be specified in each case, otherwise the beneficial consequences of an innovation cannot be used to explain its spread (Elster 1983: 20).

In seeking to explain why culture became so important in human evolution, writers working within the neo-Darwinian paradigm have pointed out several differences between cultural and genetic evolution. Artefacts do not reproduce themselves (Basalla 1988: 2), but culture has a potential advantage over genetic evolution in allowing new patterns of behaviour to be transmitted more rapidly (within the span of one generation) and more widely (beyond the parent–child relationship) than

would be possible through the natural selection of random genetic variation. If vertical transmission (transmission from parent to child) were the
only mode of transmission for cultural traits, culture would follow the
same lines as genetic transmission. The significance of cultural inheritance increases when it ceases to follow this narrow path. Cultural traits
can be transmitted horizontally (between members of the same generation) and obliquely (between generations, but not to the transmitter's own
children). A single teacher can transmit to many pupils (Cavalli-Sforza
and Feldman 1981: 54, 57, citing Rogers and Shoemaker). Two extreme
possibilities can be envisaged. In one the human makers of artefacts
deliberately create new forms that are intended better to match the
constraints of the environment than do existing equivalents. When innovations are expected to be advantageous they may be generated at a higher
rate. Intentionality can enter the process at three points, suggesting
different degrees of foresight: the future can be anticipated and acted on,
the effects of random variation in artefact-use can be monitored and
choices made, or what others do can be observed and the most common
practice copied. In the alternative view, artefacts operate as mere extensions of the body. Those who happen by chance to carry better adapted
artefacts have greater reproductive success than those who use less
appropriate implements. Artefacts are transmitted when children uncon-
sciously copy their parents' behaviour. Variants arise by chance, through
imperfect copying (see discussions in Basalla 1988: 135–9; Elster 1983:
10). Following Nelson and Winter (see 1982: 10–11), Basalla and Elster
conclude that technological change actually arises through a combination
of random and intentional behaviour. Elster argues, however, that the two
require different types of explanation. The frequency of random variations in behaviour can be explained in terms of the efficiency with which
they function, as in natural selection, as long as the feedback mechanism
through which more efficient techniques are selected is identified (Elster
1983: 22). Intentions, on the other hand, must be understood in terms of
what they hope to achieve, not their actual effects. Natural selection can
only act on existing variation, but intention can envisage imagined states.

Before an innovation can have an effect on the individual's Darwinian
fitness, it must be *adopted*, that is, translated into action (Cavalli-Sforza
and Feldman 1981: 34–5, drawing on the work of Rogers 1962, and Rogers
and Shoemaker 1971). Boyd and Richerson (1985: 132) use the term
'biased transmission' to describe the process by which alternative cultural
traits increase or decrease in frequency, as individuals choose which of
them to adopt. It is generally recognized that individuals' assessment of

cultural traits is always mediated by the local values and theories of causa-
tion they have already acquired. Cavalli-Sforza and Feldman appreciate
that sometimes we have no choice and Durham (1991: 191) stresses that
inequalities of power may compel some individuals to adopt traits which
favour the fitness of the powerful but not their own fitness. Memes can
be adopted or rejected by their carriers long before they are selected by
their consequences for reproductive success. Where there is choice, traits
which appeal to existing values can spread rapidly even if in the longer
term they prove to be maladaptive. However, Durham rejects Dawkins's
'selfish meme' model as an explanation for the spread of kuru, a degen-
erative brain disease, among the Fore. The Fore responded by struggling
to rid themselves of kuru, but did so within their own theory of causality.
Positive values attached to eating the brains of the dead impeded the
rejection of cannibalism. The odds against discovering the true cause
were so high that it took Western scientists ten years to achieve an approx-
imation (ibid. 410–2). Durham (ibid. 208) argues that, over a longer
period, guiding values are themselves likely to be selected against if they
consistently reduce their bearers' fitness. The mere existence of maladaptive cultural traits is not an argument against the theory of co-evolution,
since maladaptive genes regularly appear, and are subsequently subjected
to selection.

Boyd and Richerson (1985: 9) use the phrase 'guided variation' to
describe the process by which individuals adjust their learned behaviour
through observation and rational calculation, passing the changed pattern
on to others. They argue that, in a stable environment, the risks of learning for oneself rather than accepting the accumulated wisdom of previous generations (which they call 'social learning') will be high. They
predict that individual learning, transmitted as guided variation, will
therefore only predominate in rapidly changing environments (ibid.
95–131). However, even when those adopting cultural traits have no effective means of judging their adaptiveness, the capacity of culture to generate new variants, and to transmit them rapidly and widely, may give
culture an advantage over genetic evolution by speeding up the rate at
which random variations in behaviour are subject to selection (ibid. 199).

I argue that there are two respects in which the dual inheritance theories can be refined. More clarity is needed in identifying the environment,
social or natural, that subjects cultural traits to selective pressures. The
existence of any feedback in the relationship between culture and its environment, comparable to the way in which the worker's social environment
is changed by the appropriation of his surplus labour in Marx's theory,

also needs to be investigated. Boyd and Richerson argue that the term 'environment' should be restricted to factors such as availability of food, the climate, and the actions of predators, writing 'the social behaviour of individuals in a population is *not* part of the environment, *even though behaviour may affect individual fitness*, because it is internal to the evolving population' (ibid. 5, my emphasis). Since they later note that social structure can affect the relative predominance of alternative cultural traits, it seems more accurate to treat social structure as part of the environment which imposes selective pressures on culture (ibid. 17). The excellent case studies through which Durham develops his analysis are all cases of adaptation to aspects of the natural environment. Durham does not apply his theory to the evolution of social traits such as reciprocal altruism or territoriality (see Layton 1989).

INNOVATIONS IN MATERIAL CULTURE ON THE PLATEAU OF LEVIER

Since the turn of the twentieth century there has been a steady flow of innovations in agricultural techniques and equipment through the agricultural system of the Plateau of Levier, providing good grounds for testing the theories outlined above. Following Harrison and Barnett, the *substitution* of forms can be distinguished from the *transfer* of processes. Most of the technological innovations that have been adopted are of the first sort, the substitution of one 'thing' (an item of equipment) for another which performed the same function within an existing process or operation. In the early years of the century, the horse-drawn *râteleuse* and *faneuse* replaced the hand-rake and pitchfork. They were replaced in turn by the *râteau faneur*, which could both turn the hay and rake it into rows, but the process of turning or rowing the hay remains the same. A few local technological innovations consist of substituting an existing object to perform a different function. In one, an old wooden cart wheel has been used to form a rotating stile (*tourne à bœuf*), in another old horseshoes have been used to support the ends of poles closing the entrance to a field.

Many social innovations, in particular those where co-operative procedures have been extended to the management of new resources, are of the second sort: the transfer of a process or operation to a different resource. Social innovations will be discussed in Ch. 7.

Wagons have 'evolved' through a series of stages between the traditional horse- or ox-drawn *char[iot] à échelles* and the tractor-drawn *plate-*

PL. 17. Hub and axle of cartwheel used to construct stile

PL. 18. Horseshoes used to support poles closing gateway

forme à pneus. At each stage, a traditional component has been substituted by a new element that performs the same function. The first step was to remove the sloping sides or 'ladders' that formed a narrow V, and substitute a flat platform which could carry a larger load (see Pl. 6). This step took place before the introduction of tractors. The second was to remove the wooden-spoked wheels and replace them with pneumatic-tyred wheels recovered from old motor cars. Once tractors were introduced, the greater speed at which they travelled tended to shake the wooden-spoked wheels to pieces. The government allowed *cultivateurs* one year's grace to tow trailers on public roads before replacing their wooden wheels. The third step was to replace the traditional mechanism for allowing the front axle to turn from side to side with a mechanism akin to the rack and pinion used in a motor car.

The transition from animal to tractor power necessitated adapting many items of equipment. It was easy enough to remove the old horse-shafts and substitute a tow-bar; the problem was that horse- or ox-drawn equipment was designed to be ridden upon, whereas tractor-drawn equipment is towed behind the tractor and operated by the driver. In order to avoid having to add a tractor-driver to the workforce, *cultivateurs* resorted to a number of strategies. Muckspreading was carried out while walking beside the trailer, allowing the tractor to drive itself (see Ch. 1). Some mechanical rakes were raised by a foot-pedal (see Pl. 5) but others were activated by a vertical lever. Those lucky enough to have the second type could tie a string between the tractor seat and the lever. Many of these strategies were widespread and perhaps came into the region with the introduction of tractors. Clade observed a number of them in Haute-Saône, north of Doubs (see 1994: 27, 79). Others, such as Claude Bavarel's original method for ploughing furrows in his potato field described in Ch. 1, are genuine local innovations.

Intentionality and Lateral Transmission

When an animal species evolves it does so by a process of random muta-tion, the mutations effecting changes in the phenotype which may or may not represent appropriate responses to a changing environment. If such modifications are appropriate then the relevant genetic material stands an increased chance of being transmitted to the succeeding generation. This is a kind of transmission of information, and it is this exchange of genetic material which gives an animal population its coherence as an evolving system. Proponents of the co-evolution/dual inheritance theory point out that members of a human society also exchange information, but they exchange it in quite a different way: by direct observation of another's behaviour, by speech, by non-verbal communication. Whichever of these forms the exchange takes, people can learn from experience and they can rapidly communicate to others what they have learned. Cultural information does not have to be transmitted from parent to child, but can be passed laterally, from neighbour to neighbour.

Alexandre Maitrugue told me how he always bought new seedcorn each year, of the best varieties of oats and barley available. In 1968 he had sown his grain on a strip next to a neighbour who preferred the cheaper option of replanting some of the previous year's harvest. A short while before the harvest a hailstorm struck that end of the commune. The ears of barley on Alexandre's strip had already ripened sufficiently to hang down and swing like weather vanes against the wind, but his neighbours' still pointed upwards, catching the full force of the storm. When his neighbour arrived to help with the harvest he noticed the large number of full sacks on Alexandre's trailer and asked whether he had already harvested two strips. Alexandre was gratified to tell him that was not the case. A *cultivateur* whom I got to know in another village was a member of a local group (or CETA) which carried out research into new agricultural techniques, but he was not averse to traditional methods where he considered them worthwhile. He told me how an agricultural student had been sent to work with him during the *regain* (second hay harvest) in 1968. As he began to put the drying hay into the small stacks called *chirons*, the student asked disparagingly why he bothered with such old-fashioned methods. Well, said the *cultivateur*, we'll put half the field into *chirons* and leave half in rows, and see what happens. Surely enough, it rained both that night and the following day. By the time it was dry enough to spread the hay out again in the sun, the half which had been left in rows had rotted, but the half built into stacks had survived.

Few, if any, innovations offer an unambiguous advantage over existing techniques. When I began asking people about the sequence in which they had bought new equipment, many *cultivateurs* told me they had begun after the Second World War with oxen, then saved sufficient money to buy a horse before finally changing to a tractor. I assumed at first that horses were unequivocally better than oxen. In fact, this sequence had often been brought about by the French army's requisitioning of horses at the start of the war. The horses were soon shot by the invading Germans. Before the war, horses and oxen had existed side by side for many years. As Table 5.1 shows, the numbers of both cows and

TABLE 5.1. *Effect of the Second World War on livestock numbers in the* département *of Doubs*

	1929	1938	1945	1952
Oxen:	5,440	3,300	5,500	2,200
Cows:	78,530	84,950	59,500	78,450
Horses:	25,911	22,650	21,034	24,100

Source: Documentation française (1959).

horses fell during the Second World War, but the number of oxen increased. Cows and horses did not increase to their 1929 level until 1952, by which time tractors had begun to replace both horses and oxen.

Censuses carried out from 1688 onwards show that there were substantial numbers of horses in the villages of the Plateau of Levier (see Courtieu 1982). Although horses were generally regarded as a sign of wealth, six out of twenty-three of Pellaport's *exploitations* owned both horses and oxen during the period between 1939 and 1943. An ox was said to be as powerful as a small tractor, and easier to use in the forest. A horse was faster than an ox but it was more expensive to feed, due to its less efficient stomach. Some said a horse ate twice as much hay as an ox, although oats were normally given as a supplement to hay. One man I met in another village in 1969, who still worked with a pair of oxen, told me it was difficult for the owner of a horse to sleep at night when he could hear the beast in the stable, through the bedroom wall, eating his store of hay all night. A villager who bred the region's traditional race of horses, *le cheval Comtois*, told me that a working horse would eat 15 kilos of hay per day, but about 4 kilos of oats. This suggests the cost lay primarily in the oats rather than the hay. Pierre Bavarel recalled that his father never kept a pair of oxen for more than two years before selling them to a butcher. He always had a pair of male calves waiting to take over. 'And who ever heard of someone selling a second-hand tractor for a profit?' he added. The horse's intelligence also gave it some advantages over a tractor. The *maire*, a man famous for his traditionalism, lamented the passing of the days when one could go to market, carry out one's buying and selling, drink a few glasses of wine, and let the horse take one home.

Cultural change on the Plateau of Levier is therefore not entirely a hit-or-miss process like natural selection; it involves some degree of deliberation and calculation on the part of the participants, however partially or

wrongly informed the premisses of that deliberation may be. In a situation of general uncertainty, Boyd and Richerson argued, actors often seek
guidance from those few to whom they have access, whom they consider
to be better informed. Those who have been the first in the French village
to utilize new agricultural equipment have played this role towards their
fellow villagers.

Structure, Domination, and Choice

Choice will always be limited by the relationships into which people enter
during social life that are, in Marx's phrase, indispensable to them and
whose character is determined independently of their will. Social systems
differ in the way that social relationships are structured. Individual action
either perpetuates or transforms these relationships, but it does not take
place independently of them. One of the clearest connections between
individual action and social constraint can be seen in the relationship
between individuals who increase their milk production and the conse-
quent effect of inflation on the price of milk for all (details will be given
in Ch. 6).

The disappearance of a rural working class, the *journaliers*, during the
depopulation of the late nineteenth century, left the villages of the
Plateau of Levier in a relatively egalitarian condition. In 1969 the principal social divide was that separating *cultivateurs* from craftsmen and the
providers of other services. The adoption of technological innovations
was taking place in a social environment very different to that of contemporary Third World communities, in which the unequal distribution of
landownership had an inescapable effect on the scope and consequences
of mechanization. Lewis's study of the Mexican village of Tepoztlán
gave a classic example of the effect of mechanization on Third World
peasants. When the plough was introduced to the village, it was adopted
by the only farmers who owned deep enough soil, the aristocratic minority. Seeking labour to work this land for the cultivation of cash crops, the
ruling caciques successfully deprived poorer peasants of access to the
traditional common land, obliging them to become wage labourers for the
rich. (Lewis 1951; see also Epstein 1962; Hunter 1969; Scott 1976). In
France it was the departure of agricultural labourers for the cities that
precipitated mechanization in agriculture.

There was, none the less, a significant difference in wealth between the
largest and smallest *cultivateurs* in Pellaport after the Second World War.
Those who continued to use traditional methods during 1969 were

watching those who had mechanized steadily outstrip them in the size of their herds. Someone once remarked to me, 'There are small *cultivateurs* in this village who have better ideas than any of the large ones, but cannot afford to implement them.' While this chapter looks at individual decision-making, the following chapter will show how the window of opportunity allowing one to choose whether to adopt innovations or not moves steadily as the exchange value of milk against the franc at the village dairy declines, making it increasingly important to expand production if income is to be maintained.

INFORMATION AND MISINFORMATION

The *cultivateurs* of the Plateau of Levier are repeatedly told about new techniques for animal breeding, new varieties of crops, and new machines, all of which, according to their proponents, will enable them to work faster or more intensively. Nevertheless, experience teaches the *cultivateur* that not all innovations are as good as is claimed and he must decide whether to risk the cost of investing in each of them. The article on hydraulic grabs which appeared at the time some *cultivateurs* in Pellaport were considering buying one appeared inaccurate, even though it was cited as an authority by one garage owner to whom I spoke (see Ch. 1). Trow-Smith (1967: 188) wrote,

No decade, nearly no year, between 1845 and the end of the 1930s lacked its new prophet of animal nutrition persuading, exhorting or bullying the livestock feeder into some new regimen of diet for his animals. In retrospect, half of them now appear to have been sound enough within the knowledge of their times, a quarter nonsensical, and a quarter fraudulent. . . . The farmer, both British and Continental, had no guidance readily available to him on the comparative values of the 'concentrates' which were sold to him by millers and compounders who ranged from honest through self-deluded to unscrupulous.

Trow-Smith (ibid. 174) is equally critical of the early milking machines invented in the mid-nineteenth century, which 'used a vacuum to withdraw the milk in one continuous stream, a more destructive treatment of the delicate tissues and mechanisms of the udder being impossible to imagine'.

If the *cultivateur* buys an ineffective machine his money is wasted. If he fails to purchase an effective one he misses an opportunity to increase his level of production or reduce his workforce, which may become harder to compensate for in future. Access to further information about the characteristics of available innovations is extremely valuable. If the first to buy the machine can pass on what he has learned to others, they will be spared the risk and, perhaps, the cost of purchase. No one has complete information about all available techniques. Sometimes vital information is unavailable. In 1969 everyone in the village believed milking by hand yielded more milk than using a machine. A comparison of the quantities of milk delivered to the village dairy revealed that those using milking machines consistently gained a little more milk per cow than did those who milked their cows by hand. The rules of the dairy co-operative, however, prevented members from seeing each others' records, in order to avoid jealousy. Despite their imperfect knowledge *cultivateurs* were frequently well-informed about the available technological innovations. The following sections will explore the processes through which such information spreads through the village and region.

Local Innovators

During 1969, three individuals stood out as exemplars of the risks and benefits of innovation. All had made notable contributions to the promotion of social change within the community. Two belonged to the older generation who had experienced the Second World War. César Maitrugue bought the village's first tractor in 1952. Six years later Claude Bavarel bought the first tractor with a diesel engine, prompting everyone else to switch from petrol to diesel power. Nicolas Jouffroy belonged to the younger generation who had recently inherited *exploitations* from their fathers. When I began fieldwork he had already introduced several new types of equipment to the community.

Channels for the Flow of Information

There are a number of channels through which information about new agricultural techniques reaches the farmers of the village, but not all are of equal importance or equally widely utilized. The French government had established an office (la Chambre d'agriculture) in each *département*, to collect information on the condition of agriculture and advise local *cultivateurs* on new techniques. During the winter months a representative from the Chambre d'agriculture in Besançon visited one of the larger villages near Pellaport and several *cultivateurs* from Pellaport regularly attended his talks on the benefits to be gained from new strains of cereal or from chemical fertilizers. Once a year this official organized a visit to some other part of France, providing local people with a further opportunity to broaden their knowledge of alternative agricultural techniques. In 1969 Nicolas Jouffroy and Pierre Bavarel were the only *cultivateurs* from Pellaport to join the expedition, which visited a centre for artificial insemination and a large dairy co-operative to which the *cultivateurs* of several villages belonged. The three Chambres d'agriculture in Franche-Comté jointly publish a farmer's newspaper which was widely read in the village. Parallel to the work of this government organization run the activities of semi-autonomous bodies known as Centres for the Study of Agricultural Techniques (CETA). With government assistance these are managed by the more advanced of the local farmers. They carry out independent studies of techniques for cattle-feeding, the quality of pasture treated in a variety of fashions, and similar topics. Nicolas Jouffroy was the only farmer from Pellaport who had chosen to participate in one of these. At one meeting I attended, a report into the quality of hay artificially dried in barns was tabled, which showed it to be less nutritious than hay dried in the meadow.

The Garage Owner

Garage owners play a vital role in promoting the spread of new equipment, operating independently of local government. One might suppose that manufacturers would make great use of catalogues in spreading information about their wares but in fact little such information ever reached the farmers. One garage owner claimed that no farmers would buy a piece of equipment until they had tried it themselves. Whenever he received a new device he would therefore immediately demonstrate it to those whom he expected to be most interested, never waiting first to be invited. Both garage owners and their regular clients cultivated a personal relationship unlike the impersonality one normally associated with pure 'market' exchange. As Nicolas Jouffroy once commented, 'One would no more ask a garage owner for the loan of equipment the first time one visited him than ask for credit the first time one patronized a grocery shop' (cf. Belshaw 1965: 56–68 on shops in peasant villages).

Rogers (1962: 108) noted that awareness of an innovation spreads more rapidly than adoption, so most of a community is aware of a new trait before more than a few have put it into practice. Rogers argued that, while the impersonal forms of communication represented by mass media are well suited to creating an awareness of new possibilities, at the stage when the actor decides to try out an innovation his need is more for personal sources of information that allow a face-to-face, two-way exchange; a relationship that provides greater scope for discussion and the possibility of correcting misapprehensions that would otherwise go unnoticed. The farmers of Pellaport and the surrounding villages relied heavily upon informal discussion among themselves, and on opportunities to borrow each other's equipment, when evaluating the new devices of which they had learnt. Rogers (1962: 263) suggests that it is at the point that the actor first tries out a technological innovation that the garage-owner assumes greatest importance as an agent for the diffusion of information.

Nicolas Jouffroy experimented with two brands of rotary mower during the hay harvest of 1969. It was when his mechanical scythe broke, towards the end of the first harvest, that Nicolas decided to try out the new device. Although rotary mowers had been available since 1966 he was the first *cultivateur* in Pellaport to test one. They cost more than twice the traditional type introduced at the beginning of the century (3,500 fr. rather than 1,500 fr.) and could only be used with a tractor of at least 30 horsepower. My acquaintance, the member of the local CETA, told me that several people he knew had experimented with the new device, but none found it satisfactory. The spinning blades threw up too much loose earth, failed to accommodate themselves to hollows in the ground, and appeared dangerous to use. He had heard two reports of people in Switzerland being killed by broken blades as the metal spun through the air.

When his mechanical scythe broke Nicolas called on his regular garage at Besançon to enquire if he might borrow a rotary model. Discovering that the manager was on holiday he then visited a smaller garage in a village about 20 km. away that belonged to the brother of two farmers from a village near Pellaport. The garage-owner described himself as an expert on central heating who obtained agricultural equipment from a larger garage near Besançon to sell as a sideline. Nicolas did not find him particularly helpful: he pointedly informed Nicolas how much it would cost to replace any blades that broke and told him to return the machine after a few days. During the *regain* Nicolas contacted the garage in Besançon a second time and this time they supplied him with a *faucheuse* (see Ch. 1). After trying it out, the party returned to Nicolas's house for wine, coffee, and bread and jam, and as the mechanic was leaving Nicolas handed him a pat of butter in recompense for his help. Nicolas continued to experiment with the new *faucheuse* until the last grass had been mown, but eventually decided to revert to the reciprocating scythe. He finally bought a rotary mower the following year.

Interpersonal Exchanges of Information

Interpersonal relationships between farmers of different communities often provide channels for the spread of information that overlap in their function with the role of garage owners and the Chambres d'agriculture. Verbal accounts of past village innovations suggest that more than once the decision to adopt a new trait was taken as a result of advice from an informed outsider. During the period of my fieldwork Maurice and Étienne Maitrugue borrowed a seed-drill from a friend in the neighbouring, but technologically rather more advanced, community of Vaux. It was on the basis of their experience with this machine that Maurice was able to offer an informed opinion on the drill to a group of fellow villagers during the cereal harvest (see Ch. 1). Thirty-six per cent of *cultivateurs* living in Pellaport during the previous two generations had married girls born outside the village. Since the virtual disappearance of extended-family households, and before the rise in car ownership during the 1980s, *cultivateurs*' siblings left the village to seek work elsewhere. A number had found work in garages or in factories manufacturing equipment and (as continued to be the case in 1995) were well placed to tell kinsmen of new developments. When Claude Bavarel purchased his diesel tractor he was acting upon the advice of a cousin who at that time worked in a garage. Diesels, the cousin told him, were more expensive to buy but cheaper to run, diesel fuel being considerably cheaper even than untaxed petrol. The fuel consumption of the diesel, moreover, was only one-third of that of a petrol-engined tractor. Claude had accepted his cousin's advice and found it to be correct. CETA meetings and the annual government-sponsored expeditions themselves provide certain farmers with opportunities for establishing and maintaining friendships with members of other communities. On the occasion that I attended a committee meeting of the local CETA there was a considerable amount of discussion between the participants before and after the items on the agenda.

The Spread of Information within the Village

In 1969 some *cultivateurs* had no access to external sources of information and many relied primarily on information obtained within the village. Even so, the extent to which awareness and interest spread through the community was striking. People were often well-informed about the characteristics of equipment which at the time they had no intention of buying. Sometimes, as in the case of the milking machine, the community appeared to be universally misinformed. It was also notable how closely others modelled themselves upon the action of the innovator. César's first tractor was a diesel, but he very soon exchanged it for one with a petrol engine because he felt the diesel made too much noise (a more important consideration, perhaps, when everyone else still worked with horses or oxen). In 1955 two of the thirty-eight *cultivateurs* in Pellaport had tractors, whereas, in the neighbouring village of Vaux, twenty-nine out of fifty-two *cultivateurs* already owned one.[1] During 1956 a wave of tractor purchases flowed through Pellaport, everyone following César's example and buying tractors with petrol engines. The pattern was only broken six years later, when Claude Bavarel learnt how much cheaper diesels were to run. After 1958, all but one of those who replaced their first tractor with a more powerful model bought diesels. Subsequent stages of mechanization in the village have also tended to occur in discrete waves: the first milking machines and balers, together with the *pirouette* and *remy* which replaced the *râteau faneur*, were almost all bought between 1962 and 1970, the rotary scythe, *andaineur*, and mobile milking parlour between 1970 and 1982. Some innovations, of which the most conspicuous is the widespread practice of drying hay in the barn, have never been adopted in Pellaport.

Direct observation of his neighbour's activities has sometimes provided sufficient information to allow the *cultivateur* to evaluate the worth of his own method against its alternatives. Whenever I watched the demonstration of a new piece of equipment, *cultivateurs* not involved in the possibility of its purchase would stop to look. Étienne Maitrugue, the second in the village to buy a tractor, attributed the rapidity with which the innovation had been taken up to the fact that once the majority saw those with tractors were at home eating their supper while they were still at work in the fields, they soon made the change themselves. Sometimes a *cultivateur* is persuaded not to follow his neighbour's example. Nicolas Jouffroy got rid of his *râteau faneur* during the mid-1960s and bought a new machine. Although I never saw this device, I understand that it put the hay in rows with a series of prongs mounted on circular chains resembling bicycle chains. Nicolas was not satisfied with its performance. It remained the only one of its kind in the village until, a few years later, it broke down. Nicolas then abandoned it in favour of a *remy*. During the early 1960s Nicolas Jouffroy and Victor Jouffroy bought elevators. Although the elevator replaced the laborious task of pitchforking hay

[1] Statistic provided by the Chambre d'agriculture in Besançon, in 1969.

onto the trailer, it was unstable and difficult to manœuvre. After four or five years they sold the elevators to other farmers and replaced them with balers. One elevator was still in use, the other stood, abandoned, next to one of the tracks leading to les tartes des Fleurs. Most *cultivateurs* benefited from their experience and passed straight from the pitchfork to the baler. These two instances of 'failed' innovations illustrate how much the majority can gain from leaving others to shoulder the risks of early acceptance.

I was present at a number of discussions between those who had experimented with new machines and others who were keen to learn from their experience. Examples were given in Ch. 1. On the first occasion Nicolas Jouffroy experimented with a rotary *faucheuse*, a heifer from his stable aborted its first calf on the communal pasture to the north of the village. Two tourists brought the news back and, after the evening delivery of milk to the village dairy four other *cultivateurs* went with Nicolas to locate the carcass of the calf and to capture the cow. Afterwards Nicolas invited them into his house for a drink. The main topic of conversation was the performance of his *faucheuse*. How quickly could it cut a strip of grass? How satisfactorily did it cope with uneven ground? Did it throw up many stones? How much did it cost? In revealing the results of his experiment Nicolas repaid the others for their help.

One class of models constructed by Nelson and Winter (1982: 275–95) suggested that where competition is restrained, innovators will do better but, where competition is intense, imitators do better. They can raise their production to the same level as the innovator, and hence gain the same income, without having to bear the cost of research and development (Elster 1983: 145–6). Nelson and Winter (ibid. 281) found that the most successful strategy was often to be 'fast second', that is, the quickest to imitate an innovation developed by another firm. This raises similar issues to those dealt with in the study of reciprocal altruism, suggesting a games-theory model could also be applied to technological change (Elster 1983: 102–11).[2] Like reciprocal altruists whose rewards are undermined by opportunism or scrounging, players would be increasingly reluctant to innovate as the relative pay-offs for imitation increased. Nelson and Winter show that the costs and benefits of local innovation to someone like Nicolas Jouffroy must be carefully considered. The costs of innovation at the village level seem mainly to be incurred through invest-

---

[2] Van der Leeuw and Allen's model of a game with two strategies, the stochasts and the cartesians, is one such attempt (Allen 1989; van der Leeuw 1989).

ing in machines which the innovator later rejects, so that they need not be taken up by imitators. Chapter 6 will argue the benefits lie in keeping milk output above the average level for producers of Comté cheese. Passing on information gained is thus also, potentially, a cost to be set against the wish to stay within the network of mutual aid.

The Relative Importance of Channels of Information

Not all farmers have equal access to all sources of information. The more professional channels (CETA, Chambres d'agriculture, etc.) reach only a limited number of individuals in each community, and the remaining farmers rely very largely upon interpersonal exchanges over which government officials or representatives of manufacturers have no direct control. This shows the wisdom of the garage owner who said that he would go in search of those most likely to be interested in new equipment before being invited to give a demonstration. Once he had succeeded in feeding knowledge about a new device into the interpersonal networks though which information travels he could sit back and wait for enquiries from other *cultivateurs* to return to him!

Interpersonal exchanges of information remained important in 1995. Even in 1969 interpersonal discussion seemed to be more, rather than less, valued among the innovators of the village. They had perhaps broken to the greatest extent with the traditional mentality, hinted at in the recollections of older men such as Prosper Jouffroy and the retired postman, that confined social interaction almost entirely to members of the same community. The widening of social contacts must be an important corollary of the accelerating rate of change in the region's agricultural economy during the late 1960s. The following section considers the social position of innovators within their own community.

THE SOCIAL STANDING OF INNOVATORS AND TRADITIONALISTS

The first person in a community to adopt a new technique is likely to encounter problems which those who gain access to his experience can avoid, yet the nature of the social relationship between him and other members of his community may well influence the extent to which others can or do make use of his experience. Boichard (1960: 158) noted the 'inestimable' importance of avant-garde *cultivateurs* on the Plateau of Levier in advancing the spread of new techniques they had tested under local conditions during the 1950s. The significance of the innovator's social standing was first highlighted by Tarde. Subsequent writers revealed the complexity of the issue. Linton and Barnett both attempted to construct a universal model. Later writers have suggested that it is impossible to generalize on the scale attempted by these authors, but the processes involved exemplify the way in which structuration occurs during a period of social change.

Linton and Barnett

Linton believed that the innovator could have little to gain in a small-scale society. Where no patent offices exist, he argued, the inventor was unlikely to make any great financial gain from his innovation. Linton was unaware of cases such as that of the Arab entrepreneur in Dafur whose very profitable innovation was recorded by Barth (Barth 1967*b*). Linton (1936: 308) also doubted that the innovator could gain any prestige from his activities in a community that values tradition above change: 'Anything which departs too far from established patterns will be viewed with suspicion and is more likely to bring its inventor ridicule than prestige'. He concluded that the innovator within a small-scale society must suffer an unusual degree of discomfort under existing conditions: 'In short, he must be maladjusted' (ibid. 310, cf. Park 1928). When Linton turned from the question of innovation to that of acceptance he seemed to take a different position, arguing, 'It makes a great deal of difference, who these innovators happen to be. If they are persons whom the society admires and is accustomed to imitate, the way for general acceptance of the new trait is smoothed from the start' (ibid. 344). Barnett (1953: 325) rejected the notion that those with high social status are the best or most frequent advocates of an innovation. 'At times, and for some people,' he conceded, 'the advocacy of a trusted, idolised or feared leader is enough,' but he argued that 'against every instance of a radical change that has been carried solely by the prestige of its advocate, there could be set several others that have resulted in prestige collapse' (ibid. 319). Barnett argued those most receptive to innovations are usually the dissident, the indifferent, the disaffected, and the resentful.

It seems more likely the local innovator's standing within his community will vary according to the social and cultural contexts within which acceptance takes place. If the majority of a community is favourably inclined towards change, then the local innovator is likely on the whole to gain prestige. If not, then he will probably become the target of disapproval. If the innovation is available to all, his standing in the eyes of the majority is likely to be different to that when only a few can take advantage of the innovation.

The S-Curve

Proponents of the 'epidemic' model of diffusion have argued the rate at which innovations spread follows the same trend as the spread of an infectious disease, beginning slowly, then accelerating before finally tapering off. This 'S-curve' pattern was found to represent the rate at which epidemics spread by Hamer (1906, cited in McGlade and McGlade 1989). Tarde's editor Clark attributes the application of the S-curve model to the explanation of diffusion rates to Chapin, an American sociologist working in the tradition of Tarde (Clark 1969: 67, citing Chapin 1928). Hägerstrand (1952; 1967) popularized the concept in geography. From the late 1960s onward, other studies have criticized the model for oversimplifying the relationship between agency and structure (Lemonnier 1993; McGlade and McGlade 1989: 285, 290–1; Nelson and Winter 1982: 267–71). These critics make two points. On the one hand, innovations such as radio transmission and mechanical harvesting did not spread passively through the population but were actively promoted by their inventors (Basalla 1988: 101, 151–3). On the other, the acceptance of innovations depends on existing practices. The Japanese rapidly adopted the transistor whereas in the United States, where it was invented, firms were committed to using valve technology and resisted the cost of incorporating transistors in their products (ibid. 87). Women subverted the intended use of the telephone as a business instrument, eventually leading companies to change their charging systems. Oldenziel (1996: 63) proposes the concept of a 'trading zone', 'a going back and forth between designer and user, the designer's projected user and the real user'. The different interplay between innovations such as printing, gunpowder, and the magnetic compass, and the contexts of Chinese and European civilization are discussed in simplistic fashion by Chirot (1994: 61–8) and in more sophisticated terms by Basalla (1988: 169–76, 192–5) and Elster (1983: 115–16).

Latour's detailed study of the fate of Pasteur's ideas reveals not only the efforts Pasteur put into promoting them, but also the different reception they had among hygienists and doctors. At the time Pasteur developed his theory that diseases were transmitted by microbes, hygienists were campaigning vigorously for improved sanitation in cities, but had no idea what steps were actually needed to prevent the transmission of disease. Pasteur gave them a simple explanation, providing the fulcrum that enabled their powerful campaigns to lever practical measures into existence (Latour 1988: 34). In doing so they transformed the notion of society. Doctors, on the other hand, resisted Pasteur and his team of researchers. Unlike the hygienists, doctors were not united in a social movement but fragmented by their individual relations to patients. To have declared patients contagious would have breached the ethic of confidentiality and to reduce morbidity would have decreased the number of patients. 'Innovation takes time if those interests do not coincide or cannot be translated into a shared misunderstanding' (ibid. 120). Latour insists that we must reject not only the diffusionist model that treats Pasteur's genius as solely responsible for revolutionizing society, we must also reject the idea that ideas fail to spread because of passive resistance from groups in society. Acceptors and rejecters are agents who transform both science and society through their actions (for a review of parallel developments in archaeological theory see Dobres and Hoffman 1994).

Cancian

One of the most satisfactory attempts to generalize about the status of those who first accept innovations has been that of Cancian (Cancian 1967). Cancian based his analysis on a number of field studies and his approach has since been applied to the analysis of innovation in the art of the Asante of West Africa (Silver 1981). Cancian distinguished two phases in the process of acceptance: an initial, innovatory period during which lack of knowledge about the outcome of new practices creates a high degree of uncertainty, and a second stage that begins once there is a wider understanding of the new trait, when there is consequently less risk in accepting it.

Cancian argued the fear of accepting a practice whose consequences are uncertain has an inhibiting effect, the strength of which will vary according to the individual's place in the community. He argued that the relationship between wealth and innovativeness is more complex than Linton or Barnett had claimed. He isolated a number of conflicting considerations affecting the actor's decision. Those with higher rank might be reluctant to risk losing respect by experimenting with new and uncertain techniques, while those of lower rank (in aspiring to improve their position) might seize on any new opportunities that become available. But Cancian also pointed out that the poor often cannot afford to adopt an innovation. Hunter (1969) and Scott (1976) showed that in

Third World countries it is often those nearest the poverty line who are least willing to risk all in, for instance, adopting a new kind of seed. The introduction of innovations has often given richer farmers an opportunity to widen the gap between themselves and the poor. Cancian further pointed out that it may cost money to obtain information. Rich farmers can send their sons to agricultural college; poor farmers sometimes cannot.

Cancian (1967) reconciled these conflicting predictions by arguing that during the initial, high-risk phase those of middle social rank in a community are strongly inhibited from adopting innovations. Despite possessing the necessary wealth they have achieved a status they would fear to lose through ridicule should they be thought to have deviated from normal practice. Those of high rank, Cancian believes, are more prone to accept innovations at this stage, wanting to find some way of preserving their exclusive status and wealth. Those of low rank are inhibited by something more powerful than the middle stratum's fear of ridicule. If any innovation which requires some investment of capital were to fail, they would face possible economic extinction. If the innovation is in fact discovered to be successful then, once the initial phase has passed and the consequences of adoption become clear, the pattern changes. At this point those of the middle stratum adopt the new trait most enthusiastically.

The importance of being able to afford innovations was recognized by the villagers of Pellaport. Nevertheless, there were quite wealthy individuals, such as the *maire*, who insisted all but one of his children entered the church to conserve his landholdings, but was simply not interested in being the first to adopt new techniques. On one occasion when I watched milking at Nicolas Jouffroy's, we looked out of his stable door to see the *maire* and his wife, who had not installed water taps in their stable, struggling to lead a cow back from the village water trough. 'They're not very developed (*evolué*) across the road,' he remarked, with a smile. Another wealthy *cultivateur* had no sons and anticipated his daughters would not succeed him, so was equally content not to invest in expensive new equipment.

In order to assess the social standing of those who first accept innovations in Pellaport several questions need to be answered. What are the values held by other members of the community? Who has the resources and the inclination necessary to adopt the innovation? Who has access to sufficient information and how do they obtain it? What consequences does the adoption or rejection of a technological innovation have upon other areas of social life? The answers to these questions will reveal the significance of local culture in giving a particular trajectory to the inter-play between structure and agency.

The speed of general acceptance and the ambiguity of the innovator's status within the community in Pellaport both require explanation. Compared to the simple generalizations of Barnett and others, the ambi-guity of the innovator's status in Pellaport is striking. In attempting to decide whether the innovators of Pellaport are respected or ridiculed, whether they are integrated into community life or maladjusted, one is faced not only with the fact that different actors assess these people in different ways, but also with the fact that the same actors have over time changed their opinion. In 1969 Nicolas Jouffroy was admired by other young farmers yet mocked by older villagers. César, whose actions were both scorned and resented immediately after the Second World War, had since achieved a position of almost universal respect. The *maire* was respected for his caution and equanimity in managing village affairs yet teased by younger men for his outmoded approach to agriculture. Judge-ments are made according to the scheme described in Ch. 4, according to which a person's acts are taken to signify a disposition that is either irra-tional (*fou*) or, if accountable, deliberately antisocial (*fier*), or sociable (*gentil*). To some, Nicolas's frequent purchase of expensive equipment seemed to denote idiocy or overweening pride. To others it merely demonstrated the justifiable self-regard of a man who took care to main-tain his farm in good order: a man deserving the kind of respect the community at large accorded César Maitrugue.

One cause of this ambiguity was the relatively egalitarian nature of village society. *Cultivateurs* were not clearly differentiated among them-selves in terms of distinct classes or cultural status groups. None owned all the land they cultivated, but none (except those managing the two isolated *fermes*) was a wholly tenant farmer. Some farmers were undeni-ably wealthier than others. The Jouffroys were already among the wealth-ier *cultivateurs* of Pellaport before the Second World War. By 1969 Nicolas has five times as many cattle as the smallest-scale farmers of the village and almost twice as many as the *maire*, but he and his father had built up their herd of twenty cows from one of four or five at the end of the war. Some farmers lacked the capital to purchase the new devices favoured by those like Nicolas and it is understandable that such men should resent the latter's actions; yet others, anticipating making similar purchases themselves, were keenly interested in the experiments of local innovators. It would be difficult to point to any clear-cut division between rich and poor within the continuum of wealth among the *cultivateurs* of the community. All were members of the village dairy co-operative, all worked on their own family farms. All had participated to some extent in the process of post-war mechanization, owning at the very least a tractor and *râteau faneur*. Even though one man may consistently act as village innovator, and even if many tended to reject him as foolish or ostentatious, widely varying evaluations were made of his actions within the community of *cultivateurs*.

Although post-war technological change in Pellaport has been associated with the virtual disappearance of extended family households and a reorganization of the management of collective resources, it has not caused a restructuring of roles on the scale which followed introduction of the plough to Tepoztlán (Lewis 1951) or sugar cane to Wangala (Epstein 1962), both of which dramatically increased imbalances of wealth and power in the community. There has instead been a steady decline in the number of *cultivateurs* as families' children have moved into other careers, in offices or factories.

The innovator has rarely for long, in the case of each separate innovation, remained the only one to adopt it. If he is to maintain his position relative to other members of his community he must play the role of village innovator repeatedly. Cancian argued that the body of a community would reject innovations as long as their performance was uncertain, yet readily adopt them as soon as the apparent risks of doing so decline. Once this second phase begins evaluations of the innovator's action may change. 'When César began by buying a 20-horsepower tractor,' another of the older farmers recalled, 'everyone said, "he's crazy, we don't need such powerful tractors for small *exploitations* like ours".' But within a few years, the speaker added, many of his critics had replaced their first tractors with more powerful models. Claude Bavarel recalled how, when he had recently bought his diesel, he was stopped in the street by the *maire*, who told him, 'You're crazy to buy a diesel, think how much it will cost to replace the petrol pump!' Yet even the *maire* had purchased a diesel tractor a few years later. In the case of the rotary mower, Nicolas Jouffroy's assessment was respected by others. Yet, despite the fact that many of the other young farmers admired him, Nicolas was well aware many older people did not approve of his activities.

Whatever the extent to which others claim to be unimpressed by someone's innovation, they cannot help becoming aware of how effective it is. With the exception of the two *fermes* on the edge of the commune, all the farmhouses are located in the village rather than on isolated holdings. In

1969, each *cultivateur*'s land was divided into strips scattered among his neighbours' and this made it easy to observe both others' techniques and their results. Despite the subsequent *remembrement*, each *cultivateur* still has several fields in different parts of the commune and people often find themselves working close to their neighbours. As long as some are prepared to pay the social and financial cost of innovation, others will generally have the opportunity to assess the effectiveness of the novel technique and to adopt it themselves.

Innovators and Opinion Leaders

Rogers (1962: 79) suggested that the process of acceptance might usefully be divided into five phases: awareness, interest, evaluation, trial, and adoption; each having its own peculiar characteristics. Like much of the framework he proposes this looks like an arbitrary categorization of what is virtually a continuous process. To some extent, however, the distinctions are useful. Rogers argued that impersonal sources of information are most valuable during the early stages; later personal influence assumes greatest impact and is most sought in situations of uncertainty. In seeking information, he maintains, the actor will go to those who are more advanced than himself, but not so advanced as to create a barrier between them (ibid. 219). Rogers distinguished innovators from opinion leaders. The innovators, in Rogers's scheme, are the first 2.5 per cent of a local population to accept an innovation. He believes they are 'obsessively venturesome', drawn out of their local community into a geographically dispersed circle of like-minded friends (ibid. 169). I doubt if even Nicolas Jouffroy, among those in Pellaport, had stronger ties with outsiders than with fellow members of his own community, but it was certainly true that he, and some of the other young farmers of the late 1960s such as Pierre Bavarel, had a greater number of links with the outside world. Rogers distinguished the opinion leader from the innovator on the grounds that such a person is better integrated into his community. Although more innovative than his followers, the followers are not so greatly removed from him as they are from the innovator himself. Jurjus (1993: 110) reports that recent literature in the Netherlands refers to farmers who rely most on external sources of information about new techniques as 'forerunners', distinguishing them from others who rely more on practical experience.

In classifying people's response to innovations, Rogers takes the (sociological) observer's position as his reference point. To appreciate the diverse fashions in which the behaviour of men such as Nicolas Jouffroy is evaluated by fellow villagers, it is preferable to treat his social position as the reference point and locate 'native' observers on a continuum of responsiveness to change. For some Nicolas thus becomes an 'innovator' who is dissatisfied with culturally established traits and who favours alien alternatives; someone to whom Barnett's characterization of the innovator as dissident individual might be applied. For others it is precisely because he has greater experience of imperfectly understood techniques that he is respected; for them Nicolas is an 'opinion leader', analogous to the prestigeful advocate of Linton.

While those who are not in direct contact with such people as Nicolas Jouffroy will generally learn from those who are, there are suggestions that gaps in this network of communications have sometimes appeared. It is difficult, in retrospect, to demonstrate that actors failed to adopt an innovation simply because they were poorly informed, or rejected the advice of those who had, but I learned of two probable cases during my 1969 fieldwork. Claude Bavarel was less of a leader in village politics than César Maitrugue. His modesty led some to claim, unfairly, that he held himself apart from his fellow villagers. Despite the undoubted success of the diesel tractor such people were reluctant to acknowledge the value of his ideas. Some years after he had introduced the diesel tractor to the village, Claude's cousin lent him one of the first *pirouettes* to become available in the region. Claude accepted it 'in order to demonstrate it to the others'. He was disappointed by the lack of interest other *cultivateurs* took in the new machine, despite the fact that he once drove up to Montoiseau to help a man who had a field of hay too soaked by rain to be turned with a *râteau faneur*. After the second season he returned his *pirouette* to the garage. The following year, however, César Maitrugue bought one, and during the next three years six other farmers followed his example.

The case of Maurice Genre exemplifies the much more serious risks of social isolation. During 1969 Maurice practised some of the most traditional agricultural techniques extant in Pellaport. He was the only person who, when he sold his first tractor, bought a larger petrol-driven model. He was the only man not to join in hiring a combine harvester during the cereal harvest. According to his own account Maurice had once been an innovator but now, in Rogers's terms, he was one of the 'laggards' of Pellaport. In Rogers's scheme, the 'laggards' are the last 16 per cent of the population to adopt an innovation. 'Their frame of reference lies in the past; they are alienated from a world that moves too fast'

(Rogers 1962: 171). They are, in a sense, the most conformist of the community, yet this is a misleading view because the practices they conform to have already been abandoned by the rest of the community. Adams commented that, in a situation of rapid change, one could expect to find as many maladjusted among the conservatives as among the innovators (Adams 1951). In the eyes of the body of the community Rogers's 'laggards' are as much deviants as are the first to put new ideas into practice; indeed many in Pellaport characterized them in the same fashion: both innovators and laggards appeared to act from irrational motives and both were therefore labelled *fou* (crazy).

Maurice was not in any objective sense entirely stupid; his agricultural techniques were simply unconventional. Many of his neighbours were happy to concede that Maurice (unlike his aunt) was 'gracious enough in himself'. Despite this concession Maurice lived on the margin of the community, and lacked what was otherwise common knowledge about the operation of some forms of agricultural machinery. By 1969 it had been four years since Maurice became the only farmer not to participate in hiring the combine harvester. This was widely commented on during the cereal harvest. His behaviour was regarded as inexplicable and it was said that in 1968 Maurice lost an entire strip through being obliged to leave the crop lying on the ground after it had been cut, until it was ruined by rain. While cutting this strip with his old mechanical scythe Maurice had found himself next to some farmers working with the combine. The harvest being a communal affair, some comments on his idiosyncrasies were made at the time; but Maurice refused to change his habits. By 1969 he had apparently felt obliged to sow his cereals in corners of the commune where no one else was cultivating similar crops. Such alienation can clearly become aggravated over a number of years.

Maurice was, nevertheless, quite able to provide a rationale for his decision. He claimed he could harvest his grain whenever it was ripe and dry, whereas everyone else had to have theirs harvested on the day the combine harvester arrived, regardless of whether or not it was ripe. He believed that the old threshing machine in his barn performed a more thorough job than did the combine harvester. This was an important consideration for him, since he not only resowed the best of his own grain each year but also took some to the local mill, using the flour to bake his own bread. The combine, Maurice claimed, cut the stalks of the grain higher from the ground than his scythe, leaving much of the straw that might otherwise have been put under the cattle in the stable as stubble in the field. He had used the combine for two years; indeed, said he, he had been one of the first to switch to the new technique, but having found it unsatisfactory had reverted to his old practices, with which he was quite content.

Maurice's dilemma highlights the way in which all who depart from the norms dictated by current agricultural fashion in the community are likely to be labelled 'crazy'. Clearly Maurice's reasons are well thought out, even if his was the last household to bake its own bread, or if he was the last farmer not to purchase fresh grain at least once every two or three years. Maurice contended that, in continuing to sow a local strain, he was cultivating cereals adapted to the regional climate, whereas the others were purchasing less hardy varieties grown in the Midi. He nevertheless seemed to have condemned himself to operate, through isolation, on ill-informed premisses. The performance of the combine harvesters had almost certainly improved since he last used one and he was apparently either unaware of, or unwilling to admit this. Other farmers with whom I discussed the performance of these machines were unanimous in stating that the earlier models had been quite inefficient, despite their speed; but that later forms were greatly improved. The combine hired in 1969 had cut the stalks of the grain at a level indistinguishable from that of Maurice Genre's mechanical scythe.

Treating certain people as if they were inherently disposed to be inno-vators, opinion leaders, or laggards risks the appeal to psychological universals which Durkheim considered beyond the scope of sociology. Mary Douglas has tried to escape this problem through a 'cultural theory' that classifies both individual people and cultural systems in terms of willingness to take risks (Douglas 1996; Douglas and Wildavsky 1982). According to cultural theory, people's disposition to take risks is deter-mined by their cultural context. Individuals are bound in social relation-ships on two axes, the group which draws a boundary around its members and makes demands upon them, and the grid (network) that limits the freedom people have to constitute their social roles through exchange (Douglas and Isherwood 1996: 20–3; Douglas and Wildavsky 1983: 138–50). All four types of culture exist in any society at all times and each household belongs to a particular type (Douglas 1996: 83–7). Since the types make conflicting demands on behaviour, a household cannot strad-dle the boundary between two or more. Consumption is therefore not an expression of individual choice but of what kind of culture the actor has chosen to live in. 'Choosing commodities is choosing between cultures' (ibid. 83). Individualists situate themselves in the weak group/weak grid corner. They choose high-tech instruments, risky entertainment, and the freedom to change commitments. The individualist is driven by the principle that each person should expand his or her network of alliances. 'Hierarchists' are located within the strong group/strong grid quadrant. Their lifestyle is characterized by adherence to established traditions and institutions, a defined network of family and old friends. It is hard to expand one's personal network in a hierarchical household without intruding into the reserved times and spaces the hierarchicalist lifestyle requires. If one did expand one's network, one would have become an egalitarian. Egalitarians are those who place themselves in the strong group/weak grid quadrant. The egalitarian culture rejects authoritarian institutions, prefers simplicity and intimate friendship. The isolate, in the weak group/strong grid corner, escapes the chores of friends, is not burdened by the obligatory gifts required by the other lifestyles, nor by tight work schedules but, in trying to avoid alignment, the isolate gives offence to all. These cultures provide the bedrock of any argument; they are unquestionable premises of debate. Boholm (1996: 71) has pointed out the circularity of the approach. Like Rogers's classification of innovators and opinion leaders, it imposes a priori constructs on the community studied and its predictions are contained in its premisses.

INDIVIDUAL ACTION AND SOCIAL PROCESS

When I first analysed the spread of technological innovations, it was clear that the actions of individuals had affected their position in the network of social relationships in Pellaport, but the relative power of individual action to transform social relationships, weighed against aspects of those relationships over which they have no control, was more problematic. The *cultivateurs* of Pellaport were aware of the remorseless effect both of the declining value of milk, which compelled them to increase production, and the vanishing rural workforce, which had compelled them to replace hand labour with machines. They were repeatedly informed of new techniques that might help to alleviate these pressures. Many sources of information offered advice, but none could be completely trusted. Within the village community it was those individuals who were the first to adopt innovations who were of prime importance. They acted both as a bridge and as a buffer between their fellow villagers and the outside world by bringing detailed knowledge of innovations into the community. It was often as a result of their experience or decisions that others (saving themselves the social and economic cost of experiment) decide whether or not to adopt the new equipment.

How, then, did the actions of individual farmers such as Nicolas Jouffroy become part of a recursive pattern of social interaction in the village? The overwhelming constraints imposed by transacting within the wider market economy and conforming to state legislation were clear but it seemed that, on a local scale, actions of certain farmers could themselves shape the future course of social process. When analysing my 1969 field data, I concluded that there were two ways this could be demonstrated (Layton 1974: 71–4).

A *cultivateur* who repeatedly introduced technological innovations to the community took up a particular social position, linking him both with his local community and with outside sources of information, that appeared to exhibit an unstable equilibrium. While some of his fellow villagers accorded him friendship, the majority claimed to reject him as one who was too foolish or too proud to deserve their respect. Yet such a man was not entirely isolated. Because the sources of information and equipment that he needed if he was successfully to adapt to the changing economy lay outside his local community, and because of the importance of close, interpersonal links in the exchange of knowledge and the loan of equipment, such people had established ties with those of similar standing in other communities, through both the 'grid' of personal friendships and the group of like-minded individuals who belonged to the local CETA. At the same time he has a close relationship with at least one of the local garage owners. These relationships placed him in a good position to receive information about further innovations and thus to reinforce his present status. Others in his community were, on the other hand, themselves modernizing their farms, and once a local innovator such as César Maitrugue or Claude Bavarel ceased to introduce new items he was likely to lose his distinctive position in the community.

The situation of the laggards in some ways paralleled, and in some ways differed from that of the innovators. Those who employed the most traditional techniques also found themselves isolated from the body of their community yet, because knowledge of traditional techniques is acquired within one's community and because a network of close interpersonal ties spanning different communities appears itself to be a creation of the local innovators, those who persisted with traditional techniques were becoming genuinely isolated. The laggard ceased to be in a position fully to assess the equipment others were adopting and, as was the case with the innovator, his social position was reinforced. Since, however, the body of the community was modifying its techniques in a direction that moved increasingly further away from the laggard's, the likelihood of him becoming reassimilated into the group appeared much lower.

The social processes through which roles became attributed to individuals in Pellaport resembled the pattern predicted by the interactionist theories of Blau (1964), Berger and Luckman (1966), and Turner (1968). Out of a flux of undifferentiated behaviour, these writers had argued, shared values are negotiated and social relationships, whether of equality or domination and subordination, are transacted. Turner (1968: 553) summed up the theory in the following words: 'In any interactive setting behaviour, sentiments and motives tend to be differentiated into units which can be called roles; once roles are differentiated, elements of behaviour, sentiment and motives that appear in the same situation tend to be assigned to existing roles.' Nevertheless I stressed that if, in Pellaport, roles became differentiated as a result of social action, they did so within a pre-existing cultural structure. Roles were assigned according to the values embodied in the juxtaposed terms *gentil, fier,* and *fou.* These terms appeared to express an agreed and durable scheme against which individual dispositions could be judged (Layton 1974: 73). As Durkheim had objected, in his debate with an earlier generation of interactionists, people had never been entirely freed from traditional constraint to decide of their own free will how to constitute their social life. Bailey (1969: 95–100) acknowledged this in his analysis of the strategies for social advancement used by the distillers' caste within the persisting hierarchical structure of Indian society. The debate between the interactionists and structuralists was, as noted in Ch. 2, substantially resolved by the work of Bourdieu (1977) and Giddens (1979).

When I returned in 1995, I was interested to see whether Nicolas Jouffroy's status had undergone a similar transformation to that of César and Claude, and to find out what had happened to Maurice Genre. In fact, it turned out, Nicolas was still regarded as an innovator. People frequently remarked, 'Nicolas was never behind' or 'Nicolas was always ahead'. Not only had he been one of the first to begin milking in the fields in summer, rather than leading cattle back to the stable, he was the only *cultivateur* to take advantage of the potential offered by the *remembrement* and construct a permanent milking parlour in new farm buildings at the centre of his largest fields, even though he had not followed the implications of the *remembrement* to their logical conclusion and moved out of the village. Maurice Genre eventually became the co-operative's smallest producer, but continued farming until he died of a heart attack in 1993. A more fundamental change had taken place in the structure of cultural values themselves in the virtual disappearance of the terms *gentil, fier*, and *fou* from village discourse, reflecting the erosion of interpersonal relationships brought about by technological change (see Ch. 4).

There was a second and rather different respect in which the innovator's actions could direct future patterns of behaviour in Pellaport. Often he alone had access to certain crucial external sources of information and other *cultivateurs* relied on his experience when deciding which innovations to accept and which to reject. Since these others are prepared to allow the local innovator to shoulder the cost of selection from out of the range of potentially available innovations, the innovator was in a position to restrict as well as to promote technological change. If, in seeking a more effective means of exploiting their farms, the others adopt the alternative which the innovator pronounces to be effective, other alternatives may pass unconsidered. They will, it is true, probably adopt a viable procedure but not, perhaps, the only acceptable one. At best the community as a whole avoided the cost of mistakes; at worst the whole community laboured under a state of misinformation. For six years the farmers of Pellaport followed César Maitrugue's lead in purchasing a petrol-engined tractor and yet once Claude Bavarel learned of a more satisfactory alternative, all changed their equipment. In this fashion one individual act, embedded in a pattern of social procedure, may prove the seed that at a later date gives rise to a whole configuration of behaviour. Lemonnier (1993: 15–16) points out ways in which successful innovation inhibits further experimentation. The interesting concept of possible worlds, which extends this finding to a wider scale at which Western culture could have taken alternative and apparently equally plausible courses, such as developing steam-powered cars rather than internal combustion engines, is outlined by Basalla (1988: 189). This being the case it seems as true to maintain that social process can only be fully understood with reference to individual action as it is to emphasize that the individual's actions can be fully understood only within the context of the social and cultural systems in which (s)he participates.

CONCLUSION

The way in which the acceptance of innovations spreads through the village helps to explain the uniformity of culture within communities which Cavalli-Sforza and Feldman noted distinguished cultural from genetic variation. This uniformity is not the result of blind copying but the process Boyd and Richerson called 'guided variation'. It will be analysed further in the two remaining chapters.

Labelling people as innovators or laggards does not, in itself, explain the course of social process. While variability in individuals' strategies is crucial to understanding social continuity and change, its consequences are determined by the social environment in which different strategies are enacted, copied, or discarded. *Cultivateurs* are making their decisions in relation to a social environment, and are often quite accurate in their assessment of the risks it poses to their economic survival. They are rightly wary of exaggerated claims made by the proponents of new techniques and do not rush forward or hold back merely because of their embeddedness in a cultural matrix of grid and group nor because they are 'infected' by memes which compel them to buy ever bigger tractors.

Giddens tends to interpret structuration as a stabilizing process, the unintended consequences of actions recursively reconstituting the circumstances that initiated the action. The recent history of the Plateau of Levier shows how the recursive effects of interaction may transform the circumstances in which it takes place. Contrary to Tarde's idea of a simple chain reaction, mechanization creates the circumstances in which further mechanization becomes necessary. Chapter 6 will document the processes responsible. *Cultivateurs* find their relationships with the market for their cheese, their bank managers, and the French currency become both necessary and independent of their will, driving them further towards the regional specialization that Durkheim identified as integral to the Industrial Revolution. Innovators are valued positively by those who rely on them to identify and hence reduce risk, but regarded with suspicion by those who see them as agents of unwelcome change.

The habitus of interpersonal relations is used to make sense of a changing situation. The symbolism attributed to new technology and the messages people read from others' decisions to innovate or persist with traditional techniques, suggests a semiological analysis of the kind pioneered by Barthes (Barthes 1967), and developed by Douglas and Miller, which claims the meaning of artefacts is more important than their practical use. Douglas and Isherwood (1996) argue the most important resource people need to move up the hierarchy of Western society is information. The higher people are in social rank, the more they communicate with each other and the greater the proportion of their income they spend on the means to get information rather than on subsistence. While goods have a double role, both providing subsistence and establishing social relationships, anthropological understanding does not come from considering the practical or subsistence use of goods but rather their role as signifiers of social rank.

Although the processes described in this chapter are similar to those described by Douglas and Isherwood, there are two difficulties with using Douglas and Isherwood's theory to explain technological change on the Plateau of Levier. Access to information is vital, but the primary value of agricultural machinery is its practical capacity to increase production. It would be dangerous to accept Douglas and Isherwood's (1979: 62) advice to 'forget that commodities are good for eating, clothing, and shelter . . . and try instead the idea that commodities are good for thinking'. The following chapter will argue, moreover, that people are changing their techniques largely in order to sustain their existing economic standing rather than to become wealthier.

Miller has similarly emphasized the meaningful aspect of artefacts. He argues that, following Mauss, goods are scarce in small-scale societies and exchanged to create relationships. A gift is part of an infinite cycle of exchange, unlike the sale of a commodity which is completed in a single transaction. In industrial society consumption is, in contrast, a constant struggle to appropriate goods and services made in alienating circumstances, to transform them into emblems of personal identity. Goods are profuse, and in choosing which shampoo or cola drink to buy we invest them with a sense of self. Miller (1987: 105) accepts 'the use of artefact as symbol does not in any way detract from its significance as tool'. He also recognizes one must not be romantic about modern consumption since there are many ways goods can be used in social oppression (ibid. 206). Notwithstanding Miller's caveats, Carrier and Heyman (1997) argue that to focus on the symbolism of goods risks losing the insights earlier gained through the 'political economy' approach to industrial society. They suggest analysis of patterns of house purchase in the United States, rather than of cheap and inconsequential consumables, brings out the dangers of only considering the meaning of objects. Carrier and Heyman point out the practice of consumption is itself under threat. The purchasing power of hourly workers in the United States has declined substantially. People respond by working longer hours, and sending other people in the household, often women, out to work. I shall argue that mechanization in agriculture on the Plateau of Levier is taking place in similar circumstances. While the alienating processes discussed by Miller have clearly affected Pellaport (see Ch. 4), the most important aspects of the process are not those analysed by Miller in his work on mass consumption. Miller's (1997) more recent study of capitalism in Trinidad provides a more comprehensive analysis.

6

The Recursive Effects of Mechanization

Throughout the twentieth century, but particularly since the Second World War, agriculture on the Plateau of Levier has depended increasingly on investment in capital equipment financed by the marketing of produce. According to one interpretation of social change in rural Europe, the past twenty-five years have swept away an age-old and once changeless way of life. 'These days, revolutions follow each other in swift succession, from the steam engine to electricity, to electronics. . . . The transformation is most keenly and brutally apparent in the rural world. For the first time in centuries the countenance of our villages is undergoing a profound change . . . the rupture with the past has taken place but yesterday, and its full impact was hardly experienced before the nineteen-sixties' (Gresset 1994: 5–6). Gresset writes of the region around Pellaport, but Franklin (1969: 6) wrote similarly of post-war Europe in general, 'peasant society was caught up in a phase of economic and technical development which has resulted in a profound restructuring of rural life and what promises to be a final divorce from the existence of the preceding centuries'. Chapter 6 will look in more detail at the causes of the mechanization that has transformed rural economy and society, but it will argue that the underlying changes began well before the Second World War, agreeing with Viazzo (1989: 119) that anthropologists, geographers, and economists have been wrong to assume the Second World War was a unique turning-point in the agricultural history of Western Europe. Chapter 5 looked at the case for treating the innovator as an exceptional individual. This chapter examines the opposing (Durkheimian) case for treating the incentive to innovate as a product of collective social process. The recursive effect of producing primarily for the market is to transform the socio-economic environment of farming.

Despite the scale of the post-war transformation it did not take place in a system that had miraculously survived unchanged for centuries. The three-field rotation originated during the early Middle Ages (Ault 1972; Dahlman 1980). It was undermined during the eighteenth century by the introduction of leguminous crops that replaced the fallow phase, and by the abolition of collective grazing rights. This innovation is usually said to have spread from England to Flanders and thence to France (Bloch 1966: 38–41, 212), but Sabean (1990: 21–2) argues that intensified rotation practices had long been used in Holland and on the Rhine, often on peasant holdings. In 1863 the author of the first gazetteer of the *département* of Doubs wrote, 'Agriculture has prospered remarkably in the *département* and has undergone a veritable transformation during the last thirty years' (Rousset 1992 [1863]: 23). Mid-nineteenth–century authors urged people to continue improving their techniques. The Year Book for 1864 extolled the use of manure: 'the English use three to four times more manure than we do, not to mention all kinds of artificial fertilizer. Husbandmen (*laboureurs*) often reject such improvements, saying "it won't suit our district" but one can never use too much manure . . . The Flemish have been carefully manuring their fields for centuries, saying "after The Lord himself, manure is the little good lord, it gives every-thing." ' (Laurens 1864). In his1863 gazetteer, Rousset (1992 [1863]: 23) regretted that, despite the good work achieved through agricultural associations and shows, there were still insufficient artificially seeded pastures and few were using 'perfected agricultural instruments' in the mountains near the Swiss border.

During the first half of the nineteenth century, the improved yields achieved in agriculture were used to feed the growing rural population, but after the mid-century, migration to the towns began to transform village society in Franche-Comté. Contemporary records were quoted in Ch. 3. This was the turning-point that laid the grounds for the transformation of agriculture during the 1960s. Mechanization began as a response to the declining rural workforce. The first mechanical mowers and horse-drawn rakes appeared in Franche-Comté during the 1880s (Daveau 1959: 275), becoming more widespread between the turn of the century and the First World War. They can be seen in postcards of the period (Bouveresse 1989: 60, 62, 81–2, 146–7). It was these very instruments that the Dôle family of Dechailles were still using in 1969.

Once rural depopulation began, the rural and urban economies became caught up in an interactive process. The countryside provided the urban workforce, but the towns produced the agricultural equipment which enabled agriculture to continue without its hired labourers (OECD 1965: 37). In turn, agriculture fed the urban population. This process undoubtedly gathered pace at different times in different parts of Europe. In Ireland, according to Shutes (1993: 132), it did not begin until after the Second World War, when 'the massive and rapid re-industrialization of Europe . . . created a high demand for industrial labour. The proliferation of higher-paying industrial jobs resulted in the loss of cheap industrial labour . . . (and) a markedly higher demand for agricultural produce'. The same has been true of the Swiss Alps (Friedl 1974: 3–4).

INNOVATIONS AND THE 'FITNESS LANDSCAPE'

The acceleration of technological change in European agriculture has drawn farming into a process which had already characterized Western industry for several centuries. Has there been a higher incidence of innovations in the West than in other societies, or has the rate of innovation been the same, but a higher proportion of innovations institutionalized? The latter is almost certainly true of Western Europe over the last four hundred years and, while it is possible new variants of existing artefacts arise at a constant rate in all societies, a new attitude encouraging inventiveness also seems to have developed in Renaissance Europe (Basalla 1988: 129).

Two competing accounts have typically been offered to explain why innovations are conceived and institutionalized so much more rapidly in the West than in other historic societies. One, drawing on Adam Smith and Max Weber and retold by Chirot, is that the growth of city-based merchants, relatively free from political control, created a unique structure of opportunity, founded on a belief in one's ability to succeed by manipulating the environment and an ethic that justified the pursuit of profit for its own sake. Beginning in commerce, this culture spread into agriculture (Chirot 1994). In the second, competing account, continued innovation is made necessary by the inherent dynamic of capitalism. Labour shortage, or labour unrest, provokes the adoption of labour-saving innovations; market saturation requires the promotion of innovative products. Marx's theory that industrial technology cannot stabilize has been developed by Elster. The capitalist innovates to cut his costs and sell his goods at a profitable price. According to Marx the cost of producing goods depends on the quantity of labour put into making them. Labour-saving innovations give the capitalist an edge over his rivals. His imitators are, however, constantly catching up, driving the innovator further to improve his techniques, in order to maintain his profits. There is, however, a limit to the extent capitalists can continue to invest in a particular industry. Elster explains this in two ways. One explanation, strictly following Marx, is that the more one is forced to invest in new technology, the less income from surplus production will remain as profit. The second explanation, implicit in volume three of *Capital* and made explicit by Schumpeter, is that the market for a particular type of consumer goods ultimately becomes saturated (Elster 1983: 164–7, 178–81, cf. Marx 1977: 488–92). Kondratiev and Schumpeter identified a cyclic development in industrial production, where new markets are discovered each time existing ones are saturated. These approximately 50-year cycles can be interpreted as a strength or weakness of capitalism, depending on one's theoretical position (Basalla 1988: 111–15; Berry and Kim 1996: 215–19; Chirot 1994: 85–91).

There is a close link between economic and evolutionary theory. The utility of a strategy in economics is analogous to the contribution a behaviour pattern makes to reproductive success in evolutionary theory, while rationality (seeking the strategy which best meets the individual's economic interests) is analogous to the variable outcome of natural selection on alternative genetically determined patterns of behaviour (Maynard Smith 1982: pp. vii, 2). The argument that innovations are analogous to new genetic variants in a biological population was assessed in Ch. 5. The 'fitness landscape' is a model used in the neo–Darwinian theory of evolution to represent the effects of natural selection on a biological population which can also be used to represent the social environment in which innovations take place (see Kauffman 1993: 33–6 for a summary of the ways in which biologists have used the metaphor). Chapter 6 will explore the interaction between technological innovation and its economic landscape, while Ch. 7 will look at the effect of economic change on the management of collective resources.

In neo–Darwinian theory, random variation in genetic structures creates a variety of bodily form and behaviour (phenotypes) within a population. Environmental conditions determine which phenotypes are better able to reproduce and raise offspring to maturity than alternative forms, and it is the genes responsible for successful phenotypes that are passed on to the next generation in greatest numbers. A simple Darwinian model implies that populations will eventually stabilize around the best available adaptation to their ecological niche and does not predict cumulative, unilinear change. Van Valen showed one cause of progressive change, the 'Red Queen' scenario (van Valen 1973), where a predator population and its prey become increasingly specialized, as each exercises a selective effect on variation in the other. The idea of evolutionary landscapes takes the Red Queen scenario further, modelling interaction between many species.

In a more or less uneven landscape, peaks represent effective adaptations. Since any population (i.e. any species) contains genetic variation, the population is spread over a portion of its fitness landscape. Populations climb peaks in their landscape as they become increasingly well adapted to a particular ecological niche. Valleys in the landscape are occupied by members of a population that are poorly adapted. Genetic change can only proceed in small steps. The model predicts that once a portion of a population arrives at a peak in the landscape it will tend to stay there. Even if there were a higher peak it could climb somewhere in the vicinity, the population is unable to move because any new genetic variant would entail a descent from the lower peak into an intervening valley, and that would be a movement into a less adaptive state where the new variants would have lower reproductive success than competing members of the population located at the top of the local peak.

If there were no interaction between species, the shape of the landscape would be independent of the evolutionary process. Each population would eventually stabilize on the highest peak in its landscape, eliminating fellow members stranded on lower peaks. In practice, however, the reproductive success of each species is partly determined by the fitness of other species such as predators, with which it interacts. The evolution of other species will thus change the shape of each species' landscape and destabilize existing adaptations.

A simple Darwinian model also assumes that, while the environment exercises selective pressures on the individual organism, the organism does not transform its environment. Change in the environment is taken to be an independent variable. This assumption is transferred when Darwinian theory is applied to human cultural adaptation and society is treated as an aspect of the environment exercising selective pressure on the alternative strategies available to individuals, but the way in which the recursive effect of realizing those strategies can transform the social milieu is overlooked. The failure to identify such processes of positive feedback in biological evolution was recognized by Odling-Smee. Organisms consume resources, leave detritus, and interact socially with other members of their own species. Organisms inherit both genes which have survived the effects of natural selection, and ancestrally modified environments. Wherever organisms modify their environment, they will modify the selection pressures to which subsequent generations of the same population are subjected (Odling-Smee 1995; Odling-Smee, Laland, and Feldman 1996).

These ideas can help to clarify the forces acting on technological variation. If people living in a stable social and natural environment develop artefacts whose form converges on the best solution to living in that environment, further innovations are increasingly likely to be less effective. This may explain the relatively slow rate of technological change in a small-scale society (Basalla 1988: 66, 187; Lemonnier 1993: 6–7, 26). Those living in a changing environment will repeatedly find it advantageous to adopt new forms of artefacts. The connection between the rate of technological change and wider social process in the West therefore needs to be explored. It is largely the social rather than the natural environment that is changing. A particularly interesting situation arises when the innovations which are institutionalized *themselves* change the environment (Odling-Smee's niche construction), allowing other further innovations to be more nearly optimal. In extreme conditions, a chaotic form of uncertainty may result.

Nelson and Winter's (1982) evolutionary theory of economics uses the concept of evolutionary landscapes. Nelson and Winter distinguish their theory from economic orthodoxy on the following grounds. Orthodox theory envisages that firms choose rationally between a set of alternative production techniques about which they are perfectly informed. They will therefore always choose the best strategy. Like the simple Darwinian model outlined above, orthodox economic theory assumes that although unprofitable firms will be driven out of business, once the optimum technique has been chosen by successful firms, the industry will be in equilibrium. Drawing on Schumpeter's ideas, Nelson and Winter argue that industries are not in equilibrium, nor are firms perfectly informed about available technology. Rather than acting with self-conscious rationality, people in firms normally follow routines which resemble Bourdieu's habitus, consisting of 'relatively constant dispositions and strategic heuristics' (ibid. 15). A firm's existing routines limit but do not determine the way in which it can change. When a firm searches for innovations it is not perfectly informed about all possible alternatives, but rather draws at random from techniques similar to those it already uses. The consequences of any choice are not fully known. Different firms respond differently to the same 'murky signals' in the economic environment (ibid. 276), allowing a range of behaviours to be explored across the industry as a whole. An innovation, once adopted, may solve some problems but create other, unforeseen difficulties for the innovator, and will also transform the landscape within which other firms are operating (examples from the Plateau of Levier will be given below).

While Giddens (1984: 237) argued that agents' consciousness freed them from the blind forces of social evolution, risk and uncertainty affect intentions. When an actor can assess the probability of success or failure in following an intended course of action, (s)he weighs up the risk. Uncertainty exists when the actor simply does not know the probability of alternative outcomes arising from a course of action. Elster (1983: 70–6) points out that uncertainty plays havoc with intention. Where there is uncertainty choices between actions become increasingly random. Intentionality with regard to innovation can be recognized on at least two levels on the Plateau of Levier during the period studied; a distant one encouraged by the predictions of politicians and extension workers that only large-scale *exploitations* would survive, and the shorter-term one of earning sufficient income to repay the bank loans taken out to buy new equipment. A retrospective look at the outcome of people's intentions on the Plateau of Levier gives some idea of the degree of uncertainty with which they were faced, and the functional, or unintended consequences of their decisions.

Elster (1983: 51–61) and Allen (1997: 43–4) have suggested that intentional behaviour can overcome the problem of becoming stranded on a local 'peak' by accepting a short-term cost for the sake of crossing to a more adaptive solution, but there are clearly limits to such short cuts, since the longer one takes to cross a 'valley' the more one will be at risk from competition. It would be difficult for farmers to transform their techniques and products overnight once they have specialized in Comté production.

AGRICULTURE AND NATIONAL POLICY

Protectionism

During the 1880s, when rural depopulation was already in full flood in Pellaport and the surrounding region, European agriculture was first exposed to competition from American beef and cereals. The depopulation of the British countryside had taken place earlier, and industry was well established. Mingay (1967: 7) dates the transition of English society from one of rural self-sufficiency to dependence on food imports from the colonies to the years following 1815. By the 1880s only 12 per cent of the British population was still occupied in farming. Governments refused to protect farmers for the next forty years, by which time British agriculture had further declined. In France, 48 per cent of the population were still cultivators during the 1880s, making them a formidable political force. As in Germany, the government imposed tariffs on imported farm products to make home-grown products competitive (Tracy 1964: 38). The disruption of trade across the Atlantic during the First World War argued in favour of continuing a protectionist policy, and few inter-war French politicians dared advocate alternatives. During the inter-war period, however, non-agricultural markets expanded more rapidly than agricultural ones and an increasingly smaller proportion of the nation's income was earned by *cultivateurs*. Inflation hit farmers harder than it did factory workers, whose wages rose more rapidly, encouraging those who remained in agriculture to improve their incomes by increasing production to the point at which home markets became saturated. The surplus could not be sold abroad because it was too expensive (ibid. 187). The appearance of the first tractors in the region around Pellaport at this time (Clade 1994: 13) is symptomatic of the continuing decline in the rural labour force. Had it not been for the Second World War, the phase of 'motorization' which began in the 1950s (Franklin 1969) would probably have started ten or fifteen years earlier.

The problem was deferred by the Second World War. By the end of the war agricultural production in France had fallen by 30 per cent (Baum 1958: 16–19; Table 6.1) and the danger of relying on imported foods had been demonstrated once more.

Post-war governments continued to protect French agriculture from foreign competition. The government fixed the price of chemical fertilizers, the price of petrol and diesel was subsidized and farmers were offered loans at low rates of interest to buy new equipment (Baum 1958: 298–300; Franklin 1969: 28–30). The common agricultural policy introduced in 1957 gave *cultivateurs* living in mountainous areas additional income support (Jurjus 1993: 102). Agricultural co-operatives were promoted as a means of maintaining the viability of small-scale *exploitations* (Franklin 1969: 15). Laws authorizing the

TABLE 6.1. *Average milk production per cow*, département *of Doubs, 1929–52*

Year	1929	1938	1945	1952
Average production:	2,884	2,525	2,324	2,988

Source: *Documentation française* (1959). Figures have been converted from litres to kilos.

reorganization of fragmented landholdings through the *remembrement* were passed. None the less, the same cycle of declining incomes and over-production occurred during the 1950s and 1960s (OECD 1965: 21, 83). By the early 1960s French government policy had changed to encourage people to leave agriculture. The Fourth National Plan declared that a reduction in the active agricultural population was essential if agricul-tural incomes were to be improved. Elderly farmers were offered better pensions if they retired and gave up their land or handed it to their sons (Tracy 1964: 246; Ch. 3 above). Popular opposition defeated attempts to implement a more drastic, EC-wide programme to reduce the number of people occupied in farming (Shutes 1993: 135), eventually resulting in the accumulation of butter mountains and wine lakes, surplus produce whose prices the EC was committed to supporting even though it could not be sold. International negotiations for the 'liberalization' of world trade through a General Agreement on Tariffs and Trade (GATT) have taken place since 1986. The United States, Japan, and the former British colonies (Australia, Canada, and New Zealand) have argued for a great reduction in both import tariffs and government support for home farm-ers while the EC has opposed this. A compromise solution was reached in December 1991 (Jurjus 1993: 101).

Milk Quotas

The persistence of overproduction in dairy farming led the EC to impose quotas on milk production in 1984. Each *exploitation* now has a milk production level attached to it and is liable to the super-levy, the fine dairy farmers pay for each kilo of milk they produce over their quota (ibid. 102). During 1983, the milk produced on each *exploitation* was measured. This figure was then attached to the land, and became the quota allowed for livestock placed on it. During the reference year of 1983, the quota was therefore a measure of the productive capacity of the livestock, according to the *cultivateur's* current management policy, but thereafter it became a limit imposed on the terrain. Shutes (1993: 132) argues that milk quotas are unique, among the elements of EC agricultural policy, in the directness with which they impinge on decisions of individual farm-ers. One couple in Pellaport had reduced the size of their herd in 1983 because they were also running a bakery. By the time they had decided to give up the bakery their quota was already fixed. Another couple had recently taken over the *exploitation* from the husband's parents and, in retrospect, consider that experienced, middle-aged *cultivateurs* who had anticipated the introduction of quotas and progressively increased their production had gained more favourable quotas. During the first four years of the quota system little effort was made to monitor it. In the fifth year, however, the *cultivateurs* of Pellaport and many surrounding villages were subjected to heavy fines for overproduction. It was at this moment that several of the small-scale *exploitations* I had studied in 1969 went out of production. Each year the quota attached to remaining *exploitations* is increased, to take account of those who retire from dairy farming. The increase is, however, calculated on an EC-wide basis and is quite unpredictable at a local level. Some *cultivateurs* in Pellaport risk overproduction and gamble on their output falling within the eventual limit while one poured two months' production away into his fields rather than risk further fines.

These, of course, are not problems faced by the *cultivateurs* of Pellaport alone. EC membership encouraged a massive increase in Irish dairy farming. Farmers became eligible for subsidies which increased the price of milk, and grants and loans to improve techniques. Quotas now limit the expansion of production (ibid. 132–3). Some Dutch farmers have responded by trying to buy additional quotas, while others diversify beef production (Jurjus 1993: 110). Shutes (1993: 126–7) shows that dairy farmers in Germany and Denmark have faced similar problems. In Pellaport, some *cultivateurs* have been able to rent additional land in adjacent communes which had quotas attached. One supplemented his income by raising beef cattle but ceased when the value of beef fell dramatically. Most have followed a regional strategy of raising additional dairy calves for sale abroad. The *Montbeliarde* cow has a good reputation and a regional organization arranges their export to North Africa and Eastern Europe.

Shutes (ibid. 129) argues that anthropology has a unique capacity to illuminate the processes of post-war rural transformation, 'to demonstrate the specific set of ecological, economic and political factors that are at the source of the problem, and to do so from the point of view of real farmers having to make real decisions in a rapidly changing production climate'. The remainder of the chapter examines the operation of these forces within Pellaport.

MECHANIZATION

Mechanization takes place in response to two pressures, to replace the diminishing rural workforce and to increase output as inflation reduces the value of agricultural produce. Between 1946 and 1962 the number of people occupied in agriculture in the *département* of Doubs fell from 46,341 to 26,120. In 1993, 19,470 remained, constituting only 4 per cent of the *département*'s population (*Économie rurale*, 1967: 4–7; Agreste 1994). Since agricultural labourers had already almost entirely disappeared, the declining post-war workforce is an expression of the disappearance of smaller *exploitations*. In 1929 there were 31,149 *exploitations* in the *département* of Doubs. By 1945 16,342 survived and by 1968 the number had fallen to 9,800. In 1993, only 5,130 *exploitations* were left in the *département*. This trend parallels that in other Western European countries: in 1960 there were more than 180,000 dairy farms in the Netherlands, with a total of 1.6 m. cows. In 1984 the number of farms had fallen to 60,000 but the number of cattle had risen to 2.5 m. Mechanization had made it possible for Dutch farmers to increase herds without resorting to hired labour (Jurjus 1993: 109). Sixty per cent of Germans were employed in agriculture in 1800, 25 per cent in 1950, and only 5 per cent in 1990. Yet between 1950 and 1975 the weight of wheat harvested per hectare rose from 2,700 kilos to 4,400 kilos (Rösener 1994: 188).

The trend was readily apparent to people in Pellaport during 1969 and it was expected to continue at some speed. In 1947 there had been forty-five members of the dairy association producing 433,568 kilos of milk. By 1968 membership had fallen to thirty-one, but their total milk production had risen to 1,109,022 kilos. Pierre Bavarel predicted, as we stood outside his house overlooking the village, that the number of *cultivateurs* in the village would be halved by 1979, adding this would have to happen if those who wanted to continue were to expand their production sufficiently to remain viable. Over a drink after the demonstration of the hydraulic shovel outside Étienne Maitrugue's house (see Ch. 2), conversation turned to the pace of change. Maurice Maitrugue remarked despondently, 'In ten years' time we shall all be broken (*crevé*) and there will no more than two *cultivateurs* left in the commune.' Shortly before, a meeting had been organized by the *départemental* union of co-operatives at which the audience had been told that, within two or three years, each *exploitation* would need to have 30 milch cows if it were to remain viable. Since only one *exploitation* in the village had 20 cows at that time, the future looked bleak. Pierre's prediction proved the most accurate but all were exaggerations; the number of *exploitations* in Pellaport did not fall to half of its 1969 level until 1988, the year Maurice Maitrugue retired. There were still two viable *exploitations* with fewer than 30 milch cows in 1995. The average size of the eight surviving *exploitations* in Pellaport in

TABLE 6.2. *Pellaport and Montoiseau, total milk production and number of members in dairy co-operative, 1947–94*

Year	Total production (kg.)	No. of members	Price of milk (new fr./kg)*	Co-efficient of inflation[†]
1947	433,568	45	0.1472	23.36
1948	458,197	46	0.2251	14.73
1949	460,859	45	0.2781	14.33
1950	595,822	46	0.3037	12.90
1951	608,797	46	0.2743	11.03
1952	613,490	45	0.3406	9.86
1953	611,571	43	0.2864	9.98
1954	657,012	43	0.2853	10.02
1955	677,182	42	0.2975	9.90
1956	631,529	41	0.3228	9.71
1957	679,726	38	0.3257	9.45
1958	657,848	40	0.3452	8.22
1959	690,786	40	0.4102	7.74
1960	730,657	38	0.3772	7.46
1961	742,830	38	0.3515	7.24
1962	822,694	36	0.4652	6.91
1963	866,962	35	0.4730	6.59
1964	852,903	34	0.4904	6.37
1965	906,569	33	0.4744	6.22
1966	944,365	32	0.4735	6.05
1967	1,004,232	31	0.4844	5.89
1968	1,109,022	31	0.4686	5.64
1969		30	0.5289	5.30
1970	[records for cols. 1 and 2 for		0.6124	5.03
1971	1970–8 are missing]		0.6200	4.77
1972			0.6475	4.49
1973			0.6699	4.19
1974			0.7629	3.68
1975			0.8484	3.29
1976			0.9064	3.01
1977			1.0118	2.75
1978			1.2489	2.52
1979		20	1.1596	2.27
1980		20	1.2365	2.00
1981	1,590,752	19	1.4712	1.77
1982		19	1.6798	1.58

TABLE 6.2. *Continued*

Year	Total production (kg.)	No. of members	Price of milk (new fr./kg)*	Co-efficient of inflation[†]
1983	1,661,116	19	1.8072	1.44
1984	1,584,731	18	1.8615	1.34
1985	1,758,031	18	1.9525	1.27
1986	1,772,296	17	1.9881	1.23
1987	1,794,233	17	1.9155	1.20
1988	1,735,128	16	2.2100	1.17
1989[‡]	1,872,044	13	2.3239	1.13
1990	1,835,183	13	2.0942	1.09
1991	1,710,442	13	2.0571	1.06
1992	1,804,786	13	2.3043	1.03
1993	1,916,153	12	2.2821	1.01
1994	2,047,753	12	2.2812	1.00

* Average price for year paid to producers by the dairy co-operative.

[†] To obtain value of milk at 1994 prices, multiply actual milk price by this coefficient.

[‡] Many members were fined for overproduction in 1989.

Source: For data on inflation, INSEE (1990); *Annuaire rétrospectif de la France, séries longues 1948–1988*; and Office national des fôrets, table distributed 16 Feb. 1995 by the Director of Finance (ONF ref. 95-G-636).

1995 (70 ha.) was well above the *départemental* average in the most recent statistics (56 ha. in 1993) and the average herd size of 35 dairy cows was also above the average for 1993 of 32 cows (Agreste 1994).

MILKING AND HARVESTING

In 1969 I decided to focus my study of mechanization on two processes, milking cows and loading hay. Both are central to successful management of the *exploitation*. At the start of the year, the *exploitations* of Pellaport were divided between fifteen who milked their cows by hand and loaded hay with a pitchfork, and nine who had bought both a milking machine and a baler. The study of milking was carried out between February and April, before the cattle had been released from their stables. The study of harvesting was carried out in the second half of July, during the first hay harvest. Mike Rowlands came to the village to help me with the study of harvesting and data on five of the ten *exploitations* studied were collected by him. Such a comparative study would have been impossible in 1995, because all eight surviving *exploitations* were using the same techniques. None the less, these techniques were different to those they or their fathers had used in 1969. Milking was observed on two *exploitations* in 1986. In 1995 I studied current harvesting techniques on three *exploitations*, and milking on two.

The sequence of change in milking techniques is straightforward. Hand milking is a traditional and no doubt ancient technique. The earliest machines to be used in Pellaport had been bought in 1962 and were still in use in 1969. Only two substantial changes occurred between 1969 and 1995. During the early 1970s, people began to buy mobile milking parlours which allowed cows to be milked in the fields during the summer. Traffic on the roads leading into the village had become heavier and time was saved by driving to the cows rather than leading them to the village on foot. The second innovation was the replacement of the *pots*, into which each cow's milk was drawn, with a *pipeline* which delivered the milk directly into the stainless steel container in which milk is transported to the village dairy. The first *pipeline* was purchased in 1979. In July 1995 I watched milking with *pipelines* on two *exploitations*. Pierre Bavarel's son and daughter-in-law used a *salle des traits* (mobile milking parlour) with four stalls while on Nicolas Jouffroy's *exploitation* milking was carried out single-handedly, in a parlour equipped with six stalls.

The history of harvesting techniques is more complex. Milking itself is the major task where clearing out the stable and feeding the livestock take no more than 10 minutes each. Loading hay is, on the other hand, merely one element in a harvesting sequence that takes two days to complete. The sequence begins with cutting the grass early on the first morning and concludes with unloading the hay in the barn during late afternoon on the second day (the large, round bales produced in 1995 have to be left to dry in the open for several days before it is safe to stack them in the hayloft). Loading, or baling, occupies the first half of the second afternoon. After the grass has been cut, and before it can be loaded onto trailers, it must be turned and rowed several times. Each of these tasks has been subject to a series of mechanical innovations, the first of which appeared a century ago. The machines that had been introduced before 1969 have been described in Ch. 2. Although rotary scythes were regarded with suspicion

PL. 19. Milking by hand

PL. 20. Milking machine with *pot*

in 1969 they were adopted soon afterwards. Nicolas Jouffroy became the first in Pellaport to own one, in 1970. All the *cultivateurs* who were active in 1995 had bought one by 1978. The first *andaineurs* (mechanical rakes) also reached the village in 1970. Whereas its predecessor the *remy* is unpowered, the *andaineur* is driven by the tractor engine and functions much like a *pirouette*, except that the spinning prongs throw the hay to one side, forming rows rather than turning it over. Several types of baler have followed each other; those which produce large, round bales (*grosses boules*) were adopted in Pellaport during the mid-1980s.

No one was working entirely by hand in 1969, but hand scything on steeper hillsides remained a common practice until the 1950s. Claude Bavarel had been compelled to scythe and turn his hay by hand after the Second World War. He had no horse or ox, having sold his livestock when he was called up, and lacked the money to restock his *exploitation* when he returned from Germany to find the price of cattle had risen tenfold. Claude was therefore able to give me an indication of the time required to scythe and turn hay by hand. Additional figures have been published by Myrdal (1996). Although pitchforking hay onto the trailer is a traditional technique, the form of the trailers had changed during the 1950s and 1960s. Traditional wagons had a narrow base and sloping sides known as *échelles*

PL. 21. Delivering milk to dairy in steel *boules*

(ladders) which fitted between the large, wooden-spoked wheels (Clade 1994: 21–30). The introduction of tractors followed the transition from traditional wagons to flat platforms mounted on a chassis provided with pneumatic tyred wheels, which held more hay and were more stable. I had no opportunity to watch people working with the traditional *char à échelles*.

In 1995 I watched harvesting on three *exploitations*. All use the same techniques. Pierre Bavarel and Nicolas Jouffroy worked with their sons. Nicolas's team also included his wife Thérèse, who put the hay in rows while Nicolas transported *boules* that had been harvested earlier back to

PL. 22. *Andaineur*

PL. 23. Baling hay (large *boules*)

TABLE 6.3. *Harvesting hay: the sequence of processes and techniques*

Cut grass	Turn drying grass (at least twice)	Place in rows (at least twice)	Load	Unload
Before 1885 hand scythe	Unmechanized: pitchfork	hand rake	pitchfork	pitchfork
1885–1955 mechanical scythe	Horse- or ox-drawn equipment: *faneuse*	*râteleuse*	pitchfork	pitchfork
1955–65 mechanical scythe	Tractor-drawn equipment: *râteau faneur*	*râteau faneur*	pitchfork	pitchfork
1965–75 mechanical scythe	(More powerful tractor needed): *pirouette*	*remy*	baler (rect. bales)	elevator
1970/85–95 rotary scythe	*pirouette*	*andaineur*	baler (*boules*)	fork-lift

their barn. César Maitrugue had died two years earlier, and his *exploitation* had passed to two of his sons, who worked together. None of the three *exploitations* recruited additional labour from outside the household. One person drives an older tractor which powers the *andaineur*, putting the hay in rows, while another follows with a more powerful tractor towing the baler. The baler produces large, cylindrical bales (*boules*) which weigh about 210 kilos each. The bales are dropped onto the grass. There is a risk that fermentation within the *boule* will generate sufficient heat and flammable gas to start a fire if it is stacked in the hayloft immediately. Several days later they are loaded onto a trailer using a fork lift mounted to the front of the tractor. The trailers in use in 1995 are larger than those used in 1969, and will hold 11 or 14 *boules*.

Comparison of Techniques

In 1969, nine of the twenty-four *exploitations* in Pellaport were equipped with milking machines. Étienne Maitrugue was the first to buy one, in 1962. Nicolas, Victor, and Maurice Maitrugue bought milking machines later in the same year. The use of these machines is described in Ch. 1. Milking was not only quicker with a machine; those who used a machine

TABLE 6.4. *Average performance of three milking techniques*

Milking	Yield in kg/min.	Av. per cow, kg	Av. rate cows/hour
Hand	0.65	4.7	9
Machine, with pots	1.28	5.8	13
Machine, with *pipeline*	4.30	7.6	34

were gaining a little more milk per cow than those who milked by hand. It was not that the machine milked individual cows much more rapidly. Averages taken from two samples of 51 cows showed that it took, on average, 7 minutes to milk a cow by hand and 6.75 minutes to milk a cow with the machine. The gain lay principally in carrying out other tasks while the machine was in operation: the stable could be cleared out, a third cow could be milked by hand, or the winter cattle-feed could be prepared (the time devoted to these tasks is included in the calculations in Table 6.4).

One man, a part-time *cultivateur* who also worked in a local sawmill, had bought a machine equipped with only one *pot*. I watched milking at his stable on two occasions. On the evening he milked 4 cows, he achieved the average rate for those working by hand. When he had 7 cows to milk his rate was little better. Two *pots* greatly increased efficiency. The gain in time made by those using a milking machine was offset by the need to wash the equipment more carefully. It was said that a government inspector had removed a machine installed in a neighbouring village, after he found the vacuum pipes contaminated with stale milk.

Two arguments against buying a machine were frequently put forward by villagers. Those with smaller herds said that the time and energy needed to wash the complex equipment was too great to justify buying a machine. Both those who still milked by hand and those who had bought a machine said that they gained more milk per cow when they worked by hand. César Maitrugue, the president of the association, had kindly allowed me to consult the dairy records to discover how much milk had been obtained on each occasion I watched milking. The records suggested this claim was incorrect. César allowed me to consult the annual production figures for 1968 to gain a broader picture, and these figures also demonstrated that the stables using milking machines were obtaining slightly *more* milk per cow. My first conclusion was that the machine itself was responsible for the greater yield and that it would repay its purchase price in about four years (see Layton 1973: 507). Subsequent discussions, both in France and England, have persuaded me that the difference may as well be accounted for by differences in feeding regimes or the quality of breeding on the *exploitation*; those who are obtaining most milk will be the first who need to buy a machine (see Fig. 6.5). It remains, none the less, significant that people were deferring purchase of a machine because they were under a misapprehension about its performance.

A comparison of the average rate of milking obtained with the three techniques (Table 6.4) shows that there is relatively little difference between hand milking and the first machines, whereas the gain made by switching from the early machines to a *pipeline* is enormous. The average time to milk an individual cow using a *pipeline* is still 6 minutes. The principal reasons for the increased speed of milking are not only that more cows can be milked simultaneously but, more importantly, that milk is delivered directly to the steel *boule* and there is no need to pause and empty the *pots* into the churn.

Those who harvested their hay by hand in 1969 generally recruited a workforce of four people. One sat in the tractor seat, one pitchforked hay onto the trailer, a third stood on the trailer to receive the hay. The fourth walked behind, gathering hay which had been missed by the pitchfork and dragging it into the next row for collection. Those who had purchased a baler were able to reduce their workforce to two. One drove the tractor, the other stood on the trailer to receive the bales. If the *cultivateur* owned two tractors and had access to the labour of a third person, the task of rowing the hay could be performed simultaneously (see descriptions in Ch. 1). Some, such as Nicolas Jouffroy, considered that the efficiency of the baler and *remy* made use of the large hand-rake unnecessary.

A comparison of the three techniques studied (Table 6.5) shows that the balers used in 1969, which produced small, rectangular bales (*bottes*) speeded harvesting considerably. The baler compressed the hay, allowing more to be loaded onto a trailer and thus reducing the number of journeys between field and barn yet, even with the greater quantity loaded, it still took less time to fill a trailer. The average harvest rate was three times that for those who worked by hand. At first sight the balers used in 1995, which produced large, cylindrical bales (*boules*), speeded work in the field even further. Because the *boules* had to be loaded onto a trailer afterwards,

TABLE 6.5. *Comparison of three hay-gathering techniques*

	Ares/trailer	Mins/trailer	Ares/minute
By hand (2.5 ha.)	16.0	34.0	0.47
With baler (5.0 ha.) (small rect. bales)	39.0	24.4	1.60
With baler (12 ha.) (large *boules*)	75.7	52.4	2.33 (1.59 with loading time)

however, the time to load a trailer must be taken into account. Loading a trailer with fourteen *boules* takes about 15 minutes. Trailer size has also changed, increasing the area of the platform from 6 sq. m. to 10 sq. m. Using a 1969 trailer, the equivalent performance by a baler delivering large boules would have been 45.4 ares/trailer and 31.3 minutes/trailer. When loading times and trailer size are taken into account, the 1995 baler appears to perform no better than its predecessor of twenty-five years ago. I discussed these findings with people in the village and with staff at the Chambre d'agriculture in Besançon, and was told that the new balers have two advantages. They are less destructive, since the hay is packed more loosely and not chopped into small sections. Furthermore, a single person can in principle bale hay unaided with the current technique, whereas the technique used in 1969 demanded a minimum of two people. In this instance one of the prime advantages of the new technique appears to be to compensate for the declining workforce rather than to facilitate expansion of the *exploitation*. This was not the case with milking, where even in 1995 it remained common for two people to milk the cattle together. Although the absolute time required to harvest hay remains much the same as with the early balers, the winter ration of hay per cow has not fallen (see Table 6.6). Because the number of cattle has increased considerably, harvesting in 1995 took substantially longer than it had in 1969. The president of the dairy co-operative had negotiated with the dairyman for milk to be delivered an hour later during the harvest period. Some were still bringing *boules* back to their barns at eight o'clock in the evening. People frequently remarked to me, during the course of the harvest, that agriculture had lost the leisurely pace it possessed twenty-five years ago.

TABLE 6.6. *Feed per cow, per day, during the winter months 1968/9 and 1994/5* (kilos)

	Hay	Flour or concentrate	Yield per cow
Exploitation (a)			
1968/9	25–30	4	3,870
1994/5	20–25	6	8,676
Exploitation (b)			
1968/9	15–20	5	3,442
1994/5	16	6–7	5,366
Exploitation (c)			
1968/9	12	2.5	2,404
1994/5	20	5	7,769
Exploitation (d)			
1968/9	15	2.35	3,053
1994/5	20–1	3	6,610

What Prompts a Household to Change its Techniques?

Several considerations prompted changes in the techniques used on an *exploitation* during the period leading up to 1969. Sometimes an established technique had ceased to seem satisfactory because the *cultivateur* had learned about the benefits of an alternative. This was most strikingly the case in the change from horses and oxen to tractors. Étienne Maitrugue, who bought Pellaport's second tractor in 1954, told me that as soon as everyone realized those with tractors had gone home at the end of the day while the rest were still hard at work, they soon bought tractors for themselves. Traditional techniques were often described as *penible* (arduous). Sometimes the labour was accepted. One woman, planting beet by hand, remarked, 'C'est dur, mais tant pis!' (It's hard, but that's too bad!). On the other hand Claude Bavarel (who has a dry sense of humour) once complained to me that nowadays young men expected to lie in bed until five-thirty in the morning, whereas his father had always risen at three o'clock to milk the cattle and at two-thirty if he had to feed the oxen before working with them in the fields. And now, he added, some do not even care to sow grain by hand because the seeds become embedded in the palms of their hands.

Temporary crises in the household may make tasks suddenly more laborious. One *cultivateur* told me he had bought his milking machine when his wife was about to give birth to their second child. With twelve cows in the herd, he knew he would be unable to milk them all on his own. Another had bought his milking machine when his father retired. As the son had not yet married he would have no help to milk his eleven cows.

Behind such changes in attitude towards traditional methods, and such temporary crises, lie the constant pressures to expand the scale of production and manage with a smaller workforce, prompted by the steadily changing social and economic environment in which the villagers are working. Some said their decision to buy a milking machine was precipitated simply by the realization that their herd had steadily increased to the point where hand milking was impossible. The expectation in the community was that milking would take an hour, morning and night. As the time to milk the herd by hand steadily increases beyond the hour, purchase of a machine becomes inevitable.

CHOICE AND NECESSITY

Thanks to a convenient coincidence, all but one of the *cultivateurs* who had bought a milking machine by 1969 had also bought a baler, and the relative scale of their *exploitations* can be compared in a single table (Table 6.7). One *cultivateur* with eleven cows was still milking by hand but using a baler for the first time. It is clear from Table 6.7 that there was an important zone, between *exploitations* with seven cows and those with twelve, in which both hand and mechanized techniques are viable. Within

TABLE 6.7. *Size of* exploitations *using hand versus mechanized techniques in 1969*

		Window of opportunity	
No. of milch cows on *exploitation*	1 2 3 4 5 6	7 8 9 10 11 12	13 14 15 16 17 18 19 20
No. of *cultivateurs* milking by hand and loading hay with pitchfork	1 0 2 3 0 1	1 2 1 0 3 1	
No. of *cultivateurs* with milking machine and baler		1 0 1 0 0 1	1 0 0 1 2 1 0 1

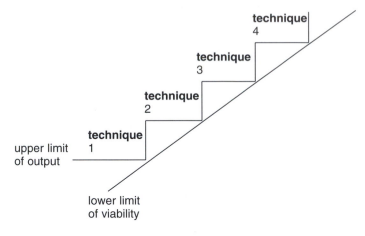

FIG. 6.1. Step model of innovation

this window of opportunity there were eight *cultivateurs* working by hand, and three who had mechanized. Among the latter, the *cultivateur* with seven cows worked part-time in a local sawmill, but all the others worked full-time on the *exploitation*. One man told me he had waited until there were sixteen cows in the herd before buying a machine! The main disincentive to buying new equipment is the cost, yet each existing technique becomes progressively less viable as the herd expands. Eventually a change in technique is triggered, establishing a new equilibrium within the demands of production. Sooner or later, if the *exploitation* is to continue, techniques will have to be changed again. As long as the window of opportunity has not moved beyond its financial scope, the productivity of the *exploitation* can thus be conceived of as proceeding in a stepwise fashion, or series of punctuated equilibria (see Fig. 6.1).

In their study of industrial innovation, Nelson and Winter similarly assume that firms will not search for new techniques if what they are doing already is sufficiently profitable, that is, if they are close enough to a peak in their 'fitness landscape' to make the cost and risk of innovating unjustifiably high. The step model is a satisficing, rather than an optimizing theory (Nelson and Winter 1982: 211; Elster 1983: 141). The step model implies a form of punctuated equilibrium, of the kind Eldredge and Gould (1972) advocated in biological evolution. It is questionable whether any direct analogue exists in natural selection, since mutation rates cannot be switched on or off, but rather similar processes may operate in an evolutionary landscape. Where a population has reached a peak in the landscape, further genetic variants cannot spread through natural selection and will not persist (see above). If, however, the co-evolution of different species erodes the peak, new genetic variants can once more be selected for.

The lower limit of production within the envelope is determined by the minimum income needed to support those working on the *exploitation*. The upper limit is set by the maximum productivity possible using current techniques with the currently available labour force and, as the above case studies show, varies with each technique. Since it is the rising cost of living that drives increased production, the rate at which the lower limit is rising can be measured in terms of the index of inflation (see Fig. 6.6). The relationship between the purchase of equipment and rising production on two actual *exploitations* can be seen in the graph at Fig. 6.2. The following paragraphs look at ways of measuring the lower limits of the envelope within which successive steps are taken.

INFLATION AND THE LOWER LIMIT OF VIABILITY

Inflation affects the value of the *cultivateur*'s produce at two levels, both in the specific value of milk and the general value of the franc. Chapuis found that, during the 1950s, the 29 per cent of *cultivateurs* in the Loue Valley who worked less that ten hectares of land could not afford the machinery that would allow them to increase output and keep pace with the incomes of factory workers. In response they had turned to full- or part-time employment outside agriculture. Even those with fifteen hectares were handicapped by the time it took them to save, since inflation eroded the value of their savings (Chapuis 1958: 180). In the early 1950s, Lambert also found that inflation had accentuated the difference between those on the Plateau of Levier working less than fifteen hectares and those with larger *exploitations* (Lambert 1953: 174–5).

The problem is not entirely due to the rising prosperity of factory and office workers. It is partly caused by the internal dynamic of agricultural production. Every summer milk production increases and the value of milk falls correspondingly. Until 1978, the monthly price was recorded in members' *carnets* and the relationship between income, production, and the seasonal cycle of inflation can be documented. The following table gives sample figures for two *exploitations*. With the exception of 1935, years have been chosen for which the records of both *exploitations* survive.

Each year, total milk production increases and this has a similar infla-

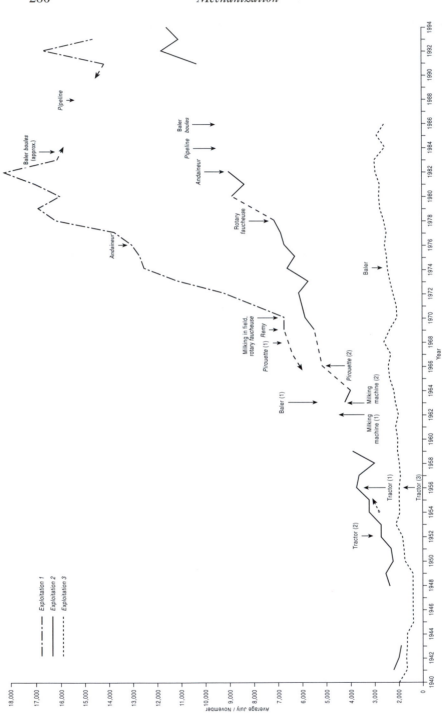

Fig. 6.2. Production and the purchase of equipment on two *exploitations*

TABLE 6.8. *Seasonal variation in the price and quantity of milk produced, 1935–75 (new fr. / kilos)*

Year	1935	1954	1967	1975
July production of milk as % of Nov. production:				
exploitation (a)	483	325	144	178
exploitation (b)		318	178	169
July value of milk as % of Nov. value	75	85	96	91

tionary effect, causing the value of milk progressively to fall in relation to the current value of the franc (see Fig. 6.3). In order to earn a constant income in relation to the current value of the franc milk production must be steadily increased, thus further decreasing the value of milk. It is only necessary for a minority of *cultivateurs* to follow this strategy for all to suffer the effect of declining value. All *cultivateurs* must follow suit, or see their income progressively eroded. This has been a particularly acute problem since the Second World War because investment in new machinery has been financed by increasing production. In 1995 Pierre Bavarel recalled how his grandfather had been wont to say it was buying machinery that ruined the *cultivateur*. The bigger the machine, the more indebted you are and, while people such as Felix Viennet and Joseph Bavarel may have had small *exploitations*, said Pierre, at least they never had to borrow money from anyone. Shutes noted that milk quotas had threatened Irish farmers' ability to repay the debts which increasing production had previously underwritten (Shutes 1993: 132–3). While the opportunity to work with more powerful equipment provided by tractors was clearly important, the pivotal change that occurred in the 1960s may well have been the arrival of a generation of farmers who could not remember the inter-war depression and the risk of bankruptcy for those unable to pay their debts. Describing change in Chanzeaux during the early 1960s, Wylie wrote that young farmers 'have gone *deeply into debt to begin mechanizing* their farms' (1966: 76, my emphasis). They 'are free of their elders' crippling fear of credit' (ibid. 117). Their attitude contrasted with that of an older farmer who 'would never borrow a penny' and feared that those who do buy equipment on credit will be dispossessed in a second great depression (ibid. 131). Gröger (1982: 123) argued that in Aveyron young farmers were more willing to borrow money because they were eligible for long-term credit. She none the less noted the reluctance

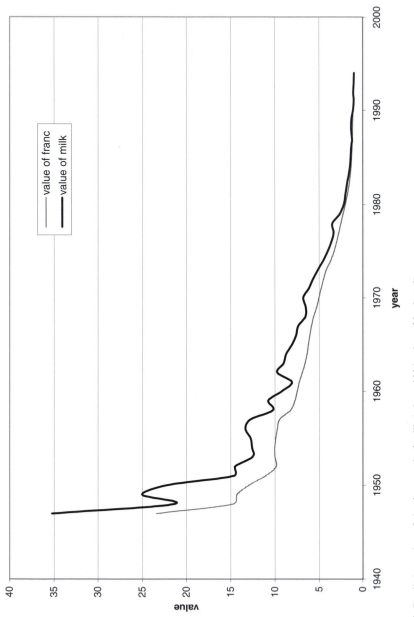

FIG. 6.3. Declining value of the franc and of milk (where 1994 value of both = 1)

of older men to invest and drew a parallel with the damaging spiral of loans and increasing production she had found on US tobacco farms (ibid. 127–8). In Brittany the arrival of the tractor 'plunged farmers into the infernal spiral of constant indebtedness. Before a new item of equipment was either worn out, paid for, or written off another version of it—newer, bigger, more powerful—had come along to render the previous one obsolete' (Segalen 1991: 245).

Figure 6.3 depicts the fluctuating value of milk against the value of the franc. While the value of milk is, in the long term, declining faster than the value of the franc, it passes through a series of peaks and troughs which are not caused solely by inflation. Étienne Maitrugue, a former president of the co-operative, explained that the peaks for 1962, 1970, and 1988 were the consequence of changing the wholesaler to whom the co-operative sold its cheeses. It was, he said, like changing your insurance agent; the new agent initially tempts you with a good rate, which becomes progressively less favourable over following years. The trough of 1976 was caused by a drought year. Production of cheese fell, bringing about a peak in prices two years later, when the effect of reduced production was experienced in the shops.

One of the three *exploitations* that have preserved their dairy records belonged to a couple whose children did not wish to take it over on their parents' retirement. Until retirement they managed the *exploitation* as the means to provide their own subsistence and undertook little mechanization. Figure 6.2 compares the growth of their production in relation to that of two *exploitations* in the forefront of mechanization.

Suppose, however, that a *cultivateur* expects to remain in production indefinitely and is aware that inflation progressively erodes the purchasing power of his production. In 1968 the average price of milk at the village dairy was 0.4686 fr. per kilo and the average annual production per *cultivateur* was 35,775 kilos, giving an average annual income of 16,764 fr. In 1994 the average price of milk at the village dairy was 2.2812 fr. per litre and the average annual production per *cultivateur* was 170,646 litres, giving an annual average income of 389,278 fr. What has this increase done to their purchasing power? A suite of machinery comprising tractor, milking machine or milking parlour, mechanical scythe, *pirouette*, *remy* or *andaineur*, and baler cost 221 per cent of the average annual income in 1968 and 131 per cent of the average annual income in 1995. Despite an increase in average milk production of 477 per cent, purchasing power has risen only by 90 per cent. Even this increase in purchasing power is overstated. It is the smaller scale *exploitations* which have gone out of

TABLE 6.9. *Cost of equipment in relation to average annual income, 1968 and 1994*

	1968 cost	% av. income		1994 cost	% av. income
Average annual income	16,764			389,278	
Tractor, 25 hp	15,750*	94			
40 hp	17,000	101	65 hp	180,000*	46
Milking machine, 2 *pots*	3,000*	18	*salle* (4 cows)	125,000	32
			(6 cows)	150,000*	39
Pirouette	3,300*	20		30,000*	8
Remy	2,000*	12	*andaineur*	15,000*	4
Baler (rect. bales)	11,400*		(*boules*)	90,000*	23
Reciprocating scythe	1,500*	9			
Rotary scythe	3,500	21		35,000*	9
Total of items marked*		221%			131%

production. The average annual income of those who remain in production in 1995 was 22,873 fr. in 1968 and the same suite of equipment would have cost 160 per cent of their annual income. Their purchasing power has only increased by 31 per cent. A *cultivateur* who had ten cows in 1969 may well have been hesitating whether to invest in this suite of equipment. Suppose he decided not to increase his herd size and to continue with his existing techniques (a small tractor and *râteau faneur*). Even if he had been able to match the others' improved yields per cow in 1994, the corresponding suite of equipment would cost him 406 per cent of his annual income. The longer technological change is delayed, the further the window of opportunity moves and the harder it becomes to invest in current machinery.

Table 6.10 shows the rank order of *exploitations* in the village at four points since 1939. The rank orders for 1968, 1980, and 1995 are based on milk production, while that for 1939/43 is based on the size of livestock holdings. In 1939 and 1943 César Maitrugue carried out a census of *exploitations* in the southern half of the village, in order to determine the scale of war requisitions. César's sons found his notebook in 1995 and allowed me to copy out his lists. Livestock were assessed according to a points system in which an ox, horse, or 2-year old heifer (i.e. one about to bear its first calf) rated two points, a cow or a 1-year old calf rated one point. A total of twenty-three *exploitations* are documented and they are ranked according to this points system in the first column of Table 6.10 (those which were surveyed on both occasions show little or no change in the size of their holdings). Since there were forty-five members of the co-operative when it was reconstituted in 1947 it seems likely that César's census provides a representative sample of about half the *exploitations* that existed at the time of the Second World War. The only new *exploitation* to appear after the war is no. 22. All the others not surveyed by César, such as *exploitations* 1 and 2, are situated in the other half of the village. No milk yields are recorded in his list, but the *carnets* of two *exploitations* survive from 1943, which show that *exploitation* 3 was producing an annual average of 1,937 kilos of milk per cow and *exploitation* 17 an average of 1,788 kilos. These give some idea of the maximum and minimum levels of milk production at the time. The dairy *carnets* for *exploitation* 17 for 1933 onwards show production was halved during the lean years of the Second World War. Pre-war production levels were not matched until the mid-1950s. Although the graph at Fig. 6.4 gives an estimate of maximum and minimum production levels for 1943 based on the above data, the curve cannot be extrapolated back-wards to the pre-war period.

Of course these data may be inaccurate (see La Thérèse's comments, in Ch. 1). I discussed the list with Claude Bavarel, who identified the people whose names I did not recognize. Claude pointed out that people were very likely to have underreported the size of their herd. 'People always tried to keep their best cows. It was normal; they were to be killed; why give your best cow? It was for the meat.' He drew my attention to the fact that *exploitation* 10 was said to have six calves under 1 year of age, but only seven cows. He thought it likely that they must have had eight cows. In many cases, however, he felt the records were broadly accurate, and only missing one or two calves from each stable.

All but one of the *exploitations* reported to own both horses and oxen in 1939–43 survived in production until 1968. Those *cultivateurs* who went out of production between 1943 and 1968 were, in general, those which did not buy tractors. The three largest *exploitations* that failed to survive belonged to families whose children left the village to find work in the cities. The man who is ranked between nos. 13 and 20 in 1939–43 was the last to work solely with oxen. He lived with his two brothers and worked as *cantonnier* until his retirement. Many of the other small *exploitations* in the 1939/43 column belonged to celibate men or women, a few of whom were still alive, albeit retired, in 1969. It is striking that all but one of the *exploitations* which have survived up till 1995 were already

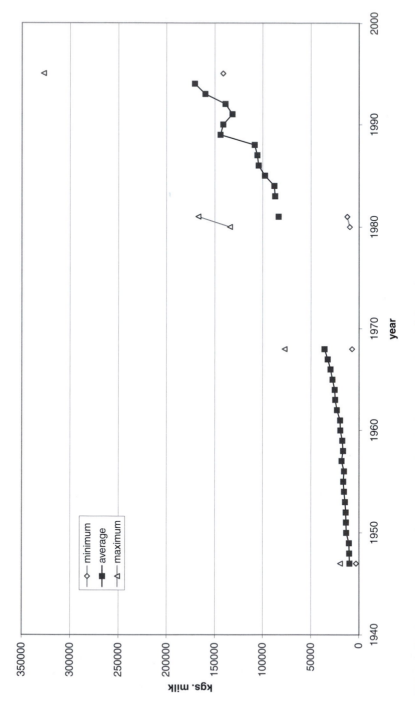

FIG. 6.4. Maximum, minimum, and average annual production per member of Pellaport's dairy co-operative, 1947–95

TABLE 6.10. *The survival of the largest?*

Rank order 1939–43	1968	1980	1995
10. (7 cows)*	**1. (20 cows)†**	2.	4. (50 cows)
— (6 cows)	**2. (17 cows)†**	4.	2. (43 cows)
— (5 cows)*	**3. (16 cows)†**	1.	13. (37 cows)
— (5 cows)	**4. (17 cows)†**	3.	1. (32 cows)
3. (5 cows)*	**5. (18 cows)†**	5.	6. (34 cows)
6. (+11.) (5 cows)*	**6. (12 cows)†**	6.	3. (28 cows)
16. (+8.) (5 cows)	**7. (13 cows)†**	7.	5. (32 cows)
— (4 cows)	8. (9 cows) [died 1980]	13.	7. (22 cows)
13. (3 cows)*	9. (8 cows) [ret'd 1979]	10. [ret'd 1988]	
— (3 cows)	**10. (9 cows)†**	14. [died 1993]	
20. (4 cows)	**11. (11 cows)**	11. [ret'd 1984]	
7. (3 cows)*	12. (8 cows)	20. [ret'd 1986]	
17. (3 cows)	**13. (11 cows)**	17. [ret'd 1987]	
12. (3 cows)	**14. (11 cows)**	19. [ret'd 1989]	
18. (3 cows)	15. (12 cows)		
23. (2 cows)	16. (6 cows)		
— (2 cows)	**17. (7 cows)**		
— (2 cows)	18. (7 cows)† [ret'd 1971]		
— (2 cows)	**19. (4 cows)**		
— (1 cow)	20. (4 cows)		
— (1 cow)	21. (3 cows) [ret'd 1976]		
— (1 heifer)	22. (3 cows)		
— (1 heifer)	23. (4 cows)		
	24. (1 cow)		

Note: **bold** type is used for those who are still active in the following column.
No. 6 in 1939–43 is the father of nos. 6 and 11 in 1968. No. 16 is still active in 1968, but his son has begun a separate *exploitation*, no. 8.

   * reported to own both horse(s) and oxen in 1939–43 (another measure of relative wealth).

   † owned both baler and milking machine in 1969 (a measure of intention to continue expanding production).

equipped with milking machines in 1969. The other survivor, *cultivateur* no. 13, bought a baler that year, but not a milking machine. While it is clearly the smallest *exploitations* which are most at risk, even large *exploitations* will cease if no children wish to perpetuate them. The position of some *exploitations* is a result of foreknowledge that they will cease with the present *cultivateurs'* retirement. Production on *exploitation* no. 3 declined during the years it was expected no child would take over. Sustained effort, on the other hand, can raise one's position in the rank order. *Exploitation* no. 13 is the most notable in this regard. In 1968 it was dominated by the elderly father. They had owned a tractor for only about three years, and were using a baler for the first time when Mike Rowlands watched them. After the father's retirement the *exploitation* began to move upwards in rank. The grandson's graduation from agricultural college in 1990 enabled it to expand even more rapidly.

LIMITS OF VIABILITY AND THE PRODUCTIVITY OF TECHNIQUES

Figure 6.1 represented the process of mechanization on an individual holding as a stepwise progression within an envelope defined by the maximum output possible using existing techniques and the minimum output required for subsistence. A general idea of the width of this envelope can be gained by comparing the actual minimum and maximum production among members of the dairy co-operative for particular years (Fig. 6.4). The following paragraphs try to quantify, as far as possible, the relationship between particular techniques and the lower limit of viability.

Milking

In 1969 the expectation in Pellaport was that each milking would take an hour. Techniques that extend milking beyond an hour should if possible be replaced. The efficacy of alternative milking techniques in the light of this expectation can be assessed from Tables 6.11 and 6.12. It is surprising to find that in 1969 it was those using a milking machine with two *pots* who were closest to the lower limit of viable production, defined by the acceptable time available for milking (see Table 6.12 col. 2: total milking time). Most were working for over an hour morning and evening. By 1986, the notional hour had been exceeded even further. In July 1986 it took Nicolas Jouffroy 1 hour 20 minutes to milk 38 cows, using four *pots*. Pierre and Renée Bavarel took 1 hour 20 minutes to milk 31 cows, using three *pots*. By 1995 the imposition of quotas had obliged both to reduce the size of their herds to the point where they could just have managed to complete milking with one hour, using this number of *pots*, but introduction of the *pipeline* has reduced their milking time even further (see Fig. 6.5 and Table 6.12).

TABLE 6.11. *Average milking rates per hour*

	Av. no.
Cows milked per hour by hand	8.9
Cows milked per hour by machine (with *pots*)	13.2
Cows milked per hour with machine and *pipeline*	34.3

I was particularly interested in the household which was still milking twelve cows by hand during 1969. They had not installed piped water to their stable and continued to lead their cows across the road to drink from the cattle trough. The last day in February, the day on which I had arranged to visit their stable, chanced to be the day I introduced myself to Prosper Jouffroy and his wife. After some initial suspicion, Prosper, his wife, and I struck up a lively conversation and they invited me to stay for lunch. Eventually excusing myself at quarter past five, I hurried up the road, feeling the effects of several glasses of wine followed by *eau de vie*. Milking had not begun at the Maitrugues' house; the first cows were emerging to drink from the stone trough across the street. I took up position in the gangway of the stable and watched while Mme Maitrugue rechained the cows in their stalls and raked out the dung. Milking of the first cow began at 5.36 p.m. and proceeded rapidly. By 6.07 p.m. Mme Maitrugue had finished milking the ninth cow and her husband had begun on the tenth. Unfortunately I was feeling increasingly dizzy, and left the stable for a moment to sit on a low wall outside. When I opened my eyes I was lying on my back in their dung heap. Up the hillside, across the road, I could see Jacques Maitrugue's father coming out of his farmhouse door. He saw me too, and hurried back indoors. Within a few minutes, Jacques had pulled me out of the dung but it was too late to return to his cousin's stable. During the next few days I learned that the couple I had been watching were teased by their neighbours, who told them it was the fetid atmosphere in their stable that caused me to pass out. They refused to let me watch their milking again. None the less, the observations I had recorded showed they had milked 9 cows in 31 minutes, indicating it would have taken 45 minutes to milk all 12. Although this was exceptionally quick they delivered only 32.1 kilos of milk to the dairy that evening, which implies they gained an average of 2.68 kilos of milk per cow, the lowest I recorded. Felicien Jouffroy and his wife, who achieved the greatest yield per cow among those milking by

TABLE 6.12. *Milking: comparison of individual performances*

Milking method	No. of cows	Total time (mins.)	Av. time per cow (mins.)	Total yield (kg.)	Rate (kg./min)
Hand (1 person)	6	51	8.5	34.5	0.68
	6	56	9.3	31.0	0.55
Hand (2 people)					
	7	40	5.7	19.5	0.49
	9	32	3.6	32.1	1.00
	6	45	7.5	29.2	0.65
	8	50	6.3	49.0	0.98
	8	62	7.8	47.6	0.77
Machine (1 *pot*)					
	4	18	5.3	—	—
	7	42	6.0	33.0	0.79
Machine (2 *pots*)					
	14	64	4.6	86.7	1.35
	13	66	5.1	81.7	1.24
	15	69	4.6	77.6	1.12
	10	42	4.2	62.5	1.49
	15	62	4.1	73.0	1.18
	16	76	4.8	80.0	1.05
	20	69	3.5	72.0	1.04
Pipeline					
	22	38	1.7	136.0	3.58
	30	54	1.8	272.0	5.04

Note: 1995 yields reflect the quantities permissible under the quota system, not the maximum possible with current techniques.

hand, took 45 minutes to milk 6 cows on the evening they gained 4.9 kilos per cow, and 62 minutes to milk 8 cows on the evening they gained 6.0 kilos per cow.

　　Table 6.12 and the accompanying graph, Fig. 6.5, compare individual performances during milking. Three stables were observed on two occasions, and each occasion is recorded separately. The two observations made in 1986 are shown on the graph but not in the table, since on these occasions I did not check milk yields. The number of cows that could be milked in one hour, given observed rates, is also shown on the graph and

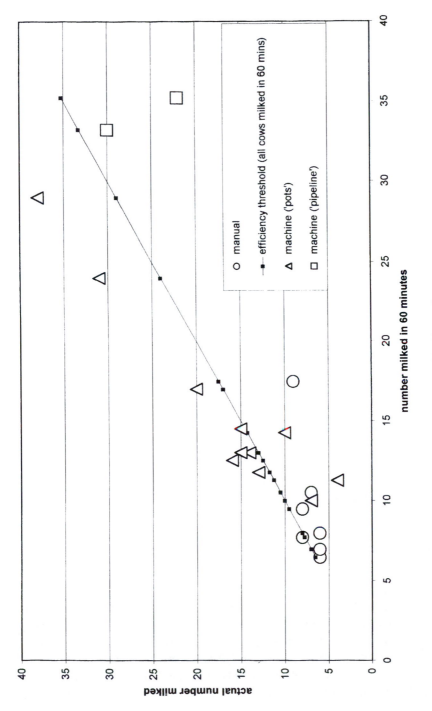

FIG. 6.5. Number of cows milked plotted against number that could be milked in one hour

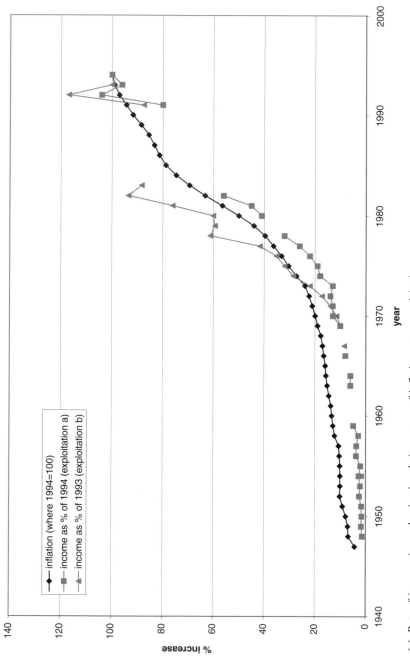

Fig. 6.6. Rate of increase in production in relation to rate of inflation on two *exploitations* in Pellaport

this curve can therefore be taken as an expression of the lower limit of viability within the envelope in the model presented above. It is striking that the performance of many using a machine and *pots* falls beyond this line, suggesting the technique became inadequate almost as soon as it was introduced.

Harvesting

When comparing the efficacy of harvesting techniques, the size of work-force required is an important variable (see Table 6.13, col. 3). The Dôle family, who used a horse to pull the trailer, had a basic workforce of three: one to pitchfork, one to receive and pack down the hay, and one to gather up loose hay with the large hand-rake. Those who replace their horse with a tractor must add one person to the workforce, to drive the tractor, although the tractor reduces the time taken to tow equipment and hay wagons between fields and house. Buying a *chargeuse* (elevator) or baler does away with the need to have someone pitchforking hay onto the trailer, and reduces the workforce by one again. Abandoning hand-raking makes it possible to reduce the workforce to two. In some cases more than one obser-vation was again made on the same *exploitation. Exploitations* are identified by number in the table, from which it can be seen that *exploitation* 1, the Dôle family, achieved a rate within the range of those who had bought trac-tors. On the basis of a single observation, the *chargeuse* offers little advan-tage in time/manpower over pitchforking by hand. It is, furthermore, powered by an unreliable auxiliary motor, and is unwieldy to use on hill-sides (cf. Clade 1994: 28). Those who continued to use a large hand-rake in conjunction with a baler achieved a lower harvesting rate per person than those who dispensed with the rake: the gain in hay harvested does not appear to justify the larger workforce. The worst performance among those using a baler was recorded on the *exploitation* that was working with a baler for the first time (see Table 6.13, col. 2: kilos of hay harvested per minute). Figures for harvesting large *boules* take into account the extra time needed to load the *boules* onto a trailer. These figures reinforce the argument that the reduction in labour requirements is one of the main gains with this technique. Since all *cultivateurs* now own two tractors, a second person can be turning the hay in another field or rowing it ahead of the baler.

It is much harder to quantify the upper limit imposed on a successful harvesting rate than is the case with milking. The speed at which hay must be harvested depends both on how many cattle there are in the stable and how much hay they are given in their winter diet, which vary considerably.

TABLE 6.13. *Harvesting: comparison of individual performances*

Exploitation	Hay harvested (kg. per minute)	Workforce	Hay (kg. per min.) number of persons
Pitchfork and horse			
1.	17	3	5.7
Pitchfork and tractor			
2.	14	4	3.5
3i.	19	4	4.75
3ii.	19	4	4.75
4.	29	4	7.25
Chargeuse (elevator)			
5.	29	3	9.7
Baler (small, rect. bales)			
6.	47	3	15.7
7.	56	3	18.7
8i.	84	3	28.0
8ii.	105	3	35.0
8iii.	140	3	46.7
9i.	91	2	45.5
9ii.	123	2	61.5
Baler (large, round *boules*)			
10.	38*	1	38.0
11i.	72	1	72
11ii.	78	1	78
12i.	81	1	81
12ii.	76	1	76

* On poor quality grass in communal pasture.

It also depends upon the year, since the number of fine days during the harvesting season is unpredictable. The first harvest extends over a period of four to six weeks but *cultivateurs* are making increasing use of the richer second hay crop or *regain*, and thus extending the harvest season. Since harvesting is a two-day process in which loading hay lasts for only half an afternoon, something like two and a half hours' loading hay correspond to two days' total harvest. Both milch cows and heifers require hay in winter (a 'cattle unit' in Table 6.14 is 1 cow or 2 heifers). As a number of approximations are built into the calculations, the results shown in Table 6.14 are little more than notional. *Exploitations* are identified with

TABLE 6.14. *Notional times required to complete harvest*

Exploitation	Cattle units	Total hay require-ment (kg.)	Aggregate harvesting rate (kg.)	Notional days required
Pitchfork and tractor				
2.	9	32,400	1,050	31
3.	6	18,360	1,425	13
4.	16	34,560	2,175	16
Chargeuse				
5.	13	40,950	2,175	19
Baler (small, rect. bales)				
6.	14	30,240	3,525	9
7.	21	66,150	4,200	16
8.	22	69,300	8,225	9
9.	26	128,700	8,025	16
Baler (large *boules*)				
10.	47	148,050	2,850	51
11.	46	136,620	5,625	24
12.	34	140,760	5,888	24

the same number as in Table 6.13 but where more than one observation was made on the same *exploitation*, the average performance has been used. Unfortunately the Dôles had to be omitted because I do not know how many cattle they had in their stable.

Where villagers told me their total harvest they had (apart from *exploitation* no. 2) harvested more, and taken longer even to complete their first harvest, than my calculations suggest. *Exploitation* no. 3 in Table 6.14 harvested 25,860 kilos over 18 days, no. 4 harvested 51,720 kilos over 24 days, no. 9 harvested 168,000 kilos over 23 ays, and no. 11 harvested 163,800 kilos (number of days not specified). Despite the variability of the samples and the imprecision of the calculations, it is still clear that, as Victor Jouffroy had told me in 1969, the early balers enabled *cultivateurs* to double the size of their herds without increasing the length of the harvest season (see Table 6.14, col. 5: notional days required to complete harvest). Although the average herd size has doubled again by 1995, the new balers have not enabled a comparable saving in time, and the length of the harvest season has now also been doubled.

THE UPPER LIMIT OF PRODUCTION AND THE SEQUENCE OF INNOVATION

In 1969 milking techniques were the critical variable that took the *culti-vateur's* methods to the limit of viability. By 1995 milking techniques had changed to give the *cultivateur* a considerable margin of safety, and harvesting (specifically hay-loading) techniques had become the critical element in the system. The upper limit on production will be determined by the element in the system of production which, at that moment, takes the longest to complete or demands the largest workforce. If innovations are available it can be predicted that they are most likely to be accepted where they increase the efficiency of this critical element, raising the upper limit of the envelope. The point was brought home to me force-fully when I was talking to Claude Bavarel about traditional harvesting techniques. Claude's recollections are largely substantiated by a number of Swedish studies carried out between 1690 and 1932 (Myrdal 1996). Claude told me that to scythe 30 ares by hand took one man a whole 10-hour day; Myrdal's data indicate that 50 ares per day was the norm, while Basalla (1988: 153) gives a figure of 40–80 ares per day for hand-reaping cereal. After each third stroke, Claude said, the blade had to be resharp-ened until it was so thin that the cutting edge could be flexed between the fingers. If you struck a stone, the sharpening took longer. The process was speeded by employing several mowers to work side by side. It is not surprising that horse- or ox-drawn mechanical scythes were the earliest pieces of equipment adopted in response to the declining workforce. The tractor-powered mechanical scythes used in 1969 had reduced the time needed to mow 1 ha. to 1 hour 46 minutes. The first machines had shorter blades and were pulled more slowly, but still reduced time and labour requirements considerably. Mechanical scythes introduced to Sweden between 1860 and 1900 took only two hours to scythe 1 ha., and cut the time to one-tenth of that needed when hand-scything. Figures quoted for early mechanical cereal reapers indicate they could also cut about 5 ha. of cereal in a 10-hour day (Laurens and Gauthier 1876: 71, Basalla 1988: 153).

Working alone, Claude needed $2^1/_2$ hours to turn 24 ares of drying hay with a pitchfork; a rate of $10^1/_2$ hours per hectare (Myrdal's figure of 4 hours per ha. is the only serious discrepancy with Claude's information). Since the hay must be turned at least twice while it dries total turning time amounts to at least 21 person/hours per hectare. Once mechanical scythes had been adopted, turning and rowing the hay would have become the critical elements in the harvesting sequence. M. Dôle, using the *faneuse* introduced shortly before the First World War to turn his hay, achieved a rate of 2 hours per ha., exactly the average time reported by Myrdal. The reduction in man/hours is again considerable. The remarkable aspect of these figures is that the earliest machines gave far greater gains over existing techniques than any of the post-Second World War innovations. The scale of the labour/time saved by the earliest machines surely contributed, together with the intervention of the Second World War, to the lengthy period that elapsed before further innovations were adopted.

TABLE 6.15. *Ideal and actual sequence of changes in technology*

Ideal sequence	Actual sequence	Date
1. Hand–scythe to mechanical scythe	mechanical scythe	1914 onwards
2. Pitchfork to mechanical fork (*faneuse*)	*râteleuse* and *faneuse*	1920 onwards
3. ? Hand–rake to mechanical rake (*râteleuse*)		
4. Tractor*	first tractor	1952–67
5. Pitchfork to baler	*râteau faneur*	1956–61
	milking machine	1962–c.1975
6. *Faneuse* } to *râteau* *Râteleuse* } *faneur*	baler (rect. bales)	1963–1974
7. *Râteau faneur* { *pirouette* { *remy*	*pirouette* *remy*	1966–70 1968–69
8. Baler (rect. bales) to baler (round *boules*)	rotary scythe	1970–78
9. *Remy* to *andaineur*	*andaineur*	1970–82
	mobile milking parlour	1970–83
	milking machine (*pipeline*)	1979–89
10. Reciprocating scythe to rotary scythe	baler (round *boules*)	1985–91

* A tractor is absolutely necessary to operate the baler and is needed to use the *râteau faneur* effectively; the earliest tractors in Pellaport were not powerful enough for balers.

Once mowing, turning, and rowing had been mechanized, the critical element became the loading of hay onto the trailer. A two–person team working with one of the early balers reduces the loading time almost to that required to mow 1 ha. with a reciprocating mechanical scythe and below the total time required to turn or row the hay with a *râteau faneur*. Rotary scythes reduce mowing time to 33 person/minutes per ha. Meanwhile the *pirouette* has reduced the time required to turn 1 ha. of hay to 30 minutes. The *remy* puts hay into rows at a rate of 1 hour per ha. and the *andaineur* further reduces this to 45 minutes per ha.

If appropriate innovations were always available at the critical time, the predicted sequence of change would, therefore, be that listed in Table 6.15 col. 1. The validity of this hypothetical sequence is generally supported by the sequence of technological change in Pellaport (Table 6.15 col. 2). The two main discrepancies are the late introduction of balers, which needed more power than the first tractors could provide, and the early introduction of rotary scythes.

CONCLUSION

Biological evolution can be explained as the effect of natural selection on genetic variation in a population, and technological change can be explained as the effect of economic selection on variations in the techniques used within a community. Although technical variations are not completely random, lack of information prevents people from making completely rational choices. The late nineteenth-century censuses from La Combe Sainte-Marie reveal some of the divergent trajectories households could follow during a period of economic change. The purchase of a machine when one's father retires or one's wife expects a baby, the necessity in the past of becoming a *journalier* if one's partner dies, also illustrate the intersection of demographic and economic variables. There will be some levels at which unpredictability in social process is important for the life-chances of individuals but relatively trivial for a sociological analysis. The cumulative effect of such small variations during a period of social instability may be more significant, precipitating social differentiation during the transformation of agriculture on the Plateau of Levier after 1850, and again after the Second World War.

Giddens objected to the use of evolutionary models in the social sciences. Chapters 5 and 6 have shown how many social scientists think otherwise and have argued that, providing the differences between learned and genetically transmitted information are kept in mind, both adaptive processes tending towards stability and interactive processes which promote cumulative change in cultural behaviour can be identified. Giddens's (1984: 237) point that societies do not have the same degree of closure as biological species is clearly applicable to any use of an evolutionary model at the level of household, village, or even the nation-state (Giddens 1984: 237), since the ramifications of agricultural change in the United States reach across the Atlantic to influence the strategies of European governments and farming households. If the cultural equivalent of a breeding population is a community among whom ideas can diffuse, then French farmers clearly belong to several communities of different scales (e.g. a smaller one for agricultural equipment, a larger one for labour-saving devices in the kitchen). Giddens also rightly criticized the treatment of cumulative changes as 'stages in history' (see conclusion to Ch. 2, above). They can better be interpreted as the outcome of more complex adaptive processes than those envisaged by Darwin, where variation in the environment is no longer an independent variable but is transformed by innovations. Giddens (ibid. 172) was also right to argue that, since people's (inter)actions generate the social order, society is not 'external' to individuals in the same sense that the physical environment is external to them, but the concepts of evolutionary landscapes and niche construction also blur Darwin's original, categorical distinction between evolving populations and their physical environment (Kauffman 1993: 173–4, Odling-Smee 1995).

Agricultural equipment must be adapted to its physical environment. The suitability of elevators and rotary mowers for the uneven terrain of the Plateau of Levier was critical to their acceptance or rejection. None the less, it is the economic, not the physical environment that determines how long use of a particular type of machine remains viable, and this environment is changed by the consequences of innovation. Despite the rise in living standards, Marx's predictions that profits are progressively reduced by increasing investment in capital equipment and that markets eventually become saturated are both supported by the post-war history of mechanization in agriculture. These processes demonstrate why a simple 'infection' model for the diffusion of technical innovations is inadequate. The population 'at risk' is heterogeneous and its condition changes. Innovations are most likely to be adopted when they best satisfy the purchaser's current needs. Nelson and Winter (1982: 325) predicted that 'a steady, gentle rain of technological advances on the industry will tend to make all firms move forward together', and much the same has been true of *exploitations* in Pellaport. None the less, Nelson and Winter's (ibid. 320) expectation that as small firms decline they cut back on their investment in research and development, thus decreasing their chances of catching up parallels the effect of the moving window of opportunity in Pellaport. There is a steady attrition of *exploitations* as the smallest tend to cease production.

Elster (1983) insisted that, in the absence of a single mechanism paralleling reproductive success, the feedback mechanisms that result in the evolution of social behaviour should be identified. The transmission of cultural traits ranges from the unconscious acquisition of habitus through copying what seems to work best under current conditions to anticipating the future and seeking out ways of coping with it. The selective mechanisms at work on the Plateau of Levier divide starkly into anticipated and unanticipated outcomes, of which the most striking are those to which villagers' strategies themselves contributed. Direct observation of alternative techniques, indirect reports (sceptically received), and monitoring one's bank balance all provide information on which the decision to continue with existing techniques or change them can be based. The performance of all innovations is to some extent uncertain, but some of this uncertainty is eliminated by the first in the village to try them out. In general terms, people were well informed about the need to increase production if their *exploitation* was to remain viable. Government propaganda had in fact led them to overestimate the rate of change. On the other hand, the tremendous effect that increased production would have on the value of their produce must, in retrospect, be seen as largely unintended. Chapter 7 will question whether, even if it had been anticipated, individual households operating in the regional economy of cheese production could have done anything about it. Only firms with a large share of the market can take account of the fact that further increases in output will lower the price of their goods (Nelson and Winter 284). In this respect the National Forestry Office's ability to regulate the sale of timber from communal forests contrasts markedly with the difficulty of regulating cheese production (see Ch. 2). Post-war economic policy has been, figuratively, to climb the adaptive peak of efficient Comté production. When the unintended consequence was to risk initiating a cheese mountain, villagers have only been able to branch out towards other peaks in the fitness landscape such as livestock breeding and new varieties of cheese to a limited extent.

7

Agency and Structuration in the Evolution of Co-operation

THE PROBLEM

This chapter returns to the issues posed by the variable social organization of villages on the Plateau of Levier that were identified in Ch. 2
and discusses them in the light of the ideas developed in Chs. 3 to 6. It
will try to identify the processes that guide the historical trajectory of
a social system, to explain why villages on the plateau, in common with
many other villages in the region of the Alps, have retained a more
highly corporate structure and a denser web of interpersonal relations
than have characterized English villages over the last two hundred
years. Examples will be given of the way in which strategies drawn
from the cultural repertoire have been implemented to cope with
changing economic and social conditions. Foremost among those
conditions are the declining proportion of *cultivateurs* and the rise of
employment outside agriculture. Strategies for managing resources in
a uniform, subsistence economy often become inappropriate as occupations diversify and agriculture becomes more specialized, but new
strategies are built from an existing cultural repertoire. Social change
is prompted by some of the same processes that drive technological
change. Like a piece of agricultural machinery, each particular institutional arrangement persists during a period of change until it
becomes untenable, and is then replaced by a new arrangement, in a
series of steps. As in mechanization, the lateral transmission of ideas
causes social strategies to converge. Communities facing the same
conditions may choose to manage their resources in different ways but
awareness of existing solutions to widely experienced problems
contributes to the similarity in the historical trajectory of neighbouring
communities.

There are also important differences between social and technological change. The decision to buy new machines is often taken within the household, but change in the management of collective resources requires political action in the commune. The procedures used by co-operatives and entrepreneurs, village council and special interest groups, CUMA and informal *ententes* provide competing strategies. Their advocates may come into conflict and will need the co-operation of others to succeed. Politics is a 'game' played in a changing arena shaped by economic and governmental processes to which villages contribute, yet which bring them into relationships beyond their control. Social change on the Plateau of Levier can take a distinctive cultural trajectory only to the extent villagers are *authorized* to enact elements from their own cultural repertoire.

This chapter will compare the social history of the Plateau with that of other regions, to identify the recursive effects of interaction in different cultural milieux which either reinforce or undermine existing social organization, helping to determine whether or not 'revolution be the same'. The third section of the chapter returns to issues raised in Ch. 3: the different effect of unigeniture and partibility on social relations inside and outside the household, the divergence of social trajectories that led to the almost universal enclosure of common land in England but its survival on the Plateau of Levier, the divisive effects of increasing participation in a market economy. In conclusion, I will reassess whether a 'science of society' of the type sought by Radcliffe-Brown can be achieved.

SOCIAL THEORY AND THE INDUSTRIAL REVOLUTION

Many classic sociological theories were originally devised to explain the causes and effects of the Industrial Revolution on European society. Durkheim's *Division of Labour in Society* is essentially an analysis of the changes that took place in French society during the Industrial Revolution (see Ch. 2). Tönnies's (1957) distinction between *gemeinschaft und gesellschaft* (social relations regulated by the mutual obligations of familial kinship and contract) tried to characterize the different quality of social relations in rural and urban communities. Chapter 4 looked at *gemeinschaft*-like relationships in Pellaport. Kropotkin (1972: 4) was inspired by the voluntary associations he found among watchmaking communities in the Swiss Jura to argue for the importance of co-operation in evolution. 'After a week's stay with the watchmakers, my views on socialism were settled. I was an anarchist.' Kropotkin (ibid. 211) also commended *fruitières* in his study of mutual aid. In analysing the evolution of co-operation, this chapter will draw particularly on the work of Marx and Darwin. Karl Marx and Charles Darwin were contemporaries. Marx's *A Contribution to the Critique of Political Economy* was published in the same year as *The Origin of Species* (1859). Their evolutionary theories none the less differed fundamentally. Marx worked within the tradition of 'progressive' evolutionists, who assumed that (social) change is driven forward by an internal dynamic, whereas Darwin saw evolution as the result of local ecological conditions acting on random genetic variation in a species.

The Marxist Paradigm

Marx took a number of ideas from Adam Smith, but set out to explain why the economic processes identified by Smith had not led, as Smith claimed they would, to universal opulence. Like Smith, Marx argued that social relationships are generated by exchange. It was A. Smith (1976: 22) who pointed out that a person can produce more than they require for their own subsistence and that the power conferred by the ownership of money is the power to buy other people's labour (ibid. 48). Marx's insight was to understand the process that progressively increased the domination of the capitalist over his workers, once the capitalist had gained control of the means of production. If a craftsman needs to work six hours to earn his subsistence, but the capitalist makes him work for eight, the extra two hours labour earns the capitalist his profit. With this he can buy more labour, or more equipment for his workshop. It is a case of positive feedback or, in Marx's (1930: 189) words, 'self-expanding value . . . a monster quick with life'.

Marx identified a second dynamic within the system. Production is ultimately limited by the tendency for workers' efficiency to decrease after many hours' labour, or even for them to die more frequently than they can be replaced. The early capitalist mode of production had therefore created a social environment in which any technological innovation that produced more from the same amount of labour would rapidly spread through the social system. As such machines were invented, the capitalist system underwent a second phase of positive feedback. Elster highlighted a third dynamic implicit in Marx's analysis, the tendency for producers' profits to fall as the market for a product becomes saturated. The implications of the third tendency for agricultural production have been discussed in Ch. 6. Here we look at the impact of such a dynamic on the management of village resources.

The principal weakness in Marx's analysis, from the perspective of this chapter, was his failure to subject collective ownership, the alternative to capitalism that he advocated, to a similarly penetrating analysis. Marx's approach to collective ownership was flawed by his treatment of it as the natural, or original human condition, thereby apparently removing the need to analyse the specific conditions that sustained it. This simple error has been responsible for the immense human suffering caused by forced collectivization during the twentieth century, including the death or deportation of five million Russian peasants (Rösener 1994: 196). The following section looks at ways in which the competing Darwinian paradigm of evolution has clarified the functionality of collective ownership of the commons, but argues that the Darwinian approach itself suffers from limitations that can be overcome only by developing Marx's analysis of feedback, or internally generated dynamics, in social process, an approach picked up by Giddens's notion of structuration and its recursive effects.

The Darwinian Paradigm

Recent work in socioecology has applied a neo-Darwinian theory to several aspects of social process. Chapter 4 looked at research on reciprocal altruism. Theories exploring parallels between the increase in frequency of adaptive genetic traits and the spread of innovations were discussed in Chs. 5 and 6. Here we will consider theories that predict the circumstances in which it is in the individual's self-interest to co-operate with others in the management of common property. As in Ch. 4, my aim is to identify objective limits to the cultural processes of structuration and habitus.

Marx's failure to analyse the dynamics of collective ownership has been addressed by several theorists. One school of thought, exemplified by Hardin (1968) holds that, unless coercion is applied by an authority, common property is inevitably less well managed than private property. A simple market model is used to support this contention. The other school, exemplified by McCay and Acheson (1987) and Ostrom (1990), use aspects of neo-Darwinian theory to argue that individual and collective ownership are both adaptive, but to different circumstances.

Hardin (1968) assumed that access to common land was normally unregulated. He drew on the work of Lloyd, a nineteenth-century writer who proposed a parallel between common grazing land and the labour market. Lloyd argued that the market was a public good to which there was open access. Where children had to fend for themselves from an early age and there were no restrictions on entry into the labour market, nothing would limit the size of working–class families. The market was flooded with labour and wages fell. It should have been in the working class's interest to restrict the number of children they had, to keep wages high. The difficulty was that if a few families produced large numbers of children, the level of wages fell for everyone, and the large families earned more than those who had showed restraint. Large families were transforming the 'niche' in which all workers tried to survive. Since others were not to be trusted, the rational strategy was for all to have large families (Lloyd 1964). Lloyd, followed by Hardin, applied the same principle to the commons. If there are no controls over access, self-restraint by some herdsmen will be undermined when others put too many stock on the commons. These 'free-riders' cause degradation of the niche on which all depend, but only they benefit from the higher numbers of stock they have pastured. The rational strategy is therefore for everyone to overstock, destroying the commons' value. Hardin argued that only sanctions imposed by government, or privatising the commons, would enable responsible management. He discounted the possibility of self-regulation among the users.

Self-regulation depends on limiting access to, and use of, a shared resource. The commons must therefore be treated as a territory. The socioecological theory of territoriality was originally developed to explain animal behaviour, and first applied to human territoriality by Dyson-Hudson and Smith (1978). The theory holds that it will be adaptive to defend the boundaries of a territory if the resources within it are sufficiently dense and predictable to outweigh the costs of defence. When resources are scarce and unpredictable, both the cost of defending a large enough area to guarantee subsistence and the risk of resources within it failing will be too great to justify defence. Hunter-gatherers living in the sparse and risky environments of tropical deserts or the Arctic generally allow neighbouring bands to forage over each other's territories, allowing the current hosts reciprocal rights to enter the guests' territory on future occasions when the distribution of local abundances has changed in the guests' favour. On the north-west coast of North America, where resources are more densely and predictably distributed, territorial boundaries were forcefully defended by the groups or individuals that owned them, even to the extent of killing trespassers. Dyson-Hudson and Smith argued that the pastoral Karimojong of East Africa defend grazing land as a tribe because the distribution of grass and water is too unpredictable to justify dividing it into small areas defended by individual lineages. Small fields of maize are, on the other hand, defended by the Karimojong households who cultivate them. Netting used the same argument in his analysis of landownership in the Swiss village of Törbel. Grass on the alpine pastures is too dispersed and unreliable to justify the cost and risk of dividing it into fields owned by individual households. Collective management is more efficient. Far from allowing open access, use of the alpine commons is closely regulated by the community. Only citizens of the village are allowed to use it and the number of cattle they can graze is controlled. Privately owned fields are located on lower, richer soils (Netting 1981: 60–7). McCay and Acheson (1987) point out that, under the medieval and post-medieval open field system, use of English commons was also generally regulated by the communities to which they belonged. Neeson (1993: 88) claims overstocking on English common land was rare and that deliberate overstocking was in fact a strategy used by wealthy landowners who advocated enclosure to justify abolishing common grazing. McCay and Acheson argue, in opposition to Hardin and Lloyd, that the English enclosures were precipitated by conditions peculiar to the rise of capitalism and not by an inherent weakness in commons management. McCay and Acheson's volume includes case studies from Japan, Ethiopia, Indonesia, and Spain, where collective management of commons is successfully practised. The conditions under which enclosure occurred in England will be assessed later in the chapter.

Even if collective management is, under certain conditions, the most effective strategy communities are not necessarily successful in sustaining joint control. Ostrom argues that Hardin's model is not wrong, but lacks the generality Hardin claimed for it. The open-access scenario proposed by Hardin is not the only possibility. The application of games theory to the study of the evolution of social strategies predicts the conditions in which individuals can form stable coalitions based on mutual trust which can avert the 'tragedy' of over-exploitation. Even if the cumulative benefits of co-operation are greater than those of cheating (free-riding), individuals who only interact once will do best to assume the other will cheat and thus avoid the costs of restraint. When individuals interact repeatedly, however, co-operation can become a stable strategy (see Axelrod 1990 and discussion of the Prisoner's Dilemma in Ch. 4). Ostrom draws on games theory to identify the conditions most likely to enable successful control of the commons by those who use them. People who interact regularly in a local context, who have developed shared norms and patterns of reciprocity, who can monitor whether their associates are adhering to the agreed level of exploitation, and who can punish free-riders, are most likely to succeed (Ostrom 1990: 184–8). Few studies have attempted to demonstrate a direct link between human social co-operation and reproductive success and, in general, theories of the evolution of co-operation are tested simply by investigating whether co-operation is most sustainable in the circumstances the theory predicts (but see Panter-Brick, Lotstein, and Ellison 1993).

Fruitful as this approach is, models that explain reciprocal aid and territoriality as adaptive to particular environments in societies as diverse as hunter-gatherers and peasants cannot of themselves account for long term processes of social transformation. Although Darwin sometimes used turns of phrase which suggested he saw evolution as a progressive force, this was not the import of his theory and classic neo-Darwinian analysis deals strictly with the adaptation of life-forms to specific ecological niches. The only criterion it uses to measure the success of evolutionary processes is their contribution to the reproductive fitness of an organism in its particular environment. This is a radical departure from the progressive models of evolution that dominated sociological thinking in the eighteenth and nineteenth centuries. Chapter 6 suggested how the concepts of evolutionary landscapes and niche construction had modified Darwin's theory to account for the instability of adaptations. Lloyd's model of commons management can be seen, in retrospect, to depend on the effect of positive feedback or, in Odling-Smee's terms, 'niche-construction' (in this case, niche degradation), and this chapter will look further at the implications of Lloyd's idea.

The evolution of commons management and dairy associations can be linked with two causes of social change familiar to Marx and other nineteenth-century writers, population growth and inflation; but it will be argued that their effect is mediated by the particular social strategies through which they are confronted. This chapter explores the effects of feedback which link population growth and inflation to policies for the collective management of resources. It looks both at processes internal to village life, and at wider processes that affect the village.

GLOBAL CYCLES

Braudelian Cycles

Braudel (1990: 15) identified cycles, each lasting several centuries, signalled by rise and fall in population levels and changes in the rate of economic activity. These have created 'a series of consecutive Frances, similar yet dissimilar. . . . In their ebb and flow, these cycles have stirred up the living mass of our history'. Braudelian cycles are driven by global variation in the scale of economic exchange, population size (i.e. supply of human labour), and technology that impinge on village life. Braudel argues the accumulation of technical knowledge is responsible for preventing his long-term cycles from returning to their starting-point. He described the period between AD 950 and 1450 as 'the first modern age' in Europe, encompassing a complete demographic cycle and corresponding growth and contraction in the economy (ibid. 128). Celtic, Roman, Merovingian, and Carolingian Gaul each corresponded to an earlier cycle (ibid. 72). The 'first modern age' began shortly before the year AD 1000, peaked in about 1350, and declined swiftly during the hundred years from 1350 to 1450. Once population growth outstripped agricultural production famine and epidemics took their toll. The cycle's downturn was associated with the Black Death, which reached Franche-Comté in 1349. High taxation, the uncertain value of currency and, above all, the Hundred Years' War, created uncertainty in the economy (ibid. 137–61).

The population of England, France, and Germany tripled between 1000 and 1340 (Rösener 1994: 49). Its growth was associated with land clearances and improved agricultural technology. Watermills, and later windmills, were the central innovations. Braudel argues the twelfth century occupies the same place in the classic cycle as the nineteenth-century Industrial Revolution does in the present cycle, but water- and windmills did not have the chain-reaction effect of stimulating further innovations. Water and wind power had been exploited to their limits by the fourteenth century and imposed a ceiling on sustainable population growth (Braudel 1990: 520). It was during the upward part of the 'classic' cycle that the Plateau of Levier and the Italian Alps were colonized. Certain preconditions had to be met: a market demand for the products of pastoralism, political stability, and an élite with sufficient wealth to sustain large flocks that were moved over long distances (Viazzo 1989: 124–6).

In the year 1300 the population of England stood at five to six million, the maximum sustainable under existing agricultural production. England was slightly ahead of the global trend. After 1350 the population of Western Europe declined. The Black Death was not, in Rösener's opinion, the initial cause. Although the climate may also have deteriorated, the cycle was not entirely a Malthusian one driven by the constraints of disease and famine. Population growth had reduced peasant holdings to a minimum size and created a class of day labourers and cottagers. The fourteenth and fifteenth centuries were a period of stagnation and crisis (Rösener 1994: 65–9). As the population declined there was less demand for agricultural produce and food prices fell, reducing income from the sale of farm products. Prices for manufactured goods, on the other hand, remained constant and craftsmen's wages rose. Rising wages drew people out of poorer rural areas into towns. The chief victims were farmers and landlords who depended on hired labour. There are clearly parallels here with the mid-nineteenth-century crisis that affected agriculture on the Plateau of Levier during the following cycle, but there is also a critical difference: in the fourteenth century technology was insufficient to replace the absent labour. Instead, farmers shifted from cereal to livestock farming, a less intensive method, producing meat that high-earning city dwellers could afford to buy (ibid. 73–7).

By 1550 the population of England had again reached its maximum of five to six million, and subsequently fell as people delayed marriage, causing the birth rate to diminish (Overton 1996: 8). As the population declined the demand for agricultural produce decreased and food prices also fell once more. When, however, population increased for a third time after 1750, agricultural techniques had improved so greatly that the Malthusian limit imposed by famine no longer applied. Between 1750 and 1850 the number of people fed by English agriculture increased by six and a half million (ibid. 198).

Population growth in the current cycle has been associated with numerous innovations in agriculture. While Braudel (1990: 271) and Netting (1981: 160–8) disagree over whether introduction of the potato between the mid-eighteenth and early nineteenth centuries was cause or consequence of population increase, the two are certainly correlated. Introduction of the potato to the Italian Alps in 1799 and to Abriès in the French Alps at about 1830 reduced mortality levels (Cole and Wolf 1974: 112; Rosenberg 1988: 90). Cereal cultivation virtually ceased in Kippel and the standard daily diet became four meals of potatoes and milk (Friedl 1974: 30–1). Planting artificial grassland containing trefoil, clover, and alfalfa was another important nineteenth-century innovation. Since it entailed abolition of the fallow phase in crop rotation, it eventually brought *vaine pâture* to an end (Braudel 1990: 279), putting pressure on the common pasture, forcing each household to guard its own livestock when they were grazing on the fields and introducing the practice of stall feeding, taking feed to livestock in their stables rather than releasing them to graze (Sabean 1990: 59).

Apart from a dip between 1760 and 1779, Neckarhausen's population followed much the same trend as that seen on the Plateau of Levier, rising continuously from 1640, when it is estimated at about 80, to 1869, when it had reached 924 (ibid. 40–1). As the population of rural Western Europe peaked again in the nineteenth century there was no longer any free land to colonize. This alone caused the cycle to follow a different trajectory to the preceding one. The eighteenth-century boundary disputes mentioned in Ch. 2 are presumably symptoms of increasing pressure on land on the Plateau of Levier. Delayed marriage and adult celibacy were adopted in response to overpopulation (Braudel 1990: 189–201) but, in Viazzo's opinion, were not sufficient to stabilize population levels (Viazzo 1989: 181–2). The adoption of such labour-intensive practices as hoe cultivation and stall feeding of cattle would have been facilitated by the increased labour capacity of the household associated with the European Marriage Pattern.

In the light of the continuing growth of the world's population, Braudel considered we were still in the midst of the cycle that began around 1450. France's population began to decline, however, during the first quarter of the nineteenth century (Bonneuil 1997: 104–5). Since then, the Braudelian link between demography and economic activity in Europe has been transformed from an *ancien régime* pattern where the population grows during a period of increasing prosperity, to a 'modern' pattern where it declines.

Industrial Cycles

The Russian economist Kondratiev developed Marx's theory that change in a capitalist economy is driven by positive feedback, encouraging the adoption of ever more efficient technological innovations whose benefits for the capitalist are eventually eliminated by saturation of the market (see Ch. 6). Kondratiev proposed that the industrial economy of the West has passed through several fifty-year cycles, the first covering the period between 1790 and 1845, the next 1845–95, and the third 1895–1930. The period between 1930 and 1950 is treated as transitional, with the fourth cycle beginning in 1950. Each cycle is produced by the adoption of a new technology which at first succeeds in generating wealth but eventually saturates demand. At the beginning of a cycle prices are high, at the end they have fallen. Berry and Kim (1996: 219) argue conditions become chaotic at the peak of each cycle, and strategies may diverge, 'beyond which clusters of innovations can move the economy on to alternative [pathways]' . Berry and Kim rely on the empirical evidence of price fluctuations in the market economy to demonstrate chaotic movement.

The rise and fall of Kondratiev cycles can deflect the trajectory of rural social systems into a new course. In 1852 the French economy emerged from a severe depression associated with the end of the first Kondratiev cycle. The start of the second cycle, coinciding with the upsurge of the French Industrial Revolution, created more urban employment and provided an unprecedented opportunity for emigration from the countryside (Rosenberg 1988: 107, 113; Wylie 1966: 50, 177–9). The Industrial Revolution radically redirected the trajectory of rural social process away from that taken during the previous, 'classic' cycle. Minot lost three-quarters of its population between 1836 and 1901 (Zonabend 1984: 5). The population on the Plateau of Levier began to decline in the 1850s, as it did in Chanzeaux and Abriès. The population of the Aveyron region peaked in 1886, during the next upturn in the French economy, but between then and 1975 it fell by one-third (Rogers 1991: 54). Depopulation did not affect the Swiss Alps until the post-Second World War economic boom characteristic of the fourth Kondratiev cycle. The population of Törbel grew more or less continuously from 1700 to 1950, while the population of Kippel continued to grow until 1960 (Netting 1981: 96; Friedl 1974: 72).

On the Plateau of Levier mechanization begins at the start of third Kondratiev cycle, while the widespread replacement of co-operative cheese production through *fruitières* by entrepreneurs took place during the third cycle's downturn. The 'disappearance of the peasantry', provoked by more intensive mechanization, has taken place during the fourth cycle. Since the 1950s, the Comté-producing region encompassing the Plateau of Levier has been locked in its own cycle of innovation and overproduction.

HISTORICAL TRAJECTORIES AND THE RECURSIVE EFFECTS OF INTERACTION

Four questions arising from the arguments of Bourdieu and Giddens were identified in the conclusion to Ch. 2. How are patterns of thought and social behaviour reproduced within and across generations? How is culture realized in the implementation of strategies? What are the recursive effects of interaction? How applicable are the ideas of evolutionary biology to cultural process? The questions can be addressed by comparing the historical trajectories of different European communities.

Giddens (1984: 190) argued that social systems are perpetuated through 'circuits of reproduction' which 'stretch' institutions across time and space. Historical and geographical comparisons between European villages reveal the circumstances in which co-evolving social strategies tend to support or undermine each other, hence enabling or inhibiting the 'stretching' of particular patterns of relationship in time. The recursive effect of using certain cultural strategies is to create the conditions in which those strategies either can or cannot readily be put into practice in future. When the realization of strategies undermines the conditions that make them possible, the social system will change. If a social system has become unstable, a single change at one point may precipitate an 'avalanche' of further changes in other parts of the system as, for example, co-operation collapses in different areas of social life (see Kauffman 1993: 242, 255, for analogous ideas in evolutionary biology). Local strategies may also be undermined by wider social processes for which village life has no responsibility.

The range of community studies carried out by Wylie (1966), Cole and Wolf (1974), Friedl (1974), Netting (1981), Zonabend (1984) and Verdier (1979), Behar (1986), Rosenberg (1988), Rogers (1991), and Ulin (1996), conducted with much the same theoretical orientation as that taken in this study, provide an excellent basis for testing hypotheses concerning the links between ecology, trade, inheritance strategies, village government, and the persistence of common land and mutual aid in production, which are raised by a comparison of the Plateau of Levier with neighbouring regions. Some of these studies are themselves comparative. Saint-Félix and Tret, studied by Cole and Wolf, are neighbouring communities with different cultural traditions, while the commune of Chanzeaux studied by Wylie and his team includes both large rented farms subject to a rule of impartibility and smallholdings transmitted through partible inheritance. Rogers compares Sainte-Foy with the very different village in Lorraine she had previously studied. A comparison of social life in Abriès before and after the French Revolution allows Rosenberg to identify the processes that destroyed the village's political integrity.

The range of social systems found in these communities shows that the various factors other authors have argued to have promoted *fruitières* on the Plateau of Levier—nucleated settlements, corporate management of village land and trade—all have important recursive effects on the probability of the social system persisting, as does the rule of inheritance. I shall discuss each in turn.

Common Property as an Adaptation to High Altitude

The forested hill slopes and high alpine pastures of the Swiss Alps and their foothills, the French Jura, are not suitable for ploughing. On the Plateau of Levier a rule of thumb holds that the better 50 per cent of land is capable of being ploughed and is privately owned, while the poorer 50 per cent belongs to the commune. Only slightly more than 11 per cent of the land in the Tyrolean valley studied by Cole and Wolf (1974: 146) is suitable for cultivation. Traces of abandoned fields on the mountainside above Saint-Félix show that current cultivation has extended private ownership to the limit of ecological sustainability (ibid. 147). Fields made by clearing and enclosing an area of common land in the Spanish village of Santa María del Monte during the mid-nineteenth century had declined in productivity to such an extent that most were abandoned by the mid-1960s, again demonstrating an ecological imperative behind the persistence of common land (Behar 1986: 230, 241). The surviving common land in Ashworthy, an English West Country village, is the poorest (Williams 1963: 13, 36). All these examples support the argument of Dyson-Hudson and Smith, and Netting, that collective ownership is more appropriate for poorer land.

Viazzo (1989: 24–5) notes that many anthropologists have argued that the virtual ubiquity in mountainous regions of village assemblies and councils of household heads, with considerable power conferred on local officials to enact community decisions and limit individual recklessness, reveals the evolution of a distinctive socio-political organization. In the Alps, the Andes, and the Himalayas economies are based on a combination of livestock rearing with cultivation of crops in small fields. The optimum ratio of herders to livestock can be as high as 1:30–40, many more animals than traditionally owned by a single household. A common herd saves labour. A rota, or the hiring of herders, releases the rest of the population to work in the fields. Communal tenure is associated with high-altitude zones where pastures, huts, and fences are more economically cared for through communal management, while lower-altitude fields and meadows are subject to individual tenure (ibid. 21–4).

The same institutional arrangements have none the less existed over a much wider area of Europe than the Alps. Open fields appeared in northern Europe between the eighth and tenth centuries and persisted for about one thousand years (Dahlman 1980: 95, Rösener 1994: 158–64; Unwin 1988: 89). The open field system combined a division of land into commons and privately managed strips of plough land in two to four large open fields (i.e. strips were not separated by hedges or fences). Private rights to strips were limited by an overriding right to graze village live-stock on the fallow and a compulsory rotation of cultivation between the open fields. While it lasted, the open field system provided the basis for corporate action in many northern European villages: 'collective property rights and communal decision making formed a very important part of the productive process' (Dahlman 1980: 95), determining which crops were to be planted and when land was to be turned over to fallow. Whereas each farmer tilled his own strips, livestock were kept together in common herds and grazed on both the fallow field and on communal pasture.

The three-field system once covered much of France north of the Loire, much of England, Germany, and Poland (Bloch 1966: 48). Other systems that distinguish common land from the fields worked by individual households and which rely on community-based procedures for regulating land-use are found in Scandinavia, on the West coast of Ireland (Fox 1978; Taylor 1987), and, formerly, in the *Mir* system of Russia (Rösener 1994: 168–70). Even in the Alps, moreover, the closed corporate community is not universal (Viazzo 1989: 280). Since they have occurred in many ecological settings, systems based on common rights to land cannot be considered an adaptation *to* high altitude, in any purposive sense. Like random genetic variations, such social systems are merely most likely to endure, that is be reproduced successfully through cultural practice, under conditions which favour the persistence of collectively managed land alongside privately worked fields.

Agency and the Perpetuation of Co-operation

While Behar (1986: 189) notes that 'the connection between communal property, co-operation and reciprocity has produced a vast body of literature over the last hundred years', she could have added that no study has shown better than her own the intricate and fragile procedures through which mutual trust is sustained. Her approach differs from that of earlier writers, who tended to assume communal property, co-operation, and reciprocity become linked independently of individual agency. Chapuis took a Durkheimian approach, 'the frequency of collective labour, especially during the hay harvest, the daily reassembling of the communal herd, imply a collective discipline which could not be better respected than by a constant *surveillance of the individual by the group*' (Chapuis 1958: 12–13, my emphasis). Bloch also suggested some form of superior will when he wrote 'the cultivators whose houses stood side by side and whose holdings were interspersed were *perforce* united . . . by all manner of bonds of common interest, and indeed by submission to common agricultural practices' (Bloch 1961: 242, my emphasis). A nineteenth-century court ruling from Besançon, on the other hand, recognized that the traditional *fruitières* depended on 'une confiance réciproque et sur la bonne foi' (mutual confidence and good faith) (Guyétant 1870: 73).

The court's interpretation is closer to current thinking on the evolution of co-operation. Co-operation and reciprocity will take root only if good faith can be rewarded (see Ch. 4). Their success depends on the scale and form of social organization. Lotteries and rotas appear to be pervasive strategies for maintaining mutual confidence. When the village assembly of Santa María del Monte decided to organize the division of common land into fields during the mid-nineteenth century, everyone worked together on the clearance. Tenure of the fields was allocated by drawing lots once the work was complete, to prevent anyone working harder on the portion that would become their own (Behar 1986: 232–4). When a set of brothers build a house together in Kippel they allocate the finished apartments by the same method, and for the same reason (Friedl 1974: 60–1). Families in Törbel agree on the division of the holding into equal portions before drawing lots to determine who will inherit each part (Netting 1981: 193–4). Lotteries are used in Pellaport to allocate wood from the communal forest and, in the past, portions of common meadow. In every case, the opportunity for favouritism or appropriation by the powerful is eliminated. The inhabitants of both Kippel and Santa María rely on the rigorous application of rotas to ensure that each household can rest assured that every other one will make a fair contribution to work on behalf of the whole group (Friedl 1974: 55; Behar 1986: 203–5). It is possible that the original *fruitières* exploited a familiarity with the application of rotas to enable each household in turn to make a cheese from all the associates' milk, each other household trusting that its own turn would come. Communal obligations and work parties persisted in Santa María 'as a result of the conscious agreement of villagers to be bound by them. . . . The rules existed to insure [*sic*] that not merely the majority, but everyone would carry out their vicinal obligations . . . whether willing or reluctant' (Behar 1986: 185). As McCay and Acheson, and Ostrom showed, such a system only works when free-riders can be detected and punished. Many were reluctant to take on the role of village headman in Santa María, since the occupant had to enforce fines on fellow villagers who failed to join collective work parties (ibid. 149). Santa María's assembly also appointed members to police the common forest. They were to fine anyone found removing wood illegally but would themselves be fined if they failed to detect offenders (ibid. 248; cf. Neeson 1993: 143). People who grazed livestock in closed fields would be publicly denounced by the hayward at meetings of the assembly (ibid. 202). The people of Santa María are more like Giddens's expert sociologists than Bourdieu's blind followers of a habitus (see ibid. 193–4).

Confidence that one's efforts will not be undermined by free-riders is essential to perpetuating the system. Such confidence depends on knowledge that the community possesses reliable strategies to enable equitable access and enforce compliance and the opportunity to detect cheaters. When everyone lives, and repeatedly interacts, with one another, in a nucleated village it is easy (some would say notoriously so) for each to check on whether their neighbours are living up to the community's standards (see Ch. 4). Rosenberg (1988: 25, 138) dismisses claims that the political apathy or 'sheep-like mentality' of people of Abriès in the recent past are natural peasant traits. She amply demonstrates they are qualities generated by the loss of control over local resources.

I was introduced to the argument that distribution of strips belonging to an *exploitation* throughout the village's terrain is a way of insuring against crop failure by Felicien Jouffroy. Felicien told me that when his father planted potatoes he always used one small *parcelle* on limestone soil and another on clay soil. If the year proved a wet one the first gave a good crop, in a dry year the second did better. When sowing wheat he would plant two *parcelles* at opposite ends of the commune so that, if one was broken by a hail storm the other was likely to survive. This custom has been widely cited (e.g. Friedl 1974: 57–8; McCloskey 1976; McCay and Acheson 1987: 17; Rosenberg 1988: 26) and explains why partible inheritance is expected to provide each heir with an equal portion of each *type* of terrain. But is it a sufficient explanation for the dispersal of a holding? Maybe, as in the choice between preserving the holding intact and providing for all children, it is a case of choosing between conflicting goals, in this case between minimizing travel time to the fields and ensuring all households have equivalent shares in the village's variable terrain. Minimizing risk may be a by-product of this political strategy, and increased travel time a cost accepted to ensure that each household gains equally from the field regime, hence promoting the good faith necessary to preserve co-operation in herding and harvesting. In Scandinavia, strips were sometimes allocated by rota, such that in a hamlet of three households, A–C, tenancy of strips in the arable fields was arranged in a regular order A/B/C/A/B/C/A/B/C (see Roeck Hansen 1996: 14, 36; Widgren 1997: 87). If strips created during medieval forest clearances were allocated by lottery, as were the fields created by the nineteenth-century clearance in Santa María del Monte, holdings would be scattered from the start, rather than becoming scattered through the cumulative effect of partible inheritance. McCloskey (1976: 128) argued that the dispersion of family holdings in the open field system was adequately explained by the wish to reduce risk. 'The alternative hypotheses, of Germanic egalitarianism or communal clearing or joint ploughing, are reduced to making arguments for action at a distance.' Important as risk reduction is, from the perspective of structuration egalitarianism is not an original condition but a precarious achievement that needs constant reinforcement.

Conditions for the Success of Fruitières

Even in the early nineteenth century, six hundred years after their appearance on the Plateau of Levier, most *fruitières* were still located in the district around Pontarlier (see Ch. 2). Nineteenth-century writers considered the harsh climate responsible for their distribution. A court ruling on the legal status of the associations, given in Besançon in 1842, began:

The *fruitières* established in the mountains without a doubt extended back into the most distant past and their indefinite continuation must be ensured since, for the inhabitants, production of cheese from the milk of their cattle is the sole means by which, in view of the climate and rigorous temperatures, they can ensure a profit from the land, particularly the pastures so extensive in most parts. (cited in Guyétant 1870: 72)

Guyétant (ibid. 58) himself argued that 'the extreme difficulty which would be experienced in successfully exploiting the pastures of the mountains of Doubs and Jura without *fruitières* undoubtedly contributed to the creation of these groups. Industry is born of need (*le besoin rend industrieux*)'.

The French geographer Lebeau argued against using environmental determinism to explain the development of *fruitières* in an essay published in 1951. He compared the plateaux on which the *fruitières* flourished with the physically very similar region of Haut-Bugey, at the southern limit of the Jura (see Fig. 1.1). During the eighteenth century, when *fruitières* on the Plateau of Levier were so successful that their members had started to construct special dairy buildings and employ full-time dairymen, the inhabitants of Haut Bugey were still practising the system of polyculture (mixed subsistence farming) typical of areas such as the Loue Valley below the plateaux. Instead of extensive pastures, all the available land in Haut Bugey was devoted to the production of cereals to feed the inhabitants. There were few cattle in Haut Bugey and those that existed were described by a contemporary observer as 'a degenerate breed, fed too parsimoniously during the winter, scarcely surviving until the season of pasturage and needing the whole summer to recover' (Lebeau 1951: 395). The cattle were used to draw ploughs and wagons and provide manure for the fields.

Lebeau argues that Haut-Bugey belonged to a different culture area. The Plateau of Levier belonged to the open field zone. Villages were nucleated, the open field system enabled everyone to put their cattle into a single herd that grazed on the commons or the fallow field, and community affairs were regulated by an assembly of household heads. Those who devised the *fruitière* took advantage of these existing customs by extending them to a new activity, the pooling of milk to make large, durable cheeses. It was only possible to take milk to a neighbour's house because homes were clustered in the village. Haut-Bugey lacked all these features. Its inhabitants lived in scattered hamlets. The only cheese they made was a soft 'blue' cheese that could be produced with the milk of single households. Bugey was surrounded by customs barriers as well as natural barriers to trade: trade passing from Bugey to Franche-Comté, Savoy, Dauphiné, and Le Pays de Gex was taxed as it left the region, while the rivers Rhône and Ain created natural barriers. Although Lebeau does not mention this, Bugey also lay in the large zone of southern France where inheritance is by unigeniture (see map in Le Roy Ladurie 1976: 39).

In Haut-Bugey even intensive polyculture could not feed the inhabitants. Analysis of surviving statistics led Lebeau (1951: 389) to conclude that the higher villages produced less than half of the grain they needed to subsist, forcing men to migrate seasonally in search of wage-labour. Ironically, some found work as carders of hemp on the Plateau of Levier (cf. Chapuis 1958: 105; Chatelain 1936). Lebeau (ibid. 399) established that at the end of the season each carder took home between 15 and 80 francs according to his skill, whereas the average (presumably annual) income per household from the sale of cheese made in *fruitières* was 160 francs. One contemporary observer wrote in 1822 that as one climbed eastwards towards Pontarlier, 'poverty disappears . . . as cereal cultivation diminishes' (ibid. 390) whereas a traveller in Haut-Bugey wrote that the inhabitants were very poor, encumbered with debt and the victims of usury. In 1789 ' the winter was terrible ... poverty was widespread'. In 1815 'the commune of Longcombe experienced dire penury following the destruction of its rye and barley by hail, obliging it to purchase grain' (sources quoted ibid. 395).

Village Government and Common Property

Villages on the Plateau of Levier are characterized by both strong local government and mutual aid between households. The corporate village was introduced to the Alps at the time villages on the Plateau of Levier were founded. The transition from seasonally occupied to permanent settlements in the Alps during the Middle Ages led former summer pastures to be converted to plough land, and new pastures to be opened by forest clearance. In some parts of Europe the open field system may have been imposed by a central authority (Nitz 1988; Roeck Hansen 1996). Other communities began as corporate groups of households who jointly organized the payment of rent to feudal lords and later purchased their freedom, others as village councils that held judicial prerogatives and acted as intermediaries between households and lords (Viazzo 1989: 126).

Although English villages now lack effective government or community cohesion, village government had been robust during the centuries when much of England, from Northumberland in the north to Dorset and Sussex in the south, was dominated by the open field system. Each village chose a jury at its village court. The court admitted new freeholders and tenants to the community, passed by-laws compelling residents to repair chimneys or clear pathways, forbidding them to encroach on access tracks by over-ploughing the edge of strips or to allow animals to graze on fields before crops had been harvested. The jury also stinted (limited) the number of animals each household could graze on commons (Ault 1972; Chibnall 1965: 231; Orwin and Orwin 1938: 154–9). Nucleated settlements grew up at the heart of the open fields. The open fields and their associated common land did not spread throughout England. Elmdon, for example, lies within the south-eastern region where scattered hamlets persisted (Williamson and Bellamy 1987: 14–16).

As on the Continent, open fields were associated in England with close-knit social organization. The villagers of Broughton went on strike against their feudal overlord in 1291 (see ibid. 42–9, where other examples are also given). The jury at Laxton regularly inspected the boundary markers of strips on the wheatfield, to ensure that no one had encroached

on common grassland. It fined both villagers who transferred their grazing rights to people from other parishes and those who grazed more than
their allotted number of animals on the commons (Orwin and Orwin
1938: 154, 157–8). The jury of Sherington passed by-laws specifying the
numbers of livestock each household could graze on common land and
threatened to fine even wealthy landowners for grazing more than their
allotted number of sheep on the fallow fields (Chibnall 1965: 169, 171,
231). Neeson gives many other examples while Ault has compiled a
collection of the by-laws passed by village juries to regulate the operation
of the open field system[1] (Ault 1972; Neeson 1993: 134–57).

Bloch contrasted these 'open' systems, with their collective obligations, to the regime of enclosed fields in the *bocage* regions of France. The
bocage comprised much of Brittany, Cotentin, Maine, Perche, Poitou, and
the Vendée, most of the Massif Central, Bugey, and the Pays de Gex. It
is to the *bocage* regions, then, that the part of the southern Jura, which
Lebeau contrasted with the Plateau of Levier, belongs, as do the villages
of Chanzeaux and Sainte-Foy. Enclosed fields in the *bocage* are almost
always associated with hamlets rather than villages and hamlets may eventually be reduced to single houses (Bloch 1966: 60). These regions were
characterized overwhelmingly by a spirit of individualism, which led each
household to look after its own livestock and undertake little co-operation
with others. Bloch cites a proposal made in 1750 to introduce a modified
form of the common herd to part of Brittany. The plan was rejected on
the grounds that 'it seems impossible to hope that reason and the community spirit could triumph among the inhabitants of the same village to
such an extent that they would be prepared to bring their sheep into one
flock under one shepherd'. 'How true it is', Bloch (ibid. 59) comments
'that all rural customs take their origin from an attitude of mind.' This
conclusion would have seemed unproblematic when Bloch originally
presented his overview of French rural history in 1926, but is called into
question by the work of Bourdieu and Giddens. The persistence of atti-
tudes of mind must be explained by uncovering the mechanisms that
reproduce a habitus or practical consciousness and transmit it from one
generation to the next. Successful transmission will depend, in turn, on
agents' ability to realize social relationships by implementing cultural
strategies.

---

[1] Mats Widgren reports that in Sweden, where open fields are commonly associated
with small hamlets, there was less community organization in their management, although
use of collective resources was, and is, carefully regulated through the *samällighet* or local
association (Widgren, pers. comm.)

The open field system broke down as farmers abandoned the fallow phase and fenced their strips to protect crops such as legumes from the livestock that habitually grazed on the fallow. Neeson (1993: 224) plots the diffusion of enclosure across Northamptonshire between 1750 and 1800. The three-field rotation was undermined in the region of the Plateau of Levier during the eighteenth century when maize, millet, and legumes were first planted in the fallow fields of villages in the Loue valley. Movable fences protected the new crops from grazing livestock (Chapuis 1958: 65). Land in Pellaport was fenced by the first municipal council in 1791 to protect crops of peas and lentils from the village herd. Yet common land was not divided and the right to graze the fallow survived for over a hundred years. Given the inherent stability of the system of collective rights it is not enough to argue it was swept aside by the simple tide of progress.

Participation in a Market Economy

Macfarlane attributed the alleged individualistic ethos of medieval England to a well-developed market in land even before the Black Death (Macfarlane 1978: 95, 101, 199). This has been disputed by other authors. Sabean found many of the land sales in the German village of Neckarhausen during the period covered by his study (1700–1870) were transactions between relatives, which strengthened rather than weakened kin networks. He argues that many studies of Medieval English village life may have underestimated the importance of kin in land sales (Sabean 1990: 355–7, 410, 412 n.). Netting found evidence of land sales in Törbel from the thirteenth century onwards (Netting 1981: 52), and yet Törbel preserved the forms of community organization which disappeared in England. Although there is plenty of evidence of a peasant land market in thirteenth-century England, records show that peasant transactions were preponderantly small in scale and would have had marginal effect on the ownership and structure of family holdings (Campbell 1984: 98; Faith 1966: 86; Howell 1976: 135; R. M. Smith 1984*a*: 14; although R. M. Smith 1984*b*: 165 appears to give a counter-example).

A market in agricultural produce is compatible with the co-operative management of resources but increased participation in market production can precipitate social change. Dietrich and Garenc (1963: 72) conclude that access to trade routes was the critical variable accounting for the success of *fruitières* on the Plateau of Levier. They point out that the more northerly Plateau of Maiche had a similar cultural history to the

Plateau of Levier but did not lie on a trade route and for many centuries failed to adopt *fruitières*. Not only did the Plateau of Levier belong to the zone of open fields, it was bounded by long-established trade routes that made it possible to export cheese for sale beyond the region. The genius of those who invented the *fruitière* was both to extend existing customs in order to exploit an opportunity for trade, and also to develop a cheese suitable for long-distance transport by wagon on rough roads. Other village studies support Dietrich and Garenc's argument that access to trade routes was crucial to the success of *fruitières* on the Plateau of Levier. The local cheese produced in the high Swiss Alpine village of Kippel has a poor reputation, and this may be because the valley was cut off from long-distance trade routes throughout the eighteenth and nineteenth centuries (Friedl 1974: 30–1). This may explain why Kippel's village dairy co-operative failed and its agriculture remained subsistence oriented, obliging people to find paid work in the towns of the Rhône Valley (ibid. 7). The French Alpine village of Abriès prospered until the late nineteenth century on the export of its distinctive ewe's cheese, a blue cheese (Bleu de Queyras) carried on foot or mule by local peddlers, to the towns of Provence. This cheese was well known and there was little poverty in the Queyras Valley, despite the decline of local textile and tanning industries. As was the case on the Plateau of Levier, there was greater prosperity at high altitude than on the neighbouring plains (Rosenberg 1988: 99). Misguided French government policy during the latter half of the nineteenth century unfortunately suppressed sheep-rearing and substituted cattle. In 1850, Abriès became the first commune in the Hautes-Alpes to manufacture Gruyère, in a government-sponsored *fruitière* employing expert women cheesemakers brought in from the Jura and Switzerland (ibid. 117)! Unfortunately villages in Switzerland and the Jura that had direct access to the railways had a competitive advantage over the Hautes-Alpes. Between 1878 and 1903, hit by the worst depression of the nineteenth century (the trough between the second and third Kondratiev cycles), most local co-operatives handed over production to entrepreneurs. During the 1930s the Nestlé company built up a monopoly, compelling farmers to accept low prices for their milk. A study by the University of Paris reported in 1959 that 'the only law regulating production in the Queyras is the price of milk set by Nestlé' (ibid. 163). When Nestlé abandoned the area in 1970, the dairy industry had been virtually destroyed.

The farmers of Sainte-Foy have been more fortunate. Sales of Roquefort cheese increased rapidly during the period of prosperity in the mid-nineteenth century and survived the later depression that so badly affected Abriès. Even though Sainte-Foyan farmers rely on milk sales to a cartel of local firms, the Roquefort cheese these firms manufacture is protected by *appellation contrôlée* regulations and has an international reputation. Milk producers formed a union in 1922 to improve contracts and stabilize prices (Rogers 1991: 62–3). Since the region within which the milk for Roquefort cheese can be collected is legally defined, manufacturers cannot play one region off against another in the way Nestlé did in the Hautes-Alpes. The intensive production of ewe's milk is best carried out on farms of intermediate size. Rapid growth of the market after the Second World War caused both small and very large farms in the district to disappear.

Partibility and Unigeniture Generate Different Social Systems

Cole and Wolf argued that the choice of partibility or unigeniture arises from the need to choose between two conflicting goals: to keep the holding intact as a material basis for perpetuating the family line, or to give all children the best possible start in life (Cole and Wolf 1974: 236, cf. Hrdy and Judge 1993). The cultural tradition to which Saint Felix belongs had chosen one, Tret's cultural tradition had chosen the other. While ecological conditions had forced a convergence of inheritance practice in the two villages, their ideologies had different consequences (i.e. recursive effects) for the distribution of authority in the household and for inter-household relations. The history of their social structures unfolding through time constituted a 'dialogue between cultural heritage and the local environment' which had generated a different fabric of social relations (Cole and Wolf 1974: 119).

The general correlation between the distribution of field systems and rules of inheritance, identified by Bloch, suggests inheritance may have a fundamental role in generating and perpetuating alternative cultural systems. Chapter 3 argued kinship and the family have a central role in generating village social structure. In all three of the communities characterized by unigeniture (Saint Felix, Chanzeaux, and Sainte-Foy) farmhouses are, as in Bugey, dispersed and each house stands in the midst of its own land. This was the pattern that developed after the enclosures in England (ibid. 240; Overton 1996: 159; Rogers 1991: 88; Wylie 1966: 91). On the other hand, all the communities practising partible inheritance consist of a nucleated village, where each household's land is intermingled with that of others in the surrounding fields. Not only is this true of

Tret, Kippel, Törbel, Abriès, Minot, and Santa María; it also occurs on those farms in Saint Felix which have been subject to division (Cole and Wolf 1974: 141) and in the hamlets around Chanzeaux where holdings are subject to partible inheritance (Wylie 1966: 77, 86).

There is a greater propensity to participate in co-operatives among those communities characterized by partible inheritance. The farmers of Sainte-Foy and Chanzeaux are generally suspicious of agricultural co-operatives (Rogers 1991: 24, 118; Wylie 1966: 223), unlike those of the village in Lorraine Rogers (1975) had previously studied. In Chanzeaux most members of the mutual aid co-operative live in one of the hamlets characterized by partible inheritance (Wylie 1966: 119, 221). As the commercialization of dairy farming gathered momentum in the Italian Tyrol, the farmers of Tret joined a local dairy co-operative while those in Saint Felix favoured entrepreneurs who arranged milk sales to a commercial dairy (Cole and Wolf 1974: 210). In Törbel the alp associations regulate numbers of livestock put on the high pasture and formerly co-ordinated the manufacture of cheese from members' livestock (Netting 1981: 25). Other associations regulate the irrigation of hay meadows. Kippel's alp and irrigation associations are carefully regulated and there were formerly arrangements for maintaining a village stud bull (Friedl 1974: 52–6).

Partible inheritance is generally associated with a dense network of mutual aid sanctioned by the threat of ostracism. In both Saint Felix and Sainte-Foy, on the other hand, unigeniture is associated with an ideal of household self-sufficiency, minimizing inter-household networks of mutual aid (Cole and Wolf 1974: 168, 243; Rogers 1991: 101). Augustins (1990: 59) and Barthelemy (1988: 199) have suggested this difference is intrinsic to the two systems (see discussion in Ch. 3). Cole and Wolf were struck by the difference, in this regard, between Tret and Saint Felix. In Tret households frequently co-operated, often shared food and wine and, while ostracizing households guilty of sharp practice, denied that a formal reckoning of debt and credit was necessary. Household heads in Saint Felix strove for complete self-sufficiency and, when help was needed from other households, kept a strict account of service rendered (Cole and Wolf 1974: 168–9, 243–4). Rogers was similarly impressed when she moved from Lorraine to the Aveyronnais village of Sainte-Foy. Instead of the reciprocal exchanges she had seen in the former village, there was little mutual aid and, where exchange between households occurred, labour flowed disproportionately from small to big holdings while equipment and money were loaned in the opposite direction, contributing to the general ethos of patronage (Rogers 1991: 106, 118). Behar describes many cases of mutual aid in Santa María; as does Friedl in Kippel. The only villages characterized by partible inheritance but little mutual aid are Törbel (Netting 1981: 19, 21) and Abriès. The situation in Törbel is hard to explain, but Rosenberg (1988: 195–9) shows the breakdown of mutual aid in Abriès resulted from the destruction of the agricultural economy by the Nestlé company.

The isolation of farms undermines co-operation. It is recognized in Pellaport that the logical outcome of a second *remembrement*, which finalized the grouping of *exploitations*, would be for each surviving *cultivateur* to move out of the village onto his own land. The geographical centre of every holding would no longer coincide in the village, and neither would the social interests of *cultivateurs*. The isolation of farms associated with unigeniture in Saint Felix and the regions of the *bocage* correlates with a minimal network of mutual aid. No *cultivateur* in Pellaport has been willing to pay this price for withdrawing from the community.

Partible inheritance is a levelling mechanism. Rosenberg (ibid. 22–3, 27) regards its levelling effect as an integral part of the democratic society that existed in Abriès before the Revolution. Both men and women inherited and bequeathed land, and widows managing property had the right to speak at the village assembly. The same is true in Santa María (Behar 1986: 116, 121). Partible inheritance in Törbel ensured that differences of family wealth were negligible and restricted the capacity of particular families to dominate village government (Netting 1981: 198).

In both Saint Felix and Sainte-Foy, on the other hand, non-inheriting children are subordinated and village politics are dominated by men who have inherited the family property. In Saint Felix they represent the domestic group in public affairs and 'all other villagers are subject to their decision-making' (Cole and Wolf 1974: 204). In Sainte-Foy a long-running campaign for control of the communal council set the traditional élite of farm-owners against the disinherited who had moved into the bourg (central settlement). As one of the former complained, 'the rejects are trying to take over' (Rogers 1991: 179).

The potential inheritance rules have to generate different structures in rural society is illustrated by Berkner's (1976) study of two adjacent regions of Germany. In the eighteenth century the south-westerly region had a rule of partible inheritance while to the north-east, as in much of Germany, unigeniture was the rule (cf. Rösener 1994: 181–3). In both districts manorial landlords were prohibited from evicting tenants but in the north-east, laws had been passed to prevent the uneconomic division of holdings through partible inheritance (Berkner 1976: 77–8). In the district where partible inheritance continued to apply, the number of peasant holdings increased four times as fast, but households employing servants were rarer. In the region converted to unigeniture siblings of the fortunate heir to the tenancy received only a share of their parents' private property. The number of holdings increased very little between 1664 and 1766. Instead a social hierarchy developed, with self-sufficient peasants at its head, often employing two or more servants. At the bottom were day labourers living on common land but without land of their own to farm. In southern France, where unigeniture is also the rule, disinherited children similarly 'run the risk of falling into the proletariat, if they are of the people; or into the church, if they come from the middle or upper classes' (Le Roy Ladurie 1976: 63). The process of social differentiation engendered by unigeniture parallels Marx's classic case of the differentiation between industrial capitalists and factory workers.

Partible inheritance seems to have been general throughout Anglo-Saxon England (Faith 1966: 79; Goody 1983: 121), but after the Norman Conquest it was displaced by unigeniture except in Kent, East Anglia, and parts of Yorkshire (Faith 1966: 81–2; Flandrin 1979: 76). Unigeniture has been the rule in much of England since the twelfth century. There is no inherent incompatibility between open field farming and partibility. Widgren (1990) shows that strip fields predate the open field system in Västergötland, Sweden, and argues that such field systems are symptomatic of a rule of partible inheritance. None the less, by the twelfth and thirteenth centuries the areas of England where open field cultivation was practised were overwhelmingly characterized by unigeniture (Faith 1966: 84–5; Goody 1983: 119; Williamson and Bellamy 1987: 43). Like the spread of the open field system itself, this appears to be a medieval example of the diffusion of an administrative innovation, but its recursive effect was to undermine the community of interest on which the open field system depended. McCloskey (1976: 128) rejected the influence of partible inheritance on the open field system, arguing that the area where partible inheritance among peasants survived the longest, the south-east of England, was among the first to consolidate holdings while the Midlands, where primogeniture began earliest, was among the last. According to Faith, however, partible inheritance survived longest in those areas of south-east England which did *not* practice the open field system, Kent and East Anglia. Within the open field zone it persisted only in parts of Nottinghamshire and the Yorkshire Dales (Faith 1966: 81–2).

Local Self-Government and Management of the Commons

Effective village self-government depends on local control of productive resources. Rétif de la Bretonne noticed this correlation in the late eighteenth century, writing: 'the little parish of Saci, since it has commons, governs itself like a large family' (quoted Bloch 1966: 180). Not only is this the case in villages with partible inheritance (Törbel, Kippel, and, until the French revolution, Abriès), it is also true of Saint Felix, the Tyrolean village with unigeniture. In the early eighteenth century Santa María successfully resisted a noble family's attempt to appropriate its commons and it has been partially successful in preventing more recent expropriation by the Spanish state (Behar 1986: 137–44, 254, 262–3). Where villages do not control their own commons, patronage replaces local democracy. The French state intervened in Abriès during the nineteenth century to prevent traditional access to the commons. Wrongly considering alpine pastures were the product of deforestation, and the absence of understorey in the pine forest the result of overgrazing, the Office national des eaux et forêts wilfully deprived villages of the right to manage their own commons, causing an economic crisis that precipitated rural depopulation and replaced village self-government with political patronage (Rosenberg 1988: 70–88, 105–6). Despite their rule of partible inheritance, the common land used by the villagers of Tret is managed by the commune council on which Tret has minority representation; Saint Felix is politically active, Tret is not. Tret's search for patrons is a realistic strategy, given the structure of the Italian state which locates political power in towns, not villages (Cole and Wolf 1974: 261–5, 275). In Sainte-Foy there are no commons and patronage is an art (Rogers 1991: 22, 111). 'Sainte-Foyans seem generally to think of the community as only a loosely connected and more or less accidental juxtaposition of relatively autonomous ostal [farm] units and people sent away from them' (Rogers 1991: 101).

A further reason for the divergence of the English village trajectory from that of France and Switzerland may have lain in the different capacity of the jury system and the assembly of household heads to defend the community's interests in land and labour against outsiders. It is possible that the principles by which political action was co-ordinated in English villages had different structural consequences. In the thirteenth century, the communal assembly already operated effectively in France and Switzerland to co-ordinate peasant resistance against feudal overlords (Bloch 1966: 168–70; Viazzo 1989: 266). In England, the village community

was 'in a position voluntarily to accept fresh responsibility, to bind itself
to the fulfilment of obligations, and to incur financial liabilities . . . (but)
its legal status is not easy to define' (Cam 1962: 79). Village juries tended
to give information that would help their lord to recover tenants who had
run away (Britnell 1990: 37; Williamson and Bellamy 1987: 42). The
English feudal structure therefore perhaps tended to turn villagers
against each other rather than unite them against the lord. Opposition
was usually by individuals or small groups, although villagers sometimes
successfully bargained collectively over the terms of their tenancies (Britnell 1990: 39–45; Hilton 1954: 79). The situation in France was quite
different. Everyone understood that public matters were resolved by
bargaining between rival centres of power: the corporate village on the
one hand, and the nobility or king on the other (Mendras and Cole 1991:
127). In 1761, a local seigneur attempted to reactivate feudal rights which,
he claimed, had belonged to earlier holders of the seigneurie and were
recorded in documents dated 1549 and 1657. Pellaport's village assembly
responded that it was an incontestable principle of French law that, to
enter into a tributary relationship with a seigneur, two-thirds of the
inhabitants must give their consent, at a freely convened meeting. The
assembly produced documentary evidence to show that in 1657 there
were between thirty and forty households in the village, yet the seigneur's
document had only been signed by seven men, some of whom were
already bound to the seigneur of the time by other obligations. Similar
arguments were used to reject the 1549 contract. The French village
assembly, then, acts to represent the interests of the village. The English
court becomes a forum for legal cases, but the jury is not a party to the
dispute.

Population Growth

The contrasting outcomes of partible inheritance and unigeniture are not
inevitable. If the size of the population is static (or declining) there will be
no practical difference between partibility and unigeniture. In a static
population, each married couple will be replaced by two children. Either
both children inherit a half share, which they combine with those of their
spouses; or one inherits all, and the other marries someone who has inherited another farm (Le Roy Ladurie 1976: 43–4; R. M. Smith 1984a:
39–53). Smith (ibid. 48–53) cites several case studies which show that
during the twelfth and thirteenth centuries there was little practical difference in England between areas with partible inheritance or unigeniture.

The full implications of unigeniture for rural social structure were only realized when the population of England was rising. Disinherited children of prosperous farmers could afford to become merchants, train for a profession, or enter university. Smallholders sent their non-inheriting children into the world penniless (Howell 1976: 151–4). From the end of the fifteenth century social differentiation increased (Campbell 1984: 103; Howell 1976: 152). In the early seventeenth century, the poor were increasingly employed as servants in wealthy households. The role of servant becomes a permanent one, rather than a temporary role for young adults (R. M. Smith 1984*a*: 83). Flandrin saw the results of this trend in Laslett's analysis of households in Goodnestone-next-Wingham (Flandrin 1976: 56–7; and see Ch. 3). Macfarlane's (1978: 165) rosy picture of English society in which the market economy can be thanked for an unusual degree of affluence that is distributed widely through the population, and where individual rights, liberty of thought, and religion are enshrined in law, sits uneasily with a sixteenth-century writer's adverse comment on the harshness with which the English gentry kept their wealth intact through unigeniture, observing that in France, Flanders, and Italy, 'you never saw younger brothers (of gentlemen) begging as you did in England' (quoted in Thirsk 1976: 185).

Chapter 3 showed that the appearance of a European marriage pattern mitigated the effect of partible inheritance. If only one son and one daughter married, family holdings would not decrease in size. A similar strategy exists in Nepal, where it has been convincingly related to the need to avoid the division of family farms through partible inheritance (see Durham 1991: 83–8). Population growth in these regions during the eighteenth and nineteenth centuries did not follow Lloyd's prediction because, as Malthus argued, subsistence was tied to a clearly limited supply of family land rather than to an open-access market. The effects of enforced celibacy were less divisive than those of unigeniture, because celibate family members remained landowners and the proportion of landless households was relatively low. Failure to limit the number of heirs can none the less quickly undermine this strategy. Social differentiation between the majority of farming households and a few small households headed by agricultural labourers can be demonstrated in eighteenth- and nineteenth-century household censuses on the Plateau of Levier (see Ch. 3). A land survey of the commune of Sombacour carried out in 1769, for example, records substantial differences in the areas of land owned by individuals (Malfroy, Olivier, and Guiraud 1981: 74–8). Among the 15 who complained they had unjustly been designated 'privileged' in accordance with laws passed by the National Assembly in 1789 (see Ch. 3), four names correspond to those of the *maire* and three councillors. When the *maire* and his council authorized the fencing of land near the village in 1791, they appointed guards to prevent animals or people trespassing on the enclosed fields.

Population growth can therefore threaten village democracy even in regions of partible inheritance. During the mid-nineteenth century, the communal assembly of Santa María del Monte began to organize the division of areas of communal forest for cultivation by the growing population. Conflict broke out between relatively wealthy villagers who wanted to keep the forest as grazing for their livestock, and poorer households who wanted to plough it. Some also argued that, since unmarried adults were not members of the village assembly, they lacked the citizen's right to a share of the village's land (Behar 1986: 238–41).

Sabean interprets the process of pauperization that took place in Neckarhausen between the third quarter of the eighteenth century and the middle of the nineteenth century, as the outcome of a combination of specific historical processes including population growth that undermined the democratic effect of partible inheritance (Sabean 1990: 22). After 1700 poor artisans and wage labourers worked increasingly outside the village. They needed land to provide a surety against breach of contract rather than for subsistence. Before long, well over 50 per cent of households held less than the minimum needed for self-sufficiency. Anyone who was declared bankrupt had their land sold to pay creditors and such land was bought by wealthier farmers (cf. Viazzo 1989: 151). By 1800 the landed farmers firmly held power.

The effect of population growth in communities applying a rule of unigeniture will, however, be particularly divisive, since siblings of the household head necessarily have no land (Cole and Wolf 1974: 201; Netting 1981: 174). Unigeniture was the rule in the German duchy of Brunswick-Wolfenbüttel. As the population grew after 1656, there were more and more local inhabitants who were not enfranchised members of the community. Often the non-inheriting sons of farmers, they lived on tiny plots of land and depended upon access to meadow and forest commons if they wanted to raise livestock. 'As long as there were not too many of them, their presence was tolerated, but with demographic expansion they found themselves increasingly excluded. . . . The upsurge in the numbers of these individuals during the eighteenth century upset the equilibrium of village life' (Rösener 1994: 153). Rösener reiterates Berkner's conclusion: 'one must stress the marked differences between [this region] . . . and the densely settled, craft-oriented communities of south-western Germany, which divided their land' (ibid. 154).

In England, rights to use common land tended to be vested in owners and tenants of farmland. During periods of population growth the effect of unigeniture was again to drive a wedge between the landed and the landless. Landless agricultural labourers rarely held rights to commons, although their use of the commons may have been tacitly allowed prior to enclosure (Ault 1972: 17; Chibnall 1965: 231; Mills 1984: 499; Orwin and Orwin 1938: 145). The structural consequences of partible and impartible inheritance are therefore, in the long run, very different.

ENCLOSURE

Enclosures in England

The eighteenth century was a critical period for the divergence of English farming from that of France, Germany, and Switzerland. The number of people fed by English agriculture doubled as the Malthusian limit imposed by medieval farming techniques was overcome (Overton 1996: 4, 198). In England, widespread enclosure sanctioned by acts of parliament created large holdings oriented towards market production (Mingay 1977; Neeson 1993; Overton 1996). Mingay, Neeson, and Overton are recent contributors to a debate whose main points were established by contemporary supporters and critics of enclosure. Proponents considered enclosure necessary to improve the land and increase output, critics considered the social cost outweighed the economic gain. Little use has been made of the evidence provided by the alternative trajectories of agriculture on the continent to test these arguments.

Enclosure also took place in parts of France. In 1793 the National Convention approved legislation permitting the enclosure of common land, providing one-third of the community's inhabitants agreed, and everyone received an equal share. The opportunity was welcomed in some regions, but not others. In mountainous areas where 'the extensive method of grazing cattle had long predominated, peasants had little interest in privatising common pasturage'. As in England, 'the change benefited only those peasants who owned land. The destruction of feudalism proved to be a bitter disappointment for the great mass of tenant farmers and agricultural labourers' (Rösener 1994: 175).

Sabean disputes the claim that innovation and experimentation in agriculture during the eighteenth century began on large English estates and was then promoted by state agencies through the rest of Europe. Intensified rotation practices had long been in use in Holland and on the Rhine, often on smallholdings. Villagers constantly introduced changes through negotiation, trial, and error. The three-field rotation system was adaptable, and did not impede these developments. In fact, highly mechanized, intensive agriculture is still carried out in Germany today on 'open fields' made up of interspersed strips (Sabean 1990: 21–2).

Mingay (1977: 12) writes bluntly that open fields in England were an obstacle to efficient farming, but grazing the fallow in the open-field villages of Oxfordshire did not prevent the introduction of legumes and sainfoin during the seventeenth century. Either agreements were reached to fence off parts of the open field until sainfoin had been harvested, or the rotation was converted to a four-field system, with one field always cultivated for sainfoin. Strips were exchanged to enable consolidation of holdings (Havinden 1961). During the eighteenth century turnips, clover, and sainfoin were introduced in the open fields of Northamptonshire with the consent of the parish. Drainage schemes were implemented by village juries (Neeson 1993: 98–9, 121–3). Proponents of enclosure were no better informed about mechanisms of disease transmission than their opponents and the marketplace was the most serious source of epidemic infection, a problem which was not changed by enclosure. Breeding in the common herd was controlled by preventing bulls from running free (ibid. 127–32). Overton recognizes that some communities which retained open fields changed their by-laws to grow clover, sainfoin, and turnips, but considers there was both significantly more innovation in enclosed villages, and a substantial rise in the number and quality of livestock as land exhausted by over-long wheat cultivation was turned into pasture (Overton 1996: 164–7). While Overton considers the main surge in agricultural production coincided with the major burst of parliamentary enclosure during the mid-eighteenth century, Neeson claims changes in agricultural practice before enclosures had already increased productivity (Overton 1996: 167; Neeson 1993: 8). The greatest growth in crop yields during the eighteenth and early nineteenth centuries may have predated enclosures by several decades (Neeson 1993: 157). These interpretations are not necessarily inconsistent, since Overton argues it was the growth of a market stimulated by increased production which made investment in land through enclosure attractive to the large landowners who advocated it.

While enclosure was clearly precipitated by a combination of circumstances I consider claims that it was imperative, in order to improve agricultural output, unproven. A more comprehensive explanation must consider the genesis of the social conditions within which it occurred.

Overton argues that, although the ability of clover and turnips to fix nitrogen in the soil enabled elimination of the fallow phase in crop rotation and increased agricultural output, those who introduced them were unaware of the cause. The 'Little Ice Age' peaked between 1660 and 1685 and the spread of turnip production during this period may have been a response to the associated summer droughts. If so, increased productivity was an unintended by-product (Overton 1996: 203). None the less, increasing output furthered the reorientation of English agriculture from subsistence to market production. During the eighteenth century rising profits from agriculture made investment in agricultural land which could be leased to tenants increasingly attractive. The recursive effect of primogeniture had been to generate a rural class structure and in the absence of machinery there was a growing demand for agricultural labour. The particularly English problem was to deprive the disinherited of self-sufficiency and turn them into labourers. After 1750, the open-field zone was progressively transformed from one of nucleated villages at the centre of the village's fields into a zone of scattered farms, each enclosed by 'ring-fences', with its farmhouse at the centre of the holding. A complex web of common rights gave way to tenancy of private property. Enclosures were directly responsible for turning those who had no land of their own, and who depended on access to the commons, into agricultural labourers. Neeson argues this was deliberate, quoting an eighteenth-century author who argued 'the inclosure of wastes would increase the number of hands for labour, by removing the *means* of subsisting in idleness' (Neeson 1993: 28, Neeson's emphasis).

The English manor jury was closely tied to the operation of the open fields, and it disappeared with the abolition of the open field system. Enclosure is not necessarily against the interests of those, such as members of the manor court's jury, who hold rights in land, since they are entitled to a portion of the commons and can fence their land against the grazing livestock of cottagers and labourers.

Population growth, combined with unigeniture, had created social divisions between a landed minority and a growing body of landless households who depended on the commons. The community of interest in the village had been fatally undermined. The greatest benefit from holding small portions of land in the open fields was the right it gave to turn stock out upon the fallow (Chibnall 1965: 231; Orwin and Orwin 1938: 145). 'This failure to protect the poorest section of the community was indeed one of the grave disadvantages of the whole enclosure movement' (Chibnall 1965: 251). In the villages studied by Neeson (1993: 202), opposition to enclosure came from small landowners and the landless. Neeson argues that large landowners could not 'tear up the contract' that favoured small and middle-scale occupiers until enclosure changed the terms of the argument (ibid. 155, 320). Following Axelrod's model for the evolution of reciprocal altruism, the possibility of enclosure suddenly enabled the end of mutual dependence to be foreseen and those who could manage without mutual aid withdrew from the social contract. Neeson argues the strength of opposition has been underestimated, since it is only visible in local records. She quotes a letter to the Marquis of Anglesey which complained, 'Should a poor man take one of Your sheep from the common his life would be forfeited by law. But should You take the common from a hundred poor mens sheep, the law gives no redress.' The Marquis replied, 'All your statements are without foundation & as your language is studiously Offensive I must decline any further communication with you' (ibid. 327).

The village assemblies of north-eastern France and Switzerland appear to have had wider powers, and therefore not only resisted enclosure more successfully, but survived the abolition of the open fields (see Bloch 1966: 43–4). In Franche-Comté it was rare for a rich farmer to be elected to the communal councils established at the time of the Revolution and the rich were never elected to the office of *maire*. 'Political power was refused to the wealthier members of the community in order to prevent them gaining control over the commonly owned lands and forest' (Mendras and Cole 1991: 128). The fate of common land, which persists in Switzerland and parts of France but disappeared in England, is evidently crucial. In France and Switzerland common pasture and forest have provided the village community with a continuing corporate identity upon which the power of the assembly and village council is based. Laxton is a unique case in England where both open fields and the jury that manages them have survived (Orwin and Orwin 1938: 149–52; Neeson 1993: 2). In León, communities continued to convene village assemblies even after their legal powers had been removed by the Spanish state. The elected officials who replaced them rarely acted without obtaining the assembly's consent (Behar 1986: 17–18, 157).

Changes in Resource Management on the Plateau of Levier

The comparative analysis of village systems in preceding paragraphs shows how change in resource management on the Plateau of Levier might be explained. The history of co-operative resource management on the Plateau of Levier suggests it has three advantages: minimizing variance, sharing costs, and taking control out of the hands of individual entrepreneurs. Collective exploitation of the pasture evens out variation in the patches available to individual households. The traditional *fruitière* originated as a way of pooling resources in order to make large enough cheeses to be exported from the region. Since each household received a cheese in turn, the *fruitière* can be interpreted as a rotating credit association. The stud bull co-operative reduced the costs to each member of keeping a bull and, like the post-war reconstitution of the dairy co-operatives, enabled younger *cultivateurs* to gain control of essential resources.

The village co-operatives of the Plateau of Levier satisfy Ostrom's conditions for success. Members interact regularly in a local context. They have developed shared norms and patterns of reciprocity, both in the wider context of mutual aid and in the specific experience of the successful management of co-operatives over a long period. They anticipate needing to co-operate for an indefinite period into the future. In the management of the common pasture opportunities exist to monitor whether associates are adhering to the agreed level of exploitation of the collective resource, and free-riders can be punished (cf. Ostrom 1990: 184–8).

Given the apparent stability and advantages of co-operative resource management, changes in the way collective resources have been managed in Pellaport and surrounding villages provide another opportunity to test theories of the evolution of co-operation. Change is caused by a different combination of circumstances to those which precipitated the English enclosures and has taken a different course. Although the proportion of *cultivateurs* in the village has been declining steadily, adjustments to the way communal resources are managed have proceeded in the step-like fashion seen in mechanization. Just as households minimize risk by adopting techniques that have been seen to work elsewhere, so communes and co-operatives tend to implement policies that have already been tried out in neighbouring villages. Whereas each household makes its own decisions about buying farming equipment, however, decisions about the management of collective resources are taken by the municipal council or at general meetings of agricultural co-operatives. Administrative changes can be implemented only through political action, and it is here that Bailey's (1969) approach to politics becomes most appropriate. Neeson (1993) gives excellent examples of the politics accompanying enclosure in England.

According to Daveau (1954: 117) the effect of agriculture becoming a minority occupation was to cause bitter divisions in some municipal councils as early as the 1950s, with *cultivateurs* and others competing to promote their special interests. During the forty or more years that followed the First World War Pellaport's municipal council invested some of the income from the communal forest by buying agricultural equipment for general use (see Ch. 2). By the 1960s it was becoming clear that spending communal income on equipment that now benefited only a minority had become unfair. In 1966 the council voted to end the practice. Other villages were making the same decision. Since the 1960s, *cultivateurs* have shared equipment either through informal *ententes* or the formal co-operatives known as CUMA (see Ch. 2).

During the 1950s, existing procedures for managing Pellaport's commons also came to appear increasingly inappropriate. As tractor-powered grass-cutters replaced hand-scythes it became impossible to mow the steeply sloping common land above la vie des Moutons. With the disappearance of horse-transport there was no longer a large market of hay and non-farmers were less interested in maintaining their rights to the commons. The procedure for allocating portions of hay was based on the number of people in the household but, since the decline of the European Marriage Strategy, the number of people per household was falling while the number of cattle rose. The primary aim of production had become, not to provide for the household's subsistence, but to take greatest advantage of the market for cheese. In the nineteenth century everyone in the village had to some extent been involved in farming, but agriculture was becoming the occupation of an increasingly specialist interest group within the community.

The commons came to be used increasingly as pasture and less as hay meadow. Although cattle placed on the commons were guarded by a cowherd (generally an elderly villager) appointed and paid by the municipal council, the commons were unfenced and in order to keep his herd from straying into the surrounding fields and forest the herdsman had to keep them together, preventing the animals from spreading out in search of the best grass. Individual households sometimes took their livestock to graze on the commons but it was rare to leave them there all day. Stall-feeding was common. To quote Claude Bavarel,

When you had five or six cows, two oxen and a horse in your stable, all you could do was give them a four hour run on the commons, then lead them back to the stable. You needed to cut some fresh grass every day and take it to the stable. It is only since the Second World War that cattle have been left to graze all day. That is why the high meadow above *Haute Source* has now been planted with fir trees; there is less demand for cut grass than there used to be.

There was no supply of water to the commons, and the cattle had to be led back to one of the village cattle troughs at midday. No chemical fertilizers were put on the commons, and no arrangement was made to level molehills or cut back brushwood. Between the First and Second World Wars, Pellaport's dairy association had periodically tried to organize work parties to clear brushwood but only some *cultivateurs* played their part and gradually no one was willing to participate.

Despite all these drawbacks, the *cultivateurs* of the village persisted with traditional procedures until they were overtaken by a crisis that triggered the 'step' into a new administrative procedure. In 1954 there was no one left willing to work all day as village cow-herd. At that moment, several of the younger farmers announced their intention of forming a new pasture co-operative. The procedures were well known through the running of the dairy co-operative, and a movement was under way throughout the district to create village pasture co-operatives. An inaugural meeting was advertised outside the dairy. Those who attended drew up a list of statutes based on government regulations for the running of co-operatives and elected a nine-man committee from the thirty-four who joined. One *cultivateur* in the village had sufficient land and few enough cattle not to need to use the commons. He was the only one not to join the new co-operative. The village council agreed to rent the largest area of commons to the association and provided it with a loan to pay for the 8 km. of boundary fence required. Now the *cultivateurs* would only need to find someone willing to bring the cattle to and from the pasture, who would be paid from the annual contribution levied on members of the co-operative. A few years later the co-operative installed a pump to take water to the pasture and bought a machine to spread chemical fertilizer. Members were invited to tender for the job of levelling molehills and cutting back brushwood. Any income they received by working for the co-operative was deducted from their annual levy. In 1967 the municipal council voted to abolish each household's traditional right to hay, and rent the remaining commons to the co-operative. Some small *parcelles* were set aside for the few non-farming households who still kept a cow and for those who wanted to scythe grass for their rabbits, but they were also required to pay a realistic rent. This was expected to prevent jealousy developing, as *cultivateurs* and other villagers all benefited from money paid into the commune's accounts. By 1969, when I began fieldwork, membership of the pasture co-operative had declined to twenty-two, but between them the members sent 206 head of cattle to graze on the commons, 73 per cent of the village's heifers and 30 per cent of its milk cows.

The comparative survey we carried out in 1972 showed management of the commons was still undertaken by the mayor and members of the municipal council in five of the fourteen villages surveyed, while pasture co-operatives had been created in six. In three others the dairy co-operative rented the pasture from the commune and arranged its management. A window of opportunity had become apparent when comparing different households' decisions to mechanize or continue with traditional techniques (Ch. 6) and, in a similar way, it was clear that no single point could be identified at which management of the commons was transferred from village council to a co-operative. Although those communes with the largest proportion of *cultivateurs* tended to leave management in the hands of the municipal council and those with the smallest proportion to set up co-operative control, the two procedures overlapped, showing that different communes were able to make different choices. In 1972 the overlapping ranges over which particular decisions had been implemented was analogous to the pattern of mechanization in individual households (compare Tables 6.7 and 7.1). In 1995, this useful parallel no longer existed. *Cultivateurs* made up respectively 17 and 4 per cent of households in the two villages where the municipal council still managed communal pasture. The *maire* of the latter village, which lies close to Pontarlier, explained that much of the demand for pasture now came not from *cultivateurs* but from households who kept horses as pets and who were content to leave management in the hands of the council. In the ten villages which now had pasture co-operatives, between 5 and 20 per cent of households were *cultivateurs*.

In most villages, the continuing decline in the number of *cultivateurs* eventually prompted the division of the commons between those who remained. In Pellaport the commons were divided in 1979, when membership of the pasture co-operative had fallen to about sixteen. Three reasons were given in favour of the division. No one suffered the risk of disease spreading from one stable's cattle to another's. On the level plateaux each *cultivateur* could decide whether to graze livestock or cut hay on his portion, and the land benefits from a rotation between meadow and pasture. People looked after the land better when they were solely responsible for their portion. One of my old friends told me in 1995 that milk production from cattle pastured on the commons had doubled since its division. In the days when the portions allocated for hay were distributed by lottery, there was no point in putting manure on your portion because someone else would (literally) reap the benefit the following year.

The division took place, however, without privatization. The commons continue to belong to the village and are rented by the co-oper-

TABLE 7.1. *The administration of communal pasture in 1972 and 1995*

1972

Method of administration	*Cultivateurs* as percentage of total households*						
Village council	55	38			30	27	
Pasture co-op.		38	37	35		25	19
Dairy co-op.			36			22	

1995

Method of administration	*Cultivateurs* as percentage of total households*							
Village council			17					4
Pasture co-op.	20	19	17	14	13	11	7	5

* Each figure represents one village.

ative, but the co-operative's role is now limited to obtaining insurance for the cattle and negotiating the current division, ensuring some flexibility as the relative needs of different *exploitations* change.

By 1995, pasture co-operatives existed in all but three communes of our survey. Eight villages, however, had divided the commons and arranged for each *cultivateur* to rent one section, either through the co-operative or directly from the council. Two further villages had divided some sections of the commons, but left the remainder as a single high pasture on which the heifers were placed together.

Following Dyson-Hudson and Smith, division of the sparse and variable pasture, either by fencing or setting a member of the household to guard each family's portion, would have been less efficient than allowing all the cattle to range across the entire pasture. As the number of people using the commons declined, however, so each remaining person gained a larger portion. This would increasingly cushion variability in the quality of the pasture available to each household, reducing the benefits of pooling cattle in a single herd and bringing to the fore the disadvantages of a single herd (the risk of transmitting disease, the inability of households to alternate between using the grass as meadow and pasture, or to

TABLE 7.2. *Variables related to the management of communal pasture in 1972 and 1995*

	Commons undivided	Commons divided
Pasture per household	1–22 ha. (av. 10 ha.)	4–33 ha. (av. 14 ha.)
Absolute no. of *cultivateurs*	5–27 (av. 16)	5–20 (av. 11)
Cultivateurs as % total households	5–38% (av. 26%)	4–20% (av. 13%)
TOTAL	16 cases*	11 cases

*Combines data for 1972 and 1995.

improve a portion). Overton (1996: 164) similarly argues that the increasing size of English farms during the eighteenth century made the risk-minimizing function of scattered strips less important and helped promote enclosure. Surprisingly, in view of this hypothesis, there is little difference between the area of commons available to each *cultivateur* in those villages that had divided their commons, and the area available where cattle still grazed in a single herd. Nor is the absolute number of *cultivateurs* in the community strikingly different. The most significant difference emerges between the proportions of households in the commune who are *cultivateurs* under the two management regimes (Table 7.2). This suggests the decision to divide the commons is as much associated with the transformation of social life in the community into special interest groups pursuing different objectives as it is with the economic benefits of division. Axelrod demonstrated the precondition of reciprocal altruism that each participant expects to need others' help at unpredictable moments in the future. Both mutual aid and the pooling of livestock will be threatened when risk and uncertainty diminish with the growth of larger, more prosperous *exploitations* (cf. McCloskey 1976: 130). Under these conditions there is less incentive to sustain a moral basis for mutal aid. There is therefore a partial parallel with English enclosures, but the effect has not been to evict large numbers of smallholders, since large-scale rural emigration had already occurred and machines had replaced manual labour.

Chapter 2 described the crisis affecting village dairy co-operatives in 1995 as the number of *cultivateurs* declined. Some co-operatives had

TABLE 7.3. *The effect of declining numbers of* cultivateurs *on the management of cheese production*

		No. of members in dairy association where			
		Association sells to entrepreneur	Co-op prod'n in village	Regrouping of co-ops	Association disbands
Village					
1.	1972		28		
	1995		17		
2.	1972		27		
	1995			23	
3.	1972		(not known)		
	1995			20	
4.	1972		26		
	1995				14
5.	1972		22		
	1995		15		
6.	1972		22		
	1995		13		
7.	1972		22		
	1995		9		
8.	1972		22		
	1995			9	
9.	1972		22		
	1995			5	
10.	1972		18		
	1995			6	
11.	1972		16		
	1995			8	
12.	1972		13		
	1995			7	
13.	1972		9		
	1995				6
14.	1972		9		
	1995			5	
15.	1972		6		
	1995				5

amalgamated, a decision foreshadowed by events in a few other villages as long ago as 1969. Since the dairy building was traditionally one of the most important foci for daily interaction between neighbours, the inflationary effects of increasing milk production had now struck at the heart of community life. Despite the declining number of *cultivateurs*, Pellaport's co-operative was still committed to remaining independent in 1995. Table 7.3 lists fifteen villages, showing the changes that have taken place in the organization of cheese manufacture between 1972 and 1995. The table strongly suggests nine members are the minimum viable for cheese manufacture in an independent dairy co-operative, at least at 1995 levels of milk production. At this point, a window of opportunity to choose between alternative strategies closes. The co-operatives in two neighbouring villages (villages 2 and 3 in Table 7.3) which have been supplying milk to the same entrepreneurs (father and son) since before 1969, had agreed to amalgamate in 1995 even though they still had twenty and twenty-three members respectively. In all other cases, amalgamation or dissolution occurred when the association had shrunk much further.

POLITICS AND CO-OPERATIVES

Changes in the management of Pellaport's resources illustrate the politics of co-operation. Even successful co-operatives, or changes in their constitution, are conceived in the factionalism of interpersonal relations. The pasture co-operative's inability to find a cowherd in 1969 had been widely discussed in the village before the co-operative's annual general meeting, and alternative solutions canvassed (see Ch. 1). Those who establish a change begin as an action set, a temporary coalition of neighbours, who implement their strategy by convening a meeting at which the majority of *cultivateurs* are persuaded to adopt their proposal. By agreeing to the statutes required by the State, a new co-operative becomes a jural entity and can take collective action.

The last entrepreneur dairyman to work in Pellaport was still alive in 1969. Like many dairymen, M. Schaltegger suffered from the resentment that built up during the German occupation (see Ch. 1). As he put it, after the war many young farmers returned filled with communist ideals, determined to reinstate co-operative control over cheese production. One of Ulin's informants, recalling the spread of wine-producing co-operatives in south-west France, had a different interpretation. In his words, many co-operatives were formed after the Second World War 'because of a profound need of men who had united to survive difficult times together, so there was a true co-operative spirit' (Ulin 1996: 174). It was César Maitrugue who took the lead in Pellaport. Not everyone was in favour of his proposal. Shortly after the men deported to Germany had returned, César called an extraordinary general meeting of the co-opera-tive. He proposed M. Schaltegger be replaced by an employee of the asso-ciation. The meeting was attended by thirty-one of the forty-five members. In retrospect, some of the absentees claimed not to have been invited but the unanimous vote in favour of César's plan was sufficient to secure a two-thirds majority. The co-operative would once again lease the dairy building from the commune. César was elected the new president, a post he held continuously for twenty-five years.

Before the Second World War Pellaport had a stud bull co-operative, but it was brought to an end by the stock requisitions of the Occupation. When the war was over, a few of the richer *cultivateurs* bought their own stud bulls and hired these out to other villagers. As the increase in milk production gathered pace during the 1960s, the co-operative was re-established by three young *cultivateurs*, only one of whom owned a bull but who were all anxious to improve the quality of their herd. According to one of the founding members, no one singly had enough money to buy a really good bull. In 1962 a notice was posted outside the dairy inviting other *cultivateurs* to a meeting where the formation of a new co-operative was proposed and accepted. All three of the proposers were elected to its committee and Claude Bavarel, widely recognized as a good judge of cattle, was chosen as president. Once the new co-operative had acquired its first bull, villagers were invited to tender for the job of stabling it. The first to succeed was an older *cultivateur* who until then had kept his own bull, but who now sold it. The following year one of the three founders entered a lower bid and displaced the older man. By implementing the co-operative, he had put himself in a position to compete with the wealthier farmer. Curiously, César Maitrugue was the only person not to join the association. He kept his stud bull until artificial insemination became available. By 1969 several people had left the co-operative and turned to the artificial insemination service provided by a regional co-operative set up with government assistance. In 1973 the village association disbanded; everyone now found it easier to telephone the regional co-operative's office in Besançon than to lead an often restless cow through the village. Before long a man would arrive on your own doorstep bringing the neces-sary equipment. One *cultivateur* had returned to keeping his own bull in 1995.

The regional culture includes knowledge of alternative administrative procedures that provide complementary or, most sharply in the case of entrepreneurs and co-operatives, conflicting means of managing resources. The analytical issues posed by such variability were discussed in Ch. 2. The local social subsystem constituted by each commune tends to swing between these methods in response to changes in social and economic conditions. Alternative cultural strategies provide the grounds for political opposition. Political competition can take place in a stable setting, but it will be enhanced by economic or social change that modifies the perceived appropriateness or practical viability of alternative procedures, or by ideological developments which bring new procedures to people's attention.

Throughout the present century, but particularly after the Second World War, agriculture has become increasingly specialized, involving a smaller proportion of the community and turning ever more intensively to the production of cheese. Changes in the balance of production, fluctuations in the market price of cheese and increased mechanization in agriculture have presented a series of problems to the commune as well as to the household. At any time, two or more potential solutions have been apparent and different villages have sometimes implemented different policies. Even if, over time, a single solution is adopted throughout the region general principles of social organization can be seen to underlie the strategies developed in particular cases which persist as possibilities, likely to be reapplied in a variety of different contexts.

The principles of collective ownership and collective management of resources have been applied again and again as solutions to particular problems, generating rather ephemeral groupings in the case of the informal sharing of machinery through *ententes* (see Ch. 2) but extraordinarily durable associations in the case of *fruitières*. The continuing use of such principles for generating administrative strategies plays an important part in giving the region its distinctive cultural style (cf. Morphy and Layton 1981: 70). Something more than a habitus, these principles are consciously invoked by people acting as agents who embody cultural strategies. In 1788 the community of Passenans wrote to the *intendant* of Franche-Comté that they were having difficulty paying their taxes. They had searched for some way to increase their income and 'after considerable investigation had found none but that of establishing a *fruitière*'. The *intendant* replied that no permission was needed; any village that wanted to set up a *fruitière* was free to do so (Latouche 1938: 776). The strategies work not only because they are familiar and tested, but because over time their use feeds back upon the ambience of social life; their recursive effect is to construct a niche in which mutual trust is sustained. In some cases the option of collective ownership and management within the village may prove unviable, as the case of the reintroduction of a stud bull co-operative suggests, and as has often been the case with CUMA, but the principle remains part of the cultural repertoire. The *fruitières*, so long a part of local culture, had virtually disappeared during the inter-war period, but were re-established after the Second World War and continue to dominate production, even though many have amalgamated to become inter-village co-operatives. The repeated application of particular principles of collective organization over time has given the regional social system of the Plateau of Levier its particular historical trajectory.

The irony of the dairy economy on the Plateau of Levier is that, despite successful management of the literal commons, the market for Comté cheese has been treated as an open-access commons. It is true the designation of Comté as a product subject to *appellation contrôlée* was a way of fencing the market. When a large industrial dairy which threatened to take business away from village co-operatives was established in the region, the regional association of dairy co-operatives successfully had the regulations modified to establish that genuine Comté had to be made in a dairy no more than a certain distance from the *exploitations* that produced the milk. This reduced the catchment area for the industrial dairy to that available to local co-operatives and destroyed its commercial advantage. None the less, as Ch. 6 showed, the steady increase in cheese production has an inflationary effect on its value. It only needs some *cultivateurs* to increase production for all to have to follow suit if their incomes are not to be eroded, just as overstocking by a few households can degrade the value of common grazing for everyone. If other households cannot increase production they will be forced out of agriculture. The consequences feed back upon the management of village resources.

The introduction of EC milk quotas in 1984 has had a damaging effect precisely because of the difficulty of monitoring free-riders. Since then each *exploitation* has a milk production level attached to it and is fined for each kilo of milk produced over their quota (Jurjus 1993: 102). The quota assigned to each *exploitation* was based on the household's production level in 1983 and is tied to the land the household was using that year. Some *cultivateurs* in Dechailles 'forgot' to declare they were using portions of common land, ensuring the entire quota was attached to their own land and rendering those portions of the commons valueless to anyone else, since they have no quota attached. Although government inspectors fined many *cultivateurs* for non-compliance five years after quotas were introduced, every dairy co-operative suspects those in neighbouring villages of cheating by accepting more milk than its associates are allowed to produce according to their quotas. Even within co-operatives the suspicion may arise that some associates have done a secret deal with the dairyman, only entering part of their production in their record book, but being paid for all the milk they deliver. The co-operative in one of the villages surveyed had disbanded in acrimony over such allegations. The introduction of refrigerated tanks, intimated in 1969 (see Ch. 1), has given *cultivateurs* who buy one a flexibility that never existed in the days of the traditional *fruitière*, allowing them to choose which neighbouring association to join. Two *cultivateurs*, one from Pellaport and one from Montoiseau, defected to Dechailles' co-operative in 1995. They now store their milk until a tanker from Dechailles' collects it. The inability to police the activities of other dairy co-operatives is the most serious problem threatening the survival of co-operation. Quotas will work only if each co-operative is assured that others' production levels are accurately monitored.

Progressive Trajectories in Social Change

There are two reasons why social change on the Plateau appears to follow a linear trajectory that looks more like 'progress' than an 'adaptive radiation' in which communities increasingly diverge as they adapt to different economic niches. Comparison of the fifteen villages in the survey shows that, at any time, several alternative strategies exist. Diversification analogous to an adaptive radiation is, however, inhibited by the uniform change in the social environment created by inflation in the price of milk, itself the consequence of strategies to increase output. The second cause (also paralleled in technological change) is the wish to avoid the risk of adopting an unfamiliar strategy. These two tendencies are responsible for what is surely the most striking difference between cultural and genetic inheritance: each human society tends to be culturally uniform but genetically diverse (Lewontin 1982: 120–3). Cultural variability occurs between populations, genetic variability occurs within populations.

Boyd and Richerson predicted that 'social learning' (adopting established strategies) would give way to 'individual learning' during periods of rapid change, increasing variability in behaviour (see Ch. 5). On the Plateau of Levier, however, as soon as an effective innovation is discovered, 'guided variation' occurs. Individuals pass on the modifications they have made to existing strategies. Lateral transmission contributes to the uniformity of culture within the population. Further experimentation is discouraged and the innovation spreads rapidly through the local culture. The process Boyd and Richerson call 'biased transmission', where households or coalitions of individuals formalized in co-operatives or municipal councils choose which alternative cultural trait to adopt, tends to inhibit cultural diversification. The same pattern can be seen at the level of the nation-state, where governments confronted with the rising cost of welfare or rising crime rates follow each other by adopting policies such as the purchaser–provider split, zero-tolerance, privatization of utilities, and so forth.

Conclusion

'The tragedy of the commons' has been attributed to the intrinsic difficulty of managing a communal resource when any individual's efforts benefit all users and no means exists to police cheaters who use the commons without contributing to their upkeep. If this argument validly explains the enclosure movement in England, then the absence of effective communal organization must be seen as the consequence of the particular historical circumstances of the eighteenth and nineteenth centuries, explicable as the outcome of inegalitarian inheritance rules combined with population growth, new farming techniques, and a growing market. It cannot be seen as a universal condition (cf. McCay and Acheson 1987: 7). Successful collective management depends not only upon the historical development of appropriate management structures, but also on the persistence of a community whose interests in the land are the same. Partible inheritance tends to create such a community, while unigeniture tends to dissolve it.

Building on the recursive effects of interaction discussed in Ch. 3, this final chapter has tried to identify correlations between several institutions in European village society. It has argued common land is more likely to survive where the quality of the land is too poor and variable to justify its division. It has also been argued that partible inheritance is associated with a nucleated settlement, where each household's land is intermixed with that of its neighbours in the surrounding fields. Rotas and lotteries play an important part in guaranteeing equality of access to agricultural land and forest in such communities. Partible inheritance is associated with a strong network of mutual aid, while unigeniture promotes self-sufficiency. A network of mutual aid enables development of the mutual trust on which successful agricultural co-operatives depend. The recursive effects of combining partible inheritance, mutual aid, and common rights to land are to create a stable system, explaining why these aspects of the cultural order on the Plateau of Levier have proved so durable. In the south of France, and in England since enclosure, unigeniture is associated with dispersed holdings. Each house stands in the middle of its own land. A historical perspective shows, however, that many English and German villages in zones where unigeniture had been imposed remained nucleated for several centuries. The dismantling of the open field system in such villages coincided with population increase and the growth of a market for agricultural produce or a demand for labour in other occupations.

While strong self-government in the village is often associated with partible inheritance, this is not so in the Breton community of Bigouden or the Italian Alpine village of Saint Felix. Strong self-government dissolved in Abriès after the French government deprived the village of control over its common land. The correlation between inheritance and self-government therefore appears more contingent than that between inheritance and mutual aid. Patronage arises where communities do not own the resources on which they depend for subsistence, while control of common land underwrites strong village government. During a period of population expansion, however, common rights come under threat. The threat is particularly acute where unigeniture undermines the equal distribution of rights to land in the village and where the growth of a market for agricultural produce has the particular effect of creating a demand for hired labour. Under these circumstances, those in power will be tempted to detach the weak from their more tenuous hold on self-sufficiency.

THE RELEVANCE OF ANTHROPOLOGICAL THEORY

Chapter 1 opened this study of continuity and change on the Plateau of Levier with a description of daily life in the village of Pellaport in 1969. Villagers were aware their routines had historical roots, but also that life in the community had changed in the past and was changing rapidly during the time I lived in the village. Chapter 2 stepped back from everyday life to take a broader historical perspective and identify the theoretical issues raised by the reproduction and transformation of social practices. I argued Bourdieu and Giddens had largely resolved the dilemmas of anthropological theory that were current during my original research, but that there was scope for refining their ideas. Bourdieu and

Giddens perpetuate the tendency of structural analysis to assume social or cultural systems are in equilibrium, and do not deal adequately with the conditions that cause instability. Both give undue attention to power and social inequality, underemphasizing the role of co-operation and mutual dependence in the generation of social relationships. Neither Giddens nor Bourdieu make much use of the idea that social behaviour may be shaped by adaptation to particular circumstances. While benefiting considerably from their work, this study has tried to show how these weaknesses can be overcome, through the analysis of village government, the organization of the household, mutual aid, and technological and social change in European villages. Although based primarily on a study of one village and those surrounding it on the Plateau of Levier, the patterns that emerge have been further explored through comparisons with other village studies that illustrate the causes of stability and instability in social process. At the end of Ch. 2 I posed four questions which can now be readdressed. How are patterns of thought and behaviour reproduced within and across generations? How is culture realized through the implementation of social strategies? What are the recursive effects of interaction? To what extent is evolutionary theory applicable to social behaviour?

How are Patterns of Thought and Behaviour Reproduced within and across Generations?

Chapter 4 demonstrated the usefulness of Bourdieu's concept of habitus for understanding the way in which the values and principles of mutual aid are learned and handed on within and between generations. Despite broad agreement, each individual holds his or her own values concerning mutual aid which express themselves through the individual's conduct in community life. Bourdieu predicted such variation without satisfactorily explaining what constrained it. Children are taught the proper way to behave, adults are praised or ridiculed, but socialization is only part of the explanation for the convergence of values and understanding. Interesting parallels emerged when the principles governing mutual aid in Pellaport were compared with those Bourdieu found among the Kabyle. I explained the relative consistency in the habitus of interpersonal relations in two ways. First, certain individuals typified the positions that people might adopt in interpersonal life. They could be referred to in discussion. Secondly, the theory of reciprocal altruism identified the strategies most likely to succeed where people wish to develop relations of mutual support, and these strategies coincide to a significant extent with the principles of mutual aid in Pellaport. The rituals of interpersonal life, while simpler in structure than verbal communication, convey vital information about a person's disposition towards neighbours and the community at large. Historical evidence shows that the symbolic actions that make up these rituals have changed, but the constructs they communicate have been more stable. The different emphasis apparent in Kabyle values correlated with a social community dominated by wealthy families where equality was precariously maintained and patronage common. I therefore questioned whether habitus was necessarily as unreflective and irrational as Bourdieu claimed.

The theme of individual differences in disposition, and the processes that cause dispositions to converge or draw apart, was developed in Ch. 5 through the study of the diffusion of innovations in agriculture. Chapter 5 revealed a complex relation between innovators or opinion-leaders and others who followed or rejected their example. The nucleated village and the intermixing of land worked by different households provided good opportunities for people to watch each other at work, while the network of mutual aid discussed in Ch. 4 provided a medium for the exchange of information, and for censure or praise of innovators and traditionalists. Individuals did not, however, blindly copy one another. They learned from the experiences of others. Decisions about new techniques and machines were taken in the knowledge that the scale of dairy production would have to increase if *exploitations* were to survive, but also in the expectation that the children of some *cultivateurs* did not intend to take over from their parents. No one is perfectly informed about the outcome of their decisions and everyone is vulnerable to economic 'selection' beyond their control, determining whether their *exploitation* will survive or fail.

Culture is Realized in the Playing of Strategies

Chapter 3 showed how local culture is realized through the implementation of strategies of inheritance and labour recruitment. The structure of the household changes as the household passes through a cycle partly determined by the birth, marriage, and death of its members. The form of the household is also guided by its needs for labour, by local inheritance rules and by the possibilities allowed in government legislation. During the mid- and late nineteenth century, production on the Plateau of Levier was labour intensive and unmechanized. The traditional rule of partible inheritance demanded that property be evenly divided among all heirs. Householders had to reconcile the additional labour large numbers of children might provide with the need to avoid fragmenting the family holding, a problem faced particularly by the majority who were *cultivateurs*. The region's population had grown steadily for two hundred years since the Thirty Years War. By the mid-nineteenth century household heads were deliberately limiting the number of heirs by enforcing late marriage or lifelong celibacy on their children, creating a relatively high frequency of extended family households and households where adult, unmarried children lived with their parents. Members of a small proportion of households were employed as agricultural labourers. Many of these were single supporting parents. Successful *cultivateurs* were able to augment their labour power without threatening the inheritance by employing labourers and domestic servants from other households.

Strategies pursued within the household thus had consequences on the wider fabric of village social organization, tending to generate a class structure most apparent in the division between landowners, *cultivateurs* who worked their own or rented land and day labourers who had to work for others. A detailed examination of census data showed this apparent class structure was partly an artefact of the household's demographic cycle. The role of domestic servant, labourer, and 'landowner' (*rentier*) were to some extent characteristic of phases in the individual's lifetime. Most domestic servants were teenagers or young adults, while many labourers and all 'landowners' were over 50 years old. The prevalence of both day labourers and *rentiers* among the elderly none the less implied these were different routes into old age dictated by relative wealth in land. A comparison of villages on the Plateau of Levier with other village studies in Western Europe showed partible inheritance has a strong tendency to generate social equality, while unigeniture, in which one child inherits most if not all the family's property, generates more marked social inequality.

During the latter half of the nineteenth century the French Industrial Revolution created unprecedented opportunities for employment in cities. The Plateau of Levier experienced a hundred years of population decline caused by emigration and a radical change in demographic strategies. Adult celibacy virtually disappeared. The introduction of contraception enabled women to begin having children earlier and then cease childbearing before the end of their natural reproductive period. The structure of farming households was transformed by the disappearance of employees and the substitution of machines for human labour. In Ch. 6 I resumed the analysis of household strategies, looking at the way house-holds used agricultural machinery to increase production, and how new household strategies had transformed local culture. I argued that the radical changes that had occurred on the Plateau of Levier since the 1950s had not caused the sudden disappearance of a tradition that had survived, unchanged, for centuries, but were the outcome of a process that began with the displacement of the open-field system in the late eighteenth century and the flight of agricultural labour after 1850. Increased productivity, the growth of an urban market for food, and the need to repay loans taken out to buy machines had created a complex pattern of positive feedback. Studies of various techniques show that the scale of the benefits provided by innovations differs greatly, and that many innovations (including that central component of post-war change, the tractor) have drawbacks as well as advantages. Surprisingly, the earliest machines, introduced in the late nineteenth century, turned out to give the greatest gain on the methods they replaced. I proposed a step model, in which each innovation lifted household production above the lower limit of viability, only to be overtaken in time by the effect of inflation on income or the decline in available labour. Chapter 7 argues a similar model could be used to explain the succession of changes in the way village resources are managed. At the start of this chapter I pointed out that the evolutionary theories of Marx and Darwin were radically different. Marx's theory, in common with most social theories of the eighteenth and nineteenth centuries, proposed an internal dynamic that caused societies to change progressively. Darwin's theory of natural selection proposed that random variation in a population was selected for or against by features of its environment. Chapter 6 noted that a simple Darwinian model implies that a population will eventually stabilize around the most effective adaptation it can achieve, while more complex models suggest interaction between species and their environments may tend to destabilize existing adaptations. Chapters 5 and 6 showed how innovation and economic change destabilized the once-efficient strategies for regulating interpersonal relations in Pellaport and managing collective resources on the Plateau of Levier. The implementation of new strategies transformed local culture.

To what extent should sociological analysis take variation in individual agents' strategies into account when studying the cause of social change? Lorenz coined the term 'butterfly effect' to express the notion that a small, chance event could displace the state of a system (Stewart 1997: 127–9). At first the effect might be imperceptible but, as the cycle progressed, the trajectory of the system diverged from what it would otherwise have followed. Nelson and Winter (1982: 15, 276) suggested that the uncertainty surrounding decisions to innovate was so great that innovations could effectively be treated as chance events, whose impact could therefore be compared to the butterfly effect. Ruelle (1991: 33) similarly argued the complexity of the universe makes free will a meaningful notion, since no one can predict the future in any detail, and it would take an impossibly long time to determine the truth or falsity of certain propositions. An actor faces both risk and uncertainty. The decision to act in a certain way is *risky* when, even though she or he knows the probability that the action will have one or another outcome, the value of those outcomes varies. Actors suffer uncertainty where they lack information about the state of their environment. This is true even in the simplest hunter-gatherer societies. A hunter faces risk when he in dangerous conditions, knowing that a certain proportion of trips will result in injury or death. He faces uncertainty when he does not know exactly where his prey will be found (Smith 1988: 230–1). In a chaotic social system the consequences of risk and uncertainty are magnified. The future state of the social system is unknowable and, to the extent that he or she can exercise free will, the actor must choose which course of action to take.

The effect of such chance events depends on the stability of the system. If each variable can only change to a limited extent, the system 'must return infinitely often to states near its original state' (Stewart 1997: 50), and the butterfly effect will be greatly reduced. The more unstable the state of the system, the greater the effect of a small, chance deflection from its current trajectory. The effect of some apparently chance event is no longer 'erased' by subsequent evolution (Ruelle 1991: 88–9, cf. T. A. Brown 1996: 121). By choosing one strategy, and thus positioning themselves in the system, agents set off along a trajectory that may diverge increasingly, and unpredictably, from the alternative routes they might have followed had they adopted a different strategy (cf. Rosser 1996: 200 and Morphy and Layton 1981: 68). The more chaotically a social system behaves, the greater the impact of variation in agents' strategies upon structuration, and the more the history of its agents' activities emerges as a separate field of study.

What are the Recursive Effects of Interaction?

Giddens' concept of structuration usefully draws attention to the need to identify the processes through which social relations are created and reproduced by human agency, rather than to take them for granted (as Radcliffe-Brown tended to do) as the mechanistic unfolding of a preordained social structure. While Radcliffe-Brown tended to assume social systems were inherently stable, I have argued structuration is as likely to transform social relations as it is to reproduce an existing social order. Radcliffe-Brown hoped to demonstrate the scientific character of structural-functionalism through the discovery of sociological laws derived from correlations between the forms of social institutions. The interactionists, followed by Giddens and Bourdieu, objected that Radcliffe-Brown treated social structure as if it had a life of its own, rather than recognizing it as the by-product of interaction among socially informed agents. Radcliffe-Brown was in effect sampling social process at particular moments in time to discover correlations between customs, but not asking how the social processes responsible for these correlations were generated. The method of structural-functionalism, developed to study small-scale, non-Western societies, can be interpreted as the observation of a long run of social events from which the anthropologist calculates the probability of certain states being repeated, hence describing the system in a probabilistic way (cf. Ruelle 1991: 5). To the extent that each cycle of events follows the same path as previous ones, this method will give an accurate account. Structural-functionalism will therefore be most appropriate to the study of simple systems, where there are few interrelated variables, and not much energy is being put into the system. The greatest failure of structural-functionalism was its failure to take account of the way colonialism was drawing the communities studied into an increasingly complex world system.

Earlier in this chapter I returned to the argument advanced in Ch. 3 that the recursive effects of partible inheritance and unigeniture are very different. I argued that the equality of access to resources promoted by partible inheritance contributed to the probable success of commons management, whereas the disenfranchisement caused by unigeniture created a conflict of interest over use of the commons. A comparative survey of European village studies led to the conclusion that partible inheritance tends to be associated with a nucleated village and a strong network of mutual aid, while unigeniture tends to be associated with isolated, self-sufficient farms exclusively working their own land. The right of a community to manage its own resources contributes to local democracy, while dispossession encourages patronage. These conclusions recall Radcliffe-Brown's search for general correlations between the form of customs. Such correlations do not, however, arise from the dead hand of social structure, obliging people to take up roles that will sustain the social order. They emerge from the *agency* of socially informed actors, even though the recursive effects of their strategies are to generate patterns of interaction beyond any individual's control.

I rejected Marx's simplistic notion that common property was part of the natural or original human condition. I reviewed two theories of commons management. The first, advocated by Hardin and Lloyd, argued that it was difficult if not impossible to regulate exploitation of the commons. Any individuals who over-exploited a common resource degraded its value for everyone. Others who showed restraint suffered the effect of over-exploitation without gaining the benefit. Ostrom, and McCay and Acheson, argued that under appropriate conditions, common resources could be regulated. The recursive effects of regulated and unregulated exploitation will clearly be different. I showed the conditions identified by Ostrom for successful management were met, not only on the Plateau of Levier and in other French, Spanish, and Alpine communities, but also in Medieval England. Successful conservation of the commons was therefore the result of particular social arrangements, enacted in appropriate conditions.

Partible inheritance was practised in Anglo-Saxon England, but during the period of population growth associated with Braudel's 'classic' cycle feudal lords increasingly imposed a rule of unigeniture. I argued that unigeniture laid the grounds for the English enclosures, but that its divisive effects were only felt to the full during a later period of population growth associated with increased production in agriculture and the growth of markets that made investment in land attractive to commercially minded landlords. English village communities became divided between the poor who depended on common land but lacked entitlement to it and the prosperous who had inherited their own land. German case studies supported the argument that partible inheritance and unigeniture generate different social structures during periods of population growth. The twentieth-century division of the commons on the Plateau of Levier had different causes. Communities here managed their common land successfully, sustaining the close-knit, effective village structure conspicuously lacking from the modern English village, but treated the market for their agricultural produce as an open-access commons. Ostrom's conditions could not be satisfied when the market for cheese was exploited by numerous independent co-operatives in different villages. Even the introduction of quotas was undermined by the suspicion of free-riding in other villages. Fewer and fewer *cultivateurs* could survive, and the benefits of common grazing gradually disappeared.

In Ch. 4 I outlined the ways in which the continued transformation of occupations in the village after 1969 had undermined the network of mutual aid. As car ownership became more common people not only commuted to work outside the village, becoming less dependent on one another, but acquired the habit of driving around the village. Fewer people met each other on foot, fewer greetings were exchanged, less gossip occurred. Television had diminished the tradition of inviting friends and neighbours to evening events. Although the surviving *cultivateurs* continued to help each other, as their numbers diminished many villages were losing their dairy buildings. Milk, cheese, and butter were no longer bought in the village. Fewer people met as milk was delivered to the dairy; where the dairy had closed, milk was collected from farmhouses by tanker. Village schools had fewer and fewer classes as the birth rate declined. School closure was widely regarded as a further blow to community life. All these trends undermined the moral community sustained by mutual aid.

To What Extent is Evolutionary Theory Applicable to Social Behaviour?

The fate of cultural behaviour—whether or not it will be successfully perpetuated—depends on its suitability to local natural conditions (such as the adaptation of a dairy economy and land management to alpine ecology), but also on the way each pattern of behaviour contributes to the organization of relations in society.

In Chs. 3, 4, and 7 I argued that Darwinian evolutionary theory can identify objective limits to the possibilities of structuration. Partible inheritance and unigeniture provide alternative solutions to two fundamentally conflicting goals: to give the best possible start in life to all one's offspring, or concentrate the resources on which they will depend in the hands of a minority and thus ensure their survival. Malthus showed how peasant farmers in the Alps could monitor the relationship between labour and resources, and maintain a balance between them through marriage strategies. Malthus's work is supported by the more detailed research of Netting. The demonstrable costs of fragmenting the holding among too many heirs, or failing to recruit sufficient labour to work the land, show how the outcome of structuration within the household can be objectively assessed. Since, however, both unigeniture and partible inheritance are practiced in the Alps, the cultural solution to particular problems cannot be predicted from the ecology. The cultural principles governing transmission of access to productive resources, moreover, complicate the issue of reproductive success. Unigeniture and partible inheritance, and employment by non-kin as servants or agricultural labourers, catch individuals in a complex web of social relationships through which some enhance their reproductive success and others are disadvantaged.

In Ch. 4 the theory of the evolution of co-operation was used to identify the strategies most likely to succeed where people wished to develop relations of mutual support, and these strategies corresponded to a significant extent with the principles of mutual aid in Pellaport. The same theory was used in Ch. 7 to predict the circumstances most likely to favour agricultural co-operatives, including the traditional *fruitières*, while the theory of territoriality was effective in predicting which types of terrain were most economically controlled by individual households and which were more efficiently managed collectively.

Bourdieu showed that the individual must be the unit of analysis in the study of habitus. Any consistency among members of a community is a problem to be explained, not something that can be taken for granted as the product of a Durkheimian collective consciousness. Bourdieu's insight invites an analogy with evolutionary theory, in which the individual organism is traditionally considered the unit of selection. The individual's success in passing on his or her genes is largely determined by the degree to which those genes create body forms and behaviour patterns appropriate to survival in their ecological niche. In Ch. 5 I briefly reviewed the large body of literature that argues in favour of analogies between the transmission of cultural and genetic traits. Chapter 6 noted the analogy between evolutionary and economic theories in which economically rational behaviour was the analogue of behaviour that contributed to reproductive success. Two vital differences between the cultural and genetic transmission of information were, however, emphasized. Genetic traits can be transmitted only from parent to child. Change can occur only through chance variation in the character of the traits transmitted during reproduction. Cultural traits can be transmitted more rapidly, enabling several changes in the course of one generation. They can also be transmitted more widely, between other relatives, between neighbours, and from teacher to pupil. Secondly, cultural traits can to some extent, although never completely, be shaped to meet perceived needs.

There are, therefore, several reasons why the complexity of social change on the Plateau of Levier argues against using a simple model of adaptation, in which random variations in a population are passed on or eliminated over successive generations, so that the population gradually becomes better adapted to its environment. I showed not only that the economic environment to which *cultivateurs* must adapt is constantly changing, rendering their current methods less effective, but also that the villagers' own strategies contribute to the transformation of this economic environment. The simple S-curve model that compares the spread of new cultural traits through a population to the spread of an epidemic assumes that susceptible individuals are randomly distributed through the population, and that their susceptibility cannot be modified by the reaction of others. Technological innovations are often more accessible to the wealthy than the poor and the effect of some adopting new techniques may be to make it harder for others to follow their example. 'Infection' with a technological innovation is, moreover, not a cost but a benefit if the *cultivateur* is to cope with a changing economic environment.

In Ch. 6 Marx's argument that a capitalist economy is characterized by repeated innovations as existing markets become saturated was found particularly helpful in explaining recent change in agriculture. The distinctive features of the spiralling growth of production, coupled with the decline in the number of producers that followed the Second World War, was the willingness of young *cultivateurs* to become indebted to banks, and the fall in the value of their produce as markets became over-supplied. These processes have been taking place through much of Western Europe, exacerbated by the protectionist policies of countries such as France, and have eventually led to the imposition of quotas on production. Although the larger-scale *exploitations* are more likely to survive, the opportunity exists for households to move up the rank order through determined and repeated innovation, or to decline as children lose interest, or random accidents force men to retire. The internal dynamic of social change repeatedly destabilized existing social adaptations, undermining the effectiveness of current farm technology, patterns of mutual aid and the management of common resources. I briefly mentioned the more complex evolutionary theories of Kauffman and Odling-Smee, which more closely model the mechanisms of social change in Pellaport and surrounding villages.

Analysis of social process on the Plateau of Levier does not argue for a science of society of the kind envisaged by Radcliffe-Brown or

Durkheim. The outcome of social processes is not entirely predictable. Households, networks of mutual aid, co-operatives, communes, even nation-states are not closed systems; they are merely eddies or turbulence in the flow of social process that coalesces around the control, use, and management of resources such as land, labour, and information. Through a dialogue between the social life and history of the Plateau of Levier, and aspects of anthropological theory, I have tried to identify how continuity in social organization is achieved, and what causes change in the way resources are managed.

REFERENCES

ABÉLÈS, M. (1991), *Quiet days in Burgundy: A Study in Local Politics*, trans. A. McDermott (Cambridge, Cambridge University Press [French edition 1989]).

ADAMS, R. N. (1951), 'Personnel in Culture Change: A Test of a Hypothesis', *Social Forces*, 30: 185–9.

AGRESTE (1990), *Le Doubs agricole et rurale, données 1990* (Besançon, Prefecture du *département* du Doubs, Direction départementale de l'agriculture et de la forêt).

—— (1994), *La Statistique agricole, données no. 2, D 25: enquête sur la structure des exploitations agricoles* (Paris, Ministère de l'Agriculture et de la Pêche).

ALEXANDER, R. (1979), 'Evolution and Culture', in N. Chagnon and W. Irons (eds.), *Evolutionary Biology and Human Social Behaviour* (North Scituate, Mass.: Duxbury), 59–78.

ALLEN, P. (1989), 'Modelling Innovation and Change', in S. E. van der Leeuw, and R. Torrence (eds.), *What's New? A Closer Look at the Process of Innovation* (London: Unwin), 258–80

—— (1997), 'Models of Creativity: Towards a New Science of History', in S. van der Leeuw and J. McGlade (eds.), *Time, Process and Structured Transformation in Archaeology* (London: Routledge), 40–56.

ANDERSON, M. (1980), *Approaches to the History of the Western Family, 1500–1914* (London: Macmillan).

ARCHER, M. S. (1985), 'The Myth of Cultural Unity', *British Journal of Sociology*, 36: 333–53.

AUGUSTINS, G. (1989), *Comment se perpetuer? Devenir des lignées et destins des patrimoines dans les paysanneries européennes* (Nanterre: Société d'Ethnologie).

AULT, W. O. (1972), *Open-field Farming in Medieval England: A Study of Village By-laws* (London: Allen and Unwin).

AXELROD, R. (1990), *The Evolution of Co-operation* (Harmondsworth: Penguin [first edition Basic Books, New York, 1984]).

BAILEY, F. G. (1969), *Stratagems and Spoils: A Social Anthropology of Politics* (Oxford: Blackwell).

BARNETT, H. G. (1953), *Innovation: The Basis of Cultural Change* (New York: McGraw Hill).

BARTH, F. (1959), 'Segmentary Opposition and the Theory of Games: A Study of Pathan Organization', *Journal of the Royal Anthropological Institute*, 89: 5–21.

—— (1966), *Models of Social Organization*, Occasional Paper No. 23 (London: Royal Anthropological Institute).

—— (1967a), 'On the Study of Social Change', *American Anthropologist*, 69: 661–9.

—— (*1967b*), 'Economic Spheres in Darfur', in R. Firth (ed.), *Themes in Economic Anthropology* (London: Tavistock), 149–74.

BARTHELEMY, T. (1988), 'Les Modes de transmission du patrimoine: synthèse des travaux effectués depuis quinze ans par les ethnologues de la France', *Études Rurales*, 110–12: 195–212.

BARTHES, R. (1967), *Elements of Semiology*, trans. A. Lavers and C. Smith, (London: Cape).

BASALLA, G. (1988), *The Evolution of Technology*, (Cambridge: Cambridge University Press).

BATESON, G. (1968), 'Redundancy and Coding', In T. A. Sebeok (ed.), *Animal Communication: Techniques of Study and Results of Research* (Bloomington, Ind.: Indiana University Press), 614–26.

BAUM, W. C. (1958), *The French Economy and the State* (Princeton: Princeton University Press).

BEHAR, R. (1986) *Santa María del Monte: The Presence of the Past in a Spanish Village* (Princeton: Princeton University Press).

BELSHAW, C. S. (1965), *Traditional Exchange and Modern Markets* (Englewood Cliffs, NJ: Prentice-Hall).

BERGER, J. (1992), *Into their Labours* (London: Granta).

BERGER, P. L. and LUCKMAN, T. (1966), *The Social Construction of Reality* (Harmondsworth: Penguin).

BERKNER, L. K. (1972), 'The Stem Family and the Developmental Cycle of the Peasant Household: An Eighteenth-Century Austrian Example', *American Historical Review*, 77: 398–418.

—— (1976) 'Inheritance, Land Tenure and Peasant Family Structure: A German Regional Comparison', in J. Goody, J. Thirsk, and E. P. Thompson (eds.), *Family and Inheritance: Rural Society in Western Europe 1200–1800* (Cambridge: Cambridge University Press), 71–95.

BERRY, J. L. and KIM, H. (1996), 'Long waves 1790–1990: Intermittency, Chaos and Control', in L. D. Kiel and E. Elliott (eds.), *Chaos Theory in the Social Sciences* (Ann Arbor: University of Michigan Press), 215–36.

BIDARDE DE LA NOE, C. (1970), *Presence de la Franche Comté, VI: 2* (Besançon: Prefecture).

BINTLIFF, J. (1997), 'Catastrophe, Chaos and Complexity: The Death, Decay and Rebirth of Towns from Antiquity to Today', *Journal of European Archaeology*, 5: 67–90.

BLAU, P. (1964), *Exchange and Power in Social Life* (New York: Wiley).

BLAXTER, L. (1971), '*Rendre Service* and *Jalousie*'. In F. B. Bailey (ed.), *Gifts and Poison: The Politics of Repution* (Oxford, Blackwell), 119–38.

BLAYO, Y. (1972), 'Size and Structure of Households in a Northern French Village', in P. Laslett and R. Wall (eds.), *Household and Family in Past Time: Comparative Studies in the Size and Structure of the Domestic Group over the Last Three Centuries* (Cambridge: Cambridge University Press), 255–65.

BLOCH, M. (1961), *Feudal Society*, trans. L. A. Manyon. (London: Routledge [French edition 1940]).

—— (1966) *French Rural History: An Essay on its Basic Characteristics*, trans. J. Sondheimer (London: Routledge [French edition 1931]).

BOHOLM, A. (1996), 'Risk Perception and Social Anthropology: A Critique of Cultural Theory', *Ethnos* 61: 64–84.

BOICHARD, J. (1960), 'La Modernisation agricole sur les plateaux du Jura: une exemple d'exploitation d'avant-garde', *Revue de Géographie de Lyon*, 35: 157–74.

BOINON, J-P. and CAVAILHÈS, J. (1988), 'Essai d'explication de la baisse du prix des terres', *Études rurales*, 110–12: 215–34.

BONNEUIL, N. (1997), *Transformation of the French Demographic Landscape, 1806–1906* (Oxford: Clarendon Press).

BORGERHOFF MULDER, M. (1987), 'Adaptation and Evolutionary Approaches to Anthropology', *Man*, NS 22: 25–41.

BOURDIEU, P. (1977), *Outline of a Theory of Practice*, trans. R. Nice (Cambridge: Cambridge University Press [French edition 1972]).

—— (1990) *The Logic of Practice*, trans. R. Nice (Stanford: Stanford University Press [French edition 1980]).

BOUVERESSE, A. (1989), *La Vie rurale en 1900 dans le canton de Vercel, Doubs* (Vesoul: IMB).

BOYD, R. and RICHERSON, P. J. (1985), *Culture and the Evolutionary Process* (Chicago: University of Chicago Press).

BRAUDEL, F. (1988), *The Identity of France*, Vol. I: *History and Environment*, trans. S. Reynolds (Glasgow: Collins [French edition 1986]).

—— (1990) *The Identity of France*, Vol. II: *People and Production*, trans. S. Reynolds (Glasgow: Collins [French edition 1986]).

BREEN, R. (1982), 'Naming Practices in Western Ireland'. *Man*, NS 17: 701–13.

BROWN, T. A. (1996), 'Nonlinear Politics', In L. D. Kiel and E. Elliott (eds.), *Chaos Theory in the Social Sciences* (Ann Arbor: University of Michigan Press), 119–37.

BUCKLEY, W. (1967), *Sociology and Modern Systems Theory* (Englewood Cliffs, NJ: Prentice Hall).

BURGUIÈRE, A. (1976), 'From Malthus to Max Weber: Belated Marriage and the Spirit of Enterprise', in R. Forster and O. Ranum (eds.), *Family and Society: Readings from the Annales*, trans. E. Forster and P. Ranum (Baltimore: Johns Hopkins University Press), 237–50.

BYRNE, D. (1997), 'Chaotic Places or Complex Places? Cities in a Post-Industrial Decline', In S. Westwood and J. Williams (eds.), *Imagining Cities: Scripts, Signs, Memory* (London: Routledge), 50–70.

CAM, H. M. (1962), *Law-Finders and Law-Makers in Medieval England* (London: Methuen).

CAMPBELL, B. M. S. (1984), 'Population Pressure, Inheritance and the Land

Market in a Fourteenth-Century Peasant Community', in R. M. Smith (ed.), *Land, Kinship and Life-Cycle* (Cambridge: Cambridge University Press), 87–134.

CAMUS, A. (1953), *The Rebel*, trans. A. Bower (Harmondsworth: Penguin [French edition 1951]).

CANCIAN, F. (1967), 'Stratification and Risk-Taking: A Theory Tested on Agricultural Innovation', *American Sociological Review*, 32: 912–27.

CARR, E. H. (1961), *What is History?* (Harmondsworth: Penguin).

CARRIER, J. and HEYMAN, J. McC. (1997), 'Consumption and Political Economy', *Journal of the Royal Anthropological Institute*, 3: 355–73.

CAVALLI-SFORZA, L. L. (1971), 'Similarities and Differences in Sociocultural and Biological Evolution', in F. R. Hodson, D. G. Kendall, and P. Tautu (eds.), *Mathematics in the Archaeological and Historical Sciences* (Edinburgh: Edinburgh University Press), 535–41.

—— and FELDMAN, M. W. (1981), *Cultural Transmission and Evolution: A Quantitative Approach* (Princeton, NJ: Princeton University Press).

CHAPIN, F. S. (1928), *Cultural Change* (New York: Century).

CHAPMAN, B. (1953), *Introduction to French Local Government* (London: Unwin).

CHAPUIS, R. (1958), *Une Vallée Franc-Comtoise, la Haute-Loue: étude de géographie humaine*, Annales Littéraires de l'Université de Besançon, 23 (Paris: Les Belles Lettres).

—— (1970), 'La Region de Levier', *Revue de Géographie de Lyon*, 45: 114–37.

CHATELAIN, A. (1936), 'La Vie rurale dans le Valromey', *Études Rhodaniennes*, 12: 41–60.

CHERRY, C. (1966), *On Human Communication* (Cambridge, Mass.: MIT Press [first edition 1957]).

CHIBNALL, A. C. (1965), *Sherington: Fiefs and Fields of a Buckinghamshire Village* (Cambridge: Cambridge University Press).

CHIROT, D. (1994), *How Societies Change* (Thousand Oaks, Calif.: Pine Forge).

CLADE, J.-L. (1994), *La vie des paysans franc-comtois dans les années 50* (Lyon: Horvath).

CLARK, T. N. (1969), 'Introduction', in T. N. Clark (ed.), *Gabriel Tarde on Communication and Social Influence* (Chicago: University of Chicago Press), 1–69.

CLOAK, F. J. (1975), 'Is a Cultural Ethology Possible?', *Human Ecology*, 3: 161–82.

COLE, J. W. and WOLF, E. R. (1974), *The Hidden Frontier: Ecology and Ethnicity in an Alpine Valley* (New York: Academic Press).

COURTIEU, J. (1982–7), *Dictionnaire des communes du département de Doubs* (Besançon, Editions Cêtre [six volumes, published at intervals from 1982 to 1987]).

CROOK, J. H. (1995), 'Psychological Processes in Cultural and Genetic Co-evolution', in E. Jones and V. Reynolds (eds.), *Survival and Religion: Biological Evolution and Cultural Change* (London: Wiley), 45–110.

DAHLMAN, C. J. (1980), *The Open Field System and Beyond* (Cambridge: Cambridge University Press).

DAVEAU, S. (1954), 'Une Communauté jurassienne au 18ième siècle: les Foncine', *Revue de Géographie de Lyon*, 29: 118–29.

—— (1959), *Les Régions frontalières de la montagne jurassienne: étude de géographie humaine*, Institut des Études Rhodaniennes, memoires et documents 14 (Lyon: Université de Lyon).

DAWKINS, R. (1976), *The Selfish Gene* (Oxford: Oxford University Press).

DERRIDA, J. (1976), *Of grammatology*, trans. G. C. Spivak (Baltimore: Johns Hopkins University Press).

DIETRICH, G. and GARENC, P. (1963), 'Le Paysage rural en Franche-Comté', *Revue Géographique de l'Est* 4: 371–83.

DOBRES, M.-A. and HOFFMAN, C. (1994), 'Social Agency and the Dynamics of Prehistoric Technology' *Journal of Archaeological Method and Theory*, 1: 211–58.

Documentation Française (1959), *Monographies Agricoles départementales: 25, le Doubs* (Paris, Ministère d'Agriculture et de la Pêche).

DOUGLAS, M. (1996), *Thought Styles: Critical Essays on Good Taste* (London: Sage).

—— and WILDAVSKY, A. (1982), *Risk and Culture: An Essay on the Selection of Technological and Environmental Danger* (Berkeley: University of California Press).

—— and ISHERWOOD, B. (1996), *The World of Goods: Towards an Anthropology of Consumption* (London: Routledge [first edition 1979]).

DUNBAR, R. (1993), 'Co-evolution of Neocortical Size, Group Size and Language in Humans', *Behavioural and Brain Sciences Evolution*, 16: 681–735.

DURHAM, W. H. (1991), *Co-evolution: Genes, Culture and Human Diversity* (Stanford: Stanford University Press).

DURKHEIM, E. (1915), *The Elementary Forms of the Religious Life*, trans. J. W. Swain (London: Unwin [French edition 1912]).

—— (1933), *The Division of Labour in Society*, trans. G. Simpson (London: Macmillan [French edition 1893]).

—— (1938), *The Rules of Sociological Method*, trans. S. A. Solovay and J. H. Mueller (London: Macmillan [French edition 1901]).

DYSON-HUDSON, R. and SMITH, E. A. (1978), 'Human Territoriality: An Ecological Reassessment', *American Anthropologist*, 80: 21–41.

EASTON, D. (1965), *A Framework for Political Analysis* (Englewood Cliffs, NJ: Prentice Hall).

ÉCONOMIE RURALE (1967), *Tableaux de l'agriculture franc-comtoise, 1ière partie: Population, structures, equipment* (Besançon, Chambres d'Agriculture de Franche-Comté, Service Interdépartemental d'Économie Rurale).

ELDREDGE, N. and GOULD, S. J. (1972), 'Punctuated Equilibria: An Alternative to Phyletic Gradualism', in T. J. M. Schopf (ed.), *Models in Palaeobiology* (San Francisco: Freeman), 82–115.

ELSTER, J. (1983), *Explaining Technical Change* (Cambridge: Cambridge University Press).

EPSTEIN, T. S. (1962), *Economic Development and Social Change in South India* (Manchester: Manchester University Press).

ERASMUS, C. J. (1956), 'Culture, Structure and Process: The Occurrence and Disappearance of Reciprocal Farm Labour in Latin America', *Southwestern Journal of Anthropology*, 12: 444–69.

—— (1965), 'The Occurrence and Disappearance of Reciprocal Farm Labour in Latin America', in D. B. Heath and R. N. Adams (eds.), *Contemporary Cultures and Societies of Latin America* (New York: Random House), 173–99.

ERWIN, H. R. (1997), 'The Dynamics of Peer Polities', in S. van de Leeuw and J. McGlade (eds.), *Time, Process and Structured Transformation in Archaeology* (London, Routledge), 57–96.

FAITH, R. J. (1966), 'Peasant Families and Inheritance in Medieval England', *Agricultural History Review*, 14: 77–95.

FIRTH, R. (1954), 'Social organization and social change' *Journal of the Royal Anthropological Institute*, 84: 1–20.

—— (1955), 'Some Principles of Social Organization', *Journal of the Royal Anthropological Institute*, 85: 1–18.

FITZSIMMONS, M. P. (1994), *The Remaking of France: The National Assembly and the Constitution of 1791* (Cambridge: Cambridge University Press).

FLANDRIN, J.-L. (1982), *Families in Former Times: Kinship, Household and Sexuality*, trans. R. Southern (Cambridge: Cambridge University Press [French edition 1976]).

FORTES, M. (1949), 'Time and the Social Structure: An Ashanti Case Study', in M. Fortes (ed.), *Social Structure: Essays Presented to A. R. Radcliffe-Brown* (Oxford: Clarendon [reprinted in M. Fortes (1970) *Time and the Social Structure and Other Essays*, London: Athlone, 1–32]).

FOUCAULT, M. (1977), *Discipline and Punish: The Birth of the Prison*, trans. A. Sheridan (Cambridge: Cambridge University Press [French edition 1975]),

FOX, R. (1978), *The Tory Islanders: A People of the Celtic Fringe* (Cambridge: Cambridge University Press).

FRANKLIN, S. H. (1969), *The European Peasantry: The Final Phase* (London: Methuen).

FRIEDL, J. (1974), *Kippel, a Changing Village in the Alps* (New York: Holt, Rinehart).

GAUTHIER, J. (1886), *Annuaire du Doubs, de la Franche Comté et du territoire du Belfort* (Besançon: Jacquin).

GEERTZ, C. (1959), 'Form and Variation in Balinese Village Structure', *American Anthropologist*, 61: 991–1012.

GENNEP, A. VAN (1946), *Manuel de folklore français contemporain, tome premier II* (Paris: Picard).

GIDDENS, A. (1979), *Central Problems in Social Theory* (London: Macmillan).

—— (1984), *The Constitution of Society* (Cambridge: Polity Press).

GILMORE, D. (1982), 'Some Notes on Community Nicknaming in Spain', *Man*, NS 17: 686–700.

GIOUD, A. (1952), 'L'Exploitation et le sciage des bois dans le Jura français', *Revue de Géographie de Lyon*, 27: 99–131.

GOFFMAN, E. (1959), *The Presentation of Self in Everyday Life* (London: Alan Lane/Penguin [US edition Anchor Books, 1959]).

GOODY, J. (1983), *The Development of Family and Marriage in Europe* (Cambridge: Cambridge University Press).

GOULD, S. J. (1999), 'Introduction: The Scales of Contingency and Punctuation in History', in J. Bintliff (ed.), *Structure and Contingency: Evolutionary Processes in Life and Human Society* (London: Leicester University Press), pp. ix–xxii.

GOURNAY, B., KESLER, J. F. and SIWEK-POUYDESSEAU, J. (1967), *Administration publique* (Paris: Presses Universitaires de la France).

GRESSET, M. (1994), 'Preface', in J.-L. Clade, *La Vie des paysans franc-comtois dans les années 50* (Lyon: Horvath), 5–6.

GRÖGER, B. L. (1981), 'Of Men and Machines: Co-operation among French Family Farmers', *Ethnology*, 20: 163–76.

—— (1982), 'Peasants and Policy: Comparative Perspectives on Aging', in R. L. Hall and C. B. Stack (eds.), *Holding on to the Land and the Lord* (Athens: University of Georgia Press), 121–30.

GUYÉTANT, C. (1870), *Traité sur les fromageries, notamment de Franche-Comté* (Paris: Cosse et Marechal).

HÄGERSTRAND, T. (1952), 'The Propagation of Innovation Waves', *Lund Studies in Geography* B4 (Lund: University of Lund).

—— (1967), *Innovation Diffusion as a Spatial Process* (Chicago: Chicago University Press).

HAJNAL, J. (1965), 'European Marriage Patterns in Perspective', in D. V. Glass and D. E. C. Eversley (eds.), *Population in History: Essays in Historical Demography* (London, Arnold), 101–43.

HAMER, W. H. (1906), 'Epidemic Diseases in England', *Lancet*, 1: 733–9.

HAMILTON, W. D. (1964), 'The Evolution of Social Behaviour', *Journal of Theoretical Biology*, 12: 1–52.

HAMPSON, N. (1963), *A Social History of the French Revolution* (London: Routledge).

HARDIN, G. (1968), 'The Tragedy of the Commons', *Science*, 162: 1243–8.

HARRIS, C. (1974), *Hennage, a Rural System in Miniature* (New York: Holt Rinehart and Winston).

HARRISON, H. S. (1930), 'Opportunism and the Factors of Invention', *American Anthropologist*, 32: 106–25.

HAVINDEN, M.A. (1961), 'Agricultural Progress in Open-Field Oxfordshire', *Agricultural History Review*, 9: 73–83.

—— (1966), *Estate village: A study of the Berkshire Villages of Ardington and Lockinge* (London: Lund Humphries).

HILTON, R. H. (1954), 'Peasant Movements in England Before 1381' in E. M. Carus-Wilson (ed.), *Essays in Economic History,* II, 73–90.

HOCKETT, C. and ASCHER, R. (1964), 'The Human Revolution', *Current Anthropology,* 5: 135–47.

HOWELL, C. (1976), 'Peasant Inheritance Customs in the Midlands, 1280–1700', in J. Goody, J. Thirsk, and E. P. Thompson (eds.), *Family and Inheritance: Rural Society in Western Europe, 1200–1800* (Cambridge: Cambridge University Press), 112–55.

HRDY, S. and JUDGE, D. (1993), 'Darwin and the Puzzle of Primogeniture: An Essay on Biases in Parental Investment after Death', *Human Nature* 4: 1–45.

HUNTER, G. (1969), *Modernising Peasant Societies* (London, Oxford University Press).

HUTSON, S. (1971), 'Social Ranking in a French Alpine Community', in F. G. Bailey (ed.), *Gifts and Poison: The Politics of Reputation* (Oxford: Blackwell), 41–68.

INSEE 1990 *Recensement générale 1990* (Paris: Institut National de la Statistique et des Études Économiques).

JOURNAUX OFFICIELS (1964), Statutes Types des Co-operatives Agricoles, No. 1221 (Paris: Journaux Officiels de la Republique Française).

JURJUS, A. (1993), 'Farming Styles and Intermediate Structures in the Wake of 1992', in T. M. Wilson and M. E. Smith (eds.), *Cultural Change and the New Europe: Perspectives on the European Community* (Boulder, Colo: Westview), 99–121.

KAUFFMAN, S. (1993), *The Origins of Order: Self-Organization and Selection in Evolution* (Oxford: Oxford University Press).

KELLY, G. A. (1963), *A Theory of Personality: The Psychology of Personal Constructs* (New York: Norton).

KIEL, L. D. and ELLIOTT, E. (1996), 'Exploring Nonlinear Dynamics with a Spreadsheet: A Graphical View of Chaos for Beginners', in L. D. Kiel and E. Elliott (eds.), *Chaos Theory in the Social Sciences* (Ann Arbor: University of Michigan Press), 19–29.

KROPOTKIN, P. (1972), *Mutual Aid: A Factor in Evolution* (New York: New York University Press [first edition 1902]).

LAMBERT, R. (1953), 'Structure agraire et économie rurale de plateau de Levier', *Bulletin de l'Association des Géographes Français,* 237–8: 170–8.

LANCASTER, L. (1961), 'Some Conceptual Problems in the Study of Family and Kin Ties in the British Isles', *British Journal of Sociology,* 12: 317–31.

LASLETT, P. (1972), 'Introduction: The History of the Family', in P. Laslett and R. Wall (eds.), *Household and Family in Past Time: Comparative Studies in the Size and Structure of the Domestic Group over the Last Three Centuries* (Cambridge: Cambridge University Press), 1–73.

LATOUCHE, R. (1938), 'La Fruitière jurasienne au xviiiième siecle', *Revue de Geographie Alpine*, 26: 773–91.

LATOUR, B. (1988), *The Pasteurization of France*, trans. A. Sheridan and J. Law (Cambridge, Mass.: Harvard University Press [French edition 1984]).

LAURENS, P. (1864), *Annuaire du Doubs et de la Franche-Comté* (Besançon: Jacquin).

—— (1873), *Annuaire de Doubs et de la Franche-Comté* (Besançon: Jacquin).

—— and GAUTHIER, J. (1876), *Annuaire du Doubs, de la Franche-Comté et du territoire du Belfort* (Besançon: Jacquin).

LAYTON, R. (1968), 'Myth and Society in Aboriginal Arnhem Land', M.Phil. thesis (University College London).

—— (1970), 'Myth as Language in Aboriginal Arnhem Land', *Man*, NS, 5: 483–97.

—— (1971), 'Patterns of Informal Interaction in Pellaport', in F. G. Bailey (ed.), *Gifts and Poison* (Oxford: Blackwell), 97–118.

—— (1973), 'Social Systems Theory and a Village Community in France', in C. Renfrew (ed.), *The Explanation of Culture Change* (London: Duckworth), 499–516.

—— (1974), 'Pellaport', in F. G. Bailey (ed.), *Debate and Compromise: The Politics of Innovation* (Oxford, Blackwell), 48–74.

—— (1981), 'Communication in Ritual: Two Examples and their Social Context', *Canberra Anthropology*, 4: 110–24.

—— (1989), 'Are Sociobiology and Social Anthropology Compatible? The Significance of Sociocultural Resources in Human Evolution', in V. Standen and R. Foley (eds.), *Comparative Socioecology: The Behavioural Ecology of Mammals and Man* (Oxford: Blackwell), 433–55.

—— (1995) 'Relating to the Country in the Western Desert', in E. Hirsch and M. O'Hanlon (eds.), *The Anthropology of Landscape: Perspectives on Place and Space* (Oxford: Clarendon), 210–31.

—— (1997*a*), 'Representing and Translating People's Place in the Landscape of Northern Australia', in A. James, J. Hockey and A. Dawson (eds.), *After Writing Culture: Epistemology and Praxis in Contemporary Anthropology*, (London, Routledge), 122–43.

—— (1997*b*), *An Introduction to Theory in Anthropology* (Cambridge: Cambridge University Press).

LEACH, R. R. (1954), *Political Systems of Highland Burma* (London: Bell).

LEBEAU, R. (1937), 'Notes sur les types d'habitations du Jura central', *Études Rhodaniennes* 13: 207–12.

—— (1949), 'Essai d'une carte des genres de vie dans le géographie du Jura français', *Revue de Géographie de Lyon*, 24: 319–30.

—— (1951), 'Deux anciens genres de vie opposés de la montagne Jurassienne', *Revue de Géographie de Lyon*, 26: 378–410.

—— (1952), 'Le Régime de l'exploitation du sol dans les Jura français', *Revue de Géographie de Lyon*, 27: 310–64.

LEEUW, S. VAN DER (1989), 'Risk, Perception and Innovation', in S. van der Leeuw and R. Torrence (eds.), *What's New? A Closer Look at the Process of Innovation* (London: Unwin), 300–29.

—— and McGLADE, J. (eds.) (1997), *Time, Process and Structured Transformation in Archaeology* (London: Routledge).

LEMONNIER, P. (1993), 'Introduction', in P. Lemonnier (ed.), *Technological Choices: Transformation in Material Cultures since the Neolithic* (London: Routledge), 1–35.

LE ROY LADURIE, E. (1976), 'Family Structures and Inheritance Customs in Sixteenth-Century France' in J. Goody, J. Thirsk, and E. P. Thompson (eds.), *Family and Inheritance: Rural Society in Western Europe, 1200–1800* (Cambridge: Cambridge University Press), 37–70.

LÉVI-STRAUSS, C. (1966), *The Savage Mind*, trans. anon. (London: Weidenfeld & Nicolson [French edition 1962]).

LEWIS, O. (1951), *Life in a Mexican Village: Tepoztlán Restudied* (Urbana: University of Illinois Press).

LEWONTIN, R. (1982), *Human Diversity* (New York: Freeman/Scientific American).

LINTON, R. (1936), *The Study of Man* (New York: Appleton-Century-Crofts).

LLOYD, W. F. (1964), 'The Checks to Population', in G. Hardin (ed.), *Population, Evolution and Birth Control* (San Francisco: Freeman [first published 1833]), 337–42.

LUKES, S. (1973), *Emile Durkheim, His Life and Work: A Historical and Critical Study* (Harmondsworth: Penguin).

McCAY, B. and ACHESON, J. M. (1987), *The Question of the Commons: The Culture and Ecology of Communal Resources* (Tucson: The University of Arizona Press).

McCLOSKEY, D. M. (1976), 'English Open Fields as Behaviour Towards Risk', in P. Uselding, (ed.), *Research in Economic History*, 1: 124–70 (Greenwich, Conn: JAI Press).

MACFARLANE, A. (1978), *The Origins of English Individualism: The Family, Property and Social Transition* (Oxford: Blackwell).

McGLADE, J. (1997), 'The Limits of Social Control: Coherence and Chaos in a Prestige-Goods Economy', in S. van de Leeuw, and J. McGlade (eds.), *Time, Process and Structured Transformation in Archaeology* (London: Routledge), 298–330.

—— and McGLADE, J. M. (1989), 'Modelling the Innovative Component of Social Change', in S. van der Leeuw and R. Torrence (eds.), *What's New? A Closer Look at the Process of Innovation* (London: Unwin), 281–99.

MALFROY, M., OLIVIER, B. and GUIRAUD, J. (1981), *Le Val d'Usier: histoire de Sombacour, Bians, Goux-les-Usiers* (Besançon: Cêtre).

MALINOWSKI, B. (1922), *Argonauts of the Western Pacific: An account of Native Enterprise and Adventure in the Archipelagoes of Melanesian New Guinea* (London: Routledge).

MALTHUS, T. (1973), *An Essay on the Principle of Population*, Books I and II (London: Dent [first published 1803]).

MARLER, P. (1998), 'Animal Communication and Human Language,' in N. G. Jablonsji and L. C. Aiello (eds.), *The Origin and Diversification of Language. Memoirs of the California Academy of Sciences*, 24 (San Francisco: California Academy of Sciences), 1–19.

MARX, K. (1930), *Capital*, Vol. I, trans. E. Paul and C. Paul (London: Dent [first published 1867]).

—— (1971), *A Contribution to the Critique of Political Economy*, trans. S. W. Ryazanskaya (New York: International Publishers [first published 1859]).

—— (1977), *Karl Marx, Selected Writings*, ed. D. McLellan (Oxford: Oxford University Press).

MAUSS, M. (1954), *The Gift: Forms and Functions of Exchange in Archaic Societies*, trans. I. Cunnison (London: Cohen and West [first published 1925]).

MAYNARD SMITH, J. (1982), *Evolution and the Theory of Games* (Cambridge: Cambridge University Press).

MENDRAS, H. and COLE, A. (1991), *Social Change in Modern France: Towards a Cultural Anthropology of the Fifth Republic* (Cambridge: Cambridge University Press).

MILLER, D. (1987), *Material Culture and Mass Consumption* (Oxford: Blackwell).

—— (1997) *Capitalism: An Ethnographic Approach* (Oxford: Berg).

MILLS, D. R. (1984), 'The Nineteenth-Century Peasantry of Melbourne, Cambridgeshire', in R. M. Smith (ed.), *Land, Kinship and Life-Cycle* (Cambridge: Cambridge University Press).

MINGAY, G. E. (1977), *Rural Life in Victorian England* (London: Heinemann).

MITTERAUER, M. and SIEDER, R. (1982), *The European Family: Patriarchy to Partnership from the Middle Ages to the Present*, trans. K. Oosterveen and M. Hörzinger (Oxford: Blackwell [German edition 1977]).

MORPHY, H. and LAYTON R. (1981), 'Choosing among Alternatives: Cultural Transformations and Social Change in Aboriginal Australia and French Jura', *Mankind*, 13: 56–73.

MYRDAL, J. (1996), *Landbon, Ladan och Lagen och Hägnaderna, Arbetstiden och Bydelaget* (Stockholm: Kunglskogs-och Lantbruksakademien).

NEESON, J. M. (1993), *Commoners: Common Right, Enclosure and Social Change in England, 1700–1820* (Cambridge: Cambridge University Press).

NELSON, R. and WINTER, S. (1982), *An Evolutionary Theory of Economic Change* (Cambridge, Mass.: Belknap).

NETTING, R. McC. (1981), *Balancing on an Alp: Ecological Change and Continuity in a Swiss Mountain Community* (Cambridge: Cambridge University Press).

NEWBY, H., BELL, C., ROSE, D. and SAUNDERS, P. (1978), *Property, Paternalism and Power: Class and Control in Rural England* (Hutchinson: London).

NITZ, H.-J. (1988), 'Introduction from Above: Intentional Spread of Common-Field Systems by Feudal Authorities Through Colonisation and Reorganisation', *Geografiska Annaler* 70B, 1.

NOWAK, M. A. and SIGMUND, K. (1998), 'Evolution of Indirect Reciprocity by Image Scoring', *Nature*, 393 (11 June 1998): 573–7.

ODLING-SMEE, J. (1995), 'Biological Evolution and Cultural Change', in E. Jones and V. Reynolds (eds.), *Survival and Religion: Biological Evolution and Cultural Change* (New York: Wiley), 1–43.

——, LALAND, K. and FELDMAN, M. (1996), 'Niche Construction', *American Naturalist*, 147: 641–8.

OECD (1965), *Agriculture and Economic Growth: A Report by a Group of Experts* (Paris: Organization for Economic Co-operation and Development).

OLDENZIEL, R. (1996), 'Object/ions: Technology, Culture and Gender', in W. D. Kingery (ed.), *Learning from Things: Method and Theory of Material Culture Studies* (Washington: Smithsonian), 55–69.

ORWIN, C. S. and ORWIN, C. S. (1938), *The Open Fields* (Oxford: Clarendon Press).

OSTROM, E. (1990), *Governing the Commons: The Evolution of Institutions for Collective Action* (Cambridge: Cambridge University Press).

OVERTON, M. (1996), *Agricultural Revolution in England: The Transformation of the Agrarian Economy 1500–1850* (Cambridge: Cambridge University Press).

PANTER-BRICK, C. (1993), 'Seasonal Organization of Work Patterns' in S. J. Ulijaszek and S. S. Strickland (eds.), *Seasonality and Human Ecology* (Cambridge: Cambridge University Press), 220–34.

—— LOTSTEIN, D. S. and ELLISON, P. T. (1993), 'Seasonality of Reproductive Function and Weight Loss in Rural Nepali Women', *Human Reproduction*, 8: 684–90.

PARK, R. (1928), 'Human Migration and the Marginal Man', *American Journal of Sociology*, 33: 881–93.

PIGALLET, M. (1912), *Annuaire départementale du Doubs* (Besançon).

PINA-CABRAL, J. (1984), 'Nicknames and the Experience of Community', *Man*, NS 19: 148–50.

POLANYI, K. (1945), *Origins of our Time: The Great Transformation* (London: Gollancz).

PUTTNAM, H. (1995), *Pragmatism: An Open Question* (Oxford: Blackwell).

RADCLIFFE-BROWN, A. R. (1952), *Structure and Function in Primitive Society* (London: Cohen & West).

REYNOLDS, P. (1968), 'Evolution of Primate Vocal-Auditory Communication Systems', *American Anthropologist*, 68: 899–921.

RIDLEY, M. (1996), *The Origins of Virtue* (London: Viking).

RINDOS, D. (1985), 'Darwinian Selection, Symbolic Variation and the Evolution of Culture', *Current Anthropology*, 26: 65–88.

ROECK HANSEN, B. (1996), *The Agrarian Landscape in Finland circa 1700, with Special Reference to Southwest Finland and Ostrobothnia* (Stockholm: Department of Human Geography, Stockholm University).

ROGERS, E. M. (1962), *Diffusion of Innovations* (New York: Free Press).

—— and SHOEMAKER, F. (1971), *The Communication of Innovations: a Cross-Cultural Approach* (New York: Free Press).

ROGERS, S. C. (1975), 'Female Forms of Power and the Myth of Male Dominance', *American Ethnologist*, 2: 727–56.

—— (1991), *Shaping Modern Times in Rural France: The Transformation and Reproduction of an Aveyronnais Community* (Princeton, NJ: Princeton University Press).

ROSENBERG, H. G. (1988), *A Negotiated World: Three Centuries of Change in a French Alpine Community* (Toronto: University of Toronto Press).

RÖSENER, W. (1994), *The Peasantry of Europe* (Oxford: Blackwell).

ROSSER, J. B. (1996), 'Chaos Theory and Rationality in Economics', in L. D. Kiel and E. Elliott (eds.), *Chaos Theory in the Social Sciences* (Ann Arbor: University of Michigan Press), 199–213.

ROUSSEAU, J. J. (1963), *The Social Contract and Discourses*, ed. G. D. H. Cole (London: Dent [French editions published 1755–62]).

ROUSSET, A. (1855), *Dictionnaire des communes de la Franche-Comté* (Besançon).

—— (1992), *Département du Doubs: géographie et dictionnaire des communes* (Paris: Res Universis/Comédit [first published as *Géographie du Doubs* (1863)].

RUELLE, D. (1991), *Chance and Chaos* (Princeton, NJ: Princeton University Press).

SABEAN, D. W. (1990), *Property, Production and Family in Neckarhausen, 1700–1870* (Cambridge: Cambridge University Press).

SALITOT, M. (1988), *Héritage, parenté et propriété en Franche-Comté du xii siècle à nos jours* (Paris: ARF/L'Harmattan).

SAUSSURE, F. DE (1959), *Course in General Linguistics*, trans. C. Bally and A. Sechehaye (London: Owen [French edition 1915]).

SCHUTZ, A. (1972), *The Phenomenology of the Social World*, trans. G. Walsh and F. Lehnert (London: Heinemann [German edition 1932]).

SCOTT, J. (1976), *The Moral Economy of the Peasant: Rebellion and Subsistence in Southeast Asia* (New Haven: Yale University Press).

SEGALEN, M. (1991), *Fifteen Generations of Bretons: Kinship and Society in Lower Brittany 1720–1980*, trans. J. A. Underwood (Cambridge: Cambridge University Press [French edition 1985]).

SHAFFER, J. W. (1982), *Family and Farm: Agrarian Change and Household Organization in the Loire Valley 1500–1900* (Albany, NY: State University of New York Press).

SHANNON, C. E. and WEAVER, W. (1949), *The Mathematical Theory of Communication* (Urbana: University of Illinois Press).

SHUTES, M. (1993), 'Rural Communities Without Family Farms? Family Dairy Farming in the Post-1993 EC', in T. M. Wilson and M. E. Smith (eds.), *Cultural Change and the New Europe: Perspectives on the European Community*, (Boulder, Colo.: Westview), 123–42.

SILVER, H. (1981), 'Calculating Risks: The Socio-Economic Foundations of Aesthetic Innovations in an Asante Carving Community', *Ethnology,* 20: 101–14.

SILVERMAN, S. (1966), 'An Ethnographic Approach to Social Stratification: Prestige in a Central Italian Community', *American Anthropologist* 68: 899–921.

—— (1974), 'Bailey's Politics', *Journal of Peasant Studies* 2: 111–20.

SMITH, A. (1976), *An Enquiry into the Nature and Causes of the Wealth of Nations* (Oxford: Clarendon Press [first published 1776]).

SMITH, R. M. (1984*a*), 'Some Issues Concerning Families and their Property in Rural England', in R. M. Smith (ed.), *Land, Kinship and Life-Cycle* (Cambridge: Cambridge University Press) 1–86.

—— (1984*b*), 'Families and their Land in an Area of Partible Inheritance: Redgrave, Suffolk 1260–1320', in R. M. Smith (ed.), *Land, Kinship and Life-Cycle* (Cambridge, Cambridge University Press) 135–95.

SPORRONG, U. and WENNESTEN, E. (1995), *Marken, Gården, Släkten och Arvet* (Stockholm: Institute of Cultural Geography, Stockholm University).

STEWART, I. (1997), *Does God Play Dice: The New Mathematics of Chaos* (Harmondsworth: Penguin [first edition 1989]).

STRATHERN, M. (1981), *Kinship at the Core: An Anthropology of Elmdon, a Village in North-West Essex in the Nineteen-Sixties* (Cambridge: Cambridge University Press).

TARDE, G. (1969), *On Communication and Social Influence,* trans. T. N. Clark (Chicago: University of Chicago Press).

TAYLOR, L. (1987), ' "The River Would Run Red with Blood": Community and Common Property in an Irish Fishing Settlement', in B. J. McCay and J. M. Acheson (eds.), *The Question of the Commons: The Culture and Ecology of Communal Resources* (Tucson: University of Arizona Press) 290–307.

THIRSK, J. (1976), 'The European Debate on Customs and Inheritance, 1500–1700', in J. Goody, J. Thirsk, and E. P. Thompson (eds.), *Family and Inheritance: Rural Society in Western Europe, 1200–1800* (Cambridge, Cambridge University Press) 177–91.

TÖNNIES, F. (1957), *Community and Society (Gemeinschaft und Gesellschaft)*, trans. C. P. Loomis (New York: Harper and Row [German edition 1887]).

TORRENCE, R. (1983), 'Time Budgeting and Hunter-Gatherer Technology', in G. Bailey (ed.), *Hunter-Gatherer Economy in Prehistory* (Cambridge, Cambridge University Press) 11–22.

TRACY, M. (1964), *Agriculture in Western Europe* (London: Cape).

TRIVERS, R. (1985), *Social Evolution* (Menlo Park: Benjamin/Cummins).

TROW-SMITH, R. (1967), *Life from the Land* (London: Faber).

TURNER, R. (1968), 'Role, Sociological Aspects', in D. L. Sills (ed.), *International Encyclopedia of the Social Sciences*, 13: 552–6 (New York: Macmillan).

ULIN, R. (1996), *Vintages and Traditions: An Ethnohistory of South-West French Wine Co-operatives* (Washington: Smithsonian Institution Press).

VALEN, L. VAN (1973), 'A New Evolutionary Law', *Evolutionary Theory*, 1: 1–30.

VERDIER, Y. (1979), *Façons de dire, façons de faire: la laveuse, la couturière, la cuisinière* (Paris: Gallimard).

VIAZZO, P. P. (1989), *Upland Communities* (Cambridge: Cambridge University Press).

VICKERY, W. L., GIRALDEAU, L.-A., TEMPLETON, J., KRAMER, D. and CHAPMAN, C. (1991), 'Producers, Scroungers, and Group Foraging', *American Naturalist*, 137: 847–63.

VIGNAU, L (1947), *Chez nous, il y a cent ans* (Besançon: Camponovo).

VIVOT, J.-N. (1994), *L'Agriculture du Doubs, un autre regard pour demain* (Besançon: Chambre d'Agriculture du Doubs).

WEILL, A. (1968), *Droit civil* (Paris: Dalloz).

WEINBERG, D. (1975), *Peasant Wisdom: Cultural Adaptations in a Swiss Village* (Berkeley: University of California Press).

—— (1976), 'Bands and Clans: Political Functions of Voluntary Associations in the Swiss Alps', *American Ethnologist*, 3: 175–89.

WIDGREN, M. (1990), 'Strip Fields in an Iron-Age Context: A Case Study from Västergötland, Sweden', *Landscape History*, 12: 5–24.

—— (1997), *Bysamfällighet och Tegskifte i Bohuslän 1300–1750* (Stockholm: Institute of Cultural Geography, Stockholm University).

WILKINS, L. (1964), *Social Deviance* (London: Tavistock).

WILLIAMS, W. M. (1963), *A West Country Village: Ashworthy* (London: Routledge).

—— (1969), *The Sociology of an English Village: Gosforth* (London: Routledge).

WILLIAMSON, T. and BELLAMY, L. (1987), *Property and Landscape: A Social History of Land Ownership and the English Countryside* (London: George Philip).

WILSON, D. and GAME, C. (1994), *Local Government in the United Kingdom* (Basingstoke: Macmillan).

WINTERHALDER, B. (1990), 'Open Field, Common Pot: Harvest Variability and Risk Avoidance in Agricultural and Foraging Societies', in E. Cashdan (ed.), *Risk and Uncertainty in Tribal and Peasant Economies* (Boulder, Colo.: Westview), 67–87.

—— (1996), 'Social Foraging and the Behavioural Ecology of Intragroup Resource Transfers', *Evolutionary Anthropology*, 5(2): 46–57.

WRIGHT, G. (1964), *Rural Revolution in France* (Stanford: Stanford University Press).

WYLIE, L. (ed.) (1966), *Chanzeaux, a Village in Anjou* (Cambridge, Mass.: Harvard University Press).

YOON, S. Y. S. (1973), 'In the Final Instance: Peasant and Gentlemen Winegrowers in Provence—a Regional Class Study', Ph.D. dissertation (University of Michigan, Ann Arbor).

YOSHIMOTO, Y. (1997), 'Cultivating Identity at the Dinner Table: Food Traditions in a French Rural Community', MA dissertation (Anthropology Department, University of Durham).

ZONABEND, F. (1984), *The Enduring Memory: Time and History in a French Village*, A. Forster (Manchester: Manchester University Press [French edition 1980]).

INDEX

DATE DUE

ILL SQP			
11353 718			
03/08/14			